For Horace, for Nuno and for Rikky
and to everybody who watches football at Molineux
These stories are our stories

All Aboard The Crazy Train

The weird thing about the appointment of Nuno Espirito Santos wasn't the strange name and the whole madness of those few weeks last Summer. It was the way he spoke to the press during his PR period when he had to glad hand and manoeuvre through the getting to know you period. What madness that must have been for him. But I think the craziest thing must have been him sitting down during his interview and probably him saying (as he stroked his beard), 'This is how we are going to play, this is how MY team will play'. I think also that his 'team' doesn't end in the eleven players he puts out every match. I suspect that the Team stretches to every member of the Wolves staff from the Owners right down to the supporter who by an off chance has been offered a ticket to a match, he hasn't been for years, but he's not going to give up the chance to see for himself what's going on up there.

Nuno came in and initiated such a sea change at the club that soon there was a right smorgasbord of names you rarely heard of moving off to pastures new. It was a Night of the Long Knives for sure. But Nuno is a man who is deeply philosophical about Football. The ethos of his game is that everybody is involved in the idea of transforming our team into something he may look at and say 'This is how it shall be done'. Maybe the staff moved out didn't fully understand or refused to understand the ideas Nuno had. They were gone quickly and with minimum fuss. Replaced by others who had that same steely glint in their eyes as Nuno himself.

We knew there was something different going on before a ball was kicked in anger. We saw the dodgy TV streams from Austria during the preseason tour before the Championship kicked off. We even saw it when at last, we, ourselves could feast our eyes on it when we played Leicester pre season. Were we not astounded? I was for sure, a little any way. But those initial moments when Nunos name was read out as the new Coach of our team made me sit up. There was a feeling there, right in the pit of my stomach. An excited one, one which made me stare out of the window for a moment and watch the clouds in the sky. It was a movement of metaphysics with the physical. Twisting around each other. I've always suspected the great footballers understand football on a metaphysical and philosophical platform and they weave into that the genetics and physicality of their athleticism to produce outstanding beautiful football.

We have seen this beautiful football and now we are taking stock of what has happened at our club. That's what this book is about. Enjoy.

Viva Nuno!
(The Chinese Revolution at Molineux)

'Madness, Badness and Sadness'

July the 16th 2017 I think it was. Was it sunny? Not in Poundstretcher it wasn't. I was in there looking for bargains. It's where all the money saving crap goes on and I was hunting. But there had been rumours. There had been words whispered to me through the ether of rumour and associated bullshit. My football club had been for sale. I had intimated a year before to somebody that the best thing that could happen to my club would be a big Chinese company coming in, so I wasn't surprised at the numbers being mentioned by the local press. Not when I was looking at Fray Bentos pies for a quid and this steamed strawberry pudding thing that looked tasty too. I noticed a security guard following me. I took my time perusing. No way was I shoplifting in Poundstretcher for fucks sake. I wasn't that bad off. But 30-40 Million quid for my club? Mental numbers. I had £4.62 in my pocket and no work on the horizon. Not for a bloke crippled by hospital; treatments. I was mentally totting up my purchases to avoid embarrassment at the till. Jesus Christ.

Wolverhampton Wanderers has been sold to the Chinese. I felt good about it. In my gut it felt right. It felt different to me. We had done the Property developer and the self made millionaire route. They were both crazy. Promotions, die offs where we tumbled down the divisions, bedsheets sprayed with black paint with swear words on. 'Moxey out' they screamed in Halfords Satin black paint.Just madness, sadness and badness. But it felt right this thing. I kept my eye on developments, things stalling at the last minute and kind of prayed for it to happen. I knew it was a good thing.

Guo Guangchang has stumped up 45 million quid for us. His name sounds like my gearbox on the van when I'm changing from first to second. I'm looking at Fray Bentos tinned pies with hardly any meat in them. Do Fosun have any meat in them? Is it all just puff pastry and a thing gravy? He wants to get us back in the Premier league. Fighting with those clubs we used to fight with back in the golden olden days when we packed the ground out and believed. But do we believe any more? Has that time passed? It's maybe a subject I'll return to. We have heard all the big lofty words and ideas to trickle down the various mouthpieces of the press direct from the dark towers of those who manage and control our club. Can we believe the hype and the bullshit again? I'm not sure. I don't really know. I'm sure I don't want to believe any more but I do want to know. I want ideas now and creativity at my club instead of the dour and expressionless football I have been watching. I want to catch my breath with a pass and a thirty yard goal, any fucking goal to be honest. That would be nice. But I want to see intent and idea fully entwined around my team. I know things are changing and I want to be part of it. I need to be part of it.

I don't really know anything about football. I've been going to the Molineux since 1972. We were playing Leeds and Billy Bremner booted the ball into the Northbank and knocked my mate out who was standing right next to me. I was hooked. I hate Leeds and I still laugh when somebody gets a good whack in the face off a booted ball. This story is not going to be coherent. A mix of Metaphysics and English Championship football will not be comfortable bedfellows. Neither will my analysis of what has actually happened this season be comfortable. It has been a mix of meeting people who I have grown to love, meeting a few I hate. It involves Hospitals, ambulances, mountains, a Druid, too many beers, often a few too many drugs, music, and total Portuguese madness.

My mind wanders during games. People talk to me during dull periods. My views are often the views of others who have concentrated in the moments when my attention has lapsed. But I am an observer, of body language and of dynamics. A metaphysical view of performance and the greater subject of ownership and the relationships between the team and our mighty stand 'The Southbank'. But it's the gaps between the stories that are important for sure. As important as the stories I think.

I remember as a kid standing in that mighty stand and watching with horror the streams of piss that used to run down the steps. The odd cigarette that used to land on your head and burn away. The violence of it, the laughter too. The crowd pressing with every attack and the air would squeeze out of you and everything would dim a little until you got air back in there. How we lived eh? How we suffered for this football thing. Of course we suffer now too. The beer and pies are expensive, the conditions can be grim at times, sterile often too. They have seats now which is weird and you can't have a roll up while you watch the game. I'm such a poor bastard thinking of the past all the time but as you get older you can't help it. The past is our lives for better or worse but the future, well it's more interesting for sure.

This book wont be about the intricacies of the tactical game and the complex variables that all fit together to make this great spectacle an occasion to laugh with joy….. or as I do most match days at the Molineux last season, watch the fucking Seagulls flying around, great swooping circles in the blue sky above the

John Ire…er Steve Bull stand. Moving from foot to foot as the cramp sets in because nothing of note has happened in the game. Underneath the seagulls, on the pitch last season I didn't feel the Kwan. Numerous players not doing their thing, a lack lustre Lambert (our ex coach) fuck around and that in my infinite wisdom I knew it would happen. I didn't like Lambert the day he turned up for the signing thing. His suit looked like a Bookies and the scruffy bastard was wearing trainers. I thought about Stan Cullis our Manager back in the mists of time, impeccable, when the Board were made up of local well suited and booted local businessmen. These Monochrome men, stern faced, what would they think of this man? I think Lambert wouldn't have got his foot on the first step of the stairs into the heart of the Waterloo Road stand. Those days we had a Commissionaire, ex Soldier, medals standing guard. He would have moved Lambert on with a quick flick of a highly polished boot up Lamberts arse crack. 'Go on piss off' The Commissionaire would have said. Piss off up your own end. And the traffic on Waterloo Road would have wound on and the seagulls would still be hawking their incessant moaning above. Someone standing next to you would do a big wet beer fart and football would still happen.

The new signings were cool. Costa could move about a bit, he looks quite normal, he says the right things to keep the Social Media knuckle biters happy albeit sounding like the kid who robs your camera while you're sunbathing on a beach in Rio. I've never been to Rio. But Helder Costa looked tiny to me. A small young man. I wondered about how he would do against the snotty lump ball lunatics he would face this season. He kept us up last season for sure as we just scraped past the finishing post gasping for air and thinking about how it had all gone wrong. Little Helder is a favourite of mine. I like him, I like his football.

Jez Moxey and Steve Morgan were the villains of the piece of course. Chief Executive Moxey was a forlorn figure then. He knew the chips were stacked against him. He had a hunted look, that look we had plastered on our faces for the years he was with us. God help us. Stoke fans had warned us about him but we knew. Yes the club was in great financial state but we were being kept alive by machines, and it was no life to lead listening to the bleep of the machines as the spreadsheets kept coming up trumps.

A new season and a new owner. We always knew Steve Morgan loved his Liverpool team. We knew it because we smelled it on him. He wasn't one of us. He could never be one of us. Now he was gone and the club was in new hands. Fosun they were called. I had never heard of them but a quick tap on the keyboard and the joys of the internet washed over me. Fosun seemed like they knew what they were doing but I didn't really have much of a clue or idea. I was lost in the sadness of the past few seasons but something was happening. Something felt different for sure. Fosun and their coterie of hard faced businessmen didn't look like sharks to me. They looked like they had just walked out of a few meetings. It looked like they had made plans, had tactics. Hard nosed? I don't know, they looked different to Tony Xia at Aston Villa and the other doughnut at West Bromich Albion.

For one, I had a strange feeling in my belly. It seemed like a positive one, where the world had shifted a little in our favour. Where Lady Luck or the Gods above had finally cocked an eye at poor old Wolverhampton and said, 'Look at those poor bastards, they could do with a bit of love so they can carry on dreaming and believing, they are at the end of their tether mate' and they were right of course, we needed it badly. Dean Saunders ex Coach, the mighty Walter Zenga had been booted out. Everything seemed up in the air again but this time I was sure we would fall into a soft bush instead of the bramble tangles we always get stuck in. Foisun seemed like a new thing. Dynamic. I closed the laptop and wondered again. There are a flurry of new signing and a look of intent on the faces of these new men replacing the worn out vestiges of the old era. Wallace, Saville are sidestepped and ignored. This is new intent and new idea.

Cavaleiro was a solid looking dude. Championship football was a fucking confusing thing to him. What were they doing? Why are my team mates running around aimlessly? Why does the ball keep flying over my head? Of course he got some neck. Maybe his heart dropped a little.....maybe I should concentrate on the metaphysical aspects of this great pantomime? I'm not sure. He was smiling now for some reason. I never knew who our new Coach was, never heard of him. I'm not mentioning his name now because I don't want it mentioned in this chapter with Moxey and Morgan. No Sir. I don't want to destroy the magic of his name with those two. Not yet.

Last season 2016-2017 was a weirdly esoteric run around. The Cup run was strange as was Coady (against Liverpool) actually running without looking like he was trying to beat the flames out. Thinking back, I know it wasn't his position but running is genetic not memetic. I would have liked to see more from him, I suspect his love and laughter may carry through to his playing if he allows his Kwan to flow. Don't forget Conor Coady, you must leap over the barriers they have placed in your way. Concentrate and forge a path in harmony with the Kwan of the team. You see July was the start point for this whole madness and Coady was one player that came out of the foggy quintessentially 'British' coaching of Lambert and Saunders and made me sit up. Made me think that there was something again that was about to explode, a feeling of anticipation when I watched Coady. Coady yes, I like him too. I may talk about him a lot.

Swapping Jed Wallace for Jota fills me with love. Jota makes my nipples go hard, Wallace made me feel like my tit was caught in a mangle. What great things his fans said when he signed for us and then? Lacklustre and often pointless meanderings, unsure, no confidence displays peppered with a peek of potential. A sideboob of a player, Look! oh. Shit no. Jota appears in the team like a great unknown. Jed never liked it here. We knew that. He couldn't find that spark amongst us and that was a shame. I watch the TV as they wax lyrics about Jota and I read things about him on the internet when it's dark and everybody has gone to sleep. Fosun buy, a Fosun man for sure. Former players are dusted off to netherworlds and we unleash a flurry of new men. Able men. I watch their YouTube videos and I am a little speechless. A jink here and there, poetic football, lithe and athletic. Moving the ball around to feet. I rarely saw a ball punked fifty feet through the air to an on running lunk of centre forward. No Sir. It was all lovely and sublime.

Saville gets up from the golden throne and while still warm enter Ruben Neves. Oh sweet stroker of the ball, that ability, that silken touch. As Saville runs as if there is an earthquake happening see Neves glide and position himself. A touch here a touch there, a stroker a veritable positioner, a much finer artiste honed in the glaring desolation of the Portuguese air where the only things of note are the ability to impress the Gods with a ball. He looks like he should be playing for another 'greater' club. I think he looks great in gold and black to be honest. It suits him. He is going to be a massive player for us.

Willy Boly. What finer example of a defensive player docs one need. As Xerxes he is. A giant among dwarves. His physical presence not yet defined but as many times last season when our defence collapsed to the ground under the shoulder of some low brow opposition team, i suspect this will not be the case under Boly. If we could put the heart of Stearman into the body of Boly there would be statues commissioned and kids starting school in five years time called Willy.

Jack Price. Wherefore art thou Jacko? This is your time my friend. A time to flourish and make that hallowed centre ground your own. A General you could be, or a great artist, the tools you have to hand this season would make Picasso blush. These Portuguese signings are your brush to define how the team plays, to stroke those broad passes, to dab a splash here and there, to hold up your hand and tell the opposition 'Thou shalt not pass' and verily it would be so. It is your time and the great Wolves players of the past sit upon the golden stairs and hold out their hands to you. Will you take them? Will your Kwan flow? All these thoughts through my little peanut head. Kwan for fucks sake, what even is Kwan?

Kwan yes. The best teams have a flowing Kwan but the Kwan is not a river it is the sparkling self belief and dare I say the telepathic ability to define your own play within the dynamics of a team. Last season we lacked Kwan. You could tell in Cavalieros face that he knew the Kwan was being diverted by the incessant dourness of the trainer wearing clown Lamberto. The style of play was the luxury sandwich they eat in the Billy Wright stand. It looked good on the menu but looking at it in your hands you wonder about the complexities of it, the strange new sauces you've never heard of. The weird bread. The way the waitresses tits jiggled as she brought it to you. The doughnuts in the other seats watching you eat it.

So this season what? What amazing things will we see from those acolytes of the demon Jorge Mendes? Agent extraordinaire What delights will our jaded eyes be assailed with? There is an assemblage here, of players who understand Kwan better than Stan Hardknock 'tackler' and midfielder of cold English Winters will never fathom. From Compton our little funky brothers like Ronan and Enkobahare will flourish if they open their minds to the blue sky cocktails on the beach football of our new additions. There will be funky jazz chords underpinned by the relentless percussion of Ronans undoubted ability. The splash of vermilion activity across our hallowed green turf from Enkobahare.....maybe.

It's chaotic isn't it? This whole chapter ricochet across a few years. There are names you are unfamiliar with and machinations you have some ignorance about. But that's ok. We are defining our relationship now and setting you up for the madness to come and for fucks sake it is a veritable stew of crazy shit. There shouldn't be a book about this madness at all really. I shouldn't really be writing about it because I'm not trained. I am not a writer just an observer, and my addled brain observes a lot differently to others and I write that madness down, for you. Maybe ask some questions too. Who are these Chinese fellas? Who is this Nuno bloke?

You have to have faith with me of course and everything will come clearer as this book goes on or maybe not. All I do is write about it the best way I can and that's by snatching little pieces of half heard conversations and opinions. Reading a few things and most of all watching. Right now I'm back in July 2016 and the season to come is again like a great unknown and in some ways I yearn for that ignorance back as now, as I write this I am broken and joyful, sad and happy. We have fought hard and well, supporters of Wolverhampton Wanderers and the team, the staff, everybody. We have been on a long fucking journey that seemed to have no end. Having climbed the mountain we look ahead and there is a new bigger mountain to climb and one after that too. All the craziness of this season will again be rolled out for our pleasure for another year. Can we take it? This mental pressure? This madness and new dogmas to adopt? I'm not sure. But lets start at the kick off yes? Lets go back to the start of the whole crazy ride.

On the bench in the garden you see, it's sunny, it's July 2017 and I've only got half a brain on the goings on at Wolves. I'm contemplating some writing although I'm not a writer. I fancy writing a book about this season. Bees are buzzing through the Wednesfield air laden with a bit of smoke from the fire my next door neighbour has decided to provoke. Fucking hell Moz you doughnut. There's one of the areas young Moms walking past and she wants a chat. That's cool too and I wax lyrical about the book idea. I'm going to document this madness you see. She fusses the dogs at my feet and I can see down her top. I'm disgusting. Turn your head away Mikey and look at something else. Talk about the fucking book idea. Do anything. Wolves. That always kills a few hours God bless 'em. Whether it's shouting at other people or whispering things I always seem to come to the same subject over and over again. The team, the owners, the days out.

'You're basically sports reporting' she said. No, this book isn't about 'sport' it's about Wolves, a subject far important than sport. But hey! A friendly against Crisptown. What a strange place Leicester is, so strange that I can actually spell it first try with right clicky red squiggles. Cool as fuck. A team full of strangers Leicester are. Like Walkers Crisps they promise (on the packaging) a taste sensation, a luxurious dip into the world of the thinly sliced deep fried potato. Until you open them and find a sad little collection of over flavoured, overpriced spud.

I haven't liked them since I was doubled over laughing in the 80's when their fans ran down a dual carriageway (at our away support) dressed in dungarees. Mad Clampett fashions. Relegation for them this season. Their Kwan is gone. Maybe. I don't know. I know it will be a good test for our new Manager. I don't know what to make of him yet of course. He's the new bloke who moved in next door. You're interested but not too interested yet. Because me and him haven't circled around each other having a sniff at each others arses like dogs do.

We seek common ground us men, that way we know we can trust whoever it is we are engaging with. Do I know this Nuno yet? No. Maybe through the medium of football we may have a tangle of possibilities that our future relationship will be rosy. I look at photos of him on the internet when I go back into the house. Maybe I could like him. He's no Lambert. He looks stylish and debonair, with a bit of a rough edge too. He looks like he plays golf but doesn't love playing it. He just does it because his mind needs to shut off for a while. Yes and intense fella.

I have a look on social media to see what goes on. See who's moaning about what. So I'm engaged with other football fans of various teams over the whole financial fair play thing. Of course I am well versed in the complexities of the regulatory initiative of European.....OK I'm not, but if you type loudly and offer perfunctory violence then the steam and fume from these strangely dressed social media-er-rers becomes muted and unsure, they start to nibble their finger nails, they start to question their own knowledge. Money is King in football, chuck enough money into a club and they will gather the necessary players to do that. 20 squillion squids on Alberto Nicetan from some sun drenched shit hole in France or Spain will be good. He sprays passes around as an afterthought, he runs like a man possessed. Welcome Alberto and the media team go 'say Wolves ay we' so the freaks on Facebook get semis. Alberto doesn't give a fuck and to be honest neither do I. What I want is Alberto to lash a few goals in, make the plays, listen to Nuno who seems like he has a fervour, or Fosun showed him videos of what happens when the third Dragon Tong from Honk Kong are called in.

I look in my inbox and there is fume and anger there already. We haven't even played a fucking game yet. Give me a break. Most of the fume is from Aston Villa fans. Who are they? I'm not sure why they are interested in us to be honest. Perhaps their fear is leaking over into their social media presence. There are only so many memes you can use before a subtle private message with promises of violence pops up in your inbox. I am amused. I'm not rolling around with you in a car park because you don't like what I said about Jack Fucking Grealish their current 'wunderkid'.

The thing is, there's no other club in the UK that deserves the thrills and spills of top quality football than Wolverhampton Wanderers. We invented football, we invented floodlit night games, we invented passion, we invented everything to do with football. So why aren't we playing the likes of Barcelona and Madrid? Let those questions drop where they may. I might even try to answer them here.

We have dumped our ex Manager Dean Saunders into the netherworld of the occasional pundit gig. Poor bastards who have to listen to that fool. Why is Dean Saunders rather than 'What is'. He's off down the M6 and Steve Morgan our former owner is too. We always knew he was Liverpool. But some look upon him with puppy eyes. 'Oh Steve why have you abandoned us to the Chinese' they wail. I couldn't give a shit. It's time for something new, something a bit more fucking viable. It's still sunny out there and I'm contemplating a few more hours in the sun watching the dogs cavort and hassling passers by with conversation.

Yes. Steve Morgan. The Scouse Mafia, The Compton Mafia a Cosa Nostra of fuck ups and circle jerks of cosy chats in offices, of glad hands, dry handshakes and knives in the back. The system is fucked up my friends. Too long have we suffered the lack of investment, watched the half dead journeyman players crack out a smile for the waiting press. Yes, we need Tony Wankle ex Manchester United defender simply because of his 'experience' and blah. Bring on Fred Swellbow too full back for Liverpool in 1995 and lately of Sheffield whatever. They are happy to get a few extra wages for playing when they should be setting up some shite sports consulting company or something. They run on the pitch and look like shadows of their former selves and we sing for them yes, that's what we do. But inside we are dying at the sorry vision of it. That vision is forged on bullshit ideas about 'experience' and the rigours of the English Football league. But deep down we know it's just bullshit. It's an old boys network and yes the echelons that pile around clubs is full of them. Did we not listen to Lambert and wonder what fucking planet he was on. We had heard it all before and that glimmering flame of hope was flickering to death in the cold wind of their redundant ideas. We trudge backwards and forwards slipping on the wet floor of the subway at the back of the Southbank regardless.

We deserved better than we got,We deserve top flight football because simply put we really are the greatest team in the world. I'm not arguing with anybody on this point. We invented the European Cuop for Gods sake. Floodlit games against Honved. Black and white newsreel footage. Putting England back on the forefront of peoples minds. What happened since I haven't the time or the memory to discuss, only that most of it was shit but interspersed with glittery happy madness we quickly forgot unless we were in the attic leafing through a box of old match day programs.

We may not have the trophies and the honours to prove it (lately) but trust me we are the fucking Godzilla of English football. Thus awake we trawl through the sludgy depths, eyes blinking at the bright lights and attention until announcing our arrival with a roar and a quick left jab at some high rise office building. Everything tends to crumble when this particular beast is unleashed. When the team we have has some sort of epiphany and goes onto that hallowed turf to dick some team or other. Oh my days what delights, and the subway reverberates to our songs.

But what about the Kwan? What about the game? I had to skip between feeds, I had to phone people, I had to stitch together uploaded videos. Leicester seemed to be very shit or had some sort of hangover from their title winning exploits. So a text message here and there from people who were there. Twitter was good, updates. The radio got kicked across the room within five minutes as they laid into this Nuno bloke. Fair play I didn't know him that well but at least he was one of us. I walked around the garden to cool off a little with my phone in my hand. Messages like 'fucking hell we look good' and 'Mikey we are all over them'. But I'm not getting ahead of myself but 'Ruben Neves is a fucking God' trouble me.

Douglas. I like the cut of his jib and at a million quid he looks like an absolute bargain. His link up play going forwards was a joy. Constantly watching the movement of players in front of him he has second sight when it comes to moving forward. No hesitation in him at all but a feeling, a metaphysical knowledge of when to move forward, when to hang back, constantly watching and probing. I haven't got a clue who he is as yet. I look up a photo of him on the internet and there he is. He doesn't look very happy for sure. But he has travelled around Europe a bit. Some of that Euro vibe must have rubbed off. You have to have courage to move to Turkey and play football. The language difficulty, the strange food, the stranger players around him. I like him. He seems dynamic. A million squid as well. Cheap. We have bought useless doughnut shaped players for four times that. He looks slick and fit.

Conor Coady. After being shifted around like a shit ornament last season he has grown. Grown or realisation? I'm not sure, but his voice booming over the pitch, shouting, giving out the orders reminded me of someone but I can't remember who at the moment but it will come to me.

Coady is a dude that will flourish under the tutelage of Nuno because A. He's not daft and B. He's not daft. Put Boly in there too and you have a unit. What is Boly? He's not human that's for sure. Playing against Boly must be like trying to wrestle telegraph poles or shuffling rubbish skips. What is Boly? Who knows so far but I tug my forelock at him. Same with Miranda, he didn't look like he gave a shit. His undoubted knowledge of his position was amazing. All of a sudden a player that had an almost telepathic understanding of how an opposition player was going to move. Who were these people? Why weren't they falling over like normal? Running into strange unthreatening positions making the defend-able undefend-able. I don't know. Next week when Boro come down here I'm seriously thinking of staying sober so I can work out what in the fuck is going on. If only so I can watch Boro players arseholes squeak when the Bolynator comes out for a fifty-fifty. It must be like getting hit by a UPS van.

Neves was a thing. A thinker obviously, undoubted athletic ability, a quality and a breath of fresh air. Searching the variables of the midfield he had it sussed in minutes and thus as all greatest workmen he crafted a pass here and a run there, a little dink of the ball on his left foot, shift weight gently and he was off again, searching, looking for movement. Of course as he envelopes the whole team and understands how they move those passes will become as natural and unconscious as the greatest teams.

But I'm confused again. Why the fuck is Neves there on the pitch? Where is Wallace or Saville? Last years flavours now resigned to the bargain bin. Neves shuffles and delights where the other pair plodded and sodded around like they didn't believe in what they were doing. I'm listening intently you see, to the radio which I have picked back up. Wolves are the drug you can't stop using. Inside my head of course I am filling in the gaps. When Neves collects the ball he makes the Leicester midfield look like fools. I see him doing it you see. Making up my own reels and frames in the great movie of this friendly. I should be there of course but buying my season ticket cost three weeks food and I'm eating custard creams and corn beef for tea. As I have a vivid imagination Neves becomes Pele for a moment because I can't remember what Ruben Neves looks like. It's still early in the season and again I don't want to hope too much. But for the moment Pele he is.

There are probably other players I should have mentioned but shout out to Jota, Cavaleiro, Saiss and a shout to Costa as well even though he's injured because I love him too. Last season was hard on this little man. He kept us up of course, single handedly. I don't entertain discussions on that subject. Helder Costa, small lithe, that Portuguese look, low centre of gravity, fast too. The radio is crackling and we score. Cavaleiro. I laugh a lot. I erupt in intense moods, fling my arms about then remember it's only a pre season friendly but, I know inside it was important. This was my team. Some rave thing comes over the airwaves, my voice shouting has moved the radio Kwan in some way. It's fucked I think. Kicking it across the room would not have given it the love it needs to stay on station. Snap crackle and fucking pop. I go to my phone and check the social medias. Yes. Belief there among the fan base. Quiet murmurs of victory and happiness. I know it's a friendly, I know the inner monologue is crisping up my positive thoughts like a Butterfly landing in the barbecue. Sizzle.

On a final note we are searching for a striker. I see that, we've had some misfires, misfits and misanthropes since Bully. This stage is set for a Hero so the picking has to be correct. What Pro striker wouldn't love to be at the sharp end of those foot juggling lunatics from Portugal. Mate, you'll be shouting for the ball running full tilt towards the Southbank and it will bonk you on the head before you get a word out. In fact I think the striker we are after should fucking pay to play with such a team. I'm excited. When I get excited I start shouting and there is nobody here to listen apart from the dogs and Moz next door fucking about with his fire.

Moz is a Walsall FC fan and has a season ticket. He is prodding his fire with an angry look on his face. I can see beads of sweat on his bald head. Oh my days. A victory. I want to hug Moz but I control myself. He wouldn't like it. He throws a sheet of plastic on the fire and an acrid odour, eye stinging attacks me. I cough and shut the window. Fucking doughnut. Typical Walsall fan.

Anyway. It's a week away. Start of the season when it all kicks off in more ways than one. What is this madness? I watch an interview with this Nuno. He is measured and calm. I like that. I'm starting to like him too although I am reticent.

I sing a Wolves song while I make a cup of tea and there in my belly a little tickle, a small butterfly trying to get out, I hope he avoids the flaming barbecue of this division. It's a harsh place full of pitfalls.. I try not to think about it. I don't want my heart broken again please. But I'm trusting. This Nuno says something about ideas and I'm interested. What ideas? What Coach at Wolves has ideas? Contain excitement, stop dancing around when you get up, stop acting like you've found a box of kittens. Time to get that stern face on. But I'm erect and ductile, proud, jolly. I shout a little at people outside when I'm talking about the match. I'm waxing lyrics at them. Like grime bars, sudden bursts of energy before I choke it back. I'm starting to believe and we haven't even kicked a ball in the league yet and we have Middlesbrough at Molineux.

The Southbank is our Church and Saint Nuno our latest Holy bringer of joys, its a fucking long season, blood will fall, icons will be torn from their alcoves, new heroes, new villains. What will happen to us? What will happen to these players we have signed? Will they collapse as soon as the Winter sets in? Will they pine for home and the sun? Will something strange happen within the club and it all goes to shit again? I'm being negative then the next second I'm positive. Outside in the garden the Bees just buzz around, the smell of burning plastic is a memory. Next week the madness is soon come. Three corned beef dinners. A few Fray Bentos pies. I run out of cigarettes on Wednesday. Drop some slabs on Thursday.

Well here we are. Saturday, brushing the sleep out of your eyes. Awake. With a face like a six year old kid at Xmas. You want to run down the subway behind the Southbank in your pyjamas smashing open the gates to see what ya got! What we gonna get?? Fuck knows. I'm old enough to know that running down the subway would be a brief knee crackling thing, a terrifying rush into the unknown. What we going to get? Beautiful jazzy slickness underpinned by a rhythmic and functional midfield? Or the disgruntled dysfunctional uninspired bootball? A defence that befits the description or a mosh pit of players running around like they have a bee in their quiff. August madness, people walking around in shorts.

There are some fucking pale looking sad legs hanging about. Like stringy blue veined horrific reminders of the short summers we have. I'm on the bus and there are loads of these stringy nightmares. Shit tattoos too. Don't think I'm being a hipster dickhead here. Mine are just as crap. Legs are brown though but I'm wearing jeans and they are new, itchy, fresh dye. I'll have blue legs later and think I've got circulation problems. First day of the season, here we go, the madness begins, the songs, too many beers, Jesus Christ help me. I'm shaking as I fondle my bus ticket watching the world go past.

I don't know. Here at the moment as a type this on my phone I'm in a pub in Wednesfield. It's crowded with 11 am early starters. They ignore their fresh morning pints for a few minutes, glancing at it, unsure whether or not to have a drink and start that slippy slide into daytime incoherent beer buzz world. Few Wolves Dads too, fresh shirts, not very fresh shoes, elbows, bellys, loud a little, excited, an undercurrent of tension. I take a sip of cold lager but it doesn't settle the nerves. Doesn't settle the tension. Don't forget in this world we live in it's the fate of those that walk into Molineux that they will end up sucking on either the honey from the Golden tit or the jug of despondency.

I'm not sure what I'll be choking on later but how often has that beautiful green lake in front of us turned into a pit of tar? How often do we have a wet wipe thrown at us and the demand that we 'finish yourself off'? But I notice I've walked the long way into town and I've gathered three very violent friends around me that I want to lose if I can. They are mates but they are lunatics. What nefarious activities they get up to as they gather a few quid who knows? I always ask them to keep it quiet, I like my ignorance, I don't want that particular knowledge. I'm happy just being in their company. For violent criminals have their own humour.

We walk through a tunnel at the back of Carvers Builders yard. It's dark for a minute and I'm still shaking a little, still a bit nervous. In my pocket my season ticket, I keep checking it like a fool. I have a crumpled tenner in the other pocket. I'm only having a couple of pints today. I want to see what's going on. See the madness unleashed.

'What the fuck were you on about? Kwan? You daft cunt'

In town, the men about town. The pubs will be rammed. Elbows, waving tenners at the bar staff in the vain hope that sexy lil thing with the pink hair and push up tits will glance at your hopeful little mush 'yes can I help you?' You forget what you want for a minute as it's hot with the scent of aftershave and sweat and beer. My mate has added her on Instagram he says. I dread to think what she's going to receive. He gently strokes her hand as he gives her some cash. She looks like she's just put her hand in sick. He's 44 years old. She's probably 20 or so. It will never work mate. Leave it alone.

New season, 'Tabula rasa' the blank slate. Everybody on nil points. Sunderland got a dicking last night. People talking about new players. Nuno, Neves, Jota, Boly and people nodding like they know who they are. But these players have yet to be coloured in with the crayons of an eventful match. They are abstract and strange, exotic. You don't want to say too much so you nod at the statements of those who still actually play football, who do actually puke on the touchline of the pitches at Fowlers park for Sunday football. What do I know? She spills your beer on your hand a little. You smile but she doesn't give a shit. I don't mind to be honest. I'm too old for that crap. My teeth are crumbling. I need to go for a piss in the night. I've got great hair though. Positives. She gives me a glance as she walks to the other end of the bar but, I look away. Outside the window of the Royal London, people streaming past to the Molineux, I smile a bit, second pint and it's still a little rancid, a little hard to get down.

Carl Ikeme Wolves number 1 and ever present Goalkeeper has got acute blood cancer. I'm thinking of him walking down the subway. Slippy. It's humid and the walls of it are slick. People are singing and bumping into me but it's cool because it's the start of the season and somebody blows smoke into my face, then a nose full of fruity vape. Beer stink, hot dogs. Mr Sizzle crackling away. Another song. Tap pocket for your season ticket, is it still there? Yeah. Cool. For fucks sake I'm shaking and the old agoraphobia is kicking in a bit but there it is. The pitch shining emerald and bright and it's open and my chest relaxes and I take a deep breath. Thank fuck for that. Carl was good, he sounded OK man. But there right at the back of my mind is that gnawing feeling and the memories of pain, that pain. It's going to be weird not seeing him in front of us in the Southbank. He always claps us and waves. It's going to be extra fucking weird. John Ruddy this big bald bloke from Norwich is in there instead. It doesn't look right and the familiar once taken away for the new has got my finding that bus ticket in my pocket and I'm ripping it into little pieces in my hands. Nervous. Shitting myself.

Middlesbrough fans are filling the bottom of the Steve Bull. What they like? Grisly bunch. Some obviously not looking at the Southbank, some obviously looking at the Southbank. I had heard some of their fans walking up. Strange gargled accent without consonants it seemed. Confident their spending in the close season would do a job and it might, or it might not. This is a skirmish of course and by the end of this season, well, we'll see where you am eh? Other than that I couldn't give a shit about Boro, but I was getting local and angry and the teams were coming out. It is of course the few seconds before battle commences that the nerves settle down and the conversations around you stop a little. Instead songs. Jeff Beck Hi-Ho Silver lining. Chunka chunka chunka chunka. Guitar chords reverberating around the packed out Molineux. Somebody has farted. It's disgusting and fresh.

There is emotion here, on mens faces who you would be hard pressed to get a whimper out of if you were hitting their balls with a mallet. I just held up my card, looked at the pitch, the only lump in my throat was Ruddy walking into the goal mouth and not Carl…..but we were off.

It took me ten minutes to work out that these fellas in Gold were actually our team. What? I hadn't had a drink before the game apart from a shit lager…who? What? The ball flicked from player to player effortless. What? Slickness and skills in abundance. Brighty gets the ball from midfield he twists, spirals, ball back to Neves the architect…he builds transitions from midfield to front line, he doesn't even look. The play book from the short time he has been with us is rote and pure dogma. He knows very little about the players around him but he knows the academics of the whole thing, what the plan is. He slips another Boro defence splitting pass and Brighty gets confused again and is dispossessed.

Danny next to me elbows me in the neck again. Bright needs to chill the fuck out but he reminds me of me. Always making something easy into something hard. He is a slalomer, in and around, jinky and low centre of gravity moving himself into positions. I want to sit him down and say 'just boot the fucking thing into the net' but what do I know? I know Brighty has that thing. That equisite balance with the ball at his feet, but he has a goldfish memory thing going on. Good for three or four seconds then the ball tumbles away. It's a mind thing with him. He doesn't believe in himself yet. That will come I hope.

Michaelangelo is attributed to have said 'what is this dance of colour and light if the plaster underneath is poor and soft'. I agree, Nuno grooves to defensive foundations at that was very much in evidence. Boly, Commander Conor Coady, Miranda all had some dodgy as fuck moments but they were moments that flickered through the mind in seconds, ethereal really as the ball moved with speed out of defence and into midfield and once again we were making moves…..hang on….no bootball. This was quality shit. I felt myself calming down after Assambalonga or whatever his face is tried to dart into our box with either Coady or Boly chewing his head. Coady amazed me. This player who I accused of running like he had broken arms shut me the fuck up. Scouse sounds echoed around as he commanded people, he's a Commander, a Captain. Now all of a sudden it's all nailed down and ship shape.

None of our defence looked massively troubled at the weight of a few million quids worth of team having a go. Boly rubbed Assambalongas head. I think Boly wanted to crush it. This territory is Boly-Land. How dare they try and rustle that ball into the net. Our net, his net maybe. He's so settled and assured with those big shoulders moving and tilting as he regains the ball effortlessly from the feet of a Middlesbrough player. Sublime art this is. I like him already.

Was it 33 minutes? A back pass that led Bonatini into the gold dreams of scoring at the Molineux BOOM! 1 fucking Nil, crowd goes wild. Danny elbows me in the head again. I'm looking for the fat Boro fan in the Steve Bull waving the fiver. Hahahahahaha you fat bastard, but he's not looking at the Southbank any more, he's looking at his shoes, rubs his face and goes up the stairs for a beer or a burger. Boro fooligans gesticulate, mime their violence. One-Nil. Ecstasy in Gold and Black it was beautiful and assured. A dink of loveliness and Bonatini wheels away in joy followed by these new boys in the team. Gorgeous. I laugh as the crowd settles and we kick off again. I roll a half time roll up. It's good, sun shining. One fucking nil. I lick the rizla paper and grin.

What happened after that? Football. Chances here and there for Boro, a few for us but it had to be Nunos day after all. His Zen like persona has gathered together some talent and the basis on which to build a lasting legacy. This! After the clown Lamberto. A dynamic and creative team with a pocket full of variables in Ivan Cavaleiro and Helder Costa, a team who know how to pass (if you ignore the first day at school nerves). Crowd shout for Nuno. Nuno waves…the noise inside the Molineux at full time was not relief, it was hope again.

Walking to the bus stop I wondered about the whole day. There was tension there, you could feel it rippling through the stand at various points of the match. Expectation is a bloody dangerous thing and yet we always cling on to hope, always. The Kwan is flowing through the team, communications and the odd pat on the back or off the ball conversations between players. Watching Nuno…Generalissimo Nuno stoic and unmoved at least on the outside. People walking through the subway were upbeat and vocal. The Zeitgeist was positive, the feeling to me at least was a good one. Nuno is a strong hand on the tiller and while other managers pray and cry out to God in the storm, Nuno demands his crew row hard towards shore.

So I lean my head on the bus window and watch Heath Town frazzle past and I'm calm and that hope that my team are ascendant gives me a little tickle on my belly, makes my legs twitch as I put my foot through the ball as I'm replaying Bonas goal on an endless loop. I look down and notice a footprint on the suede of my Adidas. I dont care..but why? Carls illness has brought a lot of my own memories back. The chemotherapy, the pain, the mad things that go through your mind, and all of a sudden I'm tired again even though it's been six years since I finished my own treatment. In my head of course I'm giving Carl Ikeme the speech I would like to give him. I have tactics you see. I'm a survivor.

What a load of shit eh Carl? That moment they tell you that insid
you have been looking after all these years is a whole bundle of Cancer
bollocks. What goes through the mind? In those few seconds and minutes after?
All the bad things, all the good things, and they are still talking but we are only
half listening. All the fears we had of 'that' illness are playing through your
head like a really shit film. But you know this so I won't dwell on it only to say
'fuck' and 'what the fuck'. Fuck. You're one of us…when you're defending the
Southbank goal and the play is up the other end it's like you are watching it
with us…that's how important you are to me and everybody else. You in
trouble bruv? You want us to kick off? How the fuck do we find this illness and
smash the fuck out of it when we can't even see it?

I have history with Cancer. I actually died from Cancer. Weird isn't it? In New
Cross Hospital on the 20th March 2010. Intensive care unit. I had been rushed
in by ambulance two days before with stomach pains and a massive infection, a
deadly infection I suppose. They said I wouldn't survive an exploratory
operation to find out what that big lump was on my Colon. But they did and I
didn't. The Cancer had eaten through my gut and for a week I had been
evacuating what was in my bowel through a massive tear in the gut wall. After
the operation about 3am my blood pressure went ballistic and my heart stopped.
By chance my Nurse Grace grabbed a passing Dr and he went into his training
and brought me back, stabbed a whole load of needles in my neck, pumped
more drugs in and I was back on the pitch. I'm not going to wax on about the
operations and the treatments after. It's gone and in the past. But it still nags at
you when it's three am and you have gone downstairs for a glass of water and
the sweat on your body is going cold in the night air.

But what about after diagnosis? I was alone, that much I knew. Despite the well
wishers and the friends, the family and the phone calls. Alone because quite
simply it is our battle. It's a personal one. Cancer is an opponent with no
fucking honour. It's a back stabber in the alley, it's the thief who steals in the
dead of night, it is not an honourable opponent. So how did I look at it? This
thing that has made everybody I love shed tears on my Hospital bed. Easy. I
had some honour, a little bit any way. I was a good guy, I mean fair enough I've
done some daft things but overall I was a good guy, like you. Why should good
guys have to suffer? Questions bowl through your mind about the validity of
the whole shebang but it's all wasted energy, questioning it, energy needed for
battle. I looked at it like that, a fight with the Bully at school, he's bigger than
us, hands like a joint of pork, big thick head, haircut like the council had
fucking strimmed it, you know the type. But we always get him in the end, we

ways find him at his most vulnerable, we always defeat the bully, always. Carl? Cancer has a shit trim and shit two stripe shoes.

So as a man of honour and a 'good bloke' what are you supposed to do now faced with such a despicable enemy? Easy mate. Carry on with your life as if nothing had happened. Eat the same stuff, do the same things you always did. How much of a thought do we give Cancer? Fucking none at all mate. Forget it. Let the Doctors and the Nurses do their thing. Do the scans, the blood tests they want. Let them be empirical and quantitative, measure the blood cells and the T-cells and whatever they want. We shouldn't allow one negative thought to enter our head because it's like worrying over the bully at school, the unpaid bill, the rattle under the bonnet of your car. Pointless. You see the day they told you that you had Cancer was the day you started to beat it. Cancer hates nothing more than ignoring it totally.

Two months after my initial operation I was at Wednesfield Plaza skatepark with a colostomy bag and the chemo shakes. Skating around gently among the other lunatics. I would slip away behind the quarter pipe to puke every ten minutes. Later on I would fall over and squash the bag at my belly and the shit would cover my trousers. Dudes ran around me with wet wipes and paper towels they had got from the local cafe. Love totally. I think you have the same love Carl, from us reprobates. If you were here now you would know our love for sure.

Carl. In the future there are going to be some bad times when it's going to be hard to lift your arm to get hold of that glass of water you want on the bedside table. Cancer has a voice and it wheezes on at you all day and night but fuck that shit. Fuck it right up. Ignore it. Put the TV on or babble at somebody about crap. Anything to shut that annoying little wanker up. Because what it says doesn't make any sense at all. the same as the whole idea of it as an illness. We destroy it with laughter and carrying on doing the same shit we do every day. We know that there will come a day when you find Cancer lacking, when you have it on the back foot and the more you love and laugh the smaller that bully gets, in fact he crouches down under your laughter curling up into a ball that gets smaller and smaller until its just a speck and then boom it just fucks off out of the whole Ikeme world.

They said I had a 1% chance of survival. When my surgeon told me I laughed in her face (as well as I could). I discovered people making decisions for me while I was ill but soon grabbed the whole subject with both hands. YOU make the decisions here Carl, you and you only. You tell people what you're going to do after you have beaten it to a fucking pulp. You will be the one laughing when the cancer skitters away down the gutter back to the darkness where it belongs. Make plans, book holidays far in the future, make those plans concrete and firm in your own mind.

Kwan is important for sure. It's not hope it's a concrete and tangible thing, it's an energy. It's what we use to get through our day and it can also be a potent weapon. Kwan is the love in the world, it's your kids laughing, your dog chasing it's tail, it's the way your partner smiles when you've done something stupid. It's sunsets, the last minute winner in an important match. It's not 'believing' it's knowing. It's not 'faith' either it's 'real'. Kwan is a plan too.

Now when you think about how many people are supporting you (and it's all of us trust me) you have to suck up that love, pull it into you and make it a weapon to use against this arsehole of an illness. You aren't alone at all because as you face Cancer if you take a quick glance behind you then you will see all of us too. Every ugly mush you see as you run up to the Southbank goal to take your position is fighting with you, every gap tooth pisshead, every fucking lunatic who stumbled through the subway. Every clap of the hands is a slap around the face of your Cancer. There will be songs too, sung for you and you only and out of that energy is power and that power is for you too. Listen to us and use that love to destroy this thing. Songs have power, that's why we have Hymns and our songs should be seen in the same light.

Be a good Warrior Carl, make every blow count against this thing, this disgrace of a thing and I will be honest, you will come out of it a different man. It's not the disease that changes you, its the battle. When everybody has gone and you're on your bed staring at the ceiling feeling that Chemo burn remember that you have all of us and if you decide to return to playing football the day you run out on that pitch there will be tears, laughter, and songs but right now our fists are clenched, fucking Wolves ay we mate.

Ah Carl. Bloody hell.

But hey another day, another no dollars and before we know it the dawn of the cups, sponsored by some fucking doughnut company you've never heard of 'The Bone &Sons Funeral Directors cup' or the 'Fresh Fred Kebab Trophy'. Whatever…league cup? Ar, I know that one, we won it a few times. Andy Gray with the hair that seemed like it was styled by a monkey with a set of Aldi hedge trimmers. Apparently it's sponsored by one of those weird Asian Energy drinks companies. Yeah, I don't drink that stuff. It sticks in the throat like a six quid bottle of Wembley stadium Budweiser. Wait till the monkey gland extract kicks in and you are outside your house shouting at lorries in your minion themed bed wear

Yeovil ay it. Never played them before apparently. One of those clubs where the fans remind you 'yeah we played you in 1985 and we battered you one nil' and you nod and smile and wonder what the fucking hell they are on about. They came down to the Molineux the other night with the Beano Book of

Football tactics, open on page one. Defend with eleven players or 'defence as Mosh pit'. What do you expect from Somersetians? The Chellini gap 4-3-3 as beautifully presented by Juventus in the 70's?

They drink Cider all the time these West Country lot. It was lumpy and ungainly, the last dance with an effalump in a Bilston nightclub, she's had too many Malibus, you cant get your arms around her...Melissa Multipack. What fucking conclusions do we draw from this match? I'm not sure. I've scouted the reports that a steal huge lumps from but even in 'PRESS CITY' the vibe seems lacklustre and has a 'going through the motions' thing. Am I being unfair? Probably

Well from what I have gathered it was like taking Melissa Multipack back to her house for some half drunk jolly time. You know you're going to hate yourself for watching it and thats why I didn't go but...nah I didn't have the cash to be fair but...Yeovil and the team we had out interlocks perfectly with Melissa taking her knickers off and you look at them on the floor draped over 'Romellos' electric 4×4 he had for xmas, draped or hung? There is the smell of takeaway food, the odd polystyrene box of half cooked rib, maybe a chicken ball, some funky noodles, kicked under the bed and forgotten. You awake with a start, what the fuck is that? It's one of Melissas hair extensions on the non too clean duvet. It looks like a deep sea creature this early on.

So our team grappled with the madness of Malibu Melissa and to be honest there's no better team to put out than the old familiar faces, the dudes that have their own chair in the proverbial Wolves pub. They scoot around the edges of this new revolution. Unsure of the language now, Portuguese maybe some broken English. It's time for our Shropshire fringe players to step up and get their groove on. Step forwards Jack Price and Dave Edwards. What better pairing to tackle the mountain of Melissa than them. Workman like and stoic I suppose, men that wouldn't think about tongue tackling the alcoholic coconut breath of Yeovil, grappling with the bra that was welded together at Thompson Chassis in 1979, peeling the defensive Yeovil knickers over that massive hump of an arse, taking a deep breath and getting stuck in...this is where you earn your money I suppose. Cup games, uninspired opposition.

Jordan Graham and Young Ronan were like onlookers really, quite happy to let Dave and Jack deal with the problem of Multipack Mel. This is to be agreed with. Graham and Jordan are cut from a finer cloth and you can tell from the ten minutes I spent looking at the highlights that they were aghast at some of the things they were being forced to watch and a couple of moments there I was again on Cannock Chase when Stan Collymores willy comes through the car window and tickles me ear. Whoah and eek went Graham and Ronan, wahey! went Dave and Jack. So fair play to them, Graham is just coming back from injury but he has the knowledge and the flair, that slick Instagram presence on the pitch…Ronan is Irish so he has a romantic literary heart which comes out in his football….but they are watching Melissas big hairy arse going up and down as the Yeovillians hear the echo of their managers voice crying after their eight something dicking at the hands of Luton a few days before. 'Euuuyyyoochoooork' Melissa goes and Ronan is searching for that open window, a slick pass, escape from the Lunt experience of a cup match, of Melissa tearing out her hair weave in passionate farting madness.

Our poor Portugeezers. Tanned little athletes, yesterday they were in Monaco or Portugal, or a Turkish beach, playing with the tight body models on the beach, later on dinner at 'Chagelle' gently fried red snapper with fresh lemon and a divine cumin, tarragon flavoured rice with a sprig of dill as an afterthought, an amusing touch, a walk along the beach later in the cool of the evening……now? Chicagos nightclub on a Friday night, grab a granny, kebab and a punch in the face while waiting for a taxi. How can you torture these poor bastards with this Nuno? Have you no heart? Or is it a tactic? Sometimes of course you have to expose these delicate egos to the horrors of war. For sure that's what Championship football and early Cup games are. It's a long haul for sure and you want the players mentally prepared and ready for the coming months. But Melissa and her cellulite wrinkly arse, the delights of Yeovil. Jesus Christ. I can see them sobbing in a fucking shell hole in some grainy black and white anti war flick. Dirt falls on them as they sob. Nuno, you are a hard taskmaster.

Here is Yeovil my young Jedis, this is the start of your war. Step forward young Salt'n'Vinagre, He's only eighteen for fucks sake! Melissa will kill him! He'll be scarred for life! Watch him struggle under the weight of Mel's knickers, how will he do?? Well, he did ok and thats what fills me with a bit of love for him. Beating players he looks up to see what's going on, not a lot. Dave and Jack are still going at it like a relentless Bank Holiday Steam Engine extravaganza, Graham and Ronan are trying to stay out of it so Vinagre does what he does, he takes the ball into space, beats a few dudes, shows us what the cut of his jib is, which is lovely to be honest and the sight of the Yeovillian/Lunt nexus going on in front of him isn't upsetting too much.

He thinks being there is enough and he's right so he's clapping and laughing at Jack and Dave knowing that yes, you can't just walk into Mordor you can also fuck it to death and that's exactly what our midfield looks like against Yeovil. But the ball is moving around for sure. Not as well as the match against Middlesbrough for sure. There are 'seagull' moments. Watching the odd solitary bird wafting around on the thermals. Somebody treads on my foor. 'Sorry mate' I say, then 'fuck' It wasn't my fault, why am I apologising? Nouha Dicko.

Nouha Nouha Nouha, what trials you have had my friend. When you collapsed in front of the Southbank with a crocked knee last season. I could have cried. Now look at you, all trim, you've dropped some weight, you look strong, you are winning headers, what's that all about? Goals, you've grabbed a couple. You looked in Melissas fridge while Dave and Jack did the Multipack dance, what was in there? Half a can of flat Coke, some chicken dinosaur shapes, an old lettuce and soldier that you are you had a swig of the coke, shoved a few dinosaur shapes in your gob and volleyed the Lettuce straight through the window and escaped. Thank You Nouha, I've never had a negative thought about you as you were playing...Nouha? Nouhas gone, through the window, legging it up the Willenhall road trying to phone Central Taxis before Dave and Jack have done what needs to be done....

So it was done. Yeovil awake to a sore head and go downstairs to get Romello, Jaden and Liam (Melissas kids) ready for the day which means throwing each of them a bag of Monster Munch for breakfast. Oh what days. I hope that these mixes Nuno provides us, ie the Latino hip pumping with the relentless gabba football we played most of last season will instigate an outbreak of beautiful football within the heads of our long standing players. Boly next to Danny Batth scared me a little, like the Yosemite Sam tattoo on Melissas tit, or the name of her dead Father inked on her neck. It will be OK though won't it? 'Big Willy Boly' is easing into this side. He's on loan at the moment, we don't know him that well yet but I have a feeling about him. He has a footballing brain for sure, a little something about him. He has ignited a little fire in my head, a smouldering cigarette down a settee kind of a fire. He moves well in that box and out of it too. Yeovil players just bounced off him as he taxed their ball away from their feet. I like him.

Derby Saturday. I'm not going. But I will provide some awful transcript to what has gone on there. Our team? They will shower themselves for a long time after the Yeovil experience, maybe the self loathing of what they had to do will mean a few tears curled up as they sit on the shower floor and later as they watch 'Cash in the Attic' on their 92″ HD Bludclaat Blu-ray surround sound TV and stretch out on the luxurious giraffe skin settee, they will think of Mel from the Lunt with some disgust but inside their hearts a little affection too.

Last week I gazed at a photo of Nuno and I swear I could feel my hair become thicker and a wind blew from somewhere and my hair was blowing back, I was like Robert Plant now and my locks were waving around. Nuno you Prophet, you Magician, your strong hand on the tiller observing the skies for bad weather, steering us to calmer more lucrative waters, barking orders, shaping events to your will. It's still only August and the weather is beautiful, everything is beautiful now and this apparent flow of happiness is down purely to the team.

The few wins have instilled a sense of order in the world again where Wolverhampton Wanderers are walking up the long drive to Premier League Mansion. There are people there we haven't seen for a while and we are fiddling with our ties, feeling the new shoes pinch a bit. Are we ready? We haven't got the official invite yet but, it's coming. I can feel it. I lick my hand and press down my hair into some sort of semi presentable mess. We won against Derby County. Jesus Christ.

What the fuck is going on? What is this particular experience? Derby choking at home to the footballing equivalent of a stranglefuck. Loud words I know but how else can one describe that show? The fluidity of passing and the sublime one touch here and there a cascade of sensuous passion, hair blowing in the wind football. Back in the day of course the whole ethos of Wolves style of play was always width, stretching the play out, attacking full backs. The pomp and circumstance of English football was Wolves in the 1950s, those monochrome warriors Flowers, Cullis, Billy Wright. So Matt Doherty and Barry Douglas these colossi of men, these gentlemen of the corner bits have risen to the task admirably dare I say like a 'Pig eatin' a tayta'. Woe betide any lollipop that dares to stand in the way of either of them as they ply their trade.

Opposition players flung here and there as wet wipes on a layby on the A5. At the end of the season there will be two trenches either side of the pitch where they relentlessly advance the cause. It will be four foot deep. Barry Douglas is the proverbial fucking bargain buy isn't he? He's a bit of a dark horse. Career locations like a Serbian people trafficker. Where you lived? Turkey? Fucking hell. Cheap tho'. Both of them are the older brothers who stare at you when you call for their Sister. The way they stare at you makes your balls shrink a little. You sit on the edge of the settee your hands sweating slightly as they too sit and stare at you. Giving you the hairy eyeball.

They are corner men really, full backs. But you wouldn't really know because they ploughed a furrow along the length of the pitch. By the end of the game I guess that the furrow was a couple of feet deep. There were times when it was fumbly again. But these fellas are getting to know each other. I can see it coming on. Seeing between the fog of championship games a real end product. It looks sexy again in parts. That ball doing hot jazz things across the fresh turf.

But overall we are within our rights to say that this spontaneous creative football is expressed and in the scheme of things must be expressed. The ease in which this team plays football is endemic of the fact that we aren't playing our football as 'hard' as we did. The football has become easier and more fluid because we aren't thinking about it as hard. Contrast Dave Edwards relentless pursuit of the ball across the pitch compared to the effortless positioning of Neves. There has become an essence of enjoyment and competition between team mates but not the competition to define the individual skill amongst his peers but the competition to see who may effortlessly mesh and integrate with the team as a whole? Last season the team (at times) was laboured and paranoid. This season it's like they have a message for the world. Garbled a little but there. Nuno is twiddling the dials, trying to get the station loud and clear, often his fingers get the frequency right and then it's back to Radio Serbia on long wave. Cheesy disco tunes, some dull piano concerto, a recipe for lard cake.

So far this season of course the periods where we do mesh and come together, where the frequencies converge are fascinating and dynamic. Bright Enkobahare splashing huge swathes of colour across the pitch as he clicks into every available space is a joy, a pure passionate beauty. Nuno has unleashed him for now and he is like a pit pony released into a pasture after a life in the mine. He flicks his mane here and there, explores the green of the pitch and it becomes less a battleground and more like a canvas for the way he personally sees his world. He's young this lad is but he has some magic, some Maverick intelligence, but he's unsure of himself. He understands football but I don't think he understands himself yet.

But how nice was it to see Derby given a solid kicking at home? Have we not tasted the bitter fruits of this tie in the past? The multiple dickings from a team that seemed to click when playing us? I sat at home packing my rucksack listening to the radio and the game, catching little bits here and there on social media. Smiling, and perhaps gloating a little too and I feel like getting a little bit drunk and maybe thinking about the team as ours apart from 'theirs'. Think about Sir Jack on the bus smiling his tits off after we won promotion, the Waterloo road rammed with a sea of Gold and Black.

There are positive vibes, feelings, and the happy moments happen when the windows of the shops up town didn't seem as grimy and the pavements not as care worn. These little thoughts creep in after a few wins, after a little bit of 'win love' and I'm going to enjoy them. I know it's a long road ahead and I know the vultures and the player pickers will be circling over the team to cherry pick our best players. There will be fume aplenty, some anger probably. Hope rises like a dawn hard on and can flicker out just as fast. But I'm 'getting it' slowly, I'm starting to understand it. Thank fuck for Nuno Espirito Santos acting as the mediator between his ideas and the fans. Through him we can begin to understand the whole thing a little better.

But we know what's going on there on the pitch and we can wax lyrical over the wheres and whys all day. There are better men and women more qualified than me who can do it. Where one match can be Melissa Multipack can one be Wendy Waitrose? Can this Derby match be that? Nuno of course walks to the podium and grips the sides of it and looks at us with the eyes of a man who has held the gaze of God. And may we say God in it's infinite abstract form has looked upon Nuno and our City with something akin to understanding? Even though the simple green shoots of the positive ethos Nuno has brought are still peeking above the dark fertile soil of Derby and Hull they are strong. Look at Nunos hands. They are strong and broad, a craftsmans hands, one who will find as much pleasure in manual labour as the construction of the 'Great Project'.

Now with the platform provided by the Fosun global business ethos and the vast 'friends' list of Uncle Jorge Mendes I sit watching the posts on social media expound love and positivity as the away matches click on relentlessly, post after post Bright Enkobahare, Coady, Neves, Cavaleiro, Jota, Saiss and Dicko. I watch the Neves goal against Hull over and over again and it takes on the magic and beauty of the Kennedy assassination, The Zapruder film. Neves pulls his foot back and to the left. Smash, no multiple shooters just him coaxing the ball to find it's path into the net. Rewind watch it again, watch the other players watch the ball float, spin, into the net, watch the goalkeeper flap. Rewind, take a sip of tea, watch the Hull team deflate. They knew that the Kwan was flowing across the pitch in an ever strengthening storm. They knew they were the bystanders on the grassy knoll destined to become witnesses as opposed to participants. The ten minutes added on was a mere post mortem to the rest of the match.

How maligned Dicko has been. Search for a striker here and there, names mentioned. We forget that we have a striker already. A leaner and fitter Dicko that looks a million miles away from the sensitivity of last season, the endless balls over his head, the fruitless lost loves scattered in front of him as another ball is spunked onto the moon head of the crisp munching byline. Nouha I never ever doubted you man. My footballing head as simple and bullet shaped as it is can't comprehend the complexities of the modern game but ever since you joined us my heart has always beaten with your presence which I deemed right and just. My soul I think understands your football better than my brain. Nouha you showed bravery and honour last season and even though you are a little dude you stand as a giant among your team mates.

As I write this we have just performed a smash and grab on Hull. 2-3 to us and the excitement of a brilliant away win is a thing, a concrete feeling that maybe the Universe has looked at it's 'to do' list and seen that we are well overdue a little glitter and pomp. It's a crazy dream isn't it? A demented hope that after all these years the team is channelling the hopes of the crowds, the fans, the great mass at the pitch edge. The zeitgeist is less a great hallucination or dream and is becoming a steam roller of intent and passion, the feeling that everything is in position to storm the plastic facades and frenzy of the Premier League. Now that freakazoid tight shirt mafia on Match Of The Day will soon have to discuss the golden juggernaut that's going to smash their cosy fucking chats to shit. I can see it, I feel it in my bones, I hear it as I walk around the streets. I can see Gary Lineker choking as he is forced to discuss my team, my City and my players. I hope we don't easily slip into the upper echelons of the Premier elite like we belong there, I hope we boot the fucking door down and put some noses out of joint immediately and we define ourselves not by how the Premier league has affected us but by how we have affected it.

Whatever….Cardiff next. Stack them up Nuno and knock them the fuck down. I sketch out the ideas of have about what to write. I'm not skilled at this I know. I'm a mover of heavy things in factories, ankle deep in building site mud. My teeth are cracked.

Neil Warnock eh? Face like a plastic carrier bag full of plastic carrier bags. Today I have to watch out what I say or this match report will just be a page full of reasons I don't like Warnock. He's a bitter twisted thing old Warnock is. I imagine him in his palatial house football bought him. He's burning leaves in his garden and poking the fire with a bit of branch. The clouds are dark and foreboding. In the distance a church bell tolls. A Crow shrieks in a barren field nearby, a skeleton held together by rotting flesh hangs from a nearby Oak…Are we too harsh on Colin Wanker? I'm not sure.

At least he grabs something creative out of me but I don't know whether or not that's just because of what a vacuous hole he is. He goes mad doesn't he? I remember my Father In Law lambasting Warnock at every opportunity. I'm in town watching the crowds walk past the windows of the Royal London pub. It's sunny and everybody has that sunshine disposition going on. That friendly sunny thing we clothe ourselves in when it's a lovely day. It is lovely. I am happy so far. I sip my Pale Ale which has cost me four quid so I sip it slowly. I'm by myself so I have a think about Warnock, he is in his garden wherever he lives…

'Ugh bastard, ugh fuckers, fucking Wolves, fuckers, bastards' he mumbles. There's a Hedgehog in there escaping the cold nights and now trying to escape the oncoming flames of the Warnockian bonfire. Nose twitching it smells the smoke, it waddles for safety but Warnock sees it's predicament, quickly getting the end of the stick under the poor wrinkly nosed mammal he flicks it back into the flames…I stop myself, this is silly. Neil Warnock isnt a Hedgehog killer is he? Even he wouldn't sink so low as to incinerate Mrs Tiggywinkle in a hot hell of smouldering leaves. I shake my head to clear it. Have a drink of beer. Swill it around a bit.

He's going to have a lot to say today and what he says will be negative, saddening and somewhat annoying. Even though he knows his football, I mean he's been in the game long enough. But it has affected him in some way. For this is 'The Warnock' the perennial miserable old bastard squeezing the veg in Aldi and muttering under his breath at the ripeness of things, the expense. He doesn't like expensive things and he looks at our team and his eyebrow twitches.

Our Colin is the epitome of the English manager of our time. He's one of these merry-go-round Coaches that appear at various clubs in times of lowly league places and threatened relegations. It's like he can smell an injured football club, his nose twitches like Mrs Tiggywinkle in that fire and then the flash of a few Iphone cameras and there he is. Resplendent in that clubs training gear. The ubiquitous 'CW' emblazoned on his tit. He reaches into the slim volume of English Coach sound bites. The players are 'Lads' and it's going to be 'tough' but I'm sure that there is 'ability'. So on and so on. Until he creeps out of the room with a wink and a nod to those in the press who are scared to ask questions, to ask proper questions.

He brings us Cardiff today. What a strange place Cardiff is, what a strange Aldi like team too. Having spent much time in that city I can honestly say I enjoy my times there. It's people are plain speaking and quick to make friends. You can also be sure that a punch up will happen at some point. Listen to the ripping sound as Warnock is unloaded from the Cardiff team coach in his travelling track suit. Don't get your hands too close to him for fucks sake! and watch out in case he shits in his hand and throws it at you! I can feel his bitter power now spreading throughout the Molineux ether, poisoning the atmosphere. Walk past his cage with a cup of tea and the milk will curdle, dogs will put their tails between their legs, babies will utter a quiet cry and old people having a nap will feel a twinge in their hips and yearn for warmer better days.

My walk up to the bus stop was shambling too. These wins we have had empower me but at the back of my head the same familiar voice. It sounds like Dean Saunders sometimes, or Glenn Hoddle. Past Wolves Coaches who have left an indelible stain in my mind. It leaves a voice also. That voice sounds slick like Jez Moxey our former Chief Executive. His lack of imagination has had me crying these past few years. A trip to watch his teams left me sobbing at the bottom of the shower while I wailed under the hot needle points of water and tried to rub soap in my eyes so I could rid my mind of it. Sorry I'm being over dramatic.

On the bus again, for I feel I will have a beer today, maybe two or three. It has been a long time since I've been allowed in the Royal London after that Leeds thing a few years ago but all is forgiven I hope. The Royal London is also a strange place. I have been joined by two of my violent friends. This is good, I felt weird standing by myself.

The Royal London yes. Catering for students in the week on match days it is full of us. Holding beers, waxing about shit. The chat is all upbeat and positive as we survey the doughnuts walking around outside. Cardiff fans mill around looking like they've just fell out of bed. Hair uncombed, shirt tails hanging out, Lonsdale trainers, tattoos on their necks, big stumpy fingers, missing teeth, missing fingers…look here come their boyfriends too…. I guess the bar staff will put on the 'football fan' CD again. Oasis, Blur, Britpop bollocks with a smattering of Ska tunes and edgy alternative 90s stuff. Yawn. But a bit better than the Great Western, a pub filled with men that look like they grew there and if the Great Western was ever knocked down they would remain in place like street furniture, still holding pints of Rancid Golden Goblin 6.7% abv. But here I've had a smile off a beautiful woman already and things are looking very good.

So the Mexican something with 'o' on the end is the lager of choice after my initial Pale Ale and I will have a few, then it's only a short amble to the back of the Southbank. Walking through the subway is an almost religious experience of course. Its all dark and musty, a light at the end which we aim for and then POP! We are out and everything is Golden and light and noisy, people milling around. Grabbed by the ankles and arse seriously slapped, get in the queue, get into the ground, quick piss and we're off! I put my arm around my mate, we are excited but pull stern man faces even if we want to run down the steps and jump around like kids setting fire to things. There is the homeless bloke with the Staffie. There is the Programme seller. There is the scratching man who is supposed to be an Albion fan. No wonder he looks pissed off. I don't buy scratchings off the enemy.

I don't say much about Saiss. He's the bloke that opens up the factory, jangling his keys. He's the dude with the lease Audi because he's clever enough to work out if it works for him. See if it saves him money. He knows how shit works. So he's checking out the doors, switching the lights on as he walks through the emerald heaven of the Molineux pitch. Work will start at 3 O'Clock bang on. Bang on he does. Pressing the shit out of the Cardiffian Nexus…'They'll be Bluebirds ooooover WHACK' .

Saiss plays a tune that is full of pain and passion. French Moroccan flavours pulsating across the match, Hard bitter contact, sweet passing across the pure Honey of the whole midfield. Ok I stood there and was lost for a while. It was romantic and a little sweaty. I felt like I had fallen in love with the whole team again. I felt a little shy as Neves slid another melodious ball through to somebody, I looked away. Jota spins, Neves catches the ball under his right foot and switches it to his left then away. The whole team has me in it's arms and for a moment I am lost, there's a Celine Dion tune playing. There are flowers and big fucking Unicorns. But hold on, what's going on here?

Warnock you little toad. You Hedgehog murderer. Prancing up and down the touchline moaning. I'm surprised he hasn't put a road cone in his technical area.

'It's mine this is! You can't step in here no, because it's mine, that's my cone. there's a law ya know, stick to your own area! Go on! Fuck off up yer own end' and for a moment I'm just watching him and I hear the soundtrack to 'Omen' Carl Orff. My knee starts to hurt and my scars start to ache and I feel old and tired and ugly and nobody loves me. Warnock is sucking the life out of me, his team is suddenly ascendant and I wonder for a second, was this all a dream? The tango with Neves? The recipes from Saiss? But what's this? Coady? Again?

Conor Coady. Sweeper. The bloke from Beatles Land, operating the shit out of defence. Control and utter fucking control. The bloke who used to run like Ghosts were chasing him, he was concentrating like he was playing 'Kerplunk'. He's quiet, not saying much, I bite my bottom lip, the madness of it. I'm beside myself and I feel the blood returning to my heart and through the mists in my eyes I see sunlight again and through the rays of the sun a Black Samurai. My Black Samurai.

> Bright Enkobahare rushes up to battle and reaches down to re energise me, me heart is beating and there he is slashing and cutting through the enemy, here now there, the Cardiffians confused and unsure, all they see are shadows that mock them. Ninja skills, shuriken balls. Tha-Donk! Boosh! Killer martial arts moves. Hold on he's fallen over again and he's Jackie Chan BUT wait! Bruce Lee moves and he jinks past a Cardiffian who just sees what he thinks is an Eagles shadow in his vision and Bright is past. But alas…we have one of 'those' Referees. A little bald one. He looks like a towel boy at a Wife Swapping Orgy running around trying not to look what's going on as Neves is getting constantly buttfucked by Cardiffians who look like they drive Vauxhalls. Bright stares at the grass as his feet are swept away. The Referee waves play on. South Wales are revitalised, they know the towel boy is a good towel boy. Our heads drop a little, we try not to look at the red rimmed eyes of Warnock. His hate has power.

Come on. We knew it was going to be a sanding the artex off the ceiling match. As the Colin Wanker virus grew into the Cardiff team, they were infected. They ran around the pitch in a frenzy not with any plan but to annihilate the beautiful play we had instigated in matches previously. Poor Neves was Brad Pitt in World War Z….darting into alleys and stairwells, at every turn the gurning twisted face of a Cardiff player, teeth dripping with black saliva, grunting and snarling.

Bright Enkobahare tumbled under the relentless press of rotted flesh, stud and elbow. Saiss taken out by the assault of a well directed elbow to the throat. Doherty and Douglas twisted here and there by the abstract and surreal tactics instigated by the sticky tendrils of the Warnock way. Goals, well they scored more which was why they won. But who was the winner today? The faux injured, the time wasting, the Jackson Pollock like spray of bootball? Warnock of course is the winner. Is it not the way of the world we live in that the deranged and the twisted football of the cursed enjoy victory over the beautiful and the divine? At least in this episode yes. As in all good dramas a defeat early on will in the end define the victory of the good and the beautiful football we play. No matter how many times you step over the security barrier and take a sharp knife to the Mona Lisa there will always be people who will repair and tend that beauty.

The defeat didn't depress me at all. I half expected it. We are in a state of flux, a state of change. The development of a Nuno-esque Butterfly from the Caterpillar of the Clown Lamberto but now at the critical stage when our football is at a chrysalis stage we are most vulnerable. Soon we will erupt from the shell of our present and into the bright future, spread our beautiful footballing wings into the sun and take flight. We will of course look below as we pass the dark valleys of Cardiff and Warnock on his throne of skulls will shake his fist at us and berate his players to more aggressions, more anti-football.

The Balled of Colin Wanker will be, in the end a dirge. A lonely song of one violin and a moaning lyric. Let us wave farewell for now to Colin Wanker and his cohesive but mentally fractured troops as they drive up the Stafford Road to the Motorway. It is a two fingered wave and the assurance that yes, we will meet again and we will have your tears Colin Wanker, yes, we will have them.

So the Bus back home was shit. Nuno had a beautiful script today. The words had a perfect cadence not unlike the effortless scintillating gorgeousness of our team and our football. But alas for the thick red marker pen of Warnock. There is something scary about Warnock that he still has the power to define what a football match should be. Would I have done the same? Probably yes. Spoil the scene with negativity, assaults, time wasting. Of course I would of. But my embarrassment would have left the whole subject there on the pitch. Warnock of course will not be able to help himself and his madness will trickle through the free buffet happiness of the assembled press as they await him.

Nuno will learn from this of course. It will just be a match on the long road of matches where he has to drill this team into some sort of coherent idea. But they have seen us now, and we cannot hide. There will be things said within the press and the broadcast media. They will know us and this Nuno. They will not like it. Colin Wankers face makes me laugh. I'm starting to like him a little.

Strange. I'm in the middle of Wales climbing a steep hill on my mountain bike. Sweat keeps stinging my eyes. My heart is reminding me of all those chopped lines in stinking toilets at away games. I think it may stop in a minute and my body will be found being pecked by birds and nibbled by animals. At the top of the mountain Nuno stands surrounded by a glow, a halo of golden light and he beckons me onwards, inspiring me to pedal harder and reach enlightenment? Nah. Not yet Nuno. Let's win first. Signals yes. A fucking phone signal so I can find out what's going on at Southampton in the Caraboon..Carabone…Carabean…the League cup. At the top of the Hill I can receive text messages and as I throw the bike down and grapple with the phone in my sweaty hand…

There are a lot of flies up here in the rarefied air of this place and as I settle down in a clump of Bilberry I waft a few flies away as they try to drink my hard sweat and moist gasping. That was a long way up here. My Chemo has made sure my muscles ache real good now and my legs are wobbly as fuck. I drink some warm water out of my drinking bottle. It tastes of plastic. I reach for an energy bar in my pocket but it's empty. I must have lost it on the way up. I'm hungry, but I see signal bars on the top of my phone screen. Wave away a fly. Connect. Yes. I send my mate a text. He's watching the game. He is my eyes and ears.

What will Nuno do today? What artistic madness has he for us? Is he 'serious' about the cup? I'm not. I want out of this division, I mean I seriously want out. Cardiff last week drained me. It took a few days to get over it for sure. I keep seeing Warnocks face under my bed leering at me and spouting some bollocks about 4-4-2 and some other inane crap.

My mate is at St Marys and texting his madness..'WE GOT THE SECOND STRING OUT' Glowing letters on the screen. Second string? My heads pumping. Danny Baath and Jack Price in my mind. Long dirge like football playing Burton and Fourth division blah ball. But I'm in a mood and tired, I'm being far too tetchy so I sit down in some heather away from this clutch of flying insect madness. Watch the sun start to dip. Welsh hills, beautiful. BEEP..I don't want to look. We have to be five/ten minutes into the game and the lack of lyrical beauty in these text messages is giving me grief. Mental grief. Cup games are unimportant to some but I understand the dynamics. My angry friend is working in Southampton so he's probably wrecked. I told him to text me updates. I'm not expecting hirsute analysis.

I imagine he's shouting at me because everything is in capitals. Exclamation marks. He's a violent man and he texts violently. I had a mad affair with a woman from Southampton and I'm twitchy now, a little like she was and I'm thinking about her, images flicking back and forth of her stark bollock naked and my team putting their boots on. Jacko thinking about the game, how he's going to define the night, me remembering her lips that tasted of Orange Tango.

'FUCKING DANNY BAATH'

Don't harsh my Wolves/Blonde mellow man. It was a two hour climb, make it worth my while. Shut my eyes and feel Nunos hand on my shoulder. The weight of it is reassuring.

'DESLANDES-MARSHALL THINK CAV STARTED'.

Cavaleiro? Good feel better, blood starting to get to important places and the black specks have stopped floating around in my vision. Breathing better. Cavaleiro yeah. Much better, I like him. Southampton fills me with dread, lost loves there, it makes me ache. But in my head there's a visual stream of hot sex and hotter football and I glean what I can from the brief messages. Cavaleiro yeah, I'm all about that. He seems to have found a comfortable place inside the philosophy Nuno has stamped within the club. His runs are powerful and energetic, but he also understands, he has the eye of a hunter. I am watching him in my minds eye terrorise the Southampton defence.

'TWO EASY CHANCES FOR THEM'

I don't know what to think. I'm wondering how and why Nuno has done this. Squad rotation? Giving the forgotten men a chance? I'm afraid but why? It's a Cup game, is it pointless? Is any cup game pointless? Doubts flying in again. Wasn't Marshall injured? I'm trying to remember who he is among the new faces but I'm having trouble. I ask about Marshall. Lambert signing he was, he was a bit thick around the middle for me, he didn't look fit. I laugh. Didn't look fit? I was nearly puking by the time I managed to cycle up here.

'FUCK NOS'

Well then, if he doesn't know then what clue do I have? I'm on top of a mountain again.

'SHOULD BE 4-0 TO US DICKO FUCKING SHIT'

Oh my days. I can see Nouha running around the box again and nothing is going his way but I know Dicko, he's relentless, he won't stop. Pulling defenders here and there allowing others to gain that yard of space, that precious few seconds to unleash a shot or a perfect weighted pass. Dicko works, team player and understanding. Nuno still has his hand on my shoulder and he squeezes it and he's gone, back to Southampton back to the madness of it all. I'm breathing in the scent of the Heather in full bloom now, perfume thick…

'FUCKING SHIT'

But I'm back in Molineux alley in 1977 and we can't get in but there are ways in of course. The huge wall at the side of the Southbank is bowed slightly and if you were tenacious and you had a bunk up you could get your fingers into the crumbling brickwork then another stretch and you could get the 4″ by 4″ wooden post with the barb wire wrapped around it. You were thirty feet up hanging onto a rotten piece of wood, feet shoved into crumbling brick and you could smell the stale piss from the open air toilet above and you stretch that hand out and the other is losing grip….

'HTIME HERE MATE PRICEY DOING IT MESSI AY HE VINEGAR BLOKE OK LOOKS OK ALL ROUND'

I stretch my legs out and the knees pop and my back is cramped, it's getting cold up here and the light is going. The only illumination is the dim sky and a light way down in the valley, a farm or something but it's too dark to make out and…

'DANNY FUCKING BAATH' What about him? Has he fucked up? Fucking hell Danny. Second string fuck ups, fourth division player he can fuck off back to Sheffield for all I'm bothered and another thing….

'HEADER 1NIL TO US'

Fucking hell. OK then. Sorry Danno. I'm emotional, I'm throwing my toys out the pram. I'm not an adult where my team are involved, I'm petulant and adolescent. Danny Baath indeed.

My hand grabs onto the post and as I remember I looked back down at the alley far below at the people going back and forth and I can hear the singing inside and the gasps, the isolated voices exhorting, challenging, shouting incoherent abuse, the noise of the game. I want to be inside and I grip hard and ease my feet up to the next piece of shit brickwork, soles of my shoes have holes in and are smooth, my grip is bad but I'm nearly there and I get my hand over the top of the wall and a leg gently creeping over and under the wire. A hand grabs my arm. Is it a Cop? They often whack your hands with a truncheon and you drop. They don't give a fuck but it's a tattooed hand and that means safe. That means he's one of us. A piss head. He grabs me and pulls me through the wire and it rakes my back but I'm in and safe. 'Ta mate' and I'm scuffing through the piss of the toilets and underneath the Southbank and I'm in and there is noise and thousands of us and we are one nil up and then I'm here again with a phone in my hand. But I'm always stuck in the 1970s lately because those days always had a tint of summer about them. Fluorescent punk socks. A pink one on one foot and a luminous green one on the other. Grandad saw them once and nearly dies laughing then calmed down and shook his head a little sad probably. Then he looked out of the window for a while. Quiet.

'FUCKING ZYRO ON'

What? Is it like that again? All these faces in new kind of places. Zyro, I liked him all those years ago when he last played for us. Was it years ago? I could hear Bats and see them in the starlight, subtle glimpses of their forms darting through the stars.

'ZYRO IS A FUCKING LUNATIC'

...but I don't know why he is and it's pitch black now and I can't see the track down at all but I have my head torch and it's cool and I know it's cool at St Marys too because Nuno knows. I know the journey down will be good and pleasant in the glow of a hard fought one nil win in the cup...

'DONOVAN WILSON GET IN 2 NIL LOOKING OK COMFORTABLE'

Who? For a moment I thought Wilson was a Saints player, own goal surely, then I remember. Academy kid I watched him at Compton once. Mobile player, good feet on him, but I have to text back and ask for sure.

'ACADEMY KID'

Yeah ok. Two Nil it is. Blondes in black latex and 0-2 Cup victories. Will we be playing Southampton next season? I may pop in and see my blonde thing. See how shit is progressing in her life. Maybe mine will now be a little more positive. The bats are going ape shit in the cobalt blue evening sky. Over the hills the sun has gone under the horizon and I can see the umbra of the sun, the shadow creep across the eart. I'm high up. High on the match. High on the technology that took me for a moment from here in the quiet to the madness of a football stadium hundreds of miles away.

I get back on my bike and I'm off back to where I'm camping. Nuno has his hands on mine making sure I get down safe. I'm not rushing. Brake softly like Nuno would. Shift my weight here and there just like Nuno would. Into the blackness of that Welsh valley I rode and my signal dies and everything is dark, dangerous, scary. Like climbing that wall back in 1977. There's always a hand, always somebody there to help as we descend into the unknown, as our hands scrabble trying to find purchase in the crumbling brickwork. Of course there is going to be a day when it's Nuno himself who will require a helping hand and I'm going to be there for him like he has been for me....so I take my fingers off the brake and pick up a little speed and turn the head torch a little brighter.

Jeff Shi is our new Boss. Chinese man, maybe forty something years of age? Hugo Boss suits the uniform of the Chinese well to do Businessman. But there is something fiery about Jeff. Something academic about him. He's quite unassuming like a Professor maybe? I'm sitting in the garden reading a paper someone has left for me in passing. I don't but the things of course. But I do like to read what twisted shit they have decided to splurge out that day. There are sniffings already within the back pages of the sports blurb. The reptiles can smell something and their noses are twitching in those plush Mayfair offices. An editorial about our Jeff. I feel protective. Me, a poor broke bastard feeling empathy with some Chinese dude I've never met. Strange feeling. But the dogs are sniffing at the doors of Molineux.

I read the hit piece with a mounting anger. I screw the fucking thing up and chuck it. Then I have to get up and put it in the recycle bin. I slam the lid and lean on the bin. Thinking. I may write a letter to Jeff. Of course I can't offer these journos a straightener in a pub car park although I am that way inclined. No, I'll write him a letter of sorts.

Grab a pen, grab a sheet of art paper, it's the only thing I can find. I scribble, I cross out, soundtrack is the ambulances that roar up and down the Lichfield road ferrying the ill to New Cross up the road. Blare and lights, the endless noise of it punctuates each line I write.

How you doing Jeff? What a mad few months this has been. You've been very busy I see sorting out transfers, running the 'business of Wolves' and trying to work out what the fuck is going on too. But not to worry, I'm going to give the low down on the zeitgeist. You see I'm Joe Wolverhampton. Normal bloke, a supporter, a dysfunctional idiot. With a pen.

I'm not a spokesman by any stretch and I don't speak for every Wolves fan at Molineux. There are some who will disagree completely with what I have to say but that's cool. They can find other ways to vent their spleens. But Ive got five minutes free and I would like to tell you a few home truths about what actually is going on here in England at the minute. You might find it interesting or not, who know? But if I don't write then I fight.

I just read the Daily Mail hatchet job on the job you and Fosun are doing here. To be honest I thought it was hilarious. The writing was poor and Daily Mailish. No real facts, a lot of hearsay, the noise of war really, fake war of course as the article was an opener in the battles to come. But why a battle? Who are we fighting? We are fighting of course the establishment. Now it's great to come out with such an easy statement when the establishment can mean all sorts of shadowy groups and sub groups and it's very easy to get caught up in a whole plethora of conspiracy theories. But here's a twisted saying I like to pontificate with at times…

What is a conspiracy? It's a set of dynamic obstacles that refuse to disappear when you stop believing in them. You see, when the 'established' English football mafia see the work that Fosun are doing in our City they don't like it. They never liked Wolverhampton any way. We are too 'lumpen' for them. We don't have the attraction of bigger more glamorous clubs, we talk funny and we are funny too. Walk into any pub full of Wolves fans and the overwhelming reaction is that we are happy, we laugh and cry in equal measures. We are emotional but stoic. We understand everything but when you can't laugh at it then it becomes an abstract and meaningless thing. 'They' don't like that because they don't understand it. Of course they will never understand us. We are a mystery to them. All they see are our gardens backing onto railway lines, washing on the line, a trampoline for the kids, a dog running around outside. They don't know us, but they think they do. They conspire against us as they whizz past.

So what's the conspiracy here? The 'establishment' want to know where the cash is going and why it isn't going in their pockets. The English FA and the Press have a great relationship, the English Press and shadowy business interests have an even greater one. It used to be forged with secret handshakes in Masonic lodges, trousers pulled up over the knee, weird aprons, weird friends these people scurry along in the corridors of power in Westminster.

But as you know Jeff the world has changed. Now the deals are done over expensive coffees and focus groups, in relationship initiatives and friendships made in Oxbridge University clubs. Even though these personalities wax lyrical about global opportunities and the global market they are in essence still deeply routed in the 'old boy network'. It's a white man dominated colossus, it's a house in Buckinghamshire, it's a Jag or two on the drive, it's the weekend cottage, the back slaps, the juicy contracts, kick backs and fucking the Personal Secretary in Travelodge. It's defunct Jeff. Has been for years.

It's a shame that they lack any real idea of how to attack a business like Fosun and you Jeff. It's a shame they are still using the tactics of the 1800's to denigrate a business idea they don't have the mental capacity to understand. I am ashamed, as an Englishman that their ideas are as lacklustre as the seats of their suit trousers and the shallow bulge of their fat guts. Jeff, I apologise.

So the article. An opening salvo in my opinion. You've stuck your face into the Boardroom and they don't like it. The easiest option for them to attack the whole Fosun dynamic is to call on that old boy network and there's no better place to do that than get in touch with the boot boys at the Daily Mail. Surreptitious is the word of the day. It's an underhanded and clumsy attack which should really fill the hearts of the troops at Fosun with joy. Indeed you should find a quiet pub somewhere Jeff, sit down and have a little giggle to yourself that the opening salvos of their angst about you and Fosun are so poor. Really? The Daily Mail?

Have Fosun lost the soul of Molineux? Well to be honest it's been kicked around the floor for a good many years. Shoved in a boot cupboard at Molineux and forgotten for a time but it's never been lost. Jeff, we are the soul of Molineux, the people who scrimp and save through the year so we can buy a season ticket. What has this years cost me? I've been eating eggs and fucking beans for four months now. When I go for a pint before a game I have a pint and that's it. It's all I can afford. Where are my holidays? A nice dry piece of forest in Wales where I don't have to pay camping fees, which is stupid because I can't afford a fucking tent.

Soul is getting up in the morning with a bit of hope in your heart that we can do something this season. Soul is being proud to say 'Wolves ay we' a much bandied about term which I think most Wolves supporters will never understand and which was born in the exchange of blows outside the stadium. Soul is pulling on your Wolves shirt to go to the shops. Soul is watching your kids run around in their Wolves replica strips with the other kids running around in Chelsea or Manchester United strips. Soul is singing your heart out while other fans are checking their fucking social media accounts or their bets. Soul is knowing that Fosun are the outsiders, the strangers from other lands, the people who talk weird, who like to kick the establishment in the balls. Soul is the team that took the piss out of the greatest teams in Europe in the 1950's.

That's what Soul is Jeff. We love Fosun not for the players, the cash or the football we are now playing (although it's beautiful and welcome). It's the fact that Fosun and you Jeff are the under dogs in the fight. We share the same position. Haven't we always been fighting for some sort of recognition? Some right to stand with the glamorous and the well heeled? This 'Post Industrial' Midlands Town has strengths that are unknown to most and only walking the streets outside those Golden halls will show you this. We have fought these battles for years and years. Walked into meetings and had our accents mimicked and made fun of. Had our teams denigrated in the national press and media. This is what the 'soul' of Molineux is, the ability to withstand the slings and arrows and stay true to our ideas and beliefs even when it seems everybody is against you.

Stand true Jeff and stand proud. Regardless of the machinations of global business and the madness of financial implications we have a chance to grab that establishment club by the lapels and to stick a gorgeous smacking forehead into the noses of them. Already they are feeling that soft warm trickle of fear. The Chinese are coming, and they have a bunch of oiks from Wolverhampton with them. It's going to be very nasty in the future Jeff but if you fall down we will be picking you right back up again.

But like I say. What do I know? I know if you go down the Tesco 24 Hour thing down the road at 8PM you can get cheap cream cakes, some Broccoli, a dodgy squashed loaf, all for £1.20. What do I know about battles between media conglomerates and ultra massive Chinese concerns. Nothing of course.

It's transfer deadline day. I put aside the letter to Jeff Shi nice and safe. I fancy a look at my phone to see what madness is happening on that particular front. I'm confused by the whole thing. I mean back in the day you would read a bit of blurb on the back of the Express and Star. Now you get Tim Spiers and the other bloke splurting rumours, gifs, the whole fucking social media arsenal. We are smashed to shit by information and rumours, locations, Instagram posts, messages, 'In the Know' accounts. Strange tanned fit looking geezers walking through town standing out from the chip shop pallor of the odd crack head in CEX. What does Tim Nash say? What fucking Tim Nash there's thousands of them on Twitter, which one do you trust? Do you even trust the real one??

Threats of violence, keyboard killers, fat Dads rolling around the car park of a shit pub because one of them slagged Dave Edwards off. Transfer deadline day is brilliant. It's dynamic and strange, fucked up, waving pink dildos on national TV, interviewing fans that are obviously stoned or pissed, it's novel and it's cool because it's a mental dysfunctional culture all of it's own and you can be any fucking colour race or creed you want to be because Transfer deadline day is Primal Man day.

Players. Grinning lunatics on official photos. Dynamic stock photos. Some You tube videos. Smashing shots into bulging nets from 45 yards. Jinking past 10 players like some insane ballet dancer. The ball stuck to his foot. Names like Scrabble tiles nailed to a clowns forehead. Dyslexic nomenclature that reminds you of Bond film villains, places in Mongolia, places in Wales if it was in Russia and you had to read everything upside down. Fucking hell. Who? I hadn't even heard of the teams they played for. Exotic. Compared to Sagbo, Holt and that other doughnut. Do we remember those transfer deadline days past when we were linked with Reginald Gonad from Hartlepool? Matthew Forehead from Scunthorpe? Steve Normal from Bury?

Jesus Christ don't I remember them all, and their faces melt into each other and it's the same dense football face, you know he has a sleeve tattoo with his kids names or dead people, dead relatives, an Arabic poem about something Arabic. He grew a beard but he thought he looked stupid and he did. He listens to garage music like his mates and his football is as good as his persona. Insipid, uninspired like the plastering job he'll be doing in 15 years time when the football money runs out.

What exotic lunatics we have mentioned with our team. I would write then down but the names are popping up and out of the golden spotlight as I speak. This is the last dance with Melissa Multipack as you gently lick the anchor tattoo on her neck and you struggle to get your arms around her waist. This is the struggle to get a player in, its the last gasp fuck in Jingles nightclub and your feet are sticking to the sugary alcohol floor and you taste roll up fags on her tongue.

You want to get away with your self image as crooked and twisted as it is away from the transfer talk and back home where you could wake up in your own bed secure in the knowledge Wolves and Nuno and Mendes have done something. That management of things they do which seems simple to us but is as complex as an algorithmic progressive jazz album. How the fuck do they do it? I don't know, it's black magic. The phone calls to agents, clubs, the player wants to come but his girlfriend doesn't. What are the add ons, the bonuses, the house, can she shop? I'm glad it's them doing it but I don't envy it. It's your feet sticking to the floor of the club as you wait for a mate and you're tired and want to go home.

But Transfer Deadline day is the car crash we can't stop staring at. And the casualties are still rising as I type. Threat and argument. But humour too I suppose. Dwight Gayle is in Wolverhampton. He's been spotted somewhere? Buying Lidl screwdriver sets? Solar Gnome lights? Walking out of Greggs? Asda? Schrodingers footballer, he's in his quantum state right now training with Newcastle but in Compton and the narrative is twisting this way and that and I understand now. He could be here, he could be there. But Dwight Gale? Jesus Christ man what's wrong with the world. We are building something new, dynamic, exotic here and Dwight fucking Gayle.

Social Media is a microcosm of madness where words become so powerful I suspect our brains aren't geared up to process it. I suspect this causes a 'blockage' then this blockage continues to back up the whole system until the slightest wrong word or context changed becomes a declaration of war. Then more insults. The day is getting foggy and the troops are gathering, there's a madness among them, because we need a striker. Quantum striker.

Whoever comes be it the exotic or the mundane. Let them look around at our ground, maybe have a walk around the museum too before they get their 200" HD telly from PC world for their new pad. Maybe they will get a feeling for the history and the passion but more importantly I hope they realise they have one mission and that's to score some fucking goals like they're supposed to.

Jesus Christ Midfielder Nazareth Academicals.

I was in Poundstretcher and 'Gary the Mastic' who I know quite well came up to me spitting and blathering about the whole Fosun thing, lack of a striker, unsure about investment, the team, the whole madness. What can I say? I was looking at Bog roll. In Poundstretcher. Crazy. There he was covered in whatever shit he messed with at work hassling me about the dealings of a Global company with interests that wriggle like the chopped off arm of an Octopus. Strikers Gary? Angel-Crease bog roll is £4 for eight rolls but you're in danger of getting a shitty finger. Softy-Bum is £6 for eight rolls and shitty finger is a problem one may forget about as you peruse the bog library.

Striker problems? What Striker problems? Dwight fucking Gayle not coming?

Some Dutch gonad pulling out at the last minute? Probably a first for him. Chasing players here and there trying to get them to sign so Norman Northbank can get at least half a semi on for transfer deadline day? I want Strikers driving up to Jeff Shi's house and banging on his door begging to play for Wolves. That's the player I want, not Doogalooo Dunrunnin from AEK Dynamo Wankspanner who scored four goals last season and one of them was an own goal. I want people who NEED to score.

But Gary Mastic is resolute and follows me up and down the aisles talking about it, mashing his gums as the mastic has rotted his teeth out. He's like the Wolves Facebook group 'Dingles Ay We' in fact he's typical of the absolute meltdown rhetoric that I used to read on there before my ban. But Gary? Who the fuck would we have bought really? Looking at the dickheads being put forward by various people had me in a depression. Is this what money brings you? Is this what transfer day really is? I was looking for Nuno interviews as an antidote to it, I was getting caught up in the madness of it. Gary was obviously in some kind of delirious state. Sky Sports had got him. I knew Gary had a big fucking telly nailed to his living room wall. I knew Gary sat in front of it with his nightly four tins of Carling Black Label. I knew his dog would be looking at him for love and attention as he constantly scanned the internet and the TV for news. It was a mess, he's a mess, I was a mess.

'Gary I think Fosun have it all under control' I said, and he nearly fell into the shelves of out of date sweeties. Anger and hostility. I felt like I was defending this multinational Global entity from Gary Mastics ire, his anger palpable and raw and I clutched the bog roll to my chest in protection as his little thin legs made the Umbro trackie bottoms he wore shake like those fan driven blow up wavy arm things outside Carpet World. Jesus Christ. I see Pringles are on offer. I don't mind the odd tube of Pringles to be honest. At night watching old football videos on YouTube, shoving them in your face one thick stack at a time. What a life we lead eh?

So the transfer window ended without a signing of a Striker. Bloody hell. Tins of Salmon for a quid. Cool. Gary followed me around singing the praises of Steve Morgan and the abyss of Moxey….or 'Moxley' as Gary called him. Remembering those halcyon days in the 4th Division when 'everything looked bright' but really it didn't did it? It was shit. It was settling for something, anything. It was the party that really failed to ignite any kind of push forward. Afobe gone. Sakho gone.

The dullness of a few seasons of making do with Kenny Charisma and Paul Lamberto. The slow relentless push for points, the dullness of work mate barbecues. Wondering whether to send a dirty private message to your mates girlfriend. Anything to pull your mind away from the resolute fucking failure to 'push on' the keyword of the post match interview. Excuses mate, they fall at our feet like a turd just rolled down your trouser leg and onto the dusty Poundstretcher concrete floor. The majority of our previous squads should have thrown themselves in Compton cut and done us all a favour.

Now the zeitgeist is different surely? Looking at the play we have developed under Nuno I feel a familiar feeling. When Neves has the ball my ballsack shrinks in anticipation. When he plays it to Jota I grab the poor bastard who stands next to me (who puts up with some madness I'll tell ya). Who else do I pick out of the roster of sexual footballing pornography Jeff Shi and Fosun have brought us. And there again I'm bigging up and defending the global and the rich. Later on I will be smashing open my piggy bank where I have £60 saved to buy this site. I'll have £22 left and people are moaning at me about 18 million quid strikers. Ruffles Raspberry Coconut bars £1 for six. Get in.

I'm not hassled mentally like Gary Mastic. What I'm about is novelty and dynamics. I want to see new ideas and new madness behind the club I love. I want just 'something' to happen whether its sexy football or raging 40 yard cross field accurate passes, a rush of players into the box, some doughnut to push it into the net so I can go home happy in the fact we got points and 2000 drongs from Shitstick United get back on the M6 with big glum sad faces. Gary Mastic is endemic of the rainy day mentality of 'some' of our support. If he read the Daily Mail then he'd probably be phoned up by Tarquin Flashtwat Sports Sub Editor for a chat about 'those fucking chinky bastards ruining our club'. Tarquin has to be a Fulham fan, it's a dead cert.

But I don't give a shit about Gary Mastic, I don't give a shit about the Daily Mail, I don't give a shit about any of the gloom squad. I don't give a shit about them simply because I'm excited and positive. For the first time in a long while I'm looking forward to the season whether we have a striker or not. Because to be fair to Dicko, as much as I tried to mentally propel him towards the madness of scoring goals for fun it was obvious that he'd had enough, and that's cool. Bye. What you going to swap him with? Of course talking to actual half insane on mastic fumes Wolves fans is a lot different to waxing in 140 characters on Twitter. It's dynamic, at least he's talking about it and not the letter from the environmental health about the state of his front garden. I see it and I feel it. I just wish he'd turn his face upwards for a few minutes and look at those lofty limbs of global brand footy instead of the Poundstretcher football we played for the last few years. Gary look up mate. Get your chin out of your chest and just fucking believe for a few moments.

Fosun can defend themselves. Jeff Shi gets paid. Everybody gets paid. Some of us just pay. I bought the Angel-Crease bog roll. I'm a risk taker, a positive thinker, a three sheet kind of bloke who likes to take risks. Whether or not we end the season with a shitty finger well…who knows? But imagine we end it with a pristine bum hole…we can but hope. It's Millwall tomorrow. I set aside my Adidas Gazelles. They were on offer at Sports Direct. They are the cleanest shoes I have. They will be on my feet most of the season. I am looking at them as it's the safest thing to do in this pub at the moment.

Millwall. Stuck in a pub surrounded by them. Millwall this and Millwall that. 'They' are Millwall, 'This' is Millwall. Soon enough you stop hearing the word itself and start hearing 'Meewuh' and everything is getting hazy and confused and you are stuck within that vortex of Londonish vowel stretching and confused random elbows as they like to dance as they talk. You wonder why you picked this pub and you remember it's because you're a lunatic, this is what you do. Know thine enemy, but you look around and they are dressed like you, same worries, hopes, dreams.

It's all very well but…nothing like Wolves social media over the last few weeks. Edgy and tense, friendships destroyed, families ripped apart over a striker, the lack of one, the wrong one, the lost one, the never had one in the first place. And the pub becomes a little distant and the noise dies down and I daydream about Steve Bull again. Even now I can't help breaking into a sweat when I see him pressing the flesh out and about. Where is the footballer that can galvanise a game like he did? Where among the smooth faced academy strikers is a diamond in the rough like Bully? But its September 2017 not 1988 and I think people don't want to be heroes any more. Am I talking about the Striker situation too much? I don't know. Probably. Nuno will know surely. I watched him on Wolves TV waxing about the game. I am beginning to trust and love him I know it. I don't want to but I do. But I'm cool. I think.

They say 'I'm trying to be cool' but I'm not. I'm a number that's all, a supporter number with access to the internet. My hands shake as I walk down the subway most matches. I need those two pints to make some sense of it all, to dull the aches and the worries. All I'm doing is talking about it. Sharing the groove. Cool? The sweat is trickling down my back. Simon (my mate) says 'YamYamism' and he's right and that statement bleeds the moisture out of the subway walls. Distilled hope. Holy water in fact, but it's slippy again. Fuck Adidas Gazelles.

I remember September. It's that time you spend looking out of the window on a Saturday morning looking at the weather. It's a bit dull in the sky and we expect Winter right now and we have the quasi Winter jacket out. The Autumnal jacket too thin for Winter but is it too much? Are we going to sweat in the pub? We don't want to be cold, we don't want to be hot. So we put the jacket on and stand in the garden for twenty minutes to see what it feels like. The Pigeon on the shed roof is looking at you funny and you say 'You What Mate?!' and he thinks 'you're gonna be too hot in that mate'.

Millwall. But Nuno has never played a back three before but again, attack is the best form of defence and I'm thinking of those team graphic tactical apps I keep seeing. Little shirts dotted here and there on your phone screen. Wingbacks, high pressing, false 9's the Chellini gap. But the variables? Neves woke up in the night, Jota feels his calf a little tight, Bonatini wired up, stoked, feeling the gnarly need to score, Marshall wanting to get forward but told to hang back for twenty minutes. Insane variables which interlock together at 3 pm and mesh with the whiteboard madness of the Millwall team talk. More variables, more tactics and it's a Mandlebrot set of chaos with the mathematical foundation of pure sweat. Boly is out that means Bennett? Batth? I can see Danny doing something good. 'Hilda' trained too, I can see him coming on but alas no.

Saville and Jed Wallace ex Wolves men. I never liked either of them while they were here. They never liked us I'm sure. We in the stands felt it and saw it. I suppose you could fool the press and the madhouse of the Molineux but us up there in the stands? Nah, we knew them, knew there lack of effort, knew their sadness at being here.

Saville still runs like he's treading on puppies. Wallace, well what can I say about him? Coming to Wolves he had a resume like his Mom wrote it. He came without colour, without the jazz. Another stoic footballer from last season when you would read his match rating in the Express and Star and you didn't realise he had played. Nearly men. Of course they will be burned by their moves to wherever Millwall is in London. Thus they will probably score one each. This is as predictable as the fat away supporter in the Steve Bull flashing his disgusting gut or the 15 year old lad in the expensive clothes miming beating somebody in the Southbank up. Get your tits out for the lads? Please don't.

The weeks previous were punctuated by the loss of Nouha (Hull) and Dave (Reading) to rivals too. Dave I wasn't that fussed about. Rubik Cube type player. Twisting, turning constantly trying to get the combo right and more often than not chucking it at the wall or putting it away in a drawer. Sometimes you'd get one side right and then it would all go to shit again. I often think what would a footballer do as a job if they didn't make it as a footy player. It gives me something to do. Dave would have been something to do with Housing administration. All the tenants love him….but they don't actually know what he does. A Lava lamp of a player, great to stare at but it doesn't really illuminate your life…sorry Dave I've called you a Lava Lamp and a Rubik Cube but nobody ever sang the Dave song as loud as me. Sorry we sent you to Reading. God Bless man. Saint Dave.

Nouha I was more aggravated about but again it was always the cusp of things, the potential not quite realised. Nouha was a firework called 'Raging Inferno'

STAND BACK 5 METERS' fucking hell, you've got visions of the shed on fire, the kids, the dog, next doors new fence and the missus on aflame, everything aflame!…and we watch as it fizzles and farts a few golden sparks into the dog shit at the top of the garden. Nouha my little puddin' what went wrong? What happened to the fuse man? We stood in the cold as you fizzled away and finally a climactic splurt of flame like a wet dog fart and you fell over into the dog egg infested wastes of Hull. Fair thee well Brother may your visits to the Molineux always be wet dog farts of a match for you…a bit like the 5-0 drubbing your new team got last night

Fuck what the Pigeon thinks. The Autumnal jacket is a thing. The Southbank will be warm as I'm sure we've sold out. But the walk is weird and I'm trapped in a group of away fans again and the Police are pushing me this way and that then a punch is thrown at somebody and well, it is Millwall so I duck my head and steer my way through the madness of stale onion, Aquascutum coats and beer odours. But I love the walk past the University art block and amongst the madness it's always good to look West and see the Clee Hills on the horizon, settles the mind a little, but the anger is palpable, the men today are simply men and the dynamic is violent and I see Nuno in the sky driving a great golden chariot, he's got hair like a rock star and I can hear singing from the stadium and the metaphysical hallucinations are replaced by the physical, the empirical, the nuts and bolts.

Score more than them. That's all. Three points for us, intangible things you can never hold in your hand, ethereal addition that will mean either nothing as we are 12 points ahead at the top of the table come May or they mean the death of the Nuno experience, Our football the beautiful melodies played during the demented point gathering frenzy of championship football. But yeah the football.

Jed and Jimmy didn't get much of a look in did they? Thank God. Saville again in that aimless discordant rhythm and Wallace still looking for….well I still don't know what he's looking for on that pitch. On the other hand we fucking smashed it right up. And here it was, the roots of the Nuno tree had taken root firmly within the grass of Molineux. The stem was still young and pliant, there were times when the blow hard football from Millwall bent the young stem, almost to the ground, well firmly to the ground as Jota got a two flipper challenge off the Millwall number 22 Aiden O'Brien. The same 22 who five minutes before was breathless and hands on hip resigned to the Brokeback Mountain love that Jota had been giving him for the previous minutes. Yes, he got bum loved purely and simply by that Jota dink here and dink there, more twists than a curly wurly this story and lo! In O'Brien goes with a two footed tango which in all honesty Jota had all week to prepare for it was that clumsy. Jota falls to the grass motionless, Saville pushes his face in, gets it pushed back out, Neves steams in, anger and hostility, it's a soap opera all of a sudden and all I'm bothered about is Jota. My little cherub. How he had the Millwall back line in confused sweats. O'Brien again physical. But Jota gets up. He's growing that dude. Growing good. It's so early in the season too.

I think we had learned all we had to learn from the Cardiff game maybe. Our team didn't have to learn much from the Colin Wanker playbook to approach this game, although not as violent as the Warnockian plague of the last home match it was still a bit snarky. Jota was a ghost through the Millwall defence, I half expected Derek Acora to start channelling his Spirit guide. I expected Yvette Fielding to start screaming on the touchline dropping her torch. Ghost Jota. He takes command of the ball deep infield and that's it, he knows his path is set, he runs, he shifts the ball over, he duffs it in the net. One-Nil. What. A. Fucking. Strike. I'm beside myself, an errant elbow knocks my glasses off and they spiral into the air. I'm still screaming, the dude next to me is screaming, everybody is screaming. I stretch a hand up and catch my glasses in a smooth Jota like grab. All is saved. Jota you sensual thing. I believe in Diogo, where ya gone, you sexy thing

Of course we ran things in the first half. Doherty and Batth are so far sucking up football knowledge via osmosis. Our Portuguese brothers have infected the training ground at Compton with football and the infection has infected. Danny Batth swapped the ball from his left foot to his right and he's past a player. I shake my head. Danny? What? Last year that ball would have been described as a clearance. A hoofed toe bunt into another opposition attack. Blob ball. But Danny has always been better than that, he is a good soldier and has done what Kenny and Lamberto told him. Fuck it off back up the pitch. Ron Bastard style centre back….what has happened? Nuno has quietly spoken golden honey like simple words into Dannys ear. 'No Danny, love the ball, stroke the ball BE the ball' and thus it was so. Apart from a few lapses into madness it was there, and he looked like a different player, they all did. Keeping possession, holding the ball, dictating the play, looking for openings, probing constantly.

The second half was a much dodgier event. It seemed as if we had watched Pink Floyd in the first half then the Latvian Pink Floyd came on in the second. It was nearly the same as the first half but something was wrong. The licks sounded yeah similar but there wasn't that really slick comfortable groove we had in the first. Maybe the sending off had some effect, altered the flow maybe, something was wrong and some changes were in the offing. The wind changed a little in the second half too. Blowing in swirls across the stand, making the seagulls cry out.

Vinagre at one point spoke animatedly with Neves and the talk started. Millwall were deep and looked to hit on the break I supposed. But half an hour of the second half had me staring at Wallace and Saville, evil glances they were as this was the thing, the point at which we had seen every one goal lead turned into a one pointer, a draw, a sick end to nail biting constant plonks at Ruddy including one through a mass of legs that Ruddy did excellent to smother. Another Millwall gut flash, another 'woman' who looked like a dude. I watched the Millwall fans for a while and it was ok but the end of the match, the final twitching corpse of it still had those heart in mouth moments, that damp hand on the back of the neck and I noticed I was gripping the arm of the dude next to me but he didn't care as he was busy chewing his finger off. We looked at each other, we had stood next to each other for five seasons and we didn't need to talk, we had the last minute equaliser stare. Shell shock, the last round knock out.

'Blow the whistle you horrible bald headed bastard'

We did it yeah. Three points, a result which will never remain as a memory of greatness and discussed over pints in dark pubs. That's the nature of growth, the incessant division of component parts into a greater all. We probably did need a Striker on the pitch. I need a big flash Mercedes to drive around in but the falling apart van I have does the job at the moment.

Bright Enkobahare had some 'Bright' moments where he forgot he had the ball again and everybody wanted a pop at those twenty yard lets bop a fan in the face shots. N'Diaye came on, total unit first touches, a run where he had three players hanging off him but never broke stride. I like the look of him but even if I didn't like him I wouldn't say anything, he's massive. But again it's all so fucking new. It's new for us seeing this madness unfold in front of our eyes. Excitement again. Dynamic movement, these are fresh green shoots of a revolution and those green shoots are susceptible to the frosts and winds of the Championship.

There will be greater nights and days to come where this Portuguese madness, this reinvigorated Doherty and Batth will force their ways through the hard packed clay of the Warnockian Championship dystopia and reach the light above. And when those shoots do untangle themselves and unfold the green leaves of the Nuno revolution some poor bastards are going to get annihilated, and they will sit within the away dressing room at Molineux and weep at the beauty of it. But now, at this moment we should nurture and provide support to this fledgling project, a bit of love too as we bend an errant branch back into the required position.

Outside the ground three Chinese fellas stopped me to grab a light for their cigarette. They were laughing and were wearing brand new club shirts. New fans maybe, who knows, maybe a few years ago I would have been a little pissed off that the club was becoming a global beast attracting these fresh faced doughnuts who had never before stepped in Wolverhampton. But this time I didn't care, I wasn't bothered about them, or the moaning from various lollipops that walked past me. I wasn't particularly bothered about the traditional Millwall post match street theatre either, or the fact Adidas Gazelles had a sole as thin as the Refs hair. It was a good feeling, a confident comfortable feeling, and I let myself be oozed along the ring road back to the car. I was thinking about Bonsai trees.

All that is gold does not glitter,

Not all those who wander are lost;

The old that is strong does not wither,

Deep roots are not reached by the frost.

Monday. I'm at the top of the Cannock Road, at the lights, Molineux in front of me, you can just see the arse end of the Northbank. It was very serene, little traffic, these big showers snake through the day, fine mists of it. Then the Sun would burst through the clouds like Doherty on a mission again. But Shaky Jake and Crackhead Dave are in the back of my van, we are going to a little job. We are the Joeys, the bodies that lift heavy things. £20 though.

While I'm waiting, and they are hacking I notice a massive rainbow stretching from Saint Peters arching right smack bang in the middle of the Molineux. I'm stunned. For a moment I forget where I am and I'm a bit fucking emotional. Against a black cloudy backdrop this beautiful arch of vibrant colour. I couldn't take it in. Shaky Jake needs his daily fix but he's singing 'Once upon a time there was a Tavern…' in that sad addicted, shattered voice, and Crackhead Dave wants to talk about conspiracy theories…I'm thinking about the Jota strike against Millwall and my glasses tumbling over and over in the air…

We are starting, I think to slowly come to terms with the horrors of the past few years. It's Post Traumatic Wolves Syndrome. Watching those stripey bastards up the road play their funeral march like football against cool top teams. Watching our fractured former squads grind out the endless litany of (often) cack football. Roger Johnson. O'Hara. Afobe gone. Sakho. How we fucking suffered. But now these horrors are starting to be discussed in constructive ways instead of anger, I think we are starting to come to terms with the 'back in the day' shit. Starting to realise that 'hope' is a tangible concept.

'Hi my name is Mikey and I've been a Wolves fan for 45 years' and everybody murmurs hello back as they twist their fingers unsure, staring at the church hall floor. I want to go for a cigarette. I feel peoples eyes on me. I too try to plait my fingers. 'You see…it all started when they hired Glenn Hoddle as Coach, then…'

It's the calm after the storm, the flirtations with relegation, the actual relegations and dare I say it some of us still haven't got over the Bhattis yet alone even started to process the madness of the Morgan & Moxey years. I can't sensibly compare it to the horror of trench warfare but once upon a time three of us were run ragged around Leeds town centre eventually finding a quiet pub where we just looked at each other, exhausted. It's like that. Relief. Maybe. Tired, angry, violent, scared, wanting to talk about it. But that sunlight through the clouds is bright and a little uncomfortable through the windscreen. The sun has made stars through the glass and if I squeeze my eyes shut all this modern architecture is gone and the old houses are still there on Molineux street. The old South bank. Molineux street stand. The North Bank.

And when the old stands were demolished we would stand there, me, a few others watching the diggers ply their trade ripping down the asbestos roof, the iron and steel, nobody saying anything but just wondering quietly to ourselves as the dark corners of Molineux were exposed to sunlight. Out of Darkness cometh light, but that light can be too bright after the darkness. I'm tapping the van steering wheel, the light is still red. I remember Robert Plant asking 'Does anybody remember laughter?' and I wished I had a stereo in the van.

Bristol City. A weird place. Quite liberal and chilled out on the one side and on the other the Dock workers, the dudes who built boats. Council haircuts. I don't even know who plays for them or who manages them. I have to be honest, I don't care. I'm watching Jota warm up. He's not even looking at the ball as he effortlessly moves it around as he's talking to Neves and Vinagre. Ruddy is catching balls, but not catching them, he's grabbing the thing like he's ripping somebodies head off, stalking up and down his line like an animal. I like Ruddy, I like the way he saved that late Millwall shot. No way was he letting that fucker in. N'Diaye is a colossus, he's standing with his legs spread shoulder width hands on hips and his chin is out. He looks like an old photo of Mussolini.

The vibe is relaxed pre match then things are getting a bit noisy and the Motorhead Volume PA is blurting out loud shit about things that aren't very interesting. Saiss is talking to Danny Batth. There are not many Bristolians made the trip here. This place scares them maybe. They haven't won here in since Moses was crucified, or something. Their warming up looks structured and energetic but not dynamic, no not easy, not slick. I hate them already, they are typical and generic. I hope they don't do a Cardiff. A Warnock. I want to be entertained.

Kick off through the expectant haze of the evening. I shout out something, words of encouragement 'fuck 'em off Wolves' and shuffle my feet, I want a piss. N'Diaye Is ascendant in midfield, already harrowing the furrow of the pitch like a plough. Fighter jet football, twisting and turning. Dog fighting and here we are. The first errant tackle by Bristol. Again late. Thrown together

Championship Mixed Football Arts. Although it's not artistic there is grappling and chasing ghosts. Jota is nonplussed. The Bristol midfield might as well join their hands together and have a seance to find out what Neves and Cavaleiro are doing.

'Neves? Are you there? Knock the table twice for yes and once for no' they whisper to the vague forms of our players, here, there, every fucking where. Cavaleiro shifts his weight from foot to foot, twists and is gone, Jotas feet seem to glide across the pitch without touching it. N'Diaye is the Wolves paywall. You have to pay him to see what final third delights Wolves back three have to offer and Bristol although determined are dragging their feet holding tight to their wallets. Shakey Jake my friend. What horrors your addiction has given you. The endless phone calls to your dealers, the networking, the shivers, the cramps. Yet through all that as he shook in the back of the van, a few days before he was almost upbeat. His team were doing well, he wanted to talk about it, wanted to discuss things and in his madness of addiction his mood was positive and hopeful.

I remembered Gary Mastic last week, sad, depressed, angry. But I had missed some play and a whistle was blown. But the juxtaposition of attitudes were glaring as the Ref pontificated about some order of rule and play while the players took a few seconds to regain composure and shape. Wolves animated and pointing out various parts of the pitch, Bristol content (for the most part) to look at the grass. The Southbank are angry at the incident I missed but I abuse the distant figure of the Ref just as much as them. Solidarity ay it.

But here we go again. Bristol City have a few digs, a few late tackles, some elbows, some moaning. It's Championship football time again folks. The Referee is a slow and dull lad, he's scared, you can see it. He can't rapidly process the information that he's seeing, the football we are trying to play. The result? Elbows on Wolves players get dismissed, tackles from behind waved on, Danny Batth taken out by a flying headbutt to the back of his neck, decisions start to pile up against us. I've seen this episode before. Cardiff. The Referee has bolstered the confidence of Bristol who see in ineffectiveness of the Ref a glimmer of light. I lose my voice 20 minutes in as my anger is directed at the Official. My language is foul and violent and I'm fucking twitching again

Neves and Cavaleiro are a marvel to me and their forensic passes of love and runs across the pitch are a joy, it's like they are stroking my hair with every kick and I feel loved with each one. Proud also, and I want to be with the Bristol City fans pointing at my team saying 'Look! This is it, look at us! Watch this beauty! This is my team!' and I'm proud yes, a word I may ponder later. But I also want to say 'Look at your team, look at the bastard in the black, he'll be your key player tonight'. And that's the reason I don't get invited into the inner sanctum of the great and good. If I bumped into the Ref I would nut him, right on the bridge of his nose as he walked past me.

At half time I roll my cigarette and hasten off to the end of the stand to shuffle and discuss the passing and the movement with whoever is there, the ex Para, the psychopath, the mate from years back, the mate I just met, the mate with the £600 coat, the mate that hasn't got a coat. Is the football pornographic? May we use abstract descriptions like 'filthy' and 'filth'? I don't think we can, the football here deserves far more respect I think. So lets try 'Unappreciated by officials and opposition teams'. My mouth is dry now and tastes of roll ups and I watch the half time fag smoke billow into the rain under the glow of the security lights.

But the cats cradle of passing movement is a joy. Doherty shifts again, slices of movement that are incisive and splitting. The rain is making things glisten and slip, the ball skips over the grass and our team have a low centre of gravity, there are corrections to the play now, and they have everything in hand. Jota to Bonatini and back again, Bright with a subtle run into box. There are units ahead of him, keep an eye on the ball and a hairy eyeball on the 14 stone of occupied space bearing down, they grab and they grapple, twist and flap. Bright is gone and they grab empty Molineux air but don't worry there's a pull back and a stray late foot, Bright goes down, Ref waves play on..

It's called traditionally the second half but really it's a coda of sorts, a finale. Bristol had run out of ideas early and our positioning was stoic, the tactical fluency of shape under Lambert replaced with the monad of rigidity of form and positions under Nuno. No matter how Bristol pried and tried to find purchase in the gaps between our players their fingers slipped and failed. The space allowed them was temporary and fleeting. The keyword was temporal. No time allowed to shake off the attentions of N'Diaye and Neves who arrived shortly after the ball was collected by a Bristol shirt. But and it's a but I keep having to insert again and again. The late tackles, the shirt pulling, the grabbing, the pushing. We aren't being allowed to play football. The difference between Bristol City and Wolves was glaring.

We were beautiful again and they were ugly. We were the artists and Bristol the epitome of the English game. Snarky, pully, arsey all the negative adjectives I can think of. Was a draw a thing? We were robbed it's simple and the result was unfair. One day we will get a Referee that understands football 'in principle' and can see the rules are there for a reason, and that reason is playing beautiful football not a Sunday Rugby match on a council pitch in Barry Island. Nuno gets spoken to by the Ref. Nuno is a Warrior artist not a 'Coach' and we are a few games into the season and he see's his creations marred again and again by some cuckold dick brained fucking idiot of a Referee and his two fucking wine gum mates running the line.

It's a harsh school Championship football, but one that this team are learning fast within. They are strangers to each other at the moment and yet the football we are playing is years ahead of last season and yet the team still galvanise, still execute and still make your stomach do a little flip. What's going to happen as they coalesce as a real familiar unit? When we get a game where the Referee understands football?

At the traffic lights I've noticed they have turned green but there are no cars behind me so I just wait for a moment with my arms on the wheel. Supporting Wolves isn't an addiction like Shaky Jakes and all the allegories and metaphors in the world wont make that so but we do share one thing and that's the love of the thing we are addicted to. I asked him months ago why he continued to score and use and he said 'because I love it, it's the first thing I think about when I wake up and the last thing at night' and I know his pain a little, a fraction. We love it because we fucking love it and we hate it because we love it. That's why the small concrete area right by our seats is polished to a high sheen.

We shake like Shaky Jake, shuffle and move, every kick of the ball marked by a twitch of the leg, a subtle jump to head a cleared ball, a corner marked by grabbing onto whoever is next to you. The great pantomime on the pitch is mirrored exactly by us, the audience. Sometimes it's a shit ending, sometimes a cliffhanger, suspense and a twist of the storyline but always a story we are part of despite the glitzy screens and the overpriced beer. 'All that is Gold does not glitter, not all those who wander are lost' Tolkien said in Lord Of The Rings. Maybe in our stand there are those who don't glitter, the ones with the crap shoes and the uncombed hair and missing teeth. But they aren't lost, we aren't lost, and we never have been. We carry our club like Shaky Jake carries the monkey on his back. Deep within us.

The lights have gone green again and my two muckers didn't even notice I had sat through the green light lost in thought. As I pulled away the sun broke through again and illuminated the stands and they did shine like Gold and that rainbow did end right there on the pitch and maybe it's only really full of Gold when we are inside and our songs are loud and our entertainment something else entirely and I'm laughing to myself. Why? Nobody would ever fucking believe in me staring at rainbows and golden stadiums but some would understand. Shaky Jake would and he would believe this too if he could read..

> *From the ashes a fire shall be woken,*
> *A light from the shadows shall spring;*
> *Renewed shall be the blade that was broken,*

The crownless again shall be king.

I don't know whether it's time to have some sort of round up. Is it too early in the book? Six or Seven games in. Are we doing OK? It's promotion level point attainment so I've been told. But that's empirical, I want to know how the Kwan is flowing in Camp Compton. Danny Batth one of our centre backs was cracking the smiles and laughs in his chat with Mikey Burrows the Wolves media man. Of course I had to rewind the fucking thing again and again trying to work out if he didn't give a shit or he was that chilled out there everything was groovy man.

He's a Vegan apparently our Danny and I applaud that, and I tell Gary Mastic this morning as he walks past with his Staffie. 'A Vegan? He's an alien then?' No Gary. But Nuno did an interview and I watched that too. Good God he's one scary powerful dude. I think if he told me to jump off a cliff I'd be scared to ask for a small cliff with ledges and shrubs to catch. But we could lose the next ten games and I would still be standing with him. Sometimes ideas take a while to catch on.

I have to contrast the zen like Kwan of THE NUNO, with the infamous Temple Street mob member 'Chelsea Tina'. I met Tina at the Rollerdrome in Temple Street. I say met, I watched her beat the shit out of two blokes at the bar. Every area of Wolverhampton had it's mobs but nobody had somebody like Tina. She had big seventies platforms on and a little sheepskin jacket. Swinging these big punches and kicks at these dudes who were cowering while I stood balancing and watching on my skates. Juxtaposition again? Nuno sitting there explaining things to us very slowly, not I suspect because of his grasp of English, that is excellent. Explaining slowly because each word and sentence has weight and he wants those words and sentences to settle on our brains gently, without alarming us too much. Osmosis again, positive potential to negative potential through a semi permeable membrane, the media. Molecule by molecule he is changing the way we perceive his communications so that we too may share in his vision. I suspect his vision is loftier than we realise and Fosun in Nuno has found somebody with the same vision they have.

But it's still early days isn't it? We haven't won a game for a while and things are itchy a little. A bit like that film with Keanu Reeves 'The Matrix' I feel plugged in like somebody is about to end this delicious fantasy with some home truths and the 'home truths' are the win ratio. The whispered conversations in the subway going back into town 'We're too fucking nice, too pretty, we have to get nasty' and I don't know. Do you stick to the path set out at game 1 or adjust your style and philosophy seven games in? It's not panic of course it's just Wolvo-genetic. It's gone to pot so many times in the past we half expect it and dare I say we are prepared for it. When you look at the subs bench and think something should change, somebody has to come on and galvanise the whole groove. When your hands are starting to sweat. The slapping of trainers on the road behind you as people start to run…

Of course the Rollerdrome was always getting heated. Rasta men, skinheads, Teds always kicking off. But it was always kicking off somewhere in those days. I couldn't walk to school without running the gauntlet of every other tit from another school chasing me down the road to give me a kicking. Or me give them one. Then at school you had the psychopathic Teacher who wasn't averse to half knocking you out with a good punch. From the small scale battles on a personal level you had certain families too, schools, then streets, then areas, then towns. It seemed like everybody hated each other but it was also a dynamic time. A time when shit happened and it was interesting shit. And Tina finishing these two fellas off throws her head back and gets her hair out of her eyes and looks around see who else fancies it.

So in retrospect these times are also interesting but from a different viewpoint. Fair enough in 1976 we were treading water in a football sense. The whole game was on the cusp of change. Socially we were starting to see factories and places of work close down. There was nothing to do. Seriously, nothing to do. Old orders were tumbling down. Youth movements polarising. Chelsea Tina had a pair of brown flares on and they flapped as I stood open mouthed, dumbstruck. And now I'm in the garden having a roll up thinking about Miranda and Batth. Wondering if I would put Saiss in there and the squad permutations are clicking away in a confused mess of faces and abilities. Competition for places. I'm wondering if the training they are doing is as hardcore as picking a team today?

Nottingham Forest eh? Tough away day traditionally. I tend to think of the (Forest) Gumps as a thing. Warburton has a face like he's trying to chew his way out of it. He's a collapsed tent of a Manager. Like a day out in Borth. He has that passing game thing going on. Taking his kebab munching players to Nunos restaurant. Of course they will attempt to behave and eat like everybody else but I 'm convinced that food will be chewed with mouths open and they wont know what to do against the delicious and provocative football Nuno wants to play.

Will it be Cardiffian childishness again? Will it be Bristolian ciderball? Who knows. We do know they play out from the back, like us. Its pure Lolaball, hang on. Lola ball? You must have heard the old Kinks song 'Lola' same thing here. In principle of course she's beautiful and standing at the bar all delicious and sexy, and you want to buy her a drink, chat some bars, wax lyrical. A few minutes in you have a weird feeling in your belly that something isn't right. Her hands are rough and big. She has a deep voice. You gently kiss her neck right next to……hang on…..a 'Nottingham Skins' tattoo???? Lola Gump you cheeky sod. Standing there looking all pretty and sexy but really you are a mirage. A fake Gump. You hear The Who song 'Won't get fooled again' and you wonder if you have been fooled by it all. But it's all pre-game nerves and you watch Nuno again. Thank fuck for Nuno. Better than watching Lamberto trying to pull his ear off again, Kenny Charisma mumbling to himself or Saunders wondering where he is and what his own name is.

I suspect that maybe 25 minutes into the game we will see that rough big hand tugging a few shirts and maybe tickling a few shins too. I don't think (I've watched two Gump games) that they are (cough) very pretty at the back. The Gump defence can get a little confused and tangled especially put under pressure….but here we go again. Tina you sit there at the front of my memories and Lola you sit there at the back, let's see what happens.

My mate Danny (who stands next to me in the South Bank) is very drunk. So I get the whole conversations about the team and the play. He's a constant commentator where the only gaps in the alcoholic monologue are a chance to check his bets on his phone, see if his betting 'acca' is coming in.

Well there we have it. The ideas were there and placed upon the pitch at Nottingham with intent and passion. Are we not entertained? My word watching the highlights was an absolute joy. Can one single out a player that can be lauded and worshipped in the emotional minefield of a Sunday morning? I'm not sure I personally can. Watching the few segments of videos and reports I am dumbstruck by the quality and passion of our play but more importantly as I quoted Nuno at the top of the page, we made our 'ideas' stronger than theirs. We set our footballing ideas in the crucible of Nottingham Forest and the alchemy did fizz and operate, it did flourish in the fire and tears of Championship football.

Am I not entertained? No it's not entertainment. Watching Wolves is far more than that. It was always a metaphysical experience with the ground and the team so entwined and tangled within our own lives, work, relationships that nearly everything that happens within and without the club has some bearing on our own lives. The ideas have flourished in the rich soil Fosun has given us to replace the deadwood tactical mess we have dealt with in the past seasons and now under the patient hand of Nuno we see it flourish and grow.

Our support is endemic of Wolverhampton as a City. We are happy to welcome and appreciate anything that makes us proud but Fosun and Nuno have only felt a small part of that love for where we live and our team. We are reticent to trust, we have seen the same things before, we have been hurt many times in the past. What Fosun and Nuno will see in the coming months is a steady building up of support, it's that time when we start to cast away that typical shroud of Wulfrunian mistrust and say yeah, maybe and yeah, OK. We can finally open our hearts fully to the work that Nuno, the team and Fosun are doing and that deluge once it is unleashed will drown the city in a hysteria the likes of which we have rarely seen in the past. All the financial figures and all the dullness of conversations about football in our city will be forgotten and maybe we will be following a bus through the City centre waving flags and scarves come May, who knows.

But the result today is a major one even if it is still early in the season. One may pick apart the tactical microcosm of the day all they wish, there is a place for that and a need. We may enjoy the madness of Jota, Neves, Vinagre etc but the most important part of yesterday was the 'Idea', the philosophy. You can't take a body of men to war without an underpinning, an essential philosophy as to why they are entering battle. That's why Redknapp has failed at Birmingham, that's why you will see a steady outflux of managers from jobs this season. They lack the philosophy to extrapolate the 'Idea' into cohesive successful football and without the philosophy you merely have a body of men, a collection of attitudes and skills. The war itself will be a long one as we know but the Nuno idea will start a deluge of passion and heartfelt support that Nuno and Fosun will feel shaking the desks they sit at. Ideas man, it's everything.

The week previous. Where do I begin? Walking past the Grand Theatre I fancy going in the Moon Under the Water but I stop for a moment to gather my post bus trip thoughts and roll a cigarette. Inside the theatre people are waiting to watch whatever delights the world of thespianism has to give them. Me I'm ready to watch what the world of Nunoism has to give us. Delights? Drama? Madness. What am I even doing walking through town when I should be sitting at home talking to the dogs and staring at my reflection in the kitchen window? Nunoism. I'm going to watch the Woo Kwan Clan, Wolverhampton Wanderers, the Wolves. I'm going up the Mol' to watch them play in the Carabi...Caraboon...Crababoo.....League cup. Bristol Rovers the opponents. They have brought many bodies with them tonight and that West Country accent thing is a thing.

Last year you couldn't have dragged me to the Molineux to watch a cup match this early on, especially against a team like Bristol Rovers. Last week we played the council haircut version of Bristolian football. This week it's Rovers, Bristol is a polarised football town. This half is the real ale hipster version, beard oil, vinyl records, they have a BMX bike or a Fixie despite being 40 something, their wives or partners have good office jobs with the local council, thinning quiffs, jackets too tight....fucking hell. They walk past me quite fast chatting, laughing, they have spoiled little kids who's names always end in 'O' and the familiar localism chunders away so I look in the foyer of the Grand to collect myself and watch the doughnuts in there wander around while I roll my fag.

I look at a poster to see what's on and it's some gormless perma tanned dude with loads of bright white teeth then I see me in the glass and I smile but half my teeth are missing, my coat is from Primark and don't get me started on the Gazelles again which are leaking slightly and my sock is damp. When I get home my big toe will look like a shrivelled dick. I think about a Just Giving page for new trainers and laugh. I'd rather walk barefoot. Three old women are staring back at me from the warmth of the carpeted loveliness of the theatre. I must look like a crackhead. A smart one with a wet sock.

I had watched the Wolves video of Coady from the Gump game. I had watched it few times as I do. Trying to work out the feelings. You can't tell with Coady as he has his vocabulary clipped and ready. His frontal lobes buzz as he receives the question, processes the variables and boom! He's off. None of it waffle. And as he talks he's processing that information rapidly, changing and adjusting his answer mid speech. His facial movements are sincere, honest, self humorous, he's always on the edge of laughing or taking the piss but when he has to be serious his jaw clenches and the muscles up the side of his head clamp that brain down tight.

I don't know why Coadys head is important enough to dedicate a few paragraphs to but it's my book and if I want to talk about his head I will. He probably wont even play tonight, but I hope he does because he epitomises the flow and the rhythm of the team. Cadence is so important in speech and the same applies to football. The cadence of our team can be relentless, a Buddy Rich percussive delight, a trill of a tight snare, pass, bang, pass, whack, pass, move, pass, subtle touch and boom. Diogo 'Thats an 'O' not an 'E" Jota. In the Coady interview he is asked about Jota in the Gump game. Coady nearly says Jota is privileged and excited to play for Wolves but then he says we are lucky to have a player like him. Yes, I suppose so, but he should be happy he's here nonetheless.

This is the Woo Kwan Clan a machine at periods in the Forest game, at least in the second half. A supergroup of sorts, a group of talented artists learning to slip and slide their own particular skills, bars and beats into a whole creation, a team effort of curvaceous lovely tracks that wind their way in and out of the opposition. But Coady I think is the stand out player for me. Yes Jota and Neves have excelled themselves in their roles so far this season, but I suspect they would have excelled anywhere under a good coach. Coady has suffered the ignominy of Lambertball and the undynamic nit picking of Jackett. Coady has improved there's no doubt about that. Being the forensic nork that I am, I hunted the YouTubez for Coady interviews. There he was reticent and quiet, maybe he was younger and more inclined to stay quiet and now his ability is shining. Maybe that Liverpool game last season gave him the belief he needed to act as anchor and foundation that he does (for me) now.

Dodging the Baghdad Taxi drivers walking across to the Royal London I let this Coady thing linger around my left side of the brain for a while as a Vauxhall Insignia nearly takes my leg off. I want to aggravate the driver but I'm chilled out, laid back. A Bristol fan laughs and says something I don't catch.

'Fogoff Grumbleweed' It's the first thing that comes to mind so don't aggravate me. But he skitters off fast past the Hogs Head and down to the ground with his weird head mates. Night football. Why do I keep tripping up and nearly getting run over? Why are there so many of these Cider quiffs?

Tonight of course the 'concert' will be something different. I'm not expecting the front men, the new faces. Tonight will be about connecting with previous seasons. So I expect Jack Price maybe fresh from the Shropshire hedgerows. He's doing something right our Jack. He's made the bench, while others have been shipped out to other clubs, discordant noisy clubs with football that matches those players drunk Uncle moves at a family wedding disco with DJ Frankie Scabies from the Lunt (originally now Wombourne). I think about Lee Evans and I can't even remember his face.

 But we are sat in the Northbank tonight and things are a little dead, a little grey, and strange. The view is excellent but the zeitgeist in here is reserved and critical. It's a moaning thing, you can hear the murmurs of the Northbank crowd barely audible like a hive of moany bees. It's five minutes in and I've shouted abuse at the Rovers the Ref and the Rovers crowd but I don't think you do that in here and instead I punch myself in the balls every time I want to stand up and be emotional.

'Radar Love' football Bristol Rovers play. Great in short bursts but the whole song? 90 Minutes of it? I think Jack Price is absorbing the metaphysical current swirling around the club. He's seen Batth, Coady, Enkobahare and Doherty developing and making dynamic moves into the new set up. Jack wants to move too and I bet he's learning fast, waiting. Maybe tonight he can do his little cameo. But I'm walking behind a fella to the ground and for some reason he stops for no reason and I crash into the back of him. 'Sorry ahk' he says. 'No, my fault ahk' I reply, but it wasn't, and we bumble down past the University Library. Jack Price eh? Lucky he wasn't shunted off to Shrewsbury but I'm watching my feet now, shuffling, watching for traffic. We try to get in the Southbank but there's a mix up, we've bought Northbank tickets instead so we rush around the ground to the barren emotional wastes of the 'other' stand

There are a few more here tonight, it's a bit elbowy but the feelings and emotions are generally happy. Hi-Ho and off. Deslandes has started, that's nice, he slices a ball early off his left foot and it's a thing already and it's cider press for five minutes as everybody tries to remember why they are there. Price harries things like a smackhead eating an apple pie. Bits falling off. Boom and again it's a sliced ball and opposition pressure.

I say pressure, it's that bloke behind you at the bar who keeps gently pushing you in the back and you look at him in the bar mirror, he's a bald evil looking little gimp. A bit like Rovers Number eight who reminds me of boiled Monkfish. The difference between our imported skill set and our partially skilled old schoolers is obvious. Price darts a ball between the cider monkeys and Bright isn't there, he raises his hands to say 'what the fuck' but Zyro is off on another run, aggravating the Rovers midfield while N'Diaye strolls back to his zone. I'm not really happy with that. He's let us down a bit. You know, us, up here watching.

My toes are cold and I want a piss again. It's the cold you know, gets in your bladder but last week somebody pissed on my foot and I'm still a bit miffed by that 18 stone of monster being unable to control his dong. Yeah, that was ten minutes as the ball pinged around a little and I went on stand by. Shake head concentrate and narrow the eyes. How do we look? I'm not sure. There's certainly a bit of effort but there's a woman eating a burger four rows in front and I watch her demolish it in builders bites, three or four bites and it's gone. How much is a burger now? Four quid? Jeff it's too fucking expensive. Sort it out. I'd love a beer at half time if it was a couple of quid.

The crowd goes 'Oooooh' and I do to but she's fished another fucking burger from somewhere and she's eating that too! Fucking hell, that's eight quid of meat bab. I'm not sure what happened on the pitch sorry. I've got a thing for girls who like to eat. Yes, fantasising over burger noshing women instead of watching the game, which is still going on apparently.

At half time I go for my roll up and she pushes past me and smiles and she has burger in her teeth. You little minx. I chat with the usual suspects and a few others who want to talk. People generally like talking to me about my writings and that's good. I only write for us but I'm waiting for that big paying writing gig that never comes. I see a few faces from the past who say hello too. This game has brought out the faces for sure. Burger girl comes past and smiles again and the burger in her teeth is gone but I'm thinking of my wet sock.

Well there's a few days talked about. Coady looked comfortable as did most of the team. But there were those 'Mom catching you having a wank' moments where you wanted to pull the duvet over your head. Young Oskar I'm looking at you. He must have had some highly infectious disease. Nobody wanted to pass to him. Off and upwards into the draw. The Bristolian hipsters didn't look too happy and they are bouncing around outside being rowdy but it's not about that tonight. Kwan is a delicious fresh burger and tonight the kwan although prevalent and raw was a Southbank concession burger. A bit dry, kind of chewy and flavourless but filling in some strange abdominal way, it might be a bit of wind. It might be stuck in our teeth a little as we probe a tongue into the gaps to get that bit of gristle out. Gristleball it was. Certain flavours shone through, Spicy Enkobahare flavours mostly. His goal a something of a thing, giving us something to cheer about.Like Thousand Island dressing in a team of grey gristle.

At times the ghosts of Lambert wafted across the pitch moaning and clanking their reserve team chains or trailing treatment room bandages like a mummy. Norris was an eye opener, how confident is he? I was quite content to see him in goal, he was vocal and not afraid to mix it up in the box. Changes a plenty really, were there eight changes in all? None of them made much of an effort apart from Norris, sandwich triangles going a bit curly at the edges. Half eaten burgers, plastic bottles underfoot.

Mid week cup games are strange affairs. They tend to be like wife swapping parties on a posh estate in Staffordshire. Nobody really knows each other and it's a little fumbly and a little embarrassing sometimes as these strangers disrobe and do their thing while you're thinking about football and why the fuck you are there in the first place. N'Diaye was certainly among those in the kitchen talking about cars and jobs with the early blowers. Zyro was interested in the buffet they had put on. Little sausage passes here and there. A few dips at goal. But I was happy to see him, bit of match time and he'll be an addition to the squad. But it was all a little Cheese cube and pineapple on a cocktail stick football. Douglas had a woman sat on his face for most of the evening. The slinky Cavaleiro had most of the attention for sure and he battled through the stockings and suspenders that were a little bit too tight with aplomb. Busy and workmanlike but it wasn't a night with the supermodels of Instagram. It was that kind of night.

I'm waiting for a lift and I'm thoughtful. Bus stop post match/mortems are a thing. I listen to the chat of the people waling past us and realise it's still upbeat. still positive. But I've noticed too that the bus to Wednesfield is a lot more positive than the bus to Bushbury. The old farts were moaning a bit, the young lads nodding and looking at their bets on their phones, an African woman in a high Vis just staring into the road. Yes, midweek cup matches in the cold mists. Shuffling along wet pavements. Wrapping up against the damp, feeling your back ache with the damp. Clutching your bus fare and checking it every few minutes. Wiping the bus window to see where the fuck you are and not recognising any of it in the dim street lights. Getting home into the warm kicking your shoes off and fussing the dogs.

'How was the match?' they ask. 'Orite' you answer. Thinking about wife swapping parties and bits of burger stuck in a fat girls teeth. 'Deslandes had a good game' you say, but the TV burbles and nobody is listening. Fourth round tho'.

Have I said enough about Conor Coady yet? I was into ten thousand words about his playing and all of a sudden I'm in love with the player I described as 'he runs like he's afraid of the grass' and now I'm castigating myself for my lack of understanding. I save the 10k words into a document. It will do for another time. Perhaps when I am sitting somewhere quiet and I can finally be dispassionate about it maybe. I doubt it.

Jota I don't have to hunt around for words for, I don't have to sit and fiddle with the thesaurus to gleam some veins of Gold in this lad. Tenacious maybe? Watching him get gnarly tackles that would stack a Sunday football meathead, watching him slide his steez all over the place. Steeze? Style with ease. Us extreme sportsmen have a word for it and it describes him perfectly. 'GnarBar' and to find out what it means watch any doughnut smash his face into the concrete on a skateboard and get up to do it again. Jota is totally GnarBar. Forget about his football for a minute and look into his eyes, there is a thousand yards of stare there, he's on the edge of the abyss and he knows it. Staring down at the limitless depths. He knows he has the skills and the silky moves and he backs up those moves with words, the words are the crunch and the smash of the errant opposition leg. And statistics are a thing.

You see I've just been talking to Alan Araldite. Now Alan is not somebody I know very well. He used to glue windows together in a dark factory in Willenhall and he was part of a group I used to go to away matches with. I avoided him pretty much, he was a fan of listening to the match commentary on the radio at matches with one single earphone stuck into his grisly hairy ear, and now you can see him in the Southbank concourse watching the match on the TVs drinking a fucking Bovril which he holds close to his face blowing it even though it has the fucking lid on it.. He takes slurping sips while he's talking to you, but he's not looking at you, he's watching the fucking telly on the wall. I feel aggravated and it annoys the shit out of me.

His Missus spends most of her day buying stuff on ebay. But Alan is a footballing expert. He stores away that much crap about football it's mental. There he is on the towpath by himself or he's haunting the concourse at half time stopping people going for a roll up. He looks like a rapist or a dog botherer. His Anorak is his second skin, the zip is broke and he's repaired it with a massive safety pin. Two stripe dude, Puma for posh events, trainer shoes for weddings and funerals which he goes to a lot of as his job kills men off eventually, stonewashed boot cut jeans, funny Tshirt from Primark. Argos clipper haircut. He fidgets as he talks, and I watch his shit shoes as he moves, I don't like looking at his face. I nod to him every match and avoid him but he thinks I'm his friend.

Barnsley I don't like. This has to do with me confusing where my Dad was from. Bolton/Barnsley, all begin with B and they are all North. Today is the Barnsley match and I'm aggravated by it all. My Kwan isn't flowing yet. Alan is talking about Coady and I'm listening but not. I'm a polite bloke, I should have kicked him in the canal for 'Coadys pass ratio has a lot to be desired and…' while I'm looking at fish in the cut. A big Pike sunning itself in the margins. I remember Blackpool, I remember a Barnsley fan going through a window of a pub and landing on the pavement in front of me while I was having an overpriced Ice cream. I don't know whether I laughed at the time and I remember my mate chatting up a couple of girls from a blind school on a jolly.

'Your blogs OK but you swear too much, I don't like swearing, there's no need'

My football knowledge isn't brilliant. I understand tactics etc but seasons that have passed I only remember the stories. The time me and Fish jumped on the bus to Blackpool after the Burnley game. The Wolves fan getting carried out of a pub with just his pants and a big foam cowboy hat. So I don't see a point to Barnsley at all, in a footballing sense, but Alan is going through their squad like Columbo on a murder case. I've seen his Missus at 'The Range' buying eight multipacks of cheap pop, loading it into their Renault 'Horrible' people carrier like a survivalist after an earthquake or a riot. The sugar is affecting him badly obviously, I feel protective of Coady now. Especially after sitting in the Northbank in the week. I could watch him from there, loved it. So quiet as well, I could hear everything Coady said, which was a lot. It was so quiet his voice echoed around the silence of the stand. 'Its like the Walking Dead in here' nah it's 'The Sitting Dead'. This is where I spent writing ten thousand words about him, that's for another day.

Alan Araldite whispers things. His voice is quiet and I'm a bit deaf so I'm hoping I'm nodding and smiling at the right parts. I listen to the cadence and pitch of his voice and mimicking his facial features which is hard, as his head reminds me of a football with a face drawn on it. It's expressionless and flat, looks like the kids over the park have been booting it around. This is the rub with running a football blog, how often can you say so and so passed to so and so but whatshisface looked jaded and his pass…..fucking hell.

But Alan has a bogie in his nostril and as he talks it's blowing in and out like a rat in a pipe. In and out, Enkobahare this, in and out, well Nuno of course, in and out, then for a minute it doesn't come out and i'm shocked for a minute. He continues about FFP and fuck, emotion, an intake of air then that fucker comes out again and it's attached to a hair!!! It's like Bungie jumping for snot and I want to laugh but I don't want to upset him! Jesus Fucking Christ. Why can't one of these fit women joggers stop to talk in their tight sporty legs? They just run a bit faster when they see me, I don't blame them. But I'm wondering what Alan is doing down here by himself…I wonder what Jota is doing now. Right now as I stare at Alans shit shoes.

Kwan is flowing and that's the truth, you could see it in the attendance today. People were busy bees. there were people there that had unfamiliar faces full of expectation and joy. Usually its faces like a Captain of a ship looking at the horizon to see if those dark clouds are coming this way, wondering whether to splice the main brace or some other sailing shit. They are expectant and that's scary as I don't personally expect anything at all except madness. Whether thats the madness of a win or some scruffy git on 'their' team grabbing a last minute winner from a (whisper it) opposition set piece. Then they will run up to the Southbank gurning. Somebody will throw a bottle at them or a coin and I'll look at the mould and algae on the roof of the stand taking a deep breath. I know my mate Horace will look after me, stop it all becoming too much, too emotional although he's as passionate as me he has a hard nosed outlook. He is the most normal person I know. In an abnormal sense.

Are we at some sort of critical mass with our side now? There are moments for sure that we have a tendency to lose grip, especially when under attack. Opposition teams tend to inflate their chests and get an extra 10% out of their facile sickly play to cause upset, we've seen it before how they do it too. Their Manager is Paul Heckingbottom who I have never heard of in my life but Alan tells me his fucking career and how he's doing at Barnsley. In the canal there are a shoal of Roach that glide past like a bunch of Japanese school kids all behaved and the Pike is watching from the reeds. When I get home I google Heckingbottom out of boredom and there he is, he doesn't look very happy. He has that Warnock vibe. Darkness, and hairless, angry mole man, obvious he would be a self employed Electrician oiling the wood on his £1000 hardwood patio set in Spring and Autumn. He is a man who religiously deletes his browser history and rarely gives out his email address because he takes Spam mail as a personal insult.

We know what our side were like today. Beautiful like a supermodel or a gorgeous pop singer, hair in the right place, bits sticking out here and there but not averse to picking their arse or dropping the odd room clearer. I thought Bright played well again, his goal against Rovers must have been a nut splosher in a metaphysical sense. Offloading some pent up rage. Yes, that's a goal Brighty, that posty thingy with the net at the back. I'm surprised he didn't dribble the ball around a bit against Rovers for that goal, then fall over. Has he lit the touch paper to his goal firework? Who knows? But maybe after that effort his goal firework has been lit.

Jota again doing 'the Jota' which is a dance only he knows and involves making the opposition behave like nippy dogs. Which is strange as Barnsley are called the Tykes for some reason. But we all know it's an old persons dog that probably shivers when it shits. As did the Barnsley team when Jota did 'The Jota' again and again. Their number 11 and 4 looked fucking knackered 20 minutes into the game, he ran them ragged, they looked like Sheep with their heads stuck in a fence. Forlorn, a bit sad. I'm suspecting the environment is putting the weight on our minds here. It certainly puts the kibosh on any thoughts of Barnsley trying to play any kind of constructive football. This is a team that has given up already. Now they are watching the bottom of the table even if it is early on. They are watching like it's a big fucking shark ready to eat them up. Every time a ball boy holds on to the ball for too long it's a stroke towards the beach for this club. Survival at all costs, even if we can't look at ourselves in the mirror any more.

Coady and Batth I can't fault, I see a team here and those variables interlock like parts of a complicated clock Nuno has made. But one errant movement, one slip of a foot and those variables amplify as Barnsley get closer to our goal, and everything is springs, cogs, screws everywhere and Coady is the one that has to make sense of it all again until the clock maker demands from the sidelines, demands and orders everything back into position. It's the typical 'Well who was the last one to use it?' and it's always Danny Batth or Coady or Miranda.

I enjoyed the Doherty thing too and Alan in his infinite wisdom calls him 'Docherty' which annoys me, and I'm just being bothered by this dude in his forensic stat laden madness he can't even call him by his proper name. But that Pike in the margins is as still as fuck, watching the little fishes. He'll make a darting run into that shoal of Roach, scattering them like Doherty does, route one machinations, the unstoppable force of the intent and passion this man has for getting shit done. The back three thing suits him, he's a bit late getting back sometimes but that's a thing he will work on through the season. Nuno will whisper magic words to him about that. Set out the groundwork for the days and matches to come.

Today again he was resolute and proud. Those runs splitting apart the Barnsley midfield like shit through a Goose. Douglas had a few moments where he forgot who he was and decided to wander the field a little, but early days for him, he'll get better with age, er time playing. But saying that he did a better job than Neves who decided that he was having a day off.

So 2-1 to us, it seems like a bit of an uninspiring scoreline which absolutely belies it's madness really. How mad? I was cooking in a Parka made for Arctic exploration. Bad coat choice Mikey. The last seconds were a mix of elation and dehydration, I was sweating as much as the team. My mate went to grab me to celebrate N'Diaye's goal and I slipped out of his arms like an errant trout I was that sweaty. The mad thing here? We won with passion and that last few seconds effort that plucked the game from the armpit of a Turkish bouncer to the cleavage of Kelly Brook. The difference? Last season that would have been a draw, now we have people who pull themselves from the clutches of the depraved draw to the madness of the walk back into town. Watching the Northbank empty itself with ten minutes to go was both sad and hilarious in many ways. The walk back out of the still full Southbank was a joy. We really are the fucking heart and soul of the Molineux.

I left Alan ruminating on something in the concourse during half time. He wasn't happy but I think he lacks understanding. The result and game will always be one to maybe forget in terms of football and desire but these are the gritty pants up your arse crack games. You can either grin and bear it while they chafe your ringhole or you can throw caution and civility to the wind and get your hand in there to dig them out. Alan Araldite will never understand the result only the quantitative aspects of it. It was definitely a 'dug out' result or a last dance with Melissa Multipack and I daresay we will see a few more, but crikey, how would that have ended up with Lamberto there?

It was funny at the Barnsley game talking to a few really horrible people, listening to their tales of what they had been up to over the past few months. I say horrible because they are nice enough to chat to but you wouldn't want to go out on a date with them. I get a bit emotional sometimes and my hands start to twitch over that strange dichotomy of the most evil of people you know and the most good.

Steve Plant is like that. The 'good un's' so to speak. At Wolves over the past few years we have all waxed lyrical over the beauty of those people we have lost, with prepare simple eulogies for them on Social Media and print but we never seem to give those who are alive our love....not in the amounts our Steve should have.

As soon as the Carl Ikeme news was announced I like many other people fell into a kind of stand by mode. We expressed our horror and our pain at the news because we loved Carl. He was our bloke, our number 1. To get that news was a low blow especially since the season was about to start and we had all these new people rushing into the club. We needed some sort of familiar face in the side to feel 'comfortable' I suppose. At least from my perspective. As brave as I was, I kind of fell into a powerless kind of funk where I didn't quite know what to do. I wrote a blog post to Carl but I was still lacking any kind of creative force to make the news digestible if you like. With the positivity that was swirling around the club it was a difficult dichotomy to try and get your head around.

But look! On the horizon! There's a bald yedded bloke on Twitter sorting shit out. There he is again on Facebook, step forward Mr Steve Plant. There are dudes in our lives that sometimes clarify and focus the pain you feel and channel it into all sorts of weird and wonderful but positive ways. Steve grabbed the bull by the horns and instantly started to get the mass of often highly dysfunctional Wolverhampton Wanderers fan base into some sort of cohesive dynamic narrative. In other words yeah you feel the Ikeme pain, right there in your gut. The fear of illness, the illness of somebody you have the utmost respect for, somebody who always knew the Southbank had his back when he trotted up to goal. And there we all were sitting moping around changing our profile photos to one of Carl. But it was all shadows and emotion, dark clouds. Steve has gathered the fortitude and intent to change all that. He has given us a focus. That pain we feel was taken away by watching people get 'waxed' on ten second Twitter videos. It was taken away by watching big fat bastards taking penalties. It was done by Steve and he did it for us as well as raising money for Leukemia charities.

This shit takes hard work, phone calls, chats at the match when you should be enjoying yourself and there was Steve running around, making sure everything is in place, everybody is singing off the same hymn sheet. Working out the details of a head shave, sussing out who needs a chest wax. Haranguing people, getting in their faces to give money not because the money was important (which it is) but knowing full well we needed a positive focus, fulfilling a need for us to give something, to be seen as 'doing' rather than being a passive spectator. As well as that he interacted with the club too, pulling that great corporate monstrosity of a global concern into the daily lives of a supporter or a fan. Vitally important at this juncture, in fact massively important.

I love people who do stuff. There's a meme flying around that when you watch the scenes of a great tragedy instead of focusing on the horror and grief look for the helpers and the people working hard to alleviate suffering. Steve is that kind of bloke. The one in the background running around making sure the subs are collected. Collecting the balls that have been booted around the pitch side, folding the nets up and trudging back through the mud holding two bags of balls and a couple of nets while everybody else is sitting in their cars moaning or having a hot shower. I wish I had his energy but all I do is type away my thoughts about how I get to the match and what coat to wear. It's easy for me but a lot harder for him.

I was thinking how funny it would be to have a kind of Southbank Resistance awards post where I make fun of what happened during the season but I think now it might make more sense to have one now seeing as I have a very clear result right now. So I would like to announce that Steve Plant is the Southbank Resistance Wolves supporter of the Year 2017-2018. Well done Steve, and no you don't get a prize, not even a beer, but you can buy me one. But Steve from all of us thank you, you are doing us proud and even though I'm broke I'm sure I will find a crinkly well worn last five quid to bung in the pot.

So. Here we are again then, sat down, roll of choccy biccies, cup of strong tea. Phone to hand for Twitter updates and lap top warmed up ready for the nights madness. It's still a little sunny outside, ambulances still whacking up and down the road. The errant screaming of a crackhead down the canal. I like it here. In Wolverhampton. I like it because there is something happening at last. Something different. I'm confused because I don't know what it is yet, this feeling I have in my belly when I think about my team and our Coach.

But I do bolt the door ready. No way I'm going to get disturbed by canal side characters unless Gaz Mastic knocks the door. I'm not going to answer it. Dogs barking, I have to untangle myself from wires, get up to listen to him moan. But while I'm waiting I'll wax some lyrics.

Last match was crazy wasn't it? Douglas is a thing and Vinagre too. Much chat about who's on the bench and who will be sitting with a big glum miserable face behind them as they aren't playing. I suspect a few things about tonight and I have had a few chats with folk about it. Douglas looked OK last match, now I know I said he looked like a lost sock for some of the game. I think I was a bit harsh and wasn't paying attention, I was probably looking at the mould on the Southbank roof again. Sorry about that. The zeitgeist says he did alright, offered some solidity. He certainly tracked back fast enough and was very hand signally but not vocal.

But what I want to talk about is not who is on the bench but what time in the match they come on. Now I don't want to get all back in the day but Kenny 'Charisma' Jackett did my head in with subs. The game would be crying out for something and he would be standing there, arms crossed, chewing the inside of his mouth not giving a shit. I'm not a coach, I don't know the variables but I felt like having him arrested for his crap street theatre statue act. The only coins I wanted to give him were a few I chucked. These biscuits are stale. Fucking Poundland again.

More goals are scored in the second half than the first. The first half is pure foreplay most the time. A touch here and there of the hand or leg. Getting to know each other. Buy her a drink. The half a lager with an umbrella in it. The crunching tackle. She laughs at your crap jokes, you listen to her story about how her Rabbits escaped once and hahahaha her Dad had to chase…..and you laugh of course. That's the first half. Tentative often weird too. The second half of course is the coffee at her place, now you know somebody is going to score (hopefully) unless it's a nil-nil thing. That's the equivalent of being thrown out of the house with your gimp suit and holding a a three foot long sparkly dildo, she's screaming, the neighbours are all coming out, the Police are on the way and you don't know where you are. You just stand on the lawn and go 'What?' Does anybody else feel that embarrassment or just me? We know we are going to score in the second half and that's where the fun happens.

The longer the second half goes on the more we expect a goal. I call this 'The Barry White Period' it's when the lights go down and the CD player gets booted up with Barrys 24 great hits of Luuurve. Brilliant, we get excited. Move the coffee cups, have a quick squint at your phone see if there's any Wolves news. She's gone for a whazz, you check for bogies or cheese cob in your teeth. The second half. The longer it goes on the more mad it gets. Here's where the substitution makes a difference. This is where Nuno becomes Artist.

Now our Sub, be it Cavaleiro or Bright or whoever has a task straight away. The player he replaces has played maybe 60-70 minutes of high tempo bongoball. It's bongoball because nobody wants to go a goal down and it's still that 'getting to know you period' and it means you have to work hard. You see you don't score in the pub or the restaurant, you score later on when the lights are getting dim and Barrys warbles are subsonically loosening blouses and buttons. But our substituted player is knackered by now, He knows her fucking family history back to front and her pets names. He's shagged and not in a good way. He's in fact mentally deranged by this point. Frothing at the neck so to speak.

Our sub on the other hand is like a dog with three dicks. Most of the digging and sniffing has been done. Now is the point where you want a forward on. The replacement of a midfielder or a wing back will be greeted with boos and groans. You see we know that the player that is going to splurge the money shot by sticking the ball in the net is going (more often than not) to be a forward.

Now you can see why Kenny Charisma and Lamberto the Clown got lambasted by the crowd when we saw Saville or Wallace trot onto the pitch. It was a great WTF moment. Fatigue is a keyword here. The legs of the opposition defence have tired by now, midfield too. Saw that with Barnsley last week. Their number 4 and 11 were shagged by the second half. They had left the target of their possible shag by herself at the table and they were thinking about squeezing through the bog windows to escape. Both of our goals had targeted and were made through the lethargy of the 11 and 4 at that point in the game. The drop off of performance was glaring and of course Nuno made full use of it by pressing the play around both players. Douglas on, and their 4 had a mare of a second half and their 11 ineffective due to Jota and Neves twisting him up like a bad pill.

What are the stats for a fresh player scoring in the second half or the dying minutes? Probably significant to be honest. Nuno isn't a slouch when it comes to subs. He knows the effectiveness of a player will degrade as the minutes tick. Wise man that he is I suspect he watches the opposition very closely during the latter part of the second half and utilises his subs with ruthless effect as seen with N'Diaye at the Barnsley match.

But back to the main menu. Sheffield United. What a godforsaken place Yorkshire is. I know that some folks will be irked by this but I'm past caring, I've had horrible times up there to be honest. The Police are like putting your fingers in electrical sockets or banging your head on a low ceiling. It's a shock. People are generally friendly but the rain I suspect makes them dull and angry, prone to outbreaks of melancholy or directionless windmilling punches. I remember playing them many times in the Stevie Bull days when they had Tony Agana or something.

The Play off final in 2003. But I woke from my afternoon nap earlier and had a dream I was fishing with Nuno and he was charming the fish by singing to them. All this Nunoism is starting to freak me out. I love him already. My dreams about Lambert were dotted with beheading scenes, nightmares, George Savillisms. No team news yet but I'm flicking my thumb across my phone screen like crazy getting past the porn accounts that dot my feed for some reason (cough).

OK the match has started and I've missed the team news and have to go to Tim Spiers a local sports Journalist account to see if he has posted anything. I don't mind Tim, he puts up with some horrendous cack and he's still young really and his forehead is growing exponentially with Wolves success. By May he will have a big shiny dome filled with knowledge I daresay.

So Conor Coady has gone home early already. Is Sheffield that bad mate? But it was a Heartbreak Ridge sacrifice. Red card, sent off. He walks off but there is still pride there and anger too. He hasn't let us down at all. We love you Conor Coady, always will I think. I keep seeing in him another Wolves player of the past. Emlyn Hughes. I knew I knew him from somewhere...

0-0 Helda gets a few minutes flying around the pitch at least while old Leon has his bristles up. It had to be though didn't it? It always does. Instead of doing the business for us, getting sold. They always come back to haunt us but it says less about the ability of the Clarkes et al than justifies the absolute disgusting people they are when they do score. Because they never did for us. What revenge have they on their minds when they do it? Do they get some sort of hard on? Fuck Leon Clarke.

But then again, it's easy to fall into that trap of being a bastard to ex players and I shouldn't get aggravated by it. Trust in Nuno I suppose. I read back what I wrote about putting subs on. Trust in Nuno to get something out of it. Anything. We are still young, fresh. I feel like I've been dragged out of the house by the cops in my gimp suit waving my dildo but instead of fun and jollity they gassed me and tasered me and are beating me in the balls with my dildo. Fucking Sheffield, a darkness there but what light? Half time now they have to find the elusive Kwan, time for Nuno to grab it by the balls and I think he will, trust, that keyword again. I suspect he will have been through similar moments. We know that Yorkshire darkness, that itching behind the eyes as we enter a ground. This time we have to grasp the game, demolish have heart and fortitude. I'm eating biscuits and there through the sounds of my angst I can hear Barry White and it doesn't feel like he's sitting on my chest any more.

Is any of this making sense? Penalty, oh Jesus Christ. What do you do to me Wolves. What heights what crazy fucking lows. I'm being pulled from pillar to post. I've eaten too many biscuits I feel sick. Neves to take. Hit's the post. The darkness falls over the pitch right now. But the light for fucks sake, the light! Where is it Nuno. Bright is on for Bonatini. My Nubian Prince what will thou doest for us tonight. Do not fall over, channel your goal firework please. This is a night of work and of graft, it is a night that defines Championship football. What character will you show against these morose and violent people of Yorkshire?

I wonder in my madness if these words can reprogramme the result. I wonder if this little blog can swing the decisions of the Gods in our favour. I'm being overly dramatic aren't I? I'm chewing my own angst in big bites but it's still just a game, still just a football match and we have loads to play…..but the character, the Kwan has to show through, it has to spark and ignite our madness tonight. We have the character…

Tim Spiers hasn't tweeted for a few minutes and I'm getting that feeling again. Fucking hell. Sweating like last week when I wore my big snow coat and nearly died in the heat of the Barnsley game. Sweating, I can feel it even though the room is cold. Leon fucking Clarke. Another set piece goal. Leon Clarke you thing, may fleas infest your hair, may the demon of wanting a piss visit you in the night.

Is it too much to think of a draw? Is it too much to hope? It's a toughie but I'm thinking of all our supporters who have travelled and trudged through the rain half pissed to that wasteland of a Yorkshire stadium. Sheffield is full of hills, it's as if the land is trying to shake off the City above. Our fans will be walking those very streets later. They are warriors. But it sounds like we are unravelling a little. What witchcraft is this? After that superb display last Saturday?

Cavaleiro for Neves, the Terminator returns, this is the tactical master stroke surely? A forward and we are down a man, this is a brave moment where Nuno surely stakes out his territory and his philosophy, beautiful substitution but to what end?

Spiers says it's a 4-2-3 system. I don't even know how that would work, I'm such a tactical imbecile. I want a cup of tea but I have a dog by me now and he's on my left arm. I feel trapped by the football, by the dogs, by the rain. Free me Nuno please. I can visualise Cavaleiro running into the box, connecting, ball smashes the back of the net, he grabs the ball and runs back to the centre circle. Somebody tell me this is happening please. If we build it they will come, random thought….but I'm thinking of all these great speeches by men of old who rallied their troops to a flag and victory over insurmountable odds, I'm being emotional again. It's still an early game. the season has only just started and I'm over emotional.

Well fuck that game, fuck it right up it's arse. Often these games pop up during the season. We should of course have put them to bed. Leon fucking Clarke, typical again. Can't be arsed to score here but love scoring against us. What have we done to you Leon? How did you coax that performance out? With hate? Dislike? Did we treat you so bad?

Nuno will know what to do, he will have all the facts in front of him within hours. The backroom team will be analysing and forming some sort of hypothesis as to how it all went wrong. You don't get to coach at these levels without a steely determination to get things right. By tomorrow morning Nuno will be sitting down relaxed but angry. He will have the culprits names in front of him with figures, quantitative analysis of the whole dog shit of a match. Conor Coady must not be blamed, I would have done the same thing. He will of course be concentrating not on the foul and the sending off, he will be analysing how the dude nearly got past in the first place. He will learn from it. It's endemic in this squad that we learn and we develop and along that learning curve will be a dip here and there, an errant game where it all goes to shit. Trust in Nuno and trust in the team and we can look to the North tonight and curse the sky over it, shout out insults and abuse but more importantly plot revenge.

Well I had another conversation about the England football team the other day. I hate getting into these conversations because I don't know what to say about it. Or not that I don't know, I just can't be arsed to circle around the most popular England Moan Memes. Why are we so shit? Five little words that are whispered and rattled about in every Pub in the country, at home in front of the massive TV you've got and at home sitting there fondling your balls while you watch another insipid knock around at Wembley. The dog farts. The can of beer at your elbow is horrible. Your Missus is on Ebay looking at garden furniture again. The kids have their faces stuck in their phones and you have 42″ of massive telly to watch and there are coloured blobs running around on there because your eyes are half closed bored, insipid TV non entertaining football wankery. Southgate comes on and his head is massive and scary.

It's our national game apparently and we are supposed to be good at it. The European Championships in 2016 was a circle jerk of a campaign where we lost to a load of part time strippers from Iceland who's national sport is lifting weights and drying fish. Iceland for fucks sake.

Fucking hell. On paper of course the team we have and the levels they play at are fabulous. It's multicultural, athletic, beards, sleeve tattoos, great cars, great Insta accounts. Expensive haircuts. They hop off the coach like men on Death Row, faces hanging like drool off a crackheads lips, eyes averted in shame at their absolute fucking boredom at being there. The England team aren't funny….

But hang on, they aren't funny? Well they aren't. Gascoigne was hilarious. He pulled the working class humour along with him into the hallowed halls of the FA, the gilded stadiums of Europe and the world. He had blokes, team mates that idolised him because his humour pulled along a team of what amounted to dysfunctional children for the most part. If we got to a major final we would always have a character in there who was a little off kilter, turned up in the papers a bit, usually naked in a 'HOT TUB ENGLAND SHAME' or some other bollocks.

But what now? Looking at the latest England team Gareth Southgate has picked I wonder to myself. OK Southgate isn't the most charismatic of people, he's like listening to your Mom talk about her day, or reading a magazine in the dentists waiting room about bread making. He's fucking dull. The team reflect his personality and you look at their poor little faces and all you see is pretty haircuts, pretty clothes, big headphones, dour miserable faces. Teenagers basically. These doughnuts haven't a fucking clue about life. You can see it in their eyes and I call it the 'two foot stare' it's that vacant narcissistic gormless blank look people have while they look at their phones. Even when they try to make themselves look a bit dynamic it's still the girls taking selfies in the mirror of the women's bogs. Pouting, slick as they can get it but ultimately generic and empty.

The only time Southgate will get a Hot tub shame headline is if someone finds an errant pubic hair in his filter system. I mean does he even have a Hot Tub? He'd look miserable like he was being boiled alive in it. See what I'm saying? We have a team of boring football players doing boring football, they're bored, you're bored, everybody is bored. It's Aldi football, it's not Cocaine football it's Lemsip football. I mean you can't blame them for being shit. All they've known is being dragged around various pitches and parks during childhood through the rain and the snow so they can maybe get somewhere in the game, get a contract and play. Now they find themselves at the top of the game, big contracts, all the perks, all the groovy photo shoots. But ultimately every single one of the England team picked by Daz Southgate are the dullest bunch of lollipops I've ever witnessed. Imagine going on a night out with them!

Now I would love to get my red flag out and start to rant about the mismanagement of the national game both at FA level and grass roots but that's not going to cut the mustard is it? Directors, owners, globalism, finances all this shit I could trowel out for five thousand words but it still wouldn't make any difference at all. TV money might have to be wheeled out as a culprit but then again it's an argument that just goes on and on like a circle jerk at the impotent mens self help group. 'Self help' hahahahaaaha.

I'll tell you what the problem is. We haven't got any nutters any more. We lack 'Mad Men'. People who have a screw loose like Gascoigne and Tony Adams, Pierce et al. This nutter dynamic is lacking at international levels. The best Players were always lunatics, always on the edge. They had normal day to day jobs in the past most the time. Plumbers, working on building sites, factories. Then given a free reign to unleash their madness on a football field they excelled. They were dynamic and fresh, novel maybe, igniting the field of play with madness and tricks, taking the piss.

The same goes on in International teams from around the world. There are always a few nutters dotted around the squad. You know they will have a six foot tall model on their arm at some point but there will also be a cocaine story, a crashed car or two. A few dodgy gangster friends in photos. The occasional fire, the random shooting incident or accusations of cannibalism. Of course you will have the Steve Armpitts and Deloney Sharelles in the team who can manage a pass or two and chip in with a goal or three until they catch themselves on the big tellys in the corners of the ground.

But to ignite a game you need a lunatic, you need an artist who has looked at the abyss of a muddy building site at 6am slipping in the ice filled ruts with an armful of breeze blocks. We need Maradona, Cruyff, Buffon, Balotelli type lunatics whose insanity is reflected in their football. Out of the chaos of their minds comes a football that is a beautiful as a still mountain pool. Ignore the occasional hotel fire and bloody street brawls these are sportsmen and women. Gladiators of our time and they need space to breathe.

The England team lacks these dynamic characters. So you can keep the excuses that are always trotted out and you need to change the narrative at the national level. You need to mute the importance of the printed press too. How many England careers have been destroyed by a dodgy backhander story or topless hot tub fun? So a player likes to get arseholed occasionally with his mates, it's great fun being drunk or stoned, it filters out the bullshit that these players operate under. The poor bastards look like kids at a Borstal, scared to step out of line in case a Screw gives them a whack. They are probably suffering some sort of post traumatic stress from being picked from obscurity to play for England. Wondering when some woman will sell her story to the Sun about how he likes to sniff amyl nitrate as she beats him with a riding crop.

England I suspect will never be successful at International level unless the FA pull their fingers out and stop treating sportsmen like children. We don't need saints like that goal hanging git Lineker, we don't need miserable gits like Shearer either, we need blokes that have looked into the abyss and seen the glaring lights of the International game as an opportunity to take the piss out of the opposition on the pitch. To breathe deep the infected wastes of political football and decided 'fuck it' lets go mental. We need to be entertained by these people but looking at that team I'm feeling a distinct lack of excitement, it's a workmate barbecue, it's flicking through Netflix football, it's fresh fades, and exotic Nikes, Beats headphones when it should be about bollocks, and laughs, and madness.

So ultimately it's all our faults. The FA, the players, TV money, Global business and us. We have to turn a blind eye to the errant and the weird, the crazy and the destructive and just love the madness of football again, bring those lunatics closer to us by supporting them through their madness and not getting involved in their lives. Let them do their art on the pitch and let them lead their lives off it. Embrace the mad and we will start to win games and trophies.

Writing the book as the match starts is a weird thing. I know I'll get tangled in wires at some point, the dogs will bite me, the lap top will end up with another dent and another crack in the screen. I'm a gloomy bastard sometimes. Usually after Wolves have been dicked by a no mark team like Sheffield United but normally it's Burton, who we play today. I've never been so sick of football as when they beat us down here. I raged out of the Southbank all boppy and angry with my coat up my face like a Fooligan. Ranting, aggravated and heated. Around the corner from the Steve Bull came the Burton fans. Moms, Dads, kids, all happy with their victory, ecstatic in fact. I felt hollow and shit. I crept back into town to see what new colours of hair the bar staff in the Royal London had that week.

This week has been punctuated by big dollops of rain dumped on us by various storms. Down the canal I lit my roll up with a lighter that disintegrated after a fart of flame I managed to catch. Then a big dollop of raindrop landed straight on the end of me roll up, extinguished it. Leon fucking Clarke I thought. It's a long journey to Burton too, short in a temporal sense but long in that waiting for your dealer way. It goes on forever that road there. Leaves a hollow in your stomach like Leon Clarke.

We play 'The Town Of The Damned' again today. At their place. Burton is strange, I say that from personal experience as I've been there a few times on business and pleasure. I met a woman in a pub. Sally Canwait. Her chat up line was 'I've got loads of food in my fridge if you want to come back to mine'. Kind of sums up the vibe of the place where that glowing heaven of bite sized delights in the corner of the kitchen is a precursor to some hefty workman like lovemaking in a strange town. I hope our team feel some love today. Last week at Sheffield Utd was a dire affair of football apparently but one that has to come along at some point, perhaps a few points.

So, Sally Canwait had a zit on her neck, not a bad one, but it kind of held the attention. Leo Bonatini is that zit. I don't mind it in a bad way he just holds my attention while he's playing and I'll explain why. Watching him move around the pitch he reminds me very much of Andy Mutch. Now I sent some big love to Andy Mutch the other week because I enjoyed his play, his link play really being that filter between Bully and whatever quality of ball came over the top or from the side via Robbie Dennison. I haven't thought about those ex Wolves greats for years. Why now I wonder? Zeitgeist Filter?

That filter is a necessity to players like Jota and Brighty who require a pretty forensic ball to be played to them. That effortless perfectly weighted pass that dips right on the foot you want at the perfect pace. I've watched him do it, that ball gets dipped off with the skill of a Snooker player. His leg whether he's in mid air or ready to receive a Warnockian 'snackle' is poised to deliver the right amount of pressure to the ball. His passes are rarely errant, often a work of pure art. He's not a 'snotter' or a 'head' but an artiste of sorts and one I think is an integral part of the way he and the team get's it's groove on.

I'm tempted to believe that he's probably the signing of the season once you look past the brilliance of Jota and the vibrancy of Neves. Jota I will have more words to say about another time but Neves? He's had some stick hasn't he? Gone off the boil a bit, not really catching fire as well as he did earlier. That gets Marvin Groin in a state straight away. Marvin would live in Burton, two bedroom house, Vauxhall car, tribal tattoos he would be married to Sally Canwait too.

You see there's nothing better than a Marvin having a rant. You can switch him on like a Duracell bunny, watch him wind up, go red in the face. All you have to mention is a certain player he doesn't like or understand and he's off. Neves is that player for Marvin. I suspect Neves is just having a bit of grief settling down. It's tough moving from a beautiful Mediterranean groove to Wolvo. We love our Wolverhampton of course because we have the proper filters in place to appreciate it. Neves of course looks like a fella having problems deciding what filters to put in place. The cadence of your life away from the training ground has some effect on how you play our football and Neves is at the moment a little polarised, maybe a little detuned to the rest of the band so his parts of the great Nuno musical hit are discordant sometimes, a little too loud and often not loud enough. But like all band leaders Count Nuno will be tapping his baton relentlessly to get everybody on the same musical wavelength, I can see it happening in the future, Nuno is too good a coach to let Neves slip into some abstract existence.

Now today we are going to have a new face in the back three. I think Boly still has a bad leg or something and I also suspect we may see Hause in there somewhere. I don't mind Hause, he has kind of lost his way again for some reason or another and maybe today will see him stake a place in the back. When I wrote 'Mad Men' the other day I was thinking about Hause a lot. Now I suspected Neves might be the mad man in the team this season, the maverick gunman, the wild bastard we need to kick start some mental football. But now I've though about it some more maybe the dynamics of the team could do with a Hause or two. He's not backward in coming forward Mr Hause. I can see him settling some rhythm down at the back, getting stuck in and bullying a few people. I hope he plays today.

'Hey! No fighting in here! Oi put those Bounties back now!' Swansea away.

Ok forget about Hause, he's not even a thing today, just saw the team announcement. Bennett, ok then, maybe he is a thing. Bonatini out too so everybody I've just bigged up in the previous words aren't even in the team. Good job I'm not a Manager or a Journo innit? Saiss in too next to Neves. I don't mind Saiss, his shots into the Southbank wake me up a bit and he's a bit gnarly too and my inner Sunday footballer enjoys this a lot. Mr Groin will be gnashing his teeth of course, he hasn't got over Dave yet. I'm liking Cavaleiro at the front too, hat trick I hope, Jota and Costa on either shoulder like bad demon/good angel whispering naughty things in his ear. Wonder if Costa is taking the Bonatini role? Its a statement of intent for sure, the art of Bonatini or the rage of Cav' who knows?

So Cavaleiro put through Jota and he scores. The journey becomes a little brighter for our loyal and brave fans that made their way up the road to nowhere. I am grinning, I am happy, fuck Leon Clarke. Fuck Sheffield. Fuck Burton Albion with their cursed last name. Fuck Nigel Clough too. Fuck Brewery towns and I'm on the fence yelling at the pitch at some ground in the 80's shouting so loud my voice just stops dead. A.L.B.I.O.N SHIT ON THEM SHIT ON THEM. For Gods sake save me, this joy erupts within me and is a fire, a fire that gives me Jota love in armfuls. Now Saiss!! We are moving the ball around too fast for the agricultural Burton, it was coming wasn't it? We knew they would click at some point. Oh my days, I have to sit down, the dogs are barking and I'm feeling that hot football sun on my head even though the skies outside are grey and sad. Sunshine super football all day my friends. Joys. Madness. Holiday vibes. Laughing babies, little puppies, little kittens!

Has Nuno sat within his office and endlessly clicked the Rubik cube of possible dynamic tactics and squad position? Has he rolled the bones at his feet and asked the Gods for aid? Who knows? But this front three are moving like a snake at the moment. I'm listening on the radio, refreshing the Twatter, texting friends in the ground. Madness, insanity. Burton fucking Albion for Gods sake. But it's working obviously. Helder Costa is a thing, is he the missing link, the bridge between the old and the new having been part of both? Is he the piece of the puzzle we had dropped down the back of the settee and now he has been found we are complete? Questions!

Burton of course wont let Wolves have it all their own way. There always has to be a drunk at the kids party falling over onto the cake, getting all emotional over something and then anger, ranting in the middle of the garden while the kids are crying and everybody should be off really it's late. Burton ball, fuck 'em off Wolves, don't take any shit.

'Cavaleiro throws himself on the floor and wins a free kick'

Burton you horrible bitter twisted non entity's, how dare you after the histrionics you showed at our ground in numerous games. You disgust me. Town of the damned you are, the Vauxhall cavalier of towns, a haven of blandness, a Nans browser history of a town.

Burton are pushing up, being pressure dynamic, moving these big crosses into our box apparently. I'm hopeful it will leave a gap as big as the ones in Sally Canwaits teeth just big enough for the 'TRIDENT OF POWER' Jota/Cavaleiro and Costa to slide in like a sesame seed. Like a sausage in a roll. Like a pound coin in a crackheads pocket. And as I type Salt'N Vinagre with a belter. I'm emotional I'll be honest. I told you they would click, I knew it. Unstoppable, European cup glory in two years, I see it. I'm over emotional, the dogs are barking and the tea is burning and I know I should be there but I'm not I'm here but that inner sun is still shining bright in my heart. 0-3. Nuno you Magi, you absolute Magician.

Half time and my phone starts buzzing with messages 'awesome' and 'brilliant ay' and 'have you got that money you owe me' OK forget that last one. But the vibe is clear now, we must have absolutely decimated those crab hand Burton bastards. I bet they are sitting in the dressing room now rubbing lotion on the burns they got from our front three running around like little burning suns. I bet the ground is heaving with the passion from our away support. I'm sad and happy. Sad I'm not there but happy we're winning. Who needs a striker anyway ay? What would those weird named non entities from Europe have given us that the Molineux Trinity of Costa-Jota-Cavaleiro haven't? Such slickness.

'AAAAAAAAA BonafuckingTini you beauty!!!!!!'

I stand here happy now, four fucking nil my friends. It's a destruction of Burton. A decimation of their intent and a reinforcement of ours. Bonatini you absolute beauty. Yes you are a part of it, get your nose in their son. Here's a paper plate, we have onion bhajjis, sausage rolls, quiche, pork pie, a bit of black forest gateaux. Eat your fill my friend, eat in the cosmic glow of the community center disco that is the cultural apex of this godforsaken place, remember this is a story you will tell your children and you will point to the East and say yes, there I slayed the one eyed blandness of that place and yes! I left them weeping into their Marmite smelling shirts.

Well there we go. Another weird day being a Wolves fan. The ignominy of Sheffield a few days ago and now the treasure of bringing back the spoils from that depressing weird place Burton. We have to have these days don't we, at least a few times in the season when everything clicks into place. The Kwan has indeed flowed today and yes it could be construed as metaphysical. It didn't flow in the week for sure but under all the chaos of the Leon Clarke retro revival there was still a belief, still a thought that there was a kind of unstoppable force to the season at Wolves. There's something moving in the sand stone geology underneath Molineux that hasn't moved for many years. I suspect it's a Dragon, a huge fiery thing that went to sleep at the end of the sixties and the success we have had since is the Dragon dreaming and moving but now I suspect the magic of Nunoism is gently prodding it slowly awake and I await with a strong heart that one day it will poke it's nostrils above the beautiful pitch and it's nostrils will quiver. It wants to see what Nuno is cooking.

I don't get invited to many civilised do's. Not because I'm a massively dysfunctional bloke (which I am) but people who know me are aware that my normal social circles are full of the highly dysfunctional too, gangsters, hooligans, crackheads and bagheads, etc. But last night I was invited to the Derek Parkin tribute dinner at the Molineux. Cold sweat time.

There would be people there. Real people who had careers and were successful. I had to get the suit out of the attic. My suit was made in 1968 by Walsh of Sheffield in a mod style. A beautiful thing. Moths had eaten a big hole in the arm but that was cool. But Derek Parkin. Full back. One of my favourite players back in the 70's and whenever a team was announced on a Saturday afternoon he was there, a lynch pin or an anchor point of the whole flowing beauty of that team. Of course there was a whole plethora of former 70's greats there. I kept bumping into them rustling between the tables in a suite in the Billy Wright stand, exchanging a few words here and there, erupting into a sweat.

Thing is, back in those days these men were Gods to us. They used to drive past us on the Waterloo road and we knew what cars they drove, where they did their shopping. We didn't stalk them but as we lived so close to the ground we always saw them and we would stop stripping the lead....er walking to school and for half an hour we would discuss that player. Last night I was bumping into these people and they would shake my hand as I stopped them. But I couldn't say anything of interest as I was struck dumb. John Richards, Phil Parkes who looked great, Willie Carr, George Berry. Here I was in my moth eaten suit talking to these men. What was I doing here? I had a tenner in my pocket I was loathe to spend.

You see, I don't move in these circles and at times it seemed highly abstract and unusual. Well out of the comfort zone initially. This environment was not mine. Everybody seemed to have all their teeth and knew what to do with the myriad of cutlery in front of them. I mistook the curly napkin display as funky bread sticks, I was concentrating on putting the chicken and mash main course in my gob. Eat with your mouth closed which was hard as my nose is shattered and I find it hard to breath through it so I had to eat holding my breath, use the right fucking spoon, right fork.

Stop swearing so much, try not to laugh too loud, don't take offence, stop sizing people up to see how they would fight later on. Fucking hell. On the pitch through the tinted viewing windows was the pitch and the empty stands lit by the movable grow lights to make the pitch happy and green. I kept glancing over to the Southbank and it was reassuring to see it standing there empty but powerful. I was wondering which bread roll to eat, the one on the left or the one on the right. One was wholemeal one was white, did you have to eat one with a certain part of the meal? The butter looked like little flower petals, what knife should I use to spread it? There was a bottle of water on the table, funky little wine glasses, should I pour the water in that?

These 70s greats eh? And they were greats. I was watching John Richards eat amazed I was, dumbstruck. I'm eating fucking dinner with John Richards. George Berry (who was my favourite player of those days) smiled at me as he brushed past. Fucking hell. Moth eaten suit, social sweats, shaking hands, trying not to swear. John fucking Richards spooning herby posh mash into his gob. George Berry laughing at something while he ate his roll. Phil Parkes moved past, Phil I loved you man and I want to grab him and hug him but you can't.

George Berry was my favourite player because he was the only one I really identified with. The other members of the squad I hero worshipped but George I always regarded as one of us lot. He made me feel a lot calmer, a lot more chilled out. When he spoke about Parkin putting an arm around him and reassuring him when he came into the team was emotional. Black players put up with some hefty shit in those days. Derek Parkin was there for him and George Berry was there for me I suppose. Other players got up on stage and had a go heaping platitudes on Derek, all deserved, all on point. But I could see George nodding and listening, laughing too and all was good.

I'm a distinctly working class bloke there's no getting away from it. My environment is bus stations waiting for buses, I know how to sew and repair my clothes. My clothes last a long time. I'm used to sneaking into the ground hiding in the train bogs when we used to travel to away games so the ticket inspector didn't get you. Territorial and lumpen I suppose. Drinking over priced beer in the rain at the back of the Southbank trying to keep your roll up alight. But here I was with the great and good. There was Steve Plant who has rode the money raising train that hard all his hair has fallen out. PR animal Russ Cockburn smashing the social thing. All the people there were men and women that had ideas and drive, they were movers and shakers within the whole Wolves thing. I started sweating again. Shit. I had last worn this suit when I collapsed teaching engineering maths to a bunch of disinterested lunatics in a Wolverhampton secondary school. I remember being on the floor as the kids freaked out, the rush of feet, the ambulance.

Now normally this weird as fuck episode would have had me heading for the doors and the bus home where I could be safe and sound away from the crowds and the madness of dinner in the Billy Wright. But it was different here. Because despite the success, the career talk and the dynamism of alcohol fuelled social occasions it was OK. These people were held together by a common thread, a common interest. We were all basically the same people. The same hopes and dreams I suppose. The atmosphere was upbeat and we were doing OK so everything was positive and cool. People were generally positive about the blog and that was good too, because it's not mine it's ours. The whole thing was ours really because without us there wouldn't be a dinner or fund raising, joy and laughter. Without us these great edifices of our club would be empty spaces, just gaps in the whole narrative. We are what fill these places with soul and love, all the emotions that we pour out fill the gaps in the abstract and the strange.

At a quiet point in the proceedings I found myself holding a pint staring at the pitch and lapsing into some sort of stand-by mode wondering why the fuck I was here really. My suit itched, my shoes didn't have enough room. John Richards laughed loud at something somebody had said. But I had strength, and that strength came from my stand, all those empty seats. There are ghosts in there you know. Because when we were kids and we were bored we would climb that wall in the alley and get into the ground. We would go and sit on the Southbank terrace in the dark because we were out of the rain, safe from a regular kicking outside from who ever fancied doing it, away from the violence of those days. Safe and sound. But we would sit there passing around a crumpled No6 fag lit with a match. Chatting about the games coming up or the ones that had gone. But between the conversations and the bullshit, if you were quiet enough you could hear things in that stand. The emotions expressed in it were powerful and they leaked into the very ground it stood on. There was blood spilled in there, and sweat and bloody tears to be honest. The whole stand was soaked in it and on some metaphysical levels they were played back when it was quiet and a few scruffy kids sheltering from the rain, bored, were witnesses to it. You could hear whispers and the odd bang from underneath. Footsteps up and down the terrace. Ghosts mate. But we weren't afraid because they were our ghosts.

I was cool here because everybody was friendly and everybody had a laugh and the atmosphere was good, funny, a bit flirty sometimes. Everything was cool now because I had a reason to be there. That reason was the ghosts, our friends. fellow supporters, family, workmates that had passed away still stood on that terrace and if you looked close enough you could see the old Southbank transparent and ethereal underneath the new build. You could just about see the figures shouting on Derek, George, and John and it might have been a reflection on the glass but there was a faint figure running across the pitch surely? Doog is that you? You would have loved this night mate.

You draw your power from the ghosts I suppose and now the moth eaten suit and the itch, the feeling that you shouldn't really be there was gone. Those Ghosts couldn't be here but I was, so I was strong for them, I experienced it for them and all of a sudden it wasn't hard to talk to people and it was easy because the ghosts out there and the life in here had the same foundation, our emotions all soaked into the same geology underneath the Molineux. It's definitely something Steve Morgan never truly understood and maybe that's where he fell short. You must have some connection to that ground, a blood connection, a spiritual connection and an emotive one too. I turned back around and joined in the chat happy now I could move around and be social, I did it for the ghosts.

But there does feel like there is another power now. Something different. Who is this Nuno? Does this book make any sense? Will it ever make sense really? I don't think any of this season has to me I'll be quite honest. I don't really understand any of it. I wish I was just a fan and this love didn't hurt so much. Who the fuck is this Nuno?

What the fuck is this? Why have you dragged us to these heady heights Nuno, it's hard to breathe, it's beautiful, it's metaphysical, it's not football as we know it! It's not! What the fuck??? I was picking on a few Villa fans on the 559 to Wolvo, they had got on at the Bluebrick…"Shiiiiiiit on the Villllaaaaa" Harangue, intimidate, right in the face, how dare you come into our fucking town!!!I calmed down, it was OK, I had a feeling…I had to follow them all the way down the back of Carvers to the ground singing at them, singing at the backs of their heads, belief…Police holding me to one side, but I have belief! I want to tell them, but they would never understand. But it's a leather clad hand around the throat from a young Copper and shoved off past the art block. Belief, that's all. But I've always hated Villa. This match is a big thing for me.

Nunoism versus the idea defunct Steve Bruce. Two men locked in a battle of the Philosophies. Nuno provokes beauty to unveil itself on the pitch, to enable his philosophy to flourish through the tools that Fosun has given him. Bruce has the stoic sense of groinball. And that groinball failed miserably. Stoicism destroyed by pure art, by philosophy, by rigorous footballing intuition

The assembly of questions Bruce asked Nuno today were blunt and involved course questioning of fine Nunoesque points. We of course watched from the sidelines, offered support, shout and yelled over particular debates on the pitch. We sang songs about 'shitting' on our opponents. In fact we sang a lot about shitting on them and we did. Often, but it was a juxtaposition to the dynamics on the pitch, the control we showed, the absolute intent. The piss taking from the Southbank and the delicious football on the pitch.

Diatribes about the Villa eh? The Squeakies. It was a bloody funny day again, an aura of seeing your favourite band who play the same venue every two weeks. Villa are the support band. Steve Bruce, Manager with a head like a steamboat sailors duffle bag, like a sack of unwashed spunky socks, like a clay head made by a man with no eyes or arms, voice like he's beating the dents out of a church bell. A face like he's been extinguishing a wheely bin fire with it. Hair like a Dogs bed. He was going to come here wasn't he? At the time I was kind of unmoved by the idea, I knew most Wolves fans didn't want him but a few Gary Foreskins did I suppose. They argued amongst themselves on Social Media happy to have a subject to tear apart with unstructured vapid boring arguments. I didn't get involved of course. It was listening to chats about fuel injectors on VW Passats. Uninspiring and a bit dull. Like the Villa team really. They have Chinese owners though, but not as dynamic as ours for sure as their owner is called 'Tony' and Tone never inspired anything apart from Pot Noodle fan pages on Facebook. He looks like a Korean Fart Porn Mogul too.

But it's Derby day and I'm not making the mistake of the 'big coat' again, not yet. It's the curse of living in the temperate climate we do and we love the onset of cold Autumns of our youth but alas climate change has thrown the match day jacket choice into a cauldron of chaos when it come to picking it. Jacket it is, I don't even want to go outside to test the temps. I'm going to wing it.

Winging it is pretty much what the Villa team did today. Already they have addled that high pitched Villa whine into some sort of incoherent buzzword laden narrative like 'we can beat them if we do this' or 'if we take the game to them' and other missives and mission statements. Weird really as for years they have been full of confidence and bollocks. But today it's all changed hasn't it? The tumble from the lush arms of supermodel teams to the sweaty bum crack of see through Primark leggings in the Championship. It's shit isn't it my little Brummie friends? Especially as you have to play those Small Heath Orcs every season. Villa can't tell the difference between piss and vinegar yet, but they will, today.

But I don't hate Villa yet, I just don't understand them. And I don't want to either. Down the canal this week I met a fella who I've talked to before. Skinny little chap with some sort of kidney disease from drinking alcohol. He shouts at you when he talks and he has those eyes like poached eggs, pickled in the cheap cider in the blue bottles he dumps by the side of the cut. Strange that Shaky Jake the Heroin addict knows him but deems him far below his class to acknowledge. 'Villa Phil' as he is known lifted up his trouser leg to show us his 'piss bag' strapped to his leg. 'We'm gonna do ya this week ar yeah, we can bost yeow up' he shouts. He wears a big pair of Panasonic headphones and listens to some bleepy dance bollocks and bobs his head up and down a lot. He decides to follow me and the dogs on our walk. While he shouts at me I try to wangle some sort of narrative, some message, but I'm stuck, I'm bereft of inspiration and that my friends is the curse of the Villa.

I had a kicking once off about five skinny Villa fans with that grey chip shop pallor on a train, I was holding a plastic cup of hot tea and none of it spilled. One of them went to hit me and smashed his knuckles into a steel handrail and screamed, another went to boot me and fell over, one did connect right on my jaw, another on my ear. I went to sip my tea but it was too hot, so I waited. No way was I wasting a cup of tea, I waited for my mates to harry them away, blowing on the beige plastic cup. Beige, there's a thing, the Villa strip should be beige, or Magnolia. The Villa team are as poetic as a pubs Artexed ceiling, have as much excitement of a day out in Walsall…Villa are in fact a massive Walsall maybe. I never spilled a drop of tea during the 'fracas'.

Coady was back, I'm happy. I love Conor Coady, I love his progression. Today he was mighty and agile, strong, a presence again. Fair play he pulled that shed thief Clarkey down at Sheffield, but hey-ho. We all have our moments don't we? That few seconds when we lose control. You see a player at this level is running a tightrope of instructions tempered with facilitating his ability and drive with clear concise instruction. It's a toughie being a player for Wolves, especially stuck down there while the Portuguese Porno-balls are being whanged around up top. Cav/Jota/Neves get the groove going early especially looking at Villas defence who were pedestrian. with all the buzz of an Invalid Scooter on charge. Why aren't we 7-0 up?

But what of the game? It certainly wasn't one of those Derby games, it was different, we made the canvas ours, the stroke of a brush here and there, a pattern emerges, Villa are actually shit or should I say they are 'there' but we made them look shit.. I suspect the Villa had some of that old Championship rub-a-dub-dub going on. Listless at times, other moments like a one legged man on an arcade Dance Mat machine. The response to our flowing beautiful rhythms a dogged resignation or an arm waving choked sympathy for their team mates. The action on Jota was worrying at times. He is a hard knock that lad. You pigeon hole and sort players into sections and I must admit I put him in the pretty as a picture section. I thought he'd be killed this season. Not so. See Jota slide and slip. See Jota manipulate the ball, sidle his way through. Action and reaction, problem and solution. Every time (or nearly) getting the ball into dynamic areas where more often than not there is a friendly foot or a flash of Gold to receive. He scores. I get another elbow in the head. That's cool. Southbank is strong and the players know it. There are voices from other stands. Jota goes down under a challenge by some Villa bloke. Voices are raised again. Filthy words and venomous but true and rightly said. I notice I've ripped my bus ticket up in my pocket and now it's full of confetti.

Cavaleiro shrugging, but not in resignation, he's shrugging off a dude I don't know, their full back, he shrugs off another Villa bloke as well. He has a low centre does Cav. That gives him room to twist and turn without that top heavy body shifting his weight, over balancing, instead he revolves around some imaginary cosmic point confusing a Villa defender who slaps his own leg in disgrace and maybe disgust. Villa are pedestrian here at the back. Sweet Magnolia defending. What are the Villa missing? Bruce teams play with belief and not a lot of nous. Square pegs smashed into round holes with the bellow of a command from the Bruce, it's not a philosophy it's a belief and 'believing' things often end in tears when the crushing reality of this Wolves team rumbles home. Coady within a trinity of sorts that back line of ours, still at odds sometimes.

It's a totally new squeeze for them still, legs in the way, arms tangled, unsure sometimes too but still slaving away over the Book Of Nuno, still memorising the tenets and the scripture. Nuno himself arms folded surveys the scenes and Neves goes over for a word. Nuno shakes his head and waves him away.

I've watched Duckens Nazon all week. He's on loan at Coventry, smashing the goals in he is. I think of him as the point of an attack using this current team. My puny brain cannot contemplate that, it is too grand an idea for me, I try to visualise it and everything erupts into a great golden joy of fragments of goal celebrations, joy, positivity, bus top parades, madness. But Bonatini, his presence is sublime and understated but he is a vibrant theme in the whole team, Duckens is fading away into the back of my mind again for another day.

Jota gets a meaty challenge. Maybe Villa are infected a little, a drowning man will often try to drown his rescuer too. Arms and drama, a few little verses from the Bruce songbook which is discordant and blaring. Bruce is funny. But I'm laughing to myself a little as Villa press, get some fuel from somewhere even as you can hear their defence creak like a tree in a Hurricane. Creaky leaky bastards they are. Big on statement but we lack the evidence lads. You can learn by reading the whiteboard and being shouted at but you only truly understand with love. Does the philosophy of Groinball flourish here, on this beautiful pitch? Here at Molineux? Of course, if the Philosophy is loud and discordant then at times yes.

The ideology of the fundamentalism of English football is represented well by Mr Bruce and Aston Villa. It's not letting the debate flourish with the wide arcs of passing that Wolves displayed today. Broad ranging play, individual acts of brilliance (and of foolishness) tempered by that Stoic football by numbers played by Villa. John Terry is not an antidote to the Portuguese melodies. These melodies entwine and caress his zone leaving him confused and lacking the correct rhythms to counteract the delicious football. Terrys songbook involves fart jokes and bawdy songs, things that are more at home in a league far below this one.

Not Warnockian dystopic football this, no, it's pretending to play football where Warnock never even tried to pretend. Going through the motions. Dancing slow, but you really don't know how, don't know how to bump and grind those hips. Terry moves one foot over to the next and back again. Jaeger bomb beats, 3am dances with elephants, a Villa defender falls to the floor twisted up like a bad pill got him. He punches the grass as he gets up. John Terry looks towards Bruce, but Bruce is looking at the floor, arms folded, imprisoned by his technical area which closes around him as the match continues, getting tighter. Bruce is thinking about Mini Pork Pies in the fridge at home where he will sit in the glow from his big expensive fridge from the USA like a pork pie Buddha, weeping probably as the pie crumbs fall to his lap. Ignoring the buzzing of his phone as his clubs owner 'Tony' send him another WhatsApp video of farting Korean girls. There's something incredibly 'wrong' with Villa, I don't know what it is yet but I feel sometime next year at the end of the season I will know.

And it's starting to resemble a juggernaut this team of ours. It's starting to get momentum going like a tiny spicy hot snowball at the beginning of the season it's now a few yards down the slippery slope of fixtures that needle and nibble away at the mass of a team as it gathers points. It's starting to gain traction and weight. With this extra weight it's going to be unstoppable and the beast that lies deep underneath the Molineux is indeed starting to open an eye and stretch out it's limbs in readiness for something. Here on the Southbank of course a swell of emotion and relief. How many Villa fans do you work with? You know, the weird fellas who buy 'Mens Health' they have 'gaming nights' on the Xbox with their dumb as dull friends from work, wear funny tshirts from Primark….

Fucking hell. This isn't a match report, it isn't even about my day, it's about our day and our stories. It isn't about who passed to who either. It's about me and Johnny Cund talking about the ways into the Molineux without paying in the 70's, it's about madness and passion, it's about singing in the subway after a game, it's about laughter and joy, it's about shitting on the Brummies. Who is this Nuno geezer? Is it him or these Portugeezers? These sexy players who knock the ball around like an STD in a knocking shop. Who is Steve Bruce? Who are Aston Villa? these pedestrian 'won a few on the trot' dickheads from Birmingham….I'm standing on the Southbank and I don't want to go home, I want to grab Bonatini and tell him how much I love him, I grab somebody else instead, I watch the Villa faithful stream out of the Steve Bull lower, sad dejected little faces all screwed up, all miserable.

I can't tell you what's going on, I can't explain it. I've talked with the greatest minds in the world but I can't fathom this, this beauty, this game where we stamp authority. Doherty jinks past a player and slices a forensic pass to Neves. Coady under pressure drops a shoulder, impresses himself on that back line, Batth clinical….Nunoism. A philosophy and pure intent. Make our ideas stronger than theirs. We did his today, everybody singing the same songs. Victory and the banishment of Brummighams. Jesus Christ.

Were we shell shocked after the Villa game? I think I am. I'm having Nuno headaches and little pangs of belief in the team. I'm not celebrating yet. No way. Those heady heights of a Derby victory wash through our veins still don't they? We are still giddy with the whole crazy few hours, the glistening victory only really dulled by the idea of Preston at home.

My ride home from the Villa match was one where I forgot what happened on the ride back, I was too busy talking to the assorted low and high lifes on the bus to notice anything outside the steamed up windows. Conversation was done by nodding furiously at affirmations about the team choice, the play, the madness and the oft shitting on those Brummie locals. Talk often phased back to other Wolves teams of the past, the Waggies, the Doogs and the Parkins, Cullis, a few Billy Wrights etc. Should we transpose these monochrome greats onto this current team? We haven't really done anything yet but over 30,000 people crowded into the stadium on Saturday with some sort of belief system in place. It's the Kwan of course. Even if most of the supporters deny some sort of metaphysical change it doesn't mean it isn't there and isn't coursing through the veins of everybody involved.

Reading through my book notes notes from the start of the season I notice there isn't really any kind of negativity in any of it, that I think should be the benchmark for the future games to come. Should be our standard really. Even as we itch a little at the though of 'November' coming up I don't think we should let those errant dark little thoughts enter our noggins. Not for one minute. Will November be just another month or one of those regular Novembers where we contemplate Adele albums and stand in the garden motionless looking at nothing at all…?

Last week, last match Jota was very much in mind. We kind of half expected him to erupt and decimate the idea of a typical Championship forward. Swashbuckling? He did the thief in the night act enough with his interlinking play with Neves and Bonatini when he did eventually come on. Jota was awesome last week, he may have been brilliant this week too but I missed those bits. So Jota.

But this Preston thing? What are they? I saw Gary Mastic after the Villa game, I'm wobbling across the Tesco 24 Hour fluorescent lit dystopic nightmare of available petrol and 24 hour shit to buy because you're bored. Fucking hell Gary. His hair is plastered to his head in some new wave madness. It is recently removed from his settee arm you can tell, His has that drool thing going on too. Sky Sports on in the background, his fat missus on Face book uploading photos of his weird looking kids who all look like him. He looks like that knobhead out of Flock Of Seagulls. He has a Goodyear Wolves shirt on.

'It's all a load of shit Mikey' he says to me.

What is Gary, life? Living in Wednesfield? Doing your mastic shit all day? I know we won but I don't need this right now. I'm still in the afterglow of Jotas goal. The Villa filing out like sad little kids looking at Coco the Clowns dead body on the floor under the bouncy castle. I want a Ginsters pastie, I don't know what Gary wants. But he's following me in. We go past the Security Guard who doesn't notice us. The Security dude has these threading a needle eyes that phone freaks have. Staring at his phone. It was a bit dysfunctional wasn't it?

This Preston thing. Of course these games will come and go during the season. Of course they will, it's a shift, a grafters job, one of those days when character and mettle come to the fore. What were Preston? I asked the same questions today as I asked Gary Mastic. Everything is coming too fast and I can't assimilate it fast enough. I remember going to my Nans funeral in Preston and her body hadn't even stopped at the bottom of the 'lift of hot fire doom' and the Vicar was getting changed into his Golfing clothes, looking embarrassed, running to his car. Preston were very much like that Vicar, at least in the second half.

I'm following Gary around Tesco because I can't find the pasties. He's already collected his shit. Five 'Hot' Pot Noodles, a loaf, some Margarine. This Noodle life. He's going on about how brilliant we were Saturday and I agree. It was a bloody eye opener. When all the orchestra played the same shit. Effortless football and easy football.

'It's all gonna go to pot mate' he says. He's juggling Pot Noodles and I can see him spooning that horrible mess onto his sticky white bread and sticking it in his face. His stick thin are cuddling the whole stack of purchases. He holds them like a baby

I don't even know who their Manager is and I don't care either. I don't even know who plays for them. We stick out practically the same team as last weekend but things are definitely looking a bit fumbly. Perhaps that was Preston taking the piss but they seemed like there was more action up our end than theirs especially in the second half. I was rocking I must admit. It was totally a Wine day. Blossom hill I think. Of course by now if I was a pro blogger or reporter you would have all these delicious facts about who came on when, who played like Messi, who played like Jed Wallace.

I would be sitting in the players lounge now chatting to Bonatini about his goal. Chatting to Nuno and laughing about zen bollocks and why N'Diaye has put so much weight on but I'm not. I walked from the match half pissed. I got on a crowded bus that smelled. I stood in a queue in a chip shop for twenty minutes waiting for a nuclear blasted meat pie while annoying little bastards screamed around their parents feet. What did I see of the match? Well I was there. I saw all the goals, I celebrated.

It was a bit physical. Conor Coady scored albeit for them. I don't care, he made some brilliant moves in that defence, probably saved a few Preston semi skimmed half chances from becoming full fat chances. I don't want to get too romantic about him but I love watching him more than Jota and Neves sometimes. But I was always the bloke that plays the chunk a chunk rhythm while everybody else doodles around, he does that too, back to the amps keeping everything flowing while Jota and Cav do the whole foot on the monitor hair rock football thing. But to be fair to Jota and Cavaleiro and to some extent Neves, they played today's football with a Preston player either on their back or jabbing some strange Morse code into their faces with their elbows. Amazing. Somebody had obviously threatened to burn Referee Steve Martins new conservatory down. He was shit, to be fair we knew it would happen, lose control, get most of the decisions wrong. But at least he didn't make it 'about him' like he did in the Cardiff match. He's just a shit Ref, you get them, like bad pints, dickheads in BMWs, tight shirts on Match of the Day. It happens, no sense moaning about it.

The brawls were funny. Fancy having neck with Preston players? What's the point? It's picking fights while waiting for your kebab at 2am, going to nightclubs on council estates called 'Frazzles' or 'Jangles'. We all love slapping people, it's often very funny but you're being paid to play football lads. If Preston players are acting like kids kicking bus shelters in then you've won the mental battle, they are destroyed lads, picking the chopped lettuce out of their hair, bleeding on their fat girlfriend. It's a won thing. Now all you have to do is stop them from putting the ball in your net. Simple. It's fighting Gary Mastic in Tesco. It's just a noodle thing.

This is certainly a writing session of post match drunkenness. One that I will stash away and forget about. Pretty much like this game. I was still happy, I clapped all the way up to the art block right next to the Molineux laughing. They pinged the ball about ok, certainly better than Villa did last week. I'll comfortably forget that when we were three up I turned around to the bloke next to me and said 'It's going to be 3-3' and I was half right I suppose. In the past seasons I would have put good money on it. Now that gap between 3 goals and 2 have some magical meaning. Some feeling of intent. It's a massive gap really, as how often have we seen a lead like that gobbled up like a crackhead eating an apple pie/ Enough bloody times thanks.

Gary is talking to me about negative things. How Jota (who he called Junta) a few times, was a goal hanging player but maybe he will come good. Gary is clinging on to his negativity like a black cloak. He can't let it go, that feeling from the past, I said before we have post traumatic stress from seasons past. I was right I think. There were times in that game against Preston when I started to get a bit sweaty, a little hot under the collar and no it wasn't the 'too thick' snow coat.

We sat back I think in the second half. Brighty and Alfred looked like Cheech and Chong in the last 15 minutes. Bright enjoying the stroll back to midfield, looking at the stars, 'Yo Preston Massif!' he says as he walks past a few Preston defenders. He's smiling and chilled. But he needs to get back to fucking defend and that Grateful Dead Stoner football ain't gonna wash mush. Slapped arse for him, but he's brilliant and I love him. Yeah goals were scored. I know Cavaleiro scored one, Bonatini too. But Nuno will have some new words to learn in English like 'dopey twat', 'you fucking knobhead' and 'for fucks sake' the set in concrete Wolves managerial handbook of words to say to players who were a bit shit.

But it's all tactical bollocks. All fizz and farts, column inches, weird shouty moments in dressing rooms. I've watched football longer than most of these doughnuts have been alive. I've watched George Best and John Richards, Wagstaff, Parkin, Dougan. Stevie Bull. It's just a day isn't it lads? Management screaming at you to get the order out but to be honest yeah you do too, but because you want to get home to sit by the fire with the dog on your lap, watching something stupid on the TV with lots of glaring colours. Lots of laughing too.

Maybe later the Missus will fancy a fuck and you can go to sleep with that flow of endorphins, a lie in too. Wolves were just that, putting a shift in, getting the order out for the pissed off truck driver who wants to miss the traffic on a motorway you never heard of. Fair enough the shit you put on the truck will fall apart probably, the pallet wrap is a bit shit and half hearted, there's a few bolts missing. But it's gone isn't it? Off down the road and you can go home happy it's all over. The grief from Preston was just that. A bit of pressure. Nothing we couldn't handle event though the lads were a bit stoned.

Gary showed me where the Pasties were. In the fucking pie section of course. £1.56 though robbing bastards. I can't even tell you what Gary was on about as we walked around the madness of Tesco. He was positive but he was still reticent, still wondering. You see this whole Wolves thing this season is waiting for the Crazy train. Some of us got on quite early and are running up and down the carriages naked with Nuno masks on playing football, half pissed, booking flights to Europe for when we are in the Champions league. Other fans are further down the track, other stations on the great endless track of the Championship football season. Gary is one of those people. He is scanning the horizon for a plume of steam and the scream of a steam whistle, the clickety clack of the wheels. He's wondering whether he has bought the right ticket and he's a bit worried. But Gary there's only one train on this track and it's the fucking Crazy Train mate and Nuno is driving it.

Is this book like a crazy ride? I'm sorry, I've told you I'm not a writer. It's all coming too fast to make sense out of any of it. I feel like Hunter Thompson in Las Vegas. Manchester City. Rich boys, cup match.

That came around quick didn't it? See off Southampton and another juggernaut comes barrelling around the corner. Of course I can't afford to go if I want to eat for the next few weeks any way. It's OK, I can deal with it.

A blast from the past this match, it reads like a 1970's teleprinter score on 'The World of Sport' with Dickie Davis. We couldn't afford tickets so it's going to be a case of watching the match through the filters of Social Media and nicking match action off Tim Spiers tweets. What is a Manchester? My Dads family are all from Salford and he was a United fan, which I found disgusting. He could have supported a local team like Manchester City or gone to support Orrel the Rugby League side.

But Salford has always been a hive for Reds. I remember my Great Nan going to watch the Rugby still wearing her Mill clogs. I'll leave the United thing for another day. I remember my Wolverhampton Nan looking at my Dad like he had done a shit in the hearth when he used to put Manchester United on the telly. I remember my Dad punching me in the face when we went to dinner with George Best because he heard me whisper to my younger brother in the car going up, 'fuck George Best'. But I've still got George Bests autograph and I still remember him standing around for three quarters of a match doing nothing. Jesus Christ on a bike. I'll get all this off my chest when we are playing United next season. Beware.

Manchester. What is a Manchester City? I don't mind them too much, I don't mind Manchester either to be honest. It was always weird being dragged up there every couple of years to touch base with the 'Manc-End' of the family. Especially as my localism and Wolverhamptoness was ingrained from birth in Low Hill. I didn't like my old man and so I hated his team with a vengeance but Uncle Steve was a City fan, he was OK. But why are we there again? The League cup. We will spill up there mob handed of course being loud and getting run over by the trams wandering aimlessly around looking where to go, looking for Wolves shirts so you can follow them to the stadium.

'Where ya from in Wolvo Bab?' You ask a couple of women in Wolves shirts

'Oh we're from Marlborough' they reply. I tell my mate,

'Where's that?' he asks. 'Back of Heath Town I think' I tell him.

'Pattingham ay it?' he says.

The media disinformation campaign against the Wolves is kicking in now. The odd article filled with bile and untruths. The Manager quotes (Yes you Steve Bruce) that have all the intellectual nous of a fucking Yoga DVD.

Love it, bring it on. You fucking Dinosaurs, how dare you. You haven't got the right to print anything about my club, you haven't earned it. And your team got beat at the Molineux? Tough fucking tit. You're all living in the past, Managers, Journos you have failed to evolve, you are old photographs, sad TV formats, you have failed to create new ways and new systems.

We are the media now.....fuck, my biscuit has fell in my tea. Yeah the disinformation, the fake articles, the men in tight suits and tighter expense accounts, the back slappers, the sidlers, idlers, the useless dregs of the old order…picking out a floating half a biscuit in hot tea, shoving it in your face while your fingers burn. Got it all out too. Kwan. Belief. Just say No to Fake Football journalism.

It's going to get much worse too once the sheeple who support other teams start to smell blood. It's bad enough now with all this FFP wankery off people with all the financial skills of a fucking scaffold plank, they're the ones who try to peel the foil off pound coins so they can eat the chocolate. Soon it's going to be one big circle jerk with us stuck in the middle of it laughing. Christ, sometimes I wish I could throw a bottle of warm piss at the lot of them.

City have some cash don't they? Oil cash isn't it? Sheikh money or something. I remember them well, knocking around the Championship/Division 1 before they got a few quid in their pockets and started buying all these funky players who could move a ball around a bit. Same as our business plan really, investment, long term planning, loyal fanbase, local roots. I don't want to big them up too much of course but this is the model we need to have in place. Growth, dynamic change, vision maybe, a global outlook. It's mad that I'm using all these keywords, I suppose one day we will see what they mean when we are playing City twice a year and nicking their Euro spot. I'm not angry about not going tonight, I've been to loads of great matches. I'm not greedy. I'm saving for the European matches in a few years. Pound in the jar.

I don't feel weird about playing them either. I know the youth have a bit of a hard on about a team that has been hanging around the top of the Premiership like a dog fart under a duvet. I get that. I also get these tasty rumblers of the ball too. I've watched a few games this year. I couldn't tell you who they are because the names are tricky to spell. But there's that little angry bloke, the big black dude, the Spanish looking fella with the bad trim, the ginger bloke 'Kev', that England player who scored that goal once….a plethora of names really that spill across my screen like a couple of packs of Panini stickers. Of course they have foil bits and are shiny. That's cool.

Manchester is a shiny place full of new buildings and shops, new ground too, the 'Eat-ya-yed' stadium or something. We're kind of looking at them with a bit of hope wondering maybe, is this our bag? Our future? But that City team always get off the bus with big glum faces and bigger headphones, handbags, Premier league things. But they also have the greatest Poet in the world at the moment. Mark E Smith of 'The Fall' and 'Kicker Conspiracy' was my anthem and he was my Messiah for a few years I'll admit. Maybe still is. We're all 'well read peasants'.

But looking at our team I don't feel aggravated at all. They can all find the space here to expand a little maybe, stretch their legs out and not fear the incessant bitchball finangling, the odd ankle kick, the pulling at shirts, the toe stamp. All the bollocks that Preston threw at us last Saturday. What a Warnockian festival of shite that was, topped off with a Refereeing display more worthy of a factory lunchtime kick about with a flat ball someone found on the roof, steel toe cap boots, fouls, apprentices for goal posts, 'stand there you little bastards and don't move'. I was a bit angry after that game even though we won it. PNE are the dirtiest team in the League at the moment. A fucking disgrace. Like looking for the TV remote in Steve Bruces hair and pulling the back of a settee out.

Jack Price, ink still wet on a new contract. Will he enter the stage as a little kid does at a school nativity play with his tea towel Shepherd outfit, little face looking all aggravated. Or will he stride on there like Richard Burton in Hamlet with Agueros skull in his hand? I hope the latter. I'm a big fan of Jacko. His passes in the Bristol Rovers game were sublime.

Will we open up the book of football Nuno has written so far at Wolves? The flowing sexual stuff? Of course. Are our ideas stronger than Pepitto Guardyacolas? Maybe. Pep looks like a bloke on the edge of a nervous breakdown. I think his players go above and beyond because they know he gets all weepy and wails like a Spanish Civil war widow when they get stuffed. Which isn't often. There's always a slim chance of course the City staff will have neglected to do their homework on our team. But I doubt it somehow. I think they are well aware of how we are on a high looking to rock somebody on their heels. Having a go at the 'big kid'. I've got biscuits at the ready 'Poundstretcher Chocolate Digestives' quid a pack. I've got my Sports Direct free mug full of tea. Roll ups. Dogs. Tim Spiers Twitter account primed. Let's fucking have it. Remember when we put Uniteds record breaking win record to the sword?

We're off. N'diaye or 'Big Alf' as I call him is doing a thing apparently, straight away. I like Big Alf. Damn weird trying to make sense of the first ten minutes of any game. It's the slow dance part, we are still in the Barry White phase with him where you are getting to know what's under the clothes, having a smooch. Big Alf has smooched somebody with a smashing tackle already. Aguero looks like the star of a beheading video from Mexico on Liveleak.

I predicted the score at full time. 0-0. I was confident we would display the same resolute and solid underpinnings that have been exposed to us for the last few weeks. It was a pure delight from start to finish. The stream of course went blah a few times but it was all there for me to see. This wasn't a 'second string' team by any means. This was another subtle materialisation of the will of Nuno and his coaching staff. A manifestation of the same idea but in different form. And yet I suppose I at least fell into the trap of thinking it was the second stringers, at least until they started to play and it became apparent that this wasn't a gathering of the dysfunctional and the forgotten.

They were the weapon Nuno and his staff chose to select to counter the threat of one of the top teams in Europe. Were we not entertained? Fucking hell, no joke there were a few times when I kind of locked into the rhythm of the whole spectacle and I saw a team that were vibrant, steadfast, agile and attack minded. A team in their rightful place.

We defended as 11 men, attacked as 11 men It was plain to see on the pitch. Manchester City threatened constantly. Ronan I will never describe as 'little Ronan' again. What a display from him. As a man he is, his stature no relation to his strength. A pure artists. He made £50,000.000 players look like snot on a bus seat.

Jack Price in everybody's face again, that beard getting in the way of attacks, nibbling away, having the occasional dig. Fair play Jack Price. Big Danny Batth, derided most of last season and now collects the ball in his own box and executes a short pass to outfield and away, his blocking, his overall play. What has Nuno done with him?It's Stepford Wives but football players from Compton. Vinagre growing into some sort of insanely creative force on the wing. Norris? He came from Cambridge as some snotnose with a good report, who is this man? This presence? Those saves? I mean he fluffed his lines a few times but he was probably nailing tiles to a roof two years ago. Give him the slack this occasion deserves. Insane player again. Love him. We are blessed.

There were times here when I actually shivered a little and the hairs on my neck stood up as our team expanded their ideas across the whole stadium. The idea I think was birthright and pedigree, history and pride. We did not seem out of place because this is our place. This is the idea our teams of the past forged in our names. Of course we played brilliantly, because that is the way we 'should' play and the tactics, at least for me pale away a little and that idea of birthright demands football that seizes back those days we had back in the past. This football reverberates back into those days and those past teams are made alive again forming this irresistible idea of beautiful Molineux football.

The misses are and should be ruminated over on other days I think. I love Brighty. The penalties are grist for the Social Media mill I suppose and I daresay someone will stop me this week and discuss it. But the beauty of it all will (I think) be the mainstay of my thoughts this week, at least until the next match. I bet Mark E Smith was entertained by it all. But for me it was an experience of a lifetime. Those fans that went, I don't envy you at all for being there and experiencing it. I've had loads of great games from the past. I'm not being greedy. I wish those penalties would have gone in just for you so you could have felt your hearts swell up but it was not to be.

Bright Enkobahare came out with some plus points. I have to talk about him for a minute if you don't mind.

He has erupted into my mind after the other night against Manchester City. This young lad kicked out the JAMS fully as he trotted onto the pitch and proceeded to confuse and kick up a stink around the 500 Billion pound city defence. Did I laugh? Damn right I did. I laughed the other week when Brighty strode around in the gaps in the play against Preston, he was chilling out, taking it easy and to be honest I never understood why. But now I think I do. I think it's not up to me to comment on why Bright does what he does. I don't want to comment because 1. I can hardly run with my knees and 2. Brights football understanding is on a totally different plane to mine.

His football is exciting and mad. He doesn't fluff scoring goals I think. Maybe he's already done all the hard work and everybody else is just struggling to keep up with the absolute avant garde football he plays. Instead of finding that player that has kept up with his groove and rhythm he often looks up after noodling a load of opposition players only to find that either there's nobody to pass to or there's a big chunk of the final ball missing. Final ball? The money shot, banging it between the keepers legs, popping it around him, sticking it in the bag so to speak.

I've watched him play in the under 21's and watched him coalesce into this team of absolute artists and he never looks out of place. I'm respectful. We are watching a pure artist but one we don't understand yet. The jumble of football he presents to us looks confused but is it really? Are we watching him wrong? Probably he himself is struggling with the absolute weight of skill he actually has, and that skill is going to click into place soon as he runs riot. I'm sure he will. He is the random variable in this team of clinical and empirical skill sets. The random variable because we lack the capacity to understand actually what he's doing. We don't know because we have never done the shit Bright does on a football field. We will never be in that position.

All you have to do is work out how far one of his probing runs were against Man City. Work out the speed, look at the opposition trying to get the ball off him. This opposition bear in mind is the fucking cream of world football really. Bright is the Compton lad. Watch him make fools of them. Watch Bright Run, watch Bright skip, watch Bright control. It was effortless and it was beautiful and it was also novel in many ways. Has he not entertained? Do you have to score goals to put that full stop on such a game? Amazed wasn't the word. I've noticed my hands shaking a lot when he gets the ball, and often falls over it. I don't really care about him falling over, I don't really care about him scoring goals. My Man City piece had a little about him not scoring and then me saying 'I don't care, I love him any way'. And I do.

He is exactly how I would play. A little dysfunctional and raw, chaotic at times, mad man. But he's not mad obviously, and his error is not that he is young and a bit daft. I think we just fail to understand him and his play. Miles Davis the famous Jazz trumpet player often hooted and blew daft riffs when playing with other jazz greats and you can hear this on many of the live club recordings he made. The errant note here and there was always a precursor to his 'team mate' whoever it was that night to try and correct the discordant Davis riff into a coherent melody. They struggled sometimes because they often lacked the capacity to understand what Miles was doing. Miles was provoking them. Now it's a tough thing to extrapolate Miles and be-bop into Bright Enobakhare football madness but it's the only way I can see. It's not a superlative prod at the subject. I'm trying to understand football so abstract and beautiful that it boggles my mind to do it.

Bright is trying to 'provoke' football maybe and his vision of what constitutes football how he plays is not shared by his team mates to a degree, not yet. But I think they are getting a handle on things and I suspect Bright is also learning that the final note you play i.e. the goal is probably the most important to the listener or the fan. It's the goal, that exuberant little melody or coda that encompasses and collects all the work that has gone on before and wraps it all up in a final triumphant finish. The thing is I don't think Bright wants to finish, I suspect he wants the whole thing to continue in some endless jam in front of the opposition box. And Jesus Christ is it some tune that kid plays. Every time he has the ball I'm grooving to the whole idea of Bright Enobakhare and what he has to say. As he's that random variable or errant note he stands out against the melodious football his mates are playing so he's seen a lot more. Centre stage. People waiting for that tune or that coda....alas.

I love Bright, I have to say he's one of my favourite players currently in the team simply because he's exciting, a maverick, a naughty boy and he appeals to me purely in that sense. I know full well that among the kids I used to teach at school there was always the one kid the teachers didn't like, who they couldn't teach, and that kid was always in the wrong place at the wrong time, always the first name mentioned when something had kicked off and more often than not getting the blame for it. I know those kids and I took them under my wing because I understood that they were simply too bloody clever for their own good most of the time. I look at Bright and I see a man that's going to pop out of that youthful madness with a plan, a plan to wipe out other teams with his own brand of skills and madness. For that's how we see these players, as being a bit crazy. I'm sure I've written elsewhere about 'mad men' and how they can galvanise a team. I think Nuno understands that Bright is exactly what this team needs to finish itself off. To make it a force that will lay waste to teams for years to come. Bright is the random variable, the bad boy who nobody will ever understand except himself. As soon as Bright does start to understand himself he is going to be unstoppable.

It's not Tubeway army you know, There's nothing cool and new wave about this. I'm looking at this dudes face, he's only about twelve inches away from my face and we are close together. He is uncomfortable because I'm uncomfortable at our proximity to each other and I think he's trying not to look me in the eye and I'm trying to ease myself into the idea....I'm two hundred foot underground on a hurtling fast underground train that stinks of many people, It's hot. He's picking up that screaming claustrophobic vibe I'm giving off and he's not happy but he can't move any where.

I'm smiling like a lunatic because I don't know what else to do with my face. I can't do the blank London look, disinterested and slack, emotionless. Horace says all the skin and hair that collects on the rails is cleaned every night so conductivity on the rails is maximised. Skin and hair. Nobody speaks. Everybody is locked into some sort of London silence. The train is rocking from side to side and I look out of the window instead of this dudes face and all I see is mine, yellow tungsten, ghostly, smiling and sick. Trepidation. A young woman walks past me and all she has on is a pair of black knickers and fishnet stockings but there's a place for that and in my football addled mind that place was not here.

Fucking London. The thing is…it was bound to happen wasn't it? Of course the hangover from Manchester was a pumper, one of those bone deep hurting ones and it was accompanied by that Cider Gollum of the West Country Ian Holloway himself, a man that epitomises the tight knot in your shoelaces you can't tease apart. It hurts your fingernails, frustration, complication, exasperation. The train screams and squeaks to a halt at Shepherds Bush tube station and I imagine for a moment that's exactly what the toilet in the Holloway household sounds like when he's having a shit. His team today played the same way, they set the teeth on edge. They played with no breath, they played like a grumbling chest infection. Haemorrhoid Holloway is sitting on my chest at that moment like a Limestone Gargoyle all dripping tongue and heavy, eyes like pissholes in the snow, his little bald head nodding. Ugh, plop, Holloway evacuates a bitter little turd into the bowl, another QPR goal.

I would love to say that they played the same strange bitter football as the Cardiffs and the Prestons but it wasn't like that at all. QPR were a poor team and it was obvious that they deserved (in part) their mid table groove. They were a rag tag bunch of weirdos for sure. A number nine that had a fatter arse than the one that pressed into my face a few times on the tube as it rocked around. Some massive tool they lumped on at half time who looked eight foot tall. Well he wasn't going to jink around the pitch like a beautiful footballer was he? Boom. The ball was incessantly lumped towards his head at every opportunity. QPRs ideas weren't stronger than ours today they were louder.

The contrast between the two sides was dysfunction in our team, an off day, a day off, a Sunday morning kick about. I think instead of the beauty of Neves and the grit of Saiss (who had a right mardy face most of the match) I suspect a pairing of N'Diaye and Price might have been more effective. It was a snotty game they would have excelled in for sure (maybe). One scans the mind for answers as we watch and the songs get quieter and the shuffling of feet is a thing.

QPR definitely rocked and creaked like those underground trains. They rocked of course our team who were in some sort of netherworld between Manchester and Cardiff. We were trapped. We were trapped in the idea of our ethos, trapped in a ground so strange I was amazed. The tube, the ground, the vibe was tight and cramped. Our team was inherently so affected by this environment their football mimicked the pyschogeography of the whole Shepherds Bush and London thing. It was edgy and dysfunctional, not massively cool and trendy. Fumbleball on many occasions. The play erupted in a game of head ping pong again and I could hear the 'bleep bleep' of the Atari every time it happened. I kept shuffling my feet and closing my eyes trying to 'will' a game of football to happen, but alas, again.

Did we not expect this? Certainly on the train down as I watched the countryside whizz past there was a feeling I admit, of trepidation. I knew two halves of a team would be glued together today. The histrionics of the dynamic gritty 'put a shift in' hero team from the Eat-Ya-Head stadium hastily welded to the bread and butter pudding sexiness of Neves and Jota et al. But I wondered whether it would come off. Yes, our ideas were definitely stronger than QPR's today but the 'Idea' was in fact a number of ideas. It was a Venn diagram that was just random circles scrawled on the paper. Nothing overlapped. All separate and all brilliant in their own way but individual skills on the pitch were lone voices and had words that just fell to their feet like the carcass of a dead pigeon. Like the emotionless stares of the cops in contrast to the happy smiling ground staff at the QPR ground.

All our disparate ideas were infinitely better than Hollowayball. All much better on paper but there were too many and not one strong theme throughout the team today. Ideas flowed everywhere of course. They were sublime and intensely sexual passes we have come to admire and wax lyrical over. There was a fucking basket full of them from all members of our team. I dare say they were all great dynamic ideas…but every one of our team today had their own personal ones. Eleven great fucking ideas when there should have been one unifying theme. I suspect minds were left in Manchester a few times. Those ideas as strong as they were failed to weld with technique and intent, failed to connect with each other. Bonatini scores from a forensic display of clockwork beautiful play. Click, click boom. The sky opens out, there is beauty there is hope, there is a breath of wind after that goal and I breathe deep, my lungs open up, it's inhaler time, the vapours of the Bonatini skill set opening those closed air passages for a moment, before it's snatched away again

Even Jota on a few occasions seemed cramped. His football was stifled by the closeness of the QPR body that was assigned to be his nemesis today. He got away a few times, made some fine chances but he knew that this match today was going to be one of them. Tube train match. Close and warm. Echoed by the strange ground which was close and small. Nuno paced the 'technical area' as big as a toilet on a train. Every time he wanted to physically display his frustration at the team he was penned in by the press of bodies around him. That dashed line around our dugout was too small to allow him space to breathe. Nuno had a straitjacket on.

No more the air and freshness of Molineux, this place was a tomb. The light that fell on the ground was close and yellow, there was no wind, no freedom and no real intent. I suspect he knew we were lost before a ball was kicked. And there's the idea of the day. We were crushed by expectation I suppose. Crushed by the negative potentials of the Holloway vibe and a QPR team that were quite happy to play their world cup game against us. Every ball they played fell in just the right place. Every knocked on ball fell at the feet of a QPR body. Just the right foot to place a weird eccentric pass that would fall perfectly at the feet of their player who, in shock, would place it at the foot of another player before the ball once again flew into the air for ten minutes of ping pong football. We look to the football Gods who have smiled on Holloway today and say is this what you wish? Is this what is rewarded? This itchy groin football, this erratic tumbling dysfunction? Is this what you want? Have we not suffered enough?

I wouldn't be surprised if Holloway said get that ball in the air a lot. We had no real answer to the pinging of the ball through the foetid London air. No wonder they keep stabbing each other to death here.. A pass that erupted into the air as it bypassed our midfield was given 2-1 odds that it would fall to a QPR player for a chance of another pass and another chance for them. We played the ball at our feet where we like it, where we know the strengths of our team lie but their idea as glaring and discordant as it is, was a lot fucking louder than ours. It was scruffy horrible crap. The Holloway doctrine of piece by piece A4 photocopied sheets of football tactics 101 were blowing around the pitch like confetti and we had no real answer to any of it. Matt Doherty at one point looked dumbfounded by it all, confused maybe but definitely pissed off. The very name Holloway reverberated around my mind as I stood in the stand watching. Hollow Way. Yes. Definitely that. Cavaleiro jumped into the air from a tackle that never was trying to get a penalty. As he sat in the box arms outstretched to the Ref in disbelief I reckoned the drama was to be a sad one.

Definitely one of those games when it failed to spark for us. The pitch and ground was small and bitter, like Holloways head. It impinged into the consciousness for sure. It was intense and negative, asthmatic at times, stuffy, wrong coat football for sure. Of course when we do get the idea right and the team do lock into some sort of comradely skill set we would have done them all day. Again we fall to a team that have all the imagination of a filthy subway wall and how many times has that happened this season?

It's not that we aren't exotic and dynamic, it's that again the psychology of the drudgeball tactic epitomised by Holloway and his ilk is one which we have no real answer for. Play football and we can win against any body, we just played Manchester City one of the best teams in Europe, had them on the back foot, we were dynamic and beautiful but today that beauty was stifled once again. We can't beat teams with no ideas. We have no answer to the negativity of the Sam Scrotum school of skirmishing football and that bothers me more than watching us play brilliantly and losing. Our ideas are stronger, our ideas are loftier, our ideas are forged in beautiful football. But when faced with this ungainly football with tactics with as much depth and gravity as a fart on a hot tube train we have little answer.

Before the game me and Horace stood for a while on the opposite side of the road to the QPR mobs favourite pub. We watched as their fellas stood outside with their beers looking menacing and angry. Phones pressed to their ears. Expensive coats, expensive drinks, inexpensive violent ideas. I half felt like just running in and throwing stuff about, even thought about just going in and ordering a drink, turning around at the bar and smiling at the ugly faces that would of course be looking straight back at you. I would have raised my glass and winked at the ugliest among them. Of course we never did. We just laughed and annoyed them a little.

Today, QPR did just that. Annoyed us a bit, winked, and we fucked off back to Wolvo grumbling and moaning. Holloway would go back to his perch on some Cathedral ledge, settling himself down amongst the pigeon shit, looking down at the people below cackling at doing us over again.

Our ideas are stronger, our team is stronger, our Coach is stronger but sometimes the numbness does bite and effect. The whole environment today was one of numbness, it was a hangover. A limpid display of idea in it's most abstract form when it failed to ignite from the simple words and names on a team sheet to a coherent and dynamic display on the day. We will have them in the future of course. These games will come and go as we plough on through the season. It's trench warfare, hand to hand combat sometimes. It's cleaning a drain out, it's getting the limescale off the toilet enamel. Our team have to realise that sometimes we have to be louder than the other team, we have to impress our ideas with volume and intent. We have to stop letting other teams scar the beautiful landscape of our football with negativity and depression.

Kwan is all powerful, but it needs room to flow and this closeness and lack of air that permeates London was an anathema to Kwan. The negativity of Londoness was too powerful for the flow to erupt onto this particular stage and yes the Kwan was stifled by skin and hair on tracks, hooligans in their pub, me and Horace wishing we had a tin of old school gas to throw in and our laughter about this fell on to the dirty pavements. On the tube back I was numb but captivated by a very beautiful woman next to me but letting the key moments of the game play through my mind. Norwich next, Nuno will have answers to this conundrum and he will address them in a quiet thoughtful manner as befitting a great coach. It was not the worst of days. Are we not a pragmatic bunch? Are we not ever hopeful? Writing about football is hard. I get too emotional I know and I'm sorry but I suppose the 'way of things' is to become more creative. It's a fucking fairy tale so far. In my mind I extrapolate football writing into a tale that may be told so to speak.

Gather around children…

Once upon a time in a land called Molineux there was a brave handsome Prince named Nuno. In that land in which he lived the people didn't smile much. It wasn't that the land of Molineux was a sad land. They were generally a happy people, singing songs, drinking beer, laughing, drinking, singing and laughing some more. Prince Nuno was a very wise and brave man. Everybody in the land of Molineux loved him and when they saw him they would all sing to him so he would wave at them, then the people of Molineux would wave back and cheer. Prince Nuno made them very happy and they made songs for Nuno and Nuno smiled too for he knew that they loveth him.

The Ruler of Molineux was King Jeff who came from a land very far away from Molineux. The people of Molineux were very happy with King Jeff because King Jeff brought sacks of gold and jewels from that far off land. This made the people glad because their last King the wicked Morgan of Scouseland was very miserly. Often he would be seen in his tower at Molineux counting his money and cackling to himself. Baron Moxey who was King Morgans Chancellor was also a wicked man and he would steal some of that money too but it wasn't called 'stealing' children, it was called 'commission' and King Morgan and Chancellor Moxey became very rich and the people of Molineux became sadder and sadder. The songs they sang became sadder too and people didn't like coming to Molineux any more. It was even rumored among them that King Morgan didn't even want to be King of Molineux at all and that he didn't love them he just wanted their money and land to build expensive houses and fill them with grey people.

One day the people of Molineux became very angry that King Morgan and his friends didn't really love the people that came to sing praises and songs of happiness every Saturday after working all week. Soon the people started calling the King horrible names and the Chancellor Moxey got called even worse ones because as well as keeping all the money he would also eat all the pies to himself. But soon King Jeff came and kicked the wicked Morgan out of his tower in a great battle and with him he brought the brave Prince Nuno and lots of Knights from sun drenched places that saw no snow or rain.

One day Prince Nuno was told he had to take his brave Knights to a dark land far away called Norfolk. Within that cold dark land was a place called Norwich which had it's own King and there was to be a battle. This battle was to gain 'magic points' and these magic points were collected all year in various battles. The points were gathered together at the end of the year and the Kingdom that had the most magic points would be allowed into the land of the Premiership where there was much Gold and jewels, enough for everybody to share. King Jeff summoned Prince Nuno to him.

'Prince Nuno! Thou shalt take your brave Knights to the Land of Norfolk and battle for these magic points for I wish that the people of Molineux should also sing my praises and I will let that Gold spill from my hands unto their hearts and the songs will be mighty and loud, verily much beer will be drunk' and King Jeff pointed to the East…'Goeth with these men I have arrayed for thee and they shalleth be called 'The Brotherhood of the Wolf' and verily you shalt have my blessings upon thy wisest of heads'… and Prince Nuno gathered his Knights and prepared set off.

The land of Norwich was ruled by a man named Balls and verily many did laugh at this and so it was the people of that land in the East became bitter and waved their lobster hands in the air as yay! they were cursed and hated the people of Molineux because we had flags of deepest Gold and Bible black and our totem was a Wolf but the people of Norwich had flags of bile green and vomit yellow and verily their Totem was a small singing bird.

They remembered too many years in the past a brave Knight of Molineux Prince Kevin of Muscat who when battling the evil no necked dwarf 'Craig of Bellamy' verily did try to snappeth off his leg. The people of Norwich did click their lobster hands in a rage when this evil dwarfs name was mentioned and verily the people of Molineux dideth mention his name much when battles were met. Much to the jollity of the Molineux but not to the sad Lobster handed peoples of Norwich.

Prince Nuno set off with songs and much praise even if he had lost his last battle with the wicked bald headed ogre of West London only a few risings of the sun before. The wicked Ogre although victorious went back into it's evil smelling cave to chew the festering bones of it's season and Prince Nuno although beaten was glad he had the knowledge of the Ogre and would be prepared the next time they met in battle. But King Jeff verily said unto Nuno...

'There are riches enough my Prince in this war and verily it will last until Spring and the coming of Summer and it is early in your battles as it is in your years, go forth with this knowledge and my blessing for I require three of these magic points today and thou wilt bring them to me so verily the people of Molineux will be triumphant and glad and we may sing songs' and Prince Nuno was pleased.

So it came to pass that the singing and happy people of Molineux dideth travel through many dark roads, passing through valleys of fear and cold until at last they came to the place of battle. Verily did the peoples of that place also cometh for did they not come to see the Gold and Black standards of the Molineux and the Brotherhood of the Wolf?? Did they not wish to see the splendour of our banners? Were we not beautiful to look upon? And the peoples of Norwich did pour from their caves to watch the Knights of Gold and Black arrive upon the battlefield and there was Sir Conor of Coady, Sir Jota of Jota, the brave young Prince Bonatini, the warriors Sir Neves of Neves, Sir Bright of Enobakhare, the laughing Cavalier Ivan of Cavaleiro and Sir Alf of N'Diaye together with others who had yet to marketh their names upon the rolls of honour.

The battle commenced and yay the hordes of Norwich did sing strange songs in the language of their caves and verily we dideth struggle to understand their plaintive wailings and yet our own songs were sung loud and clear upon the battlefield and our warriors did feel themselves heartened and strong with these voices and the leadership of Prince Nuno. For Prince Nuno did consult with the Wizards of the Kwan and they were wise with their words and it was the will of Nuno that his young Knights did run hither and thither unto the gaps between the un-named soldiers of Prince Farck who commended them in his fashion. Verily it was seen that indeed these warriors of ours were brave and forthright, for were not the songs we sang full of the glories of the past? Did we not have the right to sit at the tables of Kings and proclaim our rightful place among them?

The battle commences and what a sight to behold it was. The strategies were simple and yet eloquent, a veritable delight of linked interplays, the flashing of foot, the incisive tactics. Prince William of Boly stretched his long shanks around the pitch of battle as a storm, every attack by the men of Norwich instantly pushed back under the weight of his skill. The night sky of that cursed land was aglow with the delights of the crowds that had come to feast their eyes upon such skills and even the trolls from the surrounding ditches of Norwich did verily attend and thus the battleground was awash with the puke yellow and gangrene of their flags.

But verily and yay! They were quiet under the storm of the Wolfs again and again our Princes and Sirs battered the defence of the Norwichians and their greenbelt wizardry. But alas the flatland trolls had no answer and an attack dideth tear asunder the vanguard of the Norwichians and the black Prince of Boly did smasheth thy head upon the ball and verily that ball did'st erupt upon the back netting of the Norwichian goal. What songs we did'st sing upon this goal and verily there were limbs and much accusations that these Norwichians did'st touch themselves in sordid and sinful ways when within their caves. There were also promises of eternal brotherhood as the Wolf hordes did proclaim yay! and verily! for this is the greatest team upon the earth by far and verily Norwichian battle plans were lower than an eel and verily they were much proclamations and statements that the Norwichian hordes were 'shit' and their songs lacked the virility that was showethed by our attacks upon them. And indeed these flatlanders were silent much of the battle unless we dideth sing of Prince Kevin of Muscat whereupon much bile was released and the Norwichians didth strike themselves in the balls often and their plaintive wailings did'st fill the ground as an animal in pain.

Sir Jota of Jota did'st indeed showeth also his array of skills and set the standard of the Wolf firmly upon the middle of battle and verily dideth proclaim his own bravery and lack of fear as he danced around the Norwichian Princes and Sirs and made them look as sad burned monkeys upon a fire as the commands of Prince Nuno did'st echo indeed throughout the field of battle.

But what ends are these as Prince Bonatini took it upon himself to seize the day and settle the standard of the Wolf upon the goal of the Lime Green and Lemon yellows of the Norwichian goal? Verily he did standeth upon the green grass of that place among the blood soaked field of dreams and verily did proclaim yes! This is our power and never again shall we visiteth this place and not mention the day as it stands, a victory and a day of fired hearts, belief in the Prince of Nuno and his Holy writ…

The simple warrior Jack of Price did'st attend the battle in the later stages of it when victory seemed certain. Harried and forlorn were the men of the Norwichian flat lands and verily the support of those around did dwindle as the battle drew to it's close and the crows did circle upon the pitch ready to devour the lost dreams of those men. For is it not a thing that they too had dreamed of victory? That they, in their dreams had seen the standard of the Wolf fall upon the soaked grass to be trampled? Were not their dreams important? Verily this mere scribe did not give a shitteth and sang great goodbye songs to them as they filed from the battle with long faces and strange garbs.

The journey is at an end at least for this chapter children. And verily the journey back to King Jeff was a long and arduous one as the Norwichians in their depravity and lack of honour did'st closeth off the road leading to the fair city of Wolverhampton. Verily dideth we seek a path through the black clouds of their misfortunes at the hands of the Wolfs, verily did we seek upon the horizon that golden glow of our spires and towers. Prince Nuno it is said held the precious three points within his hands ready to present to King Jeff this gift from them who have done battle upon the darkness and the unlight of Norwich.

Let it be said as he hands those points to King Jeff that alas there will be voices from other Kingdoms this day that Prince Nuno shouldeth join with another city or another Kingdom and that he may gather around him other Princes and men so that their city will also have the joy and laughter that the Brotherhood of the Wolf haveth enjoyed. But nay! and Verily! for is it not seen that Prince Nuno has been given his own kingdom here. Do we not see that this Kingdom is not upon the concrete and steel battlements of their kingdoms and gratitudes of gold upon his purse but instead within the hearts of its people? Shall we not say that this reward is worth thrice that of golden coins? This humble scribe will say at least these Kingdoms who would offer lies and mistruths to Prince Nuno shouldeth fucketh off and that my friends is the end of this tale......for now.

OK sorry about that..mad isn't it, what this football bollocks does to a mans mind. Norwich was weird wasn't it? Me and Horace stood outside the ground pre-game sipping a Coffee and just observing the absolute madness that permeated this crazy load of fans from Norwich....OK that's a lie. It was like somebody had died.

People from Wolverhampton often shout when they talk. This is probably a result of working in places that are very loud because they 'make stuff' out of metal. That metal clangs on the floor when dropped. Machines pump and crash through great echoing factories. We shout because we are in loud places. This place is not loud. What was a Norwich? A quiet place for sure. A place where when me and Horace 'talked' it was often loud and obviously upsetting to the people walking to the ground. Yes, we were loud and the conversation was permeated with lot's of 'Yeows', 'Yams'. 'Arrs', 'Ahks' and swearing. The people of Norwich shrunk their heads further into their collars and didn't look at us. That's OK. I didn't fancy talking about anything. That journey saps the mind.

The result was a god sent thing, 'bouncebackability' they say, it's a definite promotion thing for sure. Winning after a defeat gives you the horn, after QPR it was needed, it was in fact required. Of course after the Norwich win it seemed like the Express and Star had a hard on for ploughing out a few negative stories about Nuno going, about November when we don't win. All doom and gloom of course. But why? It's not news that other teams will be after Nuno. It won't be news that a plethora of clubs will be looking to pick through our presents off Uncle Mendes either. It's a sure thing. These stories stick like shit to a duvet when ever we are doing well. I'm a bit of a paranoid fella. I often wonder what the underlying message is, what the real narrative really is. I know the press has agendas too. I suspect that the owners of a newspaper will define what that narrative is going to be before sending out their minions armed with lap tops to fill the newspaper with stories. So when I woke up Wednesday morning to see a few negative things on my social media timelines from the Express and Star my mind started working. It started defining a hypothesis as to why. Wolves and us were definitely on a high for sure. And we were being dragged back to negativity and worry.

Yes, we rarely win in November but that meme is surely dead. That was before surely?when we had a squad that lacked focus and ambition, but now, it's different isn't it? The Express and Star did a little feature about Nuno going to Everton. A non story for sure, even me in my addled state could see that Nuno wouldn't be off there but the E&S had a hard on for the story and saw an opportunity for fume. #DontGoNuno was the hashtag. It was a barely emotional plea for activity on social media. The campaign died within minutes of course, and that's the thing with letting fresh graduates of digital content blah degrees loose on the mass of lunacy that is us, the fans. We are quite happy in the golden glow of a good start to the season and we wanted to enjoy it a little. Like sitting down after xmas dinner, your belly full, eyes gently closing with the promise of 20 minutes kip while the soft xmas lights tinkle and twinkle, the dogs asleep, the kids are quiet, gently drifting into a soft, hazy,warm…..BOOM! Somebody has booted you in the bollocks and are shouting in your ear…'You've eaten too much! You'll have a heart attack! Another drink? Do you know the damage that will cause to your liver??'. Lovely, thank you. The E&S love it don't they?

I wouldn't say they had an agenda to disrupt and annihilate our little happy thoughts at this time but fucking hell I'm suspicious. The Steve Morgan hagiography when he visited the city, the big spreads about his 'return' etc. And now this, happy in the win at Norwich we suffer the next days negative bullshit from the local press. We haven't fallen for it have we? Some did I suppose. Those who still think that the local press are a viable and important part of the Wolves project. You see when we hear the word 'Local' we think that maybe, just maybe the local paper will be an important part of what it means to be a fan, they will support initiatives, provide stories that are positive and enlightening. Fully paid up members of the whole idea that at last we have momentum and intent, that the days of gloom are past. But no.

There is a gap between the Express and Star and us, the majority of fans. Years ago the paper would be bought and we would instantly turn to the back pages to see what the Wolves news is. It was sparse, as sport wasn't awash with the money it has now. So we would buy the paper and find a few paragraphs about a latest injury, the thoughts of the manager, maybe even the odd photo of our current team hero. The press is no longer the 'Press of Necessity' and the longer and faster the march of the internet goes on the more we see the printed press is unimportant, separate and mostly uninvolved with the day to day information gathering of the net linked football fan.

Now you can get information you want often at the click of a finger on a screen. The information world is fast and so is opinion too, so are conclusions I suppose. We gather the information from a variety of sources and let those bits of information leak around your network until indeed there are a number of opinions floating around. Some you don't agree with and some you do, there are some in the middle too and we read all of them, constantly reading between the lines until we have come to some sort of conclusion about a story or a rumour. This conclusion however is not set in stone, we assimilate further bits of information and our conclusions change rapidly for some, slower for others. But eventually we reach a consensus opinion which we all agree on.

The Nuno rumours took maybe an hour to rubbish and Wolves fans on Social media had already come to a viable useful conclusion it was all a load of shit within a time frame that was dynamic, fast, information heavy and maybe more true than the Express and Star rumour mill.

We shouldn't expect our local rag to be one of us just because it's the town newspaper. We have to get rid of that idea now. For too long Journalists have cherry picked the stories they want to tell and been given the keys to access backstage areas where they can pick up info here and there. They get to interview players and managers and the interviews are lacklustre North Korean type press releases, boring bollocks, stuff we already know, recycled bullshit. We should have an arena of information supply really where other new dynamic media forms are given access to Managers and Chairmen. Where we can ask questions we want answered.

Are we not Kings also? We pay the money required to tangle ourselves in the machinery of the emotional madness of football should we not be able to ask the questions we want answering? No Press pass for us. No subsidised expense account. No access. but we do have the new medias, the blogs and the webpages we set up to talk about our loves and hates, what we think from day to day. We have no axe to grind with our club, we support and love it. We may have a few things to nitpick over, we may even get emotional sometimes and that emotion may blur the edges between impartial flowing of informations to our readers and what really happened. But that's what the world is like now, people who read these missives want emotion, want clarity through that emotion, and they want to know that we are as committed to the club as the club is to us….I hope.

I've waxed about football being a global thing now, international, dynamic and fresh but I think that having a local newspaper define the narratives coming out of the club and presenting it to us behind paywalls or on dirty newsprint isn't dynamic and isn't global. It's old hat, it's fat bastards with bellies bursting through their food stained shirts with a fag in their mouth ash falling on their notebooks as they try to mangle the half baked post match thoughts into something their readers will understand. It's old shit, it's Phil Plywood Sports Journalism and it's dying a sure death thank God and alas that death is a slow painful one as we see when we finger another clickbait story purely to drive advertising revenue..

But I want to know what music Conor Coady listens to, I want to know what Nuno thinks about aliens, I want to know what Jeff Shi thinks about old British cars, I want to know what Bonatinis favourite films are, I want to know how much they pay for a haircut, what their favourite computer game is, why they get annoyed, what they love to eat, drink, what they laugh about. You see that information is the most important, it's where we fill in the gaps between the blank dull information we are spoon fed.

But we need access to the main people. When I say 'we' I mean the dickheads like me that pummel away at a laptop keyboard for a few hours after a match trying to mangle thoughts into a viable read. I want to talk to Nuno. I want to talk to Jeff Shi. I want to present their thoughts to my readers in a way that is (sometimes) honest and seen through the madness of gold and black tinted glasses. I want to tell them about us as we know about them. I want to get the whole fan-club nexus on to some sort of coherent level. I don't want the local press to be the filter between us and them. I dunno, perhaps it will never happen and the whole carousel will be tinkling around and around with the pretty lights and the jangly organ music while the members of the press cavort with players and owners alike while we stand there at the edge of darkness holding our overpriced candyfloss, but I hope not.

The journey back from Molineux last night was a circular and twisted one. Talking about the match with friends as we walked back we were animated and loud. We didn't have any plans at all where we should end up. We were concussed by what we had just seen. It was Post Traumatic Nuno Disorder. When you have watched football so beautiful and so refined it was a shock to the system, it makes your hands shake, heart swell, sweat to break out on your back, hope, love. It was a velvet club of beauty that constantly bopped us over the head as another pass from Saiss incised a feeling through our stand. Were we annihilated by it? I was. At times I was holding my breath a little as the whole team moves as one. Intent and passion was etched on that pitch with a theology not a message from Nuno himself. It was a display of such lovely football I was emotional.

This morning I was weeping at a video of Nuno hugging Captain Coady. Emotional, warm, ripped apart by love. I had to get out of the stand as quick as I could last night because I knew there was going to be some element of emotion I couldn't hold in. I wanted to grab people and ask 'what was that I just watched?'. Yes, I wanted to weep in happiness and joy. I wanted to run on the pitch and ask questions as now the whole momentum we have has taken on metaphysical properties. It is starting to seem like this fairytale has sprung to life in front of us as we watch. It grabs your heart and fills it with love. Are we not entertained? It is more than entertainment now. It is possibly a religious awakening. For we all need that figure that will galvanise and provoke such feelings.

Heresy? The Crazy Train is pulling up at another station on the journey now. That place where 'they' live. The natural order of things is about to be upset in great ways. We have a leader in Nuno and he has come down from the mountain to his people as Moses did. He is holding tablets of stone that have commandments carved on them by the Gods. Solidity, meaning, a message of sorts that say to the team in front of us commitment, love, solidarity, effort, strength words that I can sit and type all day as I heap platitudes on the head of our holy man.

Does he say anything? Does Nuno open his mouth and let fall a host of similar words that bounce back and forth between media platforms? No he doesn't. The overtures from Everton are greeted with a simple emoji. A little cartoon head of a Wolf. and the dogmas of English Championship football burn on the horizon as this simple message falls among his people. Did we understand? Head and heart for sure we understood. We understand this because we know he is us and we are him. That love we have is envied by other teams, the Warnocks and the Holloways will never know such love and they twist and turn in the flames of their unimportance.

Did we need a leader like him? Of course we did. Watch him stalk the touchline. Animated at times and at others he stands with his arms crossed like Napoleon watching his troops fight the battles he himself has dictated for them. Behind them his coaching staff cajole, inspire and whisper in his ear about events that are judged in seconds and minutes, a reply given, the twist of a tactic and the tweak of a position. Fulham have fallen under the strength of 'idea' and of 'love'. And does not love conquer all?

Have Fulham in their transparent shift football understood it? No. All they have is the slur of a few empty seats. An insult so bereft of quality and creativity it makes me sad. Is this all you have? You fat arses who watch us with envious greedy eyes, your bitter lives laid bare in front of the joy of our victory. Lower than rats you are who heap your missives about the nuts and bolts of football and you lack the heart to understand what we watch, you lack empathy and your grey faces will stutter as you speak, your lives are defunct in front of this movement, this beauty. I check my pocket for my DaySaver bus ticket. I shiver a little. I look at the fella next to me and we shared that look. We have stood in the same spot for years and walked out in tears and now? We are shell shocked by this display of football and I grab his arm and just say 'what'.

Fulham, that strange club filled with blankness that crept through and stained their football. Did they have an answer to this display? I stood in front of a Jackson Pollock painting when I was about 16 years old, Birmingham art gallery. I looked at that painting for hours just stood there trying to work out just what it was about. Those swirling lines of colour, the drips and splashes in seemingly random places. I listened to people that came and went through the morning I was there saying things like 'my dog could do better than that' and all the variations on that statement.

It was simply ignorance. I see this morning that there are bitter comments like that from other teams, broadcasters and pundits on the interwebs. I see their ignorance held forth for all to see and I am not sad about it. Yes the Nuno Revolution and the Heresy of his approach is strange to them. It's strange because they too love Nuno but they do not love us. They wonder why he is here, in Wolverhampton, they see Fosun and wonder 'why not our club?'. Thus the bitterness falls in 140 characters, it drips across Facewank, in text messages, in articles and in post match discussions.

Are they bitter and twisted? Of course they are. That is good. Millwall always harp on about how nobody likes them but we too should have a song about how we are not disliked but we are hated. We are hated by the tight shirts in satellite broadcast media. We are hated by our local media, we are hated by everybody because of our heresy. As Neves split the midfield with another pass, as Neves tries to score from his own half we see those tenets inspire our team. We see the power of the universe flow through the ideas Nuno has given us. He has welded his team together with common purpose. Willy Boly scoops another ball from the foot of a Fulham player and we attack again. Every footfall from our team is a thunder that echoes through the streets around the ground. It echoes through the Bus stop post mortems, through the spangly lights on rain splattered windscreens in traffic, in the shuffling feet waiting to get served at the bar in a pub in town. It reverberates because we understand fully what has happened here at our club. It is a sound we have not heard for many years..

We are Heretics every one of us. We are going to crash the party with a tinkle of a CS gas canister through a pub doorway and the shouts of our allegiance. You see we haven't been invited to the party. They other guests have been there for a long time and are comfortable in their appreciation of themselves and the higher orders of the football league and their sycophants are narcissistic and corrupt. They will fail to bar the door against us. Us, the people with the funny accents, who are a bit scruffy at times, we haven't really enjoyed the same universities or moved in the same circles. Sometimes rain leaks through our shoes and we lose things in the torn linings of our pockets. Simple coins are kept safe within our pockets and any amount of money we do have is sorted in a pint here and a pint there, a ticket for this and the bus fare for that.

It's a movement and a momentum they will never understand as we creep further and further into their circles. Of course the negative views on our club will get more frequent and the missives will stain the media with their bitterness. But we are allowed I think, to look at ourselves, especially after that display last night and say 'we are coming, we have a message'.

The Pollock painting. I stood there for hours as folk moved backwards and forwards glancing upon it. It was the same as standing on the Southbank. I have stood there for years and years. Like those whose ignorance slathered the hardwood floor of the art gallery I too sometimes shook my head and didn't understand our football. I didn't understand our leadership as we lost a game to Burton, Bristol, Rotherham, these teams that should have felt a fear from us but never did. The Pollock painting was a confusing swirl of madness but you see. I stood and looked at that time, then I stood back and looked and that confusing swirl of paint suddenly came alive and I saw there was a message in that painting and it was a moment of intense understanding. There in every swirl was the hand of it's maker.

The personality of Pollock was made real and concrete in the ethereal madness screwed to that wall in Birmingham. The colour was just that, and the line here and there, the splashes were true things that indeed told a message. Nuno himself has splashed his personality upon the canvas of Molineux and it is only us that truly understand what he is saying. It's only us that 'know'. The dark cobalt blue of Doherty splitting the canvas into segments, the magenta of Neves, here and there in vivid broad gashes, the scarlet of Jota dripped here and there, the background greys, blacks, silver and gold of Coady/Boly/Douglas, the sunshine yellow of Bonatini a glaring line here and there, a drop and a splash again of Cavaleiro in sanguine umber. All taken to the edges of the canvas by the artist himself, Nuno.

'They' who are 'them', the back biters and the back slappers will never understand the art and the love. They have led bitter twisted lives in the glare of finances and broadcast money. They will never understand what happens at Molineux and what it means to us waiting in bus stops counting out bus fare, seeing if you have enough for a bag of chips. But they will never know walking through the front door of your house with a happiness you never thought you would experience again. Seeing your family watching the TV or chilling out in the front room. Seeing how happy you are and the smell of a bag of hot chips, salt and vinegar, which is of course just how we like it. And they will ask 'How did they get on?' and we will smile and stuff a hot chip in our mouths as we talk about it, but no words will describe what we have and sometimes all we need is a simple emoji to explain it all.

Of course it's all getting a little frazzled now. We are only a few months into the season and already I'm starting to lose it. One minute I'm laughing and the next I'm like a worried Nan. That my friends is what football is to us. I know the whole jingly jangly fangled flashy graphics bollocks on TV and the internet is all well and good. But this is sitting in the garden stuff, looking through old programmes in the attic and feeling a bit sad. Next minute you are jumping up and down while the dog looks at you funny. You are singing songs about Portuguese fellas you don't really know. You are excited about the next match.

Now the Winter is starting to get its fingers under your shirt. Coldness creeping in. The light that has shone over us on this late Summer is going. Things are looking a little drab and dark. Our hearts echo this.

I have been thinking about our 'Sweeper' Conor Coady a lot this week. He amazes me. I am proud of him. Do we not love him? I do I'm afraid…love a funny word really. I love my dogs, I love getting on my bike but how do I equate 'loving a player'? I think it's football love. He's a fantastic Captain of our team, he is a rock in defence, a constant 'face' in the team and I am much happier when he is there and I scan the pre-game blurbs for his name on the team sheet. Thing is dear readers…

When I was in Wales this Summer I would park the bike up on a mountain somewhere and think about the season to come. There were names mentioned and they were signed, there was excitement and madness. But I would always think of what Conor Coady would do this season. I was always thinking how he would do among this influx of delicious footballing dudeness. I wasn't afraid he would get dropped of course, well, a little bit. But I did have a hope that he would excel at moving among these sexy players and he would indeed find himself lining up with them on the first game of the season and know deep within his heart that he had a right to be there and in his humility never think he would end up a giant among them.

I mean the whole idea of this book was initially ten thousand words I wrote about Coady during last Summer. Don't ask me why, I don't know. I just felt the need to pontificate on his football for a few hours and then when I did look up from the keyboard the day had turned into night and my back ached. Where would I put these words for others to see? I'll write some things, maybe for a few friends, and here it is in all it's grotty glory, this book. It's Coadys fault, all of it, blame him.

Nuno must have played a significant role in the process of Coady-development since he came to Compton, maybe in the organisation of his training and maybe even the guarantee of enjoying the total experience the player gained during the process of moving from the static un-dynamic situations he found himself under other coaches. The development of Conor is a whole process of maybe constant renewal of one's experience in the team I suppose. Probably the idea of his interaction between the football he plays and objective of learning must have been emphasised on some level or another by Nuno. But I suspect that Conor looked at Nuno on that first day and he knew deep within his heart that here was a man he could work and develop with. Maybe Nuno looked at the DVDs of the games before he arrived and looked at Coady and thought here is a base I can build upon

We played Preston and there was Coady easing an attack away from Ruddy and all the time he was shouting to his comrades to move into dangerous spaces, shut down this player, shut down that one. Arms going ten to the dozen, lunacy, intent and desire to win. You could see everybody else doing exactly what he wanted. I'll tell you why. It's all in the way he speaks and processes information. He talks fast and thinks fast, more importantly too, he can physically drive himself into spaces and incidents while he is processing the information he sees in front of him. He doesn't have to think about what his body is doing. He just does it. That is the mark of a great footballer. Eye to brain to the physical, a process for him that takes a split second.

Of course as I'm picking a decent couple of Avocados in Aldi these thoughts about Coady drift through my mind. Conor isn't even ripe yet. That head of his will still be developing into the total footballer he is about to become (if Nuno stops slapping it). I can't for the life of me think why he was moved on by other clubs he had been with. I mean I'm a bit jealous to see he has flirted with them, had his photo took in their shirts etc. I regard him as ours pretty much. I'm possessive about it. But he was stuck in a defensive midfield role. A stopper. What a strange choice. What did other Coaches think of him to put him there? I am sure that when he came here I would have said stick him in the back four. I was ignorant and lacked the skills to see what a player he is. Tall, rangy, typical back four player. I could punch myself in the balls for being so stupid.

But then we had a back four. That Stoic typical English approach to building an impenetrable wall against attack. The back four was always an anathema to me.

It just reeked of bad building work, the mortar oozing out between the bricks. It was always about tackling and snotting, Gary Mastic Sunday football bollocks. Of course Conor would have curled up and dried out in a back four.

I mean he pretty much curled up when he played in midfield for us. I don't think it was the fact he was playing midfield that took the glow off his game but the fact that we were playing with a midfield that lacked any guile and skill, any real idea of how a midfield should play. You could tell in many games he played there that that lack of inspirational football must have played on his mind a little, made him not want to understand it. Of course he played there with a 100% dedication regardless of the dullness of it. He wasn't being driven to consume the role he was given and I think the space was mentally confined and narrow. The role was part understudy and part patching the holes we had in previous seasons.

The back three espoused by Nuno has given Conor a role he can fill out. Colour in the edges and sit back, comfortable that he does have space to define his own ideas and creativity. He can play the ball out of the danger area with skill he picked up from untangling attacks, grabbing the ball back when he played midfield. But as well as that the back three gives him an intellectual challenge too. It's the area where he can operate his formidable mind into defusing attacks, rapidly appraising opposition players so that he pretty much knows what to expect from the tactics employed by many of the Championship teams we will face this season. Watching him play gives me a pleasure that I haven't felt for a long time watching a particular player at Wolves. But why pleasure?

For one he represents the old order even if he has only been here a short time. He definitely represents the flow or continuation from past teams over the past two years into this all singing all dancing group of players we have in the squad now. But more importantly for me, he has showed that progression and ability to transcend the politics and changing opinions of past Coaches at Wolves for sure. He has never let his head drop in any game I have watched him. Even in the defeats we have suffered this season he was directing and cajoling his team mates until the final whistle. I stood on the Southbank a few times and all I could hear was his voice echoing off the steel shuttering at the sides and the back. I could feel my fears evaporate, I could feel myself believing we could get something out of the game through him. Is he not the filter between the team and us? I think he is. The lubricant between the lofty ideals and screaming pistons of Nunoism and the crankcase sweat and snot of the crowd. The thing that keeps the whole Wolves machine turning.

At Liverpool last season he basically won us the game. Now I'm not arguing with anybody at this point in this post. I'm not listening to you. Conor won us that game and I think discovered within himself a rich vein of footballing ability I don't think he knew he had, or he was unaware of it. Colossal in defence? I would say so. He negated attacks with aplomb, dicing the ball up in the midst of Liverpool attacks. Same at Manchester this season. He faced the most formidable team in Europe at the moment. He made them look negated and blank. He looked as if he belonged there. He looked as if he had always played against such teams.

May we say he has a 'hunger to improve'? I think that's like saying the Titanic got sunk by some frozen water. I think the whole process of Conor becoming probably one of the greatest players to pull on a Wolves shirt is far more complicated and metaphysical than that. I think that Conor needed the intellectual hunger to become one of our best players and I think Nuno provided that arena for the footballing brain of Coady to thrive. The environment is more important than useless words and platitudes, whiteboards and rants. I suspect the holistic environment Nuno has placed at Compton has allowed players like Doherty and Coady to thrive. But I think Conor has responded to this environment a lot better than others and it's going back to the whole idea that Coady is the consummate footballing intellectual. As much as I can wax lyrical at the madmen of a team galvanising the play on the pitch I also think that this intellectual and academic basis of Coady also has a place within that particular meme.

What will we see in the future for him? He will grow into his role in that back three, I can see it, feel it and taste it. Every game he has he stores that game away in his head and uses it as an operating system for his game and every time he plays he is becoming a stronger and more intelligent player, you can see it. Positions and blocking, moving the ball from defence to midfield. The attacking ethos we have instilled in our team has given Coady the tools to base his game on the very ideas and memes that constitute a 'whole' footballer. As Captain too (of Wolves) he finds himself in a position where he can spread out and disseminate his own philosophy on how a footballer grows and develops aided and abetted by possibly one of the greatest coaches we have seen at the Wolves in Nuno. I would be inclined to give Conor the Captaincy of our team right now, officially. That's not denigrating Danny Batth at all. But I think Conor espouses the new groove within the team now and if we are building for the future we have to not only keep hold of the players we have developed but give them the intellectual framework and responsibilities they need to be that whole footballer to be that solid but effervescent personality we need to progress. I suspect handing him the Captains armband will do that. I think Coady is the leader we have craved for a long time and I think also he will be an integral part of this team in many years to come.

The greatest thing about writing about your views is that they are exactly that. My views. But my view on Coady is made from watching him play when more exciting things were happening elsewhere. I know a team is based on it's core strength and that strength is deep and 'inside'. Conor Coady is the missing piece of the jigsaw for us. I believe that with all my heart and this piece should be seen in that light. I love watching Coady play. I loved watching him play since the first time he pulled on a Wolves shirt and I'm sorry but I wont listen to anything negative said about him after people read this. I'm not going to engage in debate about it simply because when he plays I can feel it in my heart and it has become a metaphysical thing. It may be relative and subjective but I don't really care to be honest. Am I skilled at such lofty announcements? Well I predictcd thc Manchester City game to be a draw. I should be able to make money out of betting on games really but no. Coady will become one of the greatest players ever to pull on a Wolves shirt, trust me. I think about Coady on the journey down to Reading. I don't like their town.

Reading FC. Their Coach Jaap Stam eh? He says he can beat us and he's not scared. He waxes lyrical to the press about it with that Stam Steeze where his forehead wrinkles up like a Primark shirt after one wash. It's an internal dialogue where he's talking to himself really. Forget about our team Jaap. Forget about the lubrications and the magical football we play. What are your ideas? What is your philosophy? What is the platform for these ideas you have when really the idea is just a hypothesis isn't it? It's tilting at windmills like a bald headed Don Quixote hoping your words will galvanise your team into some viable opposition. You may even claw a win out of today but the question still remains. Are your ideas stronger than Nunos? I'm mixing sand and cement, thinking about the game to come and it's cold and making my back ache. I know Frazzle Dave is watching me from his kitchen window, watching me lump slabs around.

Welcome to Nunoland! Nunoland, the magical adventure kingdom where you will vomit into your lap after riding the 'Neves of Terror' the 'Jota-Train' and the 'Mean Bonatini'. Clutching your candy floss as you pass the 'Carnival of Coady' your forehead will wrinkle again and your ideas will be defunct as you power up 'The Edwards' maybe or the Bod for a final swansong against this unstoppable power and fairy dust from Nuno's Wizard cloak. Jaap Stam stops in front of a Carnival mirror and laughs at his misshapen face and head...but oh it's a real mirror.

Nuno entices you further into the maze of attractions with a wave of his hand and his top hat set at a jaunty angle. Come on in Mr Stam, and Jaap bobbles his eyes and the carnival lights reflect off his smooth head, the cards in Nunos hand skitter and tumble from hand to hand as he entices him to make a bet. The cards slip between his fingers twisting and turning, fast, so fast it's hard to see where the three of Points is...Come on Jaap lay your money down. Nunos voice is hypnotic and gentle, rhythmic and sensuous...Find the goal, it's easy. Stam picks a card and Nuno smiles and flips it over. The Joker that seems to have Dave Edwards face…. And Nuno smiles and puts the three points from Jaap into one of his many magical pockets. Try again? In the second half we were under almost constant attack and I can't bear witness to much of it as I was crouched under the seat practically. Ruddy hoofs a ball up field, it's collected by Reading and they ping two three shots at the Wolves goal and it looks like the whole script is about to be rewritten. It's sipping that eighth pint and things are curly and unsteady. Sip and hold on.

'Dave Edwards is part of the family regardless of what you think'

Family get togethers and weddings are always weird. The smelly Aunties, the Uncles who used to touch you, the cousins 'he's been to prison for nicking cable off the railway', you're on your best behaviour, turning your nose up at the crap buffet that you devour after three pints listening to Uncle Combover talk about Hank Marvin and the Shadows at Willenhall baths in 1962.

This match is like that. Dave Edwards, Uncle Dave eh? He will be polishing his angst in the mirror at the way we shifted him on. Squirting himself with 50 year old aftershave, Old Spice probably or Brut. Putting his shoes on top of the gas fire to loosen up as they have been crushed at the bottom of the wardrobe since the last family get together and now look like a deep sea fish. Wearing a suit that wouldn't be out of place on Joe Pesci in Goodfellas. You know that by the time the DJ plays 'I am the Resurrection' Dave will be white man drunk dancing in the middle of the dance floor, Dave swishes and knocks a drink out of somebodies hand, Dave knocks over a little kid and doesn't even notice as it's that bass bit in the song.

'Dum dum dumma dum dum dum dum dagga dat dat da dagga dat'

Stone Roses eh? Uncle Combover slips over in the pool of alcohol that Dave spilled and now stares at the pretty disco lights on the community centre ceiling, he thinks he's had a heart attack but it's the dodgy pork pie, always the dodgy pork pie. I am the Resurrection and I am the light.

'We treated him disgracefully. He's a Welsh International for fucks sake'

An industrial estate town, a cultural abstract, a place of potholes and wife swapping parties, holidaying at Center Parc. We left Dave and Bod there in Reading and I feel a little bad about it. I feel bad about the pre match arguments that started about Dave. He still has an effect on some peoples hearts. An old girlfriend thing. We are going to get it on with him again. Not love but fumbly touching and memories of that time you both went crazy. When one of those errant aimless runs he did made the ball bounce off his head or foot while he was in the box and it just went in. That one goal that Bod scored. Is this not love? No, I can't love them any more, as soon as they walk out the door at

Molineux they are gone, unless they did heroic things of course. Which they didn't really, not that I remember.

Oh Dave, your football was as inspiring as a book about potholes really. It reflects beautifully the diaspora of Reading. Dave is an office party fuck in the photocopier room with Denise Purplefringe from Procurement, slightly drunk with cheap wine, hands clawing wins here and there, and probably a bit of a clap after. The crumbs of a mince pie would be suck on the hairs on her upper lip as you groped your way to that five seconds of bliss and the sadness of paper towels, Dave wheeling away from a goal he scored arms outstretched…'We've got Dave Edwards! Super Dave Edwards! I just don't… want… to….. understand…'. The glass on top of the photocopier is making cracking noises as you pound away to that knee trembling festive fuck and contemplate the next twelve months of abject eye avoiding post Xmas office fuck angst. And crikey it was a fuck and a half during some points in the second half as Reading had pop after pop at our goal until at times it felt like Wolves were Denise perched on top of the photocopier getting ball after ball slammed towards us only for Boly or Coady to get a face or a foot in.

Now of course we are having a fling with that sexy Portuguese thing from Marketing, flouncing around with her sexy football, you don't know what she sees in you, she's beautiful and fit, she's making all the right noises at you, touching your hair (or bald head) telling you how much she adores you in that lubricative Mediterranean lilt, her breath smells of lemons and saffron, sunset dinners, arse like a peach…..but Denise is giving you the evils from across the office. Dave and Bod will be wearing low cut tops, tottering on heels, shouting about how many times they go to PureGym so you can hear.

Dave and Bod still love us. Probably waiting for that lil Portuguese slut to wander off not interested any more so she can say 'I told you so' if you hadn't blocked her on social media. Today will be that. I drop a slab into position and kick it up a few millimetres, stand back with my hands on me back feeling those scars ache in the cold. At Reading I watch the net bulge as Cavaleiro scores. It seems like normal service. But for a moment that cold drizzle that's falling from the sky is leaching the colour from it all, at least our play still has some brightness kind of faded and sun worn maybe. Their right back is emotionless and uninspiring, he looks like he doesn't give a shit, he lacks anything. Horace tells me Lambert loved him and tried to buy him. Blank Face. Typical.

Of course the Santa Maria football we play now is an anathema to Dave and Lambertino. Dave plays for Reading now and that's pure Denise really. Just about getting the impetus to fly into the stratosphere of Premiership football and Reading falling over on those heels at the door of the swanky nightclub, her boob has fallen out and a heel has broken off those shoes. People are laughing. Reading. What is a Reading? What is this slab? It weighs half a ton and it's a struggle as I can't grip it properly as my hands are cold. Denise Purplefringe…I could just put my hands up your jumper for a warm…Just like I will clap Dave really. It's something to do with your hands as you avoid his eyes when he runs onto the pitch. His first 'pass' rattles across the pitch for 40 yards and goes out of play. For half an hour I don't realise he is on the pitch.

Now returned from international duties some of our players will be that crowd that giggles at Denise with her tit out on the pavement. I mean Reading can play some attractive football sometimes but you just know the addition of 'Dave' and 'Bod' shows a lack of imagination and idea. But also as grey and bland as Reading is I'm sure that they will have some elements of their game, some obtuse idea of how to knock a ball around. Of course they will probably score a goal too.

I wouldn't be surprised if Frazzly Dave has put a bet on for Dave to score because Frazzly Dave loves Dave Edwards. I'm going to get £20 for laying these slabs in Frazzles garden so I could buy a beer at Reading. Dave was out in the garden most of the time avoiding his missus who has this Hyacinth Bouquet thing going on. Talking to the scum laying slabs eh? But Dave loves Dave and he wants to talk about him. Dave wears his work polo shirt on his days off. Dave bets on football. Dave has a racing bike worth 8 thousand quid he never rides. Dave owns his own printing company. Dave loves that Frazzle thing, Dave drives a BMW, his missus has a £400 hair-do and a 58p body. He eats bacon corn snacks in little bacon-y strips, little packets he scrunches in his mouth and spits the crumbs out as he talks. About Dave. Dave has a Dave Edwards shirt framed up on the wall and a little spotlight illuminating it.

'After what he did for us I think it's a disgrace we let him go, I mean yeah Nuno is doing a thing but blah blah Dave blah Wales, against Leeds blah Wales international, blah Dave, Dave Blah Dave….'

I nearly crush my finger dropping a slab down but Frazzly Dave doesn't notice that I really want to drop a slab on his head and I close my eyes as I mallet it level and Daves head is under that Mallet turning to a mush of brain and half chewed corn snack and I wish Bod and Dave were under it too. Especially if they score today. Half of Molineux is at the 'Madge' or the 'MadStad' and the surroundings are pockets of 'Ayits' and 'Ars' and 'Yeows' which sound like exotic Amazonian birdlife but are really 'Yes it is' and 'Yes' and 'You'. The feeling is stressful to me, the day is abstract, the industrial thing is thick and heavy. The Police are grumpy and leathery, the sky looks like Yodas ball sack. It's like your head being wrapped in clingfilm.

'We never understood the skill Dave has, you fuckers in the Southbank only watch one end, I see it all in the Billy Wright'

We sing because that's what we do. It's proper English folk music this is. The denigration of rivals and neighbours in song form is the purest expression of Englishness in the world. Forget Royalty and Westminster, democracy and Empire. It's all about how many fingers 'they' have. That the place where they live is a shithole. That the team that represents them are shit. There's a lot of 'shit' in these songs. That's the way it should be.

'We've never had a baggie in our seat'

The match? Well. it was 'that' kind of a match surely. This segment reflects the game perfectly. Meandering and curly with a chunk of those tactics here and there. Reading did well to get that many shots on out goal. Ruddy, immense. Doherty solid and incisive again. But I can't write about how we did this and that on the pitch when the weight of greyness that surrounded us on the way in to the stadium, it's a tragedy for sure. An endless Bentley Bridge shopping dystopia. Signs, signs everywhere a sign fucking up the scenery wasting my mind. Landscape affects the football maybe

But it was a match. I'm delirious. Yin and Yang ball surely but here and there it was a cosmic experience only countered by the wastelands that surround us on the way out of the area. What is this dystopic miasma of corrugated steel and plastic crap we have filled this country up with? A disgrace. Another three points Nuno my sweetheart. Another step up that lofty ladder to Moneyville and everything is crispy and Christmassy. A skip up the kerb outside. A heart laugh at something Horace has moaned about. Another beautiful day in Nunoland. I'm holding a load of brightly coloured balloons that all have Nuno's face on them. Could Reading have won? Maybe a few years ago this match would have been them equalising and then them scoring the winner in the last minute, their jubilant support raining abuse upon our heads….but now? This victory, as scrappy at times as it was shows us that a momentum exists now. The wins and the beautiful football we have played so far has added a weight to our intentions and that weight is now pushing games like this, that we would have lost a few years ago to a victorious conclusion. Momentum of the idea I suppose. This momentum is important in games like this when the opposition decide to stand up and be counted. They just get rolled over. No matter how brave and big they are the momentum of the Wolves is now too great. The ideas are too vast for simple tactical changes to have an effect.

We listened to Tony Pulis and enraged Albion fans on the radio on the way back to Wolverhampton and Horace kept laughing at their angry semi incoherent rants. I laughed too as we walk and move with that momentum we must also look down the road at the Birmingham clubs like West Brom/Villa/Birmingham City who have either no momentum [Villa and City] or backward momentum like West Brom. We're going to pass them aren't we? Waving at their glum faces as they stand with their faces pressed up the windows of the train to Nowhere. Looking at the pure horror of the environment around Reading I'm secure in the knowledge that despite the monochrome sadness of the place we have dug deep indeed to react and finish the match with three points and that's pure belief in a system as well as that momentum. The team need a medal for that. Onwards and upwards. I'm sure Winter is starting, I feel the titanium plates in my elbow singing softly. The damp and the rain.

It was a storm of sorts I think. The wind whipped around and coat choices were by the by really as those fingers peeled through the layers and it was Leeds. Memories of the Northbank whenever we play them. It was my first game back in 1972 when things were just becoming colour and we were leaving those black and white days behind. It was a spectacle then of course. A match was more than just a match in those days. It was indeed a spectacle, a dose of pure theatre on a Saturday afternoon.

Loads of them have come tonight and the Steve Bull is filled with 1.75 Million Leeds fans who are oddly quiet…and at the end of this match will be quieter still. Bereft indeed. The abyss of their hate filled with my love for Wolves. The Savillian dogmas burn and flutter in the flames of Nunoism. They will return to that godforsaken wasteland of Yorkshire with this new covenant blaring within their ears and making their hearts heavy.

Things now are becoming clear at Molineux and the tides and sand are shifting and are still dangerous. Reading last week showed that Stam in all his Voldemort creepiness could still change and tweak a tactic here and there to try and throw a spanner into the cogs of the Nuno Machine. What tactical nous it was well I can't tell you really. I just know all of a sudden they were pressing a lot. Getting chances. Ruddy diving around, Coady getting his vocal on, Boly being the unstoppable force and immovable object in one. Was I entertained? No not really. It's November. We would have (in another pre Nuno world) have lost that game for sure. A curling last minute free kick into the net. The roar of the home crowd and we would have run out of ideas fast. Ordinarily of course, in the past. It's not entertainment no. We are the story and the characters, the plot lines and the fables. We are tangled and wrapped in the whole Nuno machine.

Nuno utilised the tools at his disposal surely, and he was ruthless with it too. At Reading I watched as the ideas were unleashed in many ways. The input Nuno had in retaining shape and intent when Reading changed tack a few minutes into the game was a Master stroke. I was quite happy to hail the Nuno wizardry in full pelt again but it was much more than magic. It was a switch and a response made by the team that impressed me the most. In between swearing at an upside down head Reading fan yards away from me, they had angst, it was palpable and real. Every grimace and abusive comment from one of 'them' made me laugh all the louder.

Walking up to Molineux from the Blue brick pub these thoughts occupied my mind. There's a lot of Leeds fans here, at least one and a half million of them thronging the streets around the ground. I've never seen so much shit in one place. A thronging torrent of Yorkshires finest shit. I'm not apologetic about how much i don't like Leeds. Not at all. They are resurgent tonight. A few wins maybe. Their intent as shiny as their angst I suppose. But Nuno? What are your thoughts?

We are starting to look like a total unit. The squad looks like a well oiled machine in longer and longer segments during a match. At the start of the season of course, we had bursts and glimpses of the whole glorious football. Now nearly half way through the season there is more control over games and that control can stretch to ten or fifteen minutes at a time before the opposition can react. Often that reaction is total offence. Many teams we have played this season have not been bad teams. They have reacted fast and with sure fire intent as soon as they have sensed a moment of inaction from our team. We have also had reactions to this. At Reading we had a straight line of five men defending John Ruddy from an attack. Coady at the centre is growing into his role the more games he has. Boly was not just an immense presence but has a sixth sense about sudden movement. His eye for this movement is clinical, the interface between what he sees and how he moves is slick and efficient. The sense of ease in which he switches his weight from foot to foot. Springing away on his left so his right is fast to the loose ball or a clearance. I'm happy to see Douglas and Doherty within the whole backline acting just as efficiently. I don't remember us having a defensive unit like this for a long time. It's poetry at times watching them all move as one. Spooky. I wonder what strange magic Nuno and his staff had to evoke for this.

The back room staff. Dodging this awful traffic. Who are these men that wander around in the background? I'm not skilled enough to know who they are. The names unfamiliar and strange. But all highly motivated one thousand yard stares. Men you know are not going to be swayed by bullshit and excuse. I suppose the metaphysical essence of Nuno has to be balanced by the stoic empirical dogma of the bleep test and the heuristics of performance. Yin and Yang maybe.

But Helder twisting and turning after his injury. He seems like a greater presence to me, a more complete player. The injury has been negated by the back room medical staff. Can we even call them by that 'anachronistic' term any more. It smacks of black and white snotball. Surely with the global outlook we now employ as a club we may say something else? Maybe 'Technical Support' I don't know. But I do see with my eyes that they have done a job on Helder. We may contrast this idea with what may have happened under the previous staff. Helder would be a cripple probably. The whole atmosphere within the club has had a holistic effect on the injury maybe…

Cavaleiro turns shoots on the edge of the box. There is none of that meat and two veg movement here. It's a saffron tinged delight of a turn. Style and ease. It's football as art really and why not? Creativity is a driving force in any artists and that's why football will always be the greatest team sport in the world, we can create beauty and innocence through a twist of a Cavaleiro hip. Unload the vermilion joy of a well toe bunted ball into the net. The Douglas free kick. What is a Douglas? Who is he? Not an understudy for sure, to anybody. That international movement he has gleaned from his travels has done him good, extended his vision and provoked artistry like that free kick. I don't see any difference between that goal and Fred Astaire gliding across a highly polished floor with a beautiful woman in a posh frock being thrown around while those twinkle toes do their thing. But twinkle toes is surely a Jota/Neves meme. The 'Twinkle Toe' brothers for sure.

Momentum…it's become relentless now. In seasons past teams like Reading and Leeds would have steamrollered us with a nicked goal or some viable movement of the ball. Now they are crushed. You could see with ten minutes to go last night two Leeds players sitting down on the pitch. Fucked. Bereft. There was noting they could do except be a bystander to a flow so virile and strong it hurts to even think you can halt the flow of it. It was easy and steezy, all pleasey and feely. Boop, pass to Doherty, beep pass to Neves who collects, bonk, to Jota, boop to Neves again, Bonatini leaps, boop to Jota again, Cavaleiro collects, turns, shoots. Go again, 'second verse, same as the first verse' The Ramones sang.

But what is this constant struggle to win points and claw your way through the season? At first it was all that occupied my mind, especially at the start of the season and now that drudgery and madness is a distant memory nearly and we are now at the cusp of belief. Watching us slide and cajole that spherical object into the art it actually is was always the key I think. The nuts and bolts of this win against Leeds is empirically just another three points and we concrete our intentions fully into the pitch. Nuno pronounced that its the 'How, the where and the when' and when he speaks we all listen for at the end of the day he is our coach too, he galvanises us, the crowd, the fans and it's OK for now to describe 'the supporters' the same way as you describe 'the team' and we can meld and amalgamate the dynamics of both team and fans as one. In the future we will look upon these times as the very best, when we all gather together with the same voice and love perhaps.

How? Assemble a squad of players who have the capacity to unleash their ideas on the pitch. Utilise the skills they have in abundance and channel those skills into instant reaction. Provoke ideas and artistic divine football. Instil your ideas on the pitch with aplomb and beauty, planning and an idea of its conclusion. Gather the support you have into an unstoppable force, make the whole club an idea.

Where? Here at Molineux and 'there' in the idea-less dysfunctional wastes of other grounds and other places. We gather every time we play and we sing the Nuno-esque ballads. The importance of the ethos of Molineux has been gathered into the arms of the Fosun-Nuno nexus. We take Molineux with us everywhere we go. The ghosts hover at our elbows and sing with us in those strange foreign pitches. We hold the ideas firmly within our hearts everywhere we go.

When? Now of course. We have suffered enough over the past few decades when the promises and skills of those who would hold control over our club fall to the ground and are mashed in the detritus of plastic beer bottles and slippy floors. Now is the time when the planets have aligned and it has become our time and our moment. We stand, all of us at the cusp of greatness and this moment should be treasured and kept safe from the platitudes of those who would wish us nothing but disaster.

I have another bump on my head from Dannys elbow, I fell over at one point in the match. My glasses are hanging on by one arm. My Adidas have a big muddy footprint on them. I'm standing in Queens square as people sing and stagger past me and the rain has knocked off and my coat is damp and the Xmas lights are shining and magical. I'm looking up at Prince Albert on his great bronze nag and for a moment as the wind moves the lights strung across the street I see a shadow move across Alberts face but it's not Albert for a precious second, it's Nuno and he is proud, gallant, and resolute and that sword is his idea and his legacy for this town. Onwards as ever and who knows what the future may hold and for once I don't care what the future holds because right now I feel that pride in the place where I live and every foot step I take is light and free. 'How, where and when' Nuno has said, and we listen to every word he says. Fuck the future, the time and the beauty is now.

I don't like it when people say they like my writings. You see I'm not a writer really. I don't understand how to do it. I'm self taught in the way that I can see if some words don't fit and some do. I like the nice words but sometimes they think it's me and it's not at all correct. What is any of this shit without all of us? The faces in the stories are ours in all their madness. So yeah…fuck Bolton. What even is a Bolton? We are playing them today and I'm bereft of feeling about it. Positive feeling anyway.

I know 'what' it is as my Dad was born there and in all his sins and misdeeds the two things I most admire him for, well the only two things I admire him for are that he moved away from Bolton at a young age and the other he decided to support ManUFuckingnited. Jesus Christ what a godforsaken place Bolton is. That Godforsaken of course, one would abandon the team of their town or city of birth and prostrate themselves to the colossal red wankery of Manchester United. There is only one team of Wanderers though and it's correct that not all that wander are lost, any more anyway.

Have we not seen the path towards greatness? Will those who pretend to stand on the same mountain top as us try to shove us away? Is the top of this mountain our rightful place? We're Wolverhampton! We're top of the league and we sing it like we don't quite believe it.

But it's been snowing which is freaky. Outside Poundland the kids were laughing and the old 'uns having a moan as I popped in to get some Polo mints. The bus stop windows on the main road outside are steamed up so I draw a big dick on it for old times sake and an old fella sees me and shakes his head sadly. Big dicks on steamed up dirty windows. I have to get home quick as our Vinny is giving me a lift up town.

It's dead good being a 'writer' though. I had dinner with Alex Rae last week. He was sat at my left side. I watched him dunk a bread roll in his soup while he waxed lyrical about things. It's dead fucking civilised having dinner with these ex footballers. They are used to it and are relaxed and cool. I'm thankful for the nosh. I don't want to talk about football I want to talk about expensive old guitars and fast old cars then remember I'm not in a Nickleback song but listening to Alex talk about things football and I told him about when I got stabbed at Millwall. It went quiet after that. yeah being a writer is a weird experience for sure when mere words you type can get you eating a dinner with such company when normally I would be outside looking in, now I suppose there's still a large part of me still outside in the rain. Always will be. Wondering if I pull that knife out of my knee will I get done for possession? The cop directs me to an ambulance but the wound is shallow and the knife practically falls out. I think I was kicked in the balls as well Alex, but he's talking about the mortgage on his farm in Pattingham, so I shut up.

The North. Well we fucked off Leeds didn't we? Their horrible little faces were a joy to behold. They are a people who would star in a dangers of fried food commercial. Four-One eh. My Grandfather was called 'Bill the Bastard'. Bill the Bolton Bastard. On the way to the match I think about McGinlay a little. Only a little bit. If I think too much I want to start writing those letters again and my shrink said I should start to accept he still exists. All the bad shit floats to the surface of a Wolves fans mind when you mention that cursed name. Then things aren't all jolly and Holy. Nuno would come up and say 'Lads it's cool come on, let's go. leave it behind' in that soft voice of his. But Nuno…back off. This is raw revenge shit, this is thievery and dishonour, this is a lack of justice and the story of our town. This is shit that as much as you are our saviour and our Holy man you have to step aside and let this thing be settled by those who have walked the evil paths of those days long ago.

But then that's the most Wolves thing ever isn't it. Getting riled up and pissy. Not really thinking well of course Nuno knows how we feel about it. These fixtures with enemies come around a couple of times a season. We get all riled up and sweaty, we may even run around the ring road with our hoods up nearly getting run over. Angry yeah. Angry and stupid. Stupid because we have underestimated our Coach. We've underestimated him because he doesn't give a shit about history and the past. He believes in the now. He approaches every game like a local derby. Meticulous planning, immaculate idea. Every game for him is the penultimate battle because it is the battle of the present and not of the past. But it's Bolton and I hate Bolton.

Shall we move on too? Throw away that secret Voodoo altar in the shed where you have that little doll of McGinlay with his porky little face. You like to burn him over a black candle just little touches of flame and you hope somewhere that bitter little fat man is having that voodoo twinge as he watches Colin Wanker roast Hedgehogs on a garden bonfire. It's VHS tape scratchy and jumpy and Colins face is a little yellow and the camera gets real close to his face and he says 'The Wolves don't like ugly under the counter stuff'. League of gentleman football. Once you get trapped in the village of Snotball-on-dull it's hard to get out. Colin Wanker is the Mayor of that shitty little town and it's populated by bitter little twisted men who define the hate mantras of the Warnockian way.

Again we have a plethora of ideas that are kind of bouncing around in the darkness of the void engineered by vapid pointless opposition tactics for sure. This Bolton football reminiscent of pussy grab courting, great lolloping tongues that taste of cheap alcohol and trying to find your clothes in the dark. Bolton are pretty shit to be honest, a bit like their fan writing too. Big words and tactics they don't quite understand but are trying. Their team look like gas fitters, a lads night out, a lads day at Cheltenham races, shit trims, tight suits and fat arses.

So fuck Bolton. How are they doing in general? I have a little look at them on Youtube. Very shit. It was like watching madmen chase balloons. It's only what they deserve. I don't know who plays for them except Karl Henry. But here at the footy they look kind of mobile in that mutton dressed as lamb groove they have. They look like they are pretending to play attractive football but the scent of the shithouse follows them around as Neves looks a bit confused by Bolton but another incisive pass through the fat of the fried spam Bolton philosophy delights again. It's all very deep fried this Bolton thing. And they've had a 'resurgence' lately have they? Cavaleiro is ratcheting around like a lunatic again. He believes again doesn't he? His link up with Bonatini is a thing for me. This whole Doherty thing is a thing too. I love their fume about our players. The snide comments about Mendes. You see we are not allowed to dream. We are too Wolverhampton for glitzy football they think. More FFP fume and grief. Every word the grey faces type gives me joy.

More control here. Saiss is beautiful. Commanding in midfield. How did Lambert denigrate this man so? He glides between Bolton players and another gorgeous stroke of foot and again it's a runner. Helder down the side. Trembling with anticipation we bang our shins on the seats in front. Alas a fruitless run but beauty in itself. Costa I think I lurve you. It's not 'filthy' football. It's romantic candlelit dinner football. Dunking a fresh roll in your soup football. It's having dinner with ex pros and wondering whether you have cabbage in your teeth. Privileged I am I suppose to watch it. Even though they aren't moving out of second gear....what? Yeah no way were Wolves in top flow. The turbo didn't even kick in and we were smashing them all over the place. See Neves run, see Jota twist.

Even if we were just jogging along we were taking the piss totally and lo and behold what happens? Bolton decide to act like little girls at a party and shit wasn't going their way was it. A little pull here and there, an errant late foot, and poor Jota spent that much time in the air I'm quite tempted to fly 'Jota Airlines' next time I fly. Little Jotty baby I thought. He's a lil soul isn't he? Nah. Jota comes from hard stock. Jota is a hardnut, a lad, a piece of work, a head and a tough nut. He didn't give a shit about Liam Softcock and his Bert Boilknob book of Championship Football tactics (all five pages of it, and three of them pages are Warnocks foreword talking about Wolves).

What a disgrace Bolton are really. They don't deserve the name of Wanderers. Notlob Disunited I name them. I'm glad their syncophants high in the corner of the Northbank were far away so I couldn't see them. I've had my fill of 'North' this week. Oh there's Jota in the air again, he rubs his leg and gets up and seconds later he's giving little fat Bolton boy a lesson in Nunoism. Nuno of course is sent off in the next few minutes. It's a Coach-tastic rumble in the jungle on the touchline. I'm violent at this point. If Nuno gets touched I'm going around the front after the match and getting angry. Don't touch my Nuno. Nobody touches the Nuno.

So Nuno alights into the sanctum of the Billy Quiet. The Northbank still think they have to pay extra for time added on and on 90 minutes they have gone home. Somebody should tell them they don't have to pay extra ya know. It's cruel.

Five goals. Five delicious slices of Nuno cake. And we weren't even on fire. We will see in he next few weeks the attention I warned about early in the season. Now the words on most football fans minds will be Wolverhampton Wanderers. Articles are being prepared right at this moment. Maps are being consulted about where we are. Stories will be made up, rumours and propaganda. It's ok for us to languish in some post orgasmic joy about our football, the ideas, the beauty and the moments. But we must also be prepared for the ugly and the dark as the world turns it's eyes on us. We must be brave also and listen to what Nuno has to say to his team and we must also do what he says. Don't worry about the league position. Take it one game at a time. Make every game a cup final. Control your opponents. Make your ideas stronger than theirs.

I'm waiting in the Chippy down Stubby Lane and the dude serving has a Wolves shirt on and he's explaining the game to some of his customers. But he's like all of us at the moment. We find it hard to explain what we are seeing and experiencing. We are struggling to find words and emotions that accurately narrate something like Cavaleiro/Jota/Costa/Douglas/Coady/Boly/Doherty and the madness of their methods. We don't really understand any of this yet. Don't understand why the journey to the bus stop takes 10 minutes when we win and twenty when we don't.

He can't explain it because we don't really know what we are experiencing at all. The algorithms are all clicking through the orders with clinical efficiency. Each player we have is uniquely suited to the tasks required. Nearly every pass and shot is weighted perfectly. Every knocked on loose ball has a Wolves player there to collect…and we stand there mesmerised by the whole thing. The Jota chip made my lower lip tremble and I though I was going to just start weeping and letting the stress of the previous decades just pour out.

And this is Bolton for fucks sake. What's going to happen in the next few months as we consolidate our position and get stronger and stronger? What happens when the atmosphere is that permeated with victory and promotion? When we are standing there watching our team celebrate…I don't think we are strong enough to deal with it. The team are, but me personally? This beautiful football is going to give me that much joy I may go totally insane. But I put the kettle on and dunk a tea bag in there. Give it a pump. Two sugars. Make sure when you put the milk in it's the same colour as a good tan. I watch the birds on the feeder outside for a minute or two. It's good this football shit. I feel calm. Five goal calm. But that can change...

Are we insane yet? Endlessly checking your phones for news on Wolves. Bumping into things, the Missus talking to you and you can't tear your eyes away from that Neves pass to Cavaleiro. 'Yeah I'm listening for fucks sake' we say. But the outside of that right foot has become the full Kelly Brook thing and we hear Beethoven or Elgar. At least Ed Elgar was a Wolf. I can't eat properly. I'm staring at the moon outside in the frost cold and thinking about it all. There is a darkness out there. Underneath the silvery glitter of frost and stillness. It's something that dirties the memories of the last week watching us dismantle Leeds and Bolton. Like little cracked finders pawing at the mind muddying the waters. An unease. Yes. Birmingham City. The Lulus.

Normally I would start waxing some half baked rant about the next match and opposition but now standing outside all I feel is an abyss of idea. Birmingham City leech the creative forces out of me. They suck the joy from me. West Bromwich Albion are comical and funny, clowns and the objects of intensely funny humour due to their inherent shitness. But City aren't funny at all. They are psychic vampires sucking any joy out of our existence. I though it would be funny extrapolating their support into a quasi Lord of the Rings type scenario but. No. Orcs scurrying from their holes carrying their bitterness and hate, their lack of idea, their lack of beauty.

Instead of holes they have Small Heath, Kings Heath…names that you really only see driving as fast as you possibly can through Birmingham on dirty road signs. Feet slapping on the road, the dull thud of the odd punch. You can't just walk into Mordor but you can sing your way out of it. If I was going to the match I would be eloquent and waxative but here now, in the warm front room of my house I just feel blankness and greyness. They could be Cardiff or Bristol City really. The faces of the team all have that same generic blank beard/quiff/tattoo thing going on. They have a Jota but not a JOTA. I remember watching a video on Twitter of City fans on the 'Party boat' on the Thames, bumbling from foot to foot drinking expensive beer wondering what the fuck they are doing there.

It would have been too light a waxing for something so void of joy. My babies will be going there to play within that darkness and it makes me feel sad and unhappy. That their beautiful feet should press upon that cursed ground makes me want to weep. That they should perform their beauty and rhythms in front of Philistines and the ignorant makes my heart twinge and I am angry and this is what the metaphysical aspects of this derby really are.

We are used to presenting the ideas of Nuno to people that have a little understanding and empathy for this philosophy, as monkeys watching an ant hill they understand to some extent the concepts displayed on the pitch. But this? David Davis the exiled one. Your ministrations to the Southbank after your goal isn't forgotten but it doesn't really affect us in our hearts Dave. It was just you. Your whole ethos was defined by that display. Taking on the blue and white cloak of depravity you expected limnal griefs from us, but all we did was sigh and look to the heavens. Accusing the Gods of terrible metaphysical banter that you should present Dave Davis to us in this way. Diggah, you will fade into future headlines about assaults and traffic violations and the press will lament your fall, but not us. We are driven by muscle and skill but directed purely by strong minds. Birmingham, you lack honour.

The walk through Birmingham to the ground is a Psychogeographical exercise in survival. Not only from the offer of physical violence but that of mental violence. This dystopian madness in those sad streets that surround the ground are relentless. Pressing on your mind as soon as you leave the sterility of the city centre. What are Small Heath? Why are they a thing? I'm not sure. Aside from the various matches we have met and the shenanigans that have gone on. On my part it isn't the violence and jollity that goes on in the after-party, it's the lack of any identity they have that bothers me.

They are a lumpen lot Birmingham City. I would have expected more of them being 'second city' and all that bollocks. I forget Aston Villa for a moment as I don't really see them as having anything to do with us. But Small Heath. Yes, they are a thing for me. Outside the house the bats have given up chasing the few insects but the moon is shining as well as it can through the haze of traffic fumes and the odd vapid cloud. What is a Birmingham? I have some good memories of Birmingham but they are wrapped up in punches and kicks, Moseley Road, having illicit sex with blond WPC's, Steve Bull half killing Citys goalkeeper, spinning him around like a traffic cone booted by a drunk 1st year undergraduate.

Over the past ten years I have watched them with interest. They have paraded a series of Managers that I had a keen dislike for. Every time I go to Saint Andrews I get a vibe there. It's not the doughnuts whacking the odd 'dingle' or West Midlands Police getting their weekly hard on. It's the area and the people. They look dejected. Even when they play us and enter the Golden Dragon they look pissed off and grey. They file in with a cursory song or two. Half hearted and sad. This makes me sad because I want their little faces to be angry and shouty. To put some vim into the whole away support thing. But it's never like that. I suspect the darkness of their ends is a weight upon them. I feel like it's a good job I'm not going really.

Pre-game mind propaganda from Steve Coterill is interesting 'Wolves are the best team in the Championship' yeah well we know that. But why are you talking about our team and not your own? At the Tesco one stop this morning putting some diesel in the van another decrepit Transit turned up full of Joeys and their van had a big Birmingham City sticker on the side. It was a dirty thing. I drew a cock on the grimy back just because I could (and they were too busy heaping Pot Noodles into the thing). Steve Cotterill eh. He's about as dynamic as a shit Ford Transit. His whole team shout out Ford Transit in fact. On paper they look handy, until you open the back doors and a few crackheads fall out in plaster covered tracksuits and Moms woolly hats. One sits at the front cramming crisps into his face and crumbs of fried potato are falling all over him. The pump display is getting close to the £20 I'm putting in but my eyes are shocked by the fact he's eating his crisps with gloves on. Amazing. Birmingham.

But what is the rub here, what's the angle with City? I can't find one. They dull the imagination both here in front of the lap top and even watching them play. There's a dichotomy of course between us. We have more or less the same attendances, we play 20 miles apart, both owned by Chinese global entities...but the difference. Lack of idea. We have a plan and a transformative algorithm. We have erupted from the nothingness of Moxey and Morgan et al with an idea and a dream I suppose, underpinned by business nous and a philosophy. But them? What idea can they drag from Small Heath? What philosophy? Silk purses from pigs ears?

There is nothing in the geography of that place that gives any idea at all, any underpinning of intent by structured concrete thought. It's all crisp packets blowing down the road. It's potholes and fast food take aways run by angry middle easterners. It's Kevin Phillips scoring a goal, it's walking through Digbeth at 3am with your head pounding from that dodgy pill. It's being herded together by West Midlands Police and truncheon tickled when you step off the kerb. It's temporary traffic lights, it's chavvy little fucks bouncing on their Air Max. It's a metaphysical black hole that sucks any joy out of you unless it's three points and a fast route out of the place.

I expect our team to again lash the Book Of Nuno tight with our attack and to not allow the Cotteralism of City to look further than their stadium. Their team will only perform if they forget what they are. There will be a moment when they remember their lives before Birmingham. Like a convict in a dungeon seeing a square of blue sky above him while he sits in the squalor of his existence. This little blue sky thinking will jolt them from their depressions and they will remember football, and playing it. They will remember those few joys they had playing before they entered this chasm of unjoy. Will they remember? Who knows. Maybe their football will be eating crisps with gloves on, being cramped up in the back of a transit with no real idea of how you are going to get out of it and start your life anew. We do inspire minds with our football, but how do you inspire others who have such an abject experience of it?

Our job is to confuse and blind them with our light and we will. The match will be a battle against light and darkness and it's a darkness we remember too although the dark crept around our pitch under the lamentations of Paul Lambert it was held back by the light from our support. We never wavered and never stopped hoping. We know that we deserve the rarefied atmosphere of academic and structured football, but them? What history do they have? Pitch invasions and throwing seats. The vacant Jasper Carrot blankness. The City is theirs they call out to their Villa rivals…of course it is lads. All yours, every grey street of it, every pothole, every errant mistimed tackle, every coin flung skywards.

Our team must be vigilant. Our plan and philosophy must be strong and applied with beauty and strength and as Nuno says 'our ideas must be stronger' and they must be here. Because here is where we must plant our flag firmly within the centre circle. It's not filthy porn football any longer for how long does that sexual act last? ten, twenty, thirty minutes? Beware that as we display our football we will also inspire City to play too. They will glimpse the meadows of our hearts in every ball played, every switch of play from the left to the right, the way our front three prowl and hunt the goals, the way our defence is hewn into shape under the masterful hand of our Captain. They will look into our golden light and want it very badly and this will galvanise them into some semblance of a team. The ministrations of Cotterill will be forgotten for a moment as they watch us and want to be us, and this is a most dangerous thing when our own beauty and passion becomes their inspiration too.

I'll be back after this match has gone and I can sit and squeeze superlatives in between the meat of the whole derby sandwich but I had to say something before hand, had to write some madness down. Best of luck out there troops. Don't let the darkness into your minds as you walk through Digbeth. Be brave, remember our idea. The dude who owns the Birmingham City transit can't start his van and you can hear the battery struggling to turn the starter motor. He looks around with that blank look for somebody to fall out of the heavens to help him and I grab my starter leads from the back of my van and step out into the cold to help him. I'm not a total bastard but as I go around the side of the van I write in the dirt encrusted to it 'FWAW' and that's the right thing to do as well. So what happened?

It was a job wasn't it? Going into the garden to pick dog shit up and the grass has grown a little too long. It's a bit of an Easter egg hunt looking through the tussocks for those little shrivelled turds. You get the shit bag in your hand and try to tease the soft shit from the tussocks and the musty shitty smell of dogshit rises pungent into your quivering nostril. Earthy and protein rich, cloying and clinging you gag as you feel warmth through the bag onto your hand. It's repulsive and yet weirdly warming. You tie a knot into the bag and notice you've got a little bit on your finger. You bend down to wipe it on the grass and find you've wiped it through a whole pile of hidden dog shit and now your hand is covered. You stand back to shout at the Gods and fuck. You've trod in another load.

The above is the match report. Sometimes gaining points away is simply 'picking up the dog shit' an maybe even treading in it too.

How was it walking through those wastes tonight? The car fumes, the industrial stink, the misty can't be arsed rain that makes your skin feel greasy. See what I mean about light? Tonight that light was a lot brighter than Birmingham city for sure. The darkness of that place didn't prevail and it was a major point in the Wolves campaign. Why? It's the top of the climb. While tackling Welsh Hills on my bike this summer I know how key parts of the season will work out, I think. This is a tough match. It is an effort.

The hardest part of the attempt to get to the top of the hill is the start. At this point our muscles are not warmed up. You may not have used them for a while, or maybe ever. They are a group of strangers you have to get working together to get to the top of the hill. Some of these muscles are strong and fit, some of your muscles are a bit crap. But get them all working together and that strength can be taken up by the weaker. Pedalling at the start is strange. Start of the climb. Sometimes you get the wrong gear and almost stop. Cardiff. Bristol City. Sheffield. But eventually you get the gear right and the climb is slowly starting. You ease yourself into various positions to find the best one and here it is. Before you know it the going is steeper. You are maybe a quarter of the way up and those muscles are feeling it. The groove is relentless. QPR, Norwich, Leeds, Bolton. Sometimes you lose concentration too.

This match was the halfway way point of the whole climb. Not physically but mentally. Backroom work, health work, strange scientific shit to do with performance analysis. This has made this team ninja ready. Super fit. But mentally there has been a lot to get their heads around. The personalities in the dressing room have settled into some social hierarchy and the groups communication and display dynamics would have settled down. Everybody will be happier now there is order.

Nuno would have had a lot to do with that. He is an Alpha, wise, quick to erupt in temper but also quick to placate and reforge bonds. Unconsciously the team understand this and the trust between them will get stronger. It's beyond white boards and tactical slashes in blue and red wipe off marker pen. You can't really coach this team any more. My mate saw Nuno at a driving range. He set the ball down. Boom. 250 yards straight down the line. Ball down. Boom. Again 250 yards. He kept hitting them spot on, hard, fast, accurate, concentrating. Again and again. Nuno has told them their roles and he trusts them to fulfil that role in the manner in which their skill level and mental state allow. His role at the side of the pitch to remind and cajole performance, tweak the idea a little, maybe swap the idea completely? Who knows what magic goes through the whole set up?

But here tonight is where that light of intent was tested. The teams vision will have narrowed in the madness of Birmingham. I've described elsewhere the psychogeographical aspects of this 'derby'. The hollowness of it. Coady and Doherty will understand it. Not simply because they understand rivalries as Cavaleiro, Jota and Costa do too. Football rivalries exist all over the world and the spectrum of discontent they cause are apparent and visible. But this isn't Rangers and Celtic, United or City pick any one you want. This is a battle between light and darkness where hate just becomes an abstract thing and the battle I suppose looking at a stadium full of Golden light and then descending into the dystopic miasma of Digbeth is a dichotomy you can't ignore. Coady will understand it because it's a uniquely English thing. Doherty because the Irish experience is heavy with that dichotomy too.

Tonight that light was glaring. Cavaleiro has a gentle and big emotional part of his being. This emotion is contained by him much of the time. He knows that his love is too big to show the world in case the world throws his love back at him. Tonight he was quiet and refined. His runs effortless and powered. His heart straining to keep back that power and emotion trying to channel it into physical exertion. He is susceptible to darkness but still he ran on and on into space, closing down players.

Football as well as emotions have a full spectrum. It is a range of ability and skill and the one end and at the other drive and ambition and this was visible tonight in all it's glory. But with all the spectrum there are areas at either end that we don't have the sense to understand. Wolves are like that tonight. Some of it is ugly, some so beautiful it makes my heart ache. There are things I simply don't have the capacity to understand here. That communication Saiss has with the ball. It's not an inanimate object for him it is a system of meaning. He certainly stamped his meaning all over that pitch tonight.

Bonatini a revelation again. Those runs of steeze like an Iron Maiden bass riff at times, thundering and punchy runs into the Birmingham half. Shrugging off the ministrations of the Godless city midfield and defence with aplomb and grace. I don't want to talk about the other end of the spectrum, the Warnockian wavelengths. A little pulling here and there. Don't these people learn their lessons? The more you hump the motionless body of your skill set by kicking the shit out of our team the more resilient they become. What doesn't kill you makes you stronger. The Cardiffian model has been tested out on us by other teams since that day and have been found wanting. You can't blank out this light. Jota crumples under a late foot. He stands almost immediately and doesn't even look at the Referee who has become a mere bystander to the strength of this teams intent.

These games are never pretty. Orc ball. Birmingham started to get inspired by our football I think. Our beauty was taken in initially after some Neanderthal tackles. Mad derby times. They had Ron Forehead sent off. There were some differences of opinion and tribal stuff going on but still we were in control. They had some moments of clarity through the dark mist of their football but no real chance to dim the light. Jota, what a marvel he is, what a nutter! If he walked into my front room now and did a shit on the rug I would just pick it up and get him to sign it.

Marvellous on loan Boly, the giant Coady, the able and skilled Bennett. What light they did shine despite the darkness that crept into their hearts as the match progressed. This Birmingham thing reflected in Costas ripped sleeve. The warrior spirit of N'Diaye awakened. Nuno becoming more demanding, more virulent in his ideas because now at this point this team is about to crack open their shell and erupt into the world like a Gold and Black Eagle…

It's done this Birmingham thing. Now our people their will be walking back through the streets of that place and will be in a glow of sorts but wary. I will take this 3 points in the spirit it was taken, with a bit of an edge, a bit of in your face belief and anger. Sometimes that's what you have to do at these places. But us? Our team will have new belief now, to get a result in that place is a milestone and now you're pedalling slow and you think it's levelling out a bit and you're right. The rest of the season will be all down hill now. Fresh air blowing in your face football. We can look back at this match as just one of those dark forest chapters which every hero has to travel through.

Right bear with me as I can hardly see anything. It's been a liquid day. An amber day. A day of struggling with alcohol again. I struggle because everything is a struggle. These games are coming thick and fast now and I don't think my mind can take it.

It was cold down the canal especially going East. Bitter bone biter of a thing. Nuno has got December Manager of the month then eh? The curse! ooooooh. Nuno doesn't give a shit about these things but on the Compton photo shoot with the award he wasn't actually touching it. As well as having some dude hold the actual trophy Nuno had all of his back room staff around him in the snow cold. Nuno although pragmatic and again stoic knew the Kwan had to be protected. The Kwan and the team Juju would be affected negatively by that whole Sky Sports thing. Nuno glad he had won it, less glad to get tangled in the black tentacles of the Sky Sports curse.

There is a fella in the woods at the side of the canal moaning and groaning to himself, he's staring at the sun through the trees and my dogs don't like it and growl sub audibly almost, deep back in their throats. The bloke has got a faded WBA pink woolly hat on. There's half a foot of snow. Now he's laughing, he's holding a blue bottle of mad cider. Frosty Jack is a killer cider. Never seen an apple in it's life. This poor bastard is nearly as blue it's that cold.

Sunderland in the snow cold. I've wrapped up warm today and there is no argument about coat choice. Snow coat. Boots. No Football Factory 80's Adidas bollocks. Good grippy boots. Warm. What are a Sunderland? Coleman has just joined them. Coleman looks like he smells nice but also looks like he worries a lot. He's going to be an hour down the motorway and think 'fuck…did I leave the oven on?'. I wondered where Sunderland were in the league so I had a look. Oh dear. Coleman is going to look at lot more worried having to face us today. That Alan Hansen tan he rocks is going to look very pale. I wonder what happened to Alan Hansen? But I know how Coleman feels, I felt like it last Monday against City. Trepidation. I don't want to talk too much about Sunderland but I wonder again if Coleman can galvanise those dejected well paid but highly dysfunctional team into some sort of shape to face this team of ours? What are you going to do Coleman you little Taff git?

Molineux has a thin layer of snow around it and that is purely a testament to how hard the ground staff have worked putting the game on. That's the idea isn't it? Last year there may have been a cursory sweep around but now, Nunoism even smashes the weather conditions. People with shovels, smiles on their faces, energy to get the game on.

Nuno is changing now. Gone is the peaceful Philosophy of the start of the season. The reasoning and thoughtful expressions he used to get his ideas to us. Then he was placating and reassuring, stressing the importance of bonds between club and support. Gently outlining his plans and desires. Now Nuno stands erect and is reiterating major points with a stab of his chin and head held back, commands rather than answers. Three Thousand years ago he would probably have been a great Greek General. But he looks like a man now firmly gripping the fur of the Wolf as he rides upon it and the accelerating beast rushes him through the dark forests of the Championship. Hold tight to that Wolf Nuno.

What may Coleman say to this figure? What idea will Coleman present to us on this cold Saturday afternoon? There are names within that team I am loathe to mention. My Southbank brothers have stories to tell about their fans too. The North East is strange to us, there is both beauty and desolation within it's borders. Their fans are quiet and their songs flutter quietly into the sky before they get to me.

The match starts with a customary exchange of pleasantries. But Neves starts by being Neves. Ultimate footballer for me. We're at the top of the hill but I don't think we have seen the best of him yet. He's understated for sure. He collects the ball like he has an affinity to it. He wants the ball, needs it, but as soon as it's collected it's gone again across the pitch.

I'm stood by the canal again listening to the lunatic cry. I ask him if he's ok but he looks at me with eyes that have absolute terror in them. The snow still Falls on him and he takes another swig of his cider and has another plaintive wail. Here at Molineux our team look fresh but bruised. Doherty slashing pieces out of the pitch on one of his few runs.

How was it all? You've been in the bath and shaved off all those errant pieces of hair. Plucked your nose hairs. Plastered what's left of your hairline into some semblance of a trendy fashionable haircut. Have a pout in the mirror. You pick up the 40 squid bottle of aftershave you rarely use. Spray a bit on. You are sexy as fuck. Put your pants on, the ones with the fewest holes and the most lively elastic. Clean pair of socks. Put some nice clothes on, you don't really like them but she does. She'll be downstairs doing something . You are fit as fuck, hold your gut in. You sidle down the stairs and get Barry Whites 50 greatest Lurve songs...is it too early for that? Maybe George Michael? Ah fuck it, Barry White, go in for the kill. You put the LED lamp on you got from Untouchables. It's supposed to change colour from red to green but it's stuck on green. She comes into the room and she looks like the Incredible Hulk in the lamp light. Fuck. Press play. Barry White oozes from the Argos Bluetooth speaker hifi thing. You do a little shimmy and your hip clicks. Fuck. She is more than half way down the Prossecco now. She is playing with the hairs on her arms and looking at you in that way that hides her squint. You sit next to her on the settee and make an attempt to smooch and groove but she's not having any of it. Barry gets turned off and as she gets up to turn the telly on she lets out a vicious fart. Ant and Dec, Celebrity Jungle. And it's all a fucking comedy really as you go and stare out at the snow in the back garden...

That match was like that. Ready for some smooth moves and some funky foot play. Fair enough it was sexy and it was beautiful, and it smelled nice. The day was cold and crisp. Football weather. Gloves and scarves, jolly pre Christmas faces. But it just wasn't to be. We did well to hold on to our concentration that's all I'll say. The movement of Jota was again a joy to behold. And Neves? What football from him. Pure funk in slices of hot Neves bass. He runs his own set list that dude. Faced with a Sunderland back five to unlock he was proudly reticent to inflict his football on it. But Wolves clicked the tumblers to the safe trying to unlock the meaty tumblers of Sunderland. Those meathead, long necked pale Northern mother fuckers. They are the Plumber that never turns up and the Gas Fitters hairy arse crack. What a fucking task Coleman has, and fair play to him he did a job today. A point for his team. A clean sheet too. But it wasn't pretty Gary. It wasn't real football. It's supposed to be dynamic and brave combat full of thrills and madness that makes you want you scream and shout in joy and horror. But this was not that.

But it was a dip in the landscape I think. An intake of breath perhaps after the trials of the past month. But it's important that we too had our part today and were lacking. It was quiet and reserved. The ambience was laid back and chilled out. It was football as sitting back in bed lighting a cigarette after hot sex. Everything is good. We have extended our lead at the top of the table for a bit at least. We are doing good and in January we will do better. I sense movement of players in and out. If Fosun are wise and Nuno demands then we will see a strengthening of this side of ours. Maybe here and now is the time to rest a few players, let some others have a go. Or is it a momentum that can't be stopped and Jota, Cavaleiro, Neves, Bonatinni must play and must 'crack' on?

These next few weeks are important. These are the times when many of these young men that play for us have to spend Christmas away from families and loved ones. I know they are paid handsomely but still, it's a time when you need people around you that you love and want to be with. They will have moments in the next few weeks when they will be a little slower and a little less committed because that's the nature of the human being. Us? We must forgive these moments as we would deal with them in the same way as our players, a little selfish sometimes, a little sad.

My Albion fan is still in the trees and he's downed half the bottle. He's as pissed as a fart but he can see me and the dogs and he's just watching me watching him while the dogs sniff things. Yeah sometimes I suppose these games come along in a season. It's a bit of a shock though after the battering of Leeds and Notlob which is I suppose a Barometer of how well we have been playing. Onwards. I leave him behind and can still hear him shouting two hundred yards away. We will freshen up this team in January add to the already practically unstoppable impetus, new momentum and maybe new ideas too. Nuno is not one to sit back static and unmoving but constantly learns and acts on ever changing conditions. Yeah I'm not fussed by Nil-Nil. Learn and move on.

One thing I have noticed over these past few months as we wax lyrical over the beauty of this team and watched them home and (thanks to Horace, away too) is the way in which we tend to define ourselves regardless of the opposition. In fact the Ideas of the Nuno have become that strong we have made the opposition team not an 'opposition' because there's simply no way to describe this Sheffield Wednesday team as an equal partner in last nights football. Tenacious yes. Their movement was an attempt to define themselves, their passing was often eloquent and refined for sure but it lacked conviction. Again we warmed up by running in formation across the pitch before the second half started and the Wednesday players looked on. Hands on hips, staring into the Gold and Black or just simply the blank sky waiting for the whistle to start the game. They lack ethos. I remember Danny Batth held aloft by their fans when they got promotion. Odd feelings here.

Sheffield is normally a cold place any way and I was a two coat man. Boots too. The rigours of an English winter. I have a mate from Norway who when he visited one cold November sat in his car dithering. I was like well, You are used to this cold surely and he said 'Your Winter is different, it gets in your bones first'. After being thrown out of the first pub we went into by a barmaid that looked like the spirit medium from 'Poltergeist' we decamped and made our way to another pub. Hills everywhere here. The Barmaid here had skin like an old Kipper. She looked nicotine stained. I think if you waxed enough bars and got her into bed she would get naked and on that skin unseen there would be sanskrit spells tattooed on her back. She was nice. We were foreigners and the locals kept their jollity to a minimum.

The Wednesday ground is a soulless place and of course their star player Forestieri is a thing. Apparently he doesn't want to play there any more and I don't blame him. This whole place lacks idea. Last year the Conor Ronan cameo. The way he was hacked down a few times. We came away with a 0-0 and back down an icy M1 with most of our love trampled into the ice that settled around the ground. Then of course, my hopes were pinned on the Ronans and the whispers from the academy of this or that player you'd never heard of. Wondering whether they would burst onto the pitch with the grace and fervour of Stevie Bull. That was year Zero really for us. That was Fosun looking closely at the whole model of Wolves before they started to make decisions, weighty decisions on players and ethos.

Tonight we watched a completely new meme and one where Momentum/Idea/Progress were the buzzwords of the night. But why? Around us, in the stand there were dissenting 'football managers' again. Horace was looking around at them with his angry 'I'm about to kick off' face. What say you? As you watch this football? Single out players for your ire. That computer game you play has infected you and your football is full Matrix. You have sold your souler to the Xbox controller. Cavaleiro my beauty. How you ran around getting busy. You were running around for 90 minutes and the strength and passion you had is clear to me. But 'he's having an off night'. He wasn't.

What is clear to me now sitting in the afterglow of that match. How we have defined Nunos ideas so well and so effortlessly that we don't see the hard work and the academic bones of the whole idea. We play and we impress. We are not 'playing' another football team and dare I say it although we have 3 points in the bag and extended our lead at the top of the table. This is not football as we know it. Tonight an errant challenge here and there. Bennett getting involved in glad handing the opposition. Jota hacked down again. Neves 'passing' or 'threading' the ball into the goal. It wasn't football no.

Maybe it wasn't beautiful at times either. Yorkshire has an ugliness to it, a sense of entitlement over art and creativity. Wolves last night used them like an old wet wipe. Opposition teams are simply a framework by which Nuno imposes these ideas of his. Sheffield Wednesday were simply the medium by which Nuno like a Japanese Zen Calligrapher watches and meditates upon. Sitting there cross legged with his brush loaded with ink. He may sit for hours contemplating the blankness of Sheffield. Contemplating his materials. The Jota, The Neves, The Coady, The Boly and these players are like strings of pearls strewn across those wastes last night. Eventually of course. A burst of activity from Nuno the artists and he throws himself to the paper in front of him and slashes the brush across the paper and the ink is perfectly loaded, the paper just absorbent enough. The calligraphy is abstract and is simple, but beautiful at the same time. Nunos thought transcribed perfectly in simple movement. Nuno sits back and closes his eyes to contemplate the art.

There is Kwan, the ever flowing momentum of idea and grace but there is also Chi an energy which also winds it's way around the monad of Kwan. Both of these things intertwine and melt into each other. I watch Boly collect the ball, and a Wednesday player approaches him full pelt to do one of 'those' tackles. You know the one, the Warnockian 'I've fucking run out of ideas so I'm going to clatter the big bastard' tackles. The player bounces off the immovable Boly who didn't even look at his enemy twisting around on the floor like somebody flicked one of his bollocks. He passes to Coady who imposes his own unique brand of Nunoist skills, he dips a shoulder and his eyes constantly scan the ground in front of him to unload the ball and continue momentum. We move and pass in possession. We move and block when without the ball. We push on and are relentless and even their Managers ministrations at half time which to some extent galvanises his squad fall onto the pitch in empty late challenges. Intent but lack of idea. Momentum but negative momentum as Coady again places himself in positions of power and strength.

I love Vinagre. Some of his play was sublime too. Somewhat rough maybe a little too grand a flourish when a simpler movement would have sufficed but the ways of the youth eh? Next year he will be immense. When we are playing our trade with the money counters and the voids of the Premiership. His idea of course will be strengthened and forged in the cold flames of games like this. He will be a Warrior for us. The Wednesday defence is a Cats cradle of bodies that move from left to right as we prime an attack. Intent. We have three of our attacking forwards moving and twisting in the box and Neves waits, one step, then two. The bodies in the box are moving like a shoal and Cavaleiro is dictating that movement with his positioning.

I am watching and holding my breath. I can feel a dribble of liquid from my burst ear drum trickle down my neck. Then there it is. Neves collects the ball and the movement is complete and all it requires is the Coda or the epilogue. The players in the box part and there is a gap, not much, maybe four foot of space between them. Neves hardly looked up. It was if he sensed that the gap would open for him. He felt the Kwan tighten and his Chi rear up like an Eagle hunting a small bird in the sky. Perfect position, perfect weight, and he digs the ball straight through that gap and the prey is captured and torn asunder on the cliff edge. Beautiful. It may have been the cold, my ear, the Jaeger bombs. I don't know. Perhaps it was the whole season which started in the rarefied mountain atmosphere of Austria in preseason which seems years ago now. But I had a little weep to myself in that cold stand. My brothers and Sisters singing and shouting and we had won the game.

Can we start to believe? Is it possible? The game was dictated by idea and intent for sure. The medium, the opposition rough and pockmarked with scars but still the art stood out upon it. This was again a game where we would have conceded a late goal, a final kick in the teeth. In the second pub we went into before the game the Landlord came around the bar to chat. It was a nice gesture. He spoke a little about our team and then waxed about his own for 15 minutes and the talk from him was all negative and sad. The things that had gone wrong with his team, the dynamics of their football. It was all so similar of course. On the way up we had chatted about Lambert and Saunders, McCarthy, Clipboard and those names lacked power and were seen in the NunoLight as wanting and derelict. We are looking down from a lofty position at the places we ourselves had sat despondent and angry. It still 'feels' and it still hurts but those tragedies at Burton and Rotherham and all those Godforsaken shit holes we have visited in the past are (for now) being forgotten and the traumas and shadows are being chased away by these strands of sunlight trickling through the gap between the Southbank and the Billy Wright.

Ethos. The power of the Nuno Espirito Santo to cajole and inspire through his own strength of idea and his own philosophy. He demands respect and that respect is laid upon a foundation of trust. His team are 'HIS' team.

Pathos. Nuno has the heart of a Lion and the emotions he holds onto would be a torrent not many could withstand. He demands also that his players channel that emotive part of their combative and forensic football into the mold of his idea.

Logos. The connection between this team and us, here in the stands, waiting at Bus stops in the rain, feeling the trickle of pus running down your neck as you watch them, walking into work proud of your team.

Constantly improving and fortifying our intentions as the season goes on and the dissenting puerile voices of other commentators, supporters, members of the press will fall like ash on the wind for sure. As we walked out of the ground we saw Nathan Judah with his video camera in hand to capture the zeitgeist from the fans. Of course, we would never be asked our opinions, us, those ragged loud, often swearing and proud. We have too may things to say and they would be punctuated by superlatives that can't exist within the confines of the digital medium just like our football can't be confined any longer to the Championship. Our voices are loud as we walk past the disgruntled Wednesday fans but we don't give a shit. McCarthy next. Come on Big Nose, lets see what weird ideas you have for us as the snow falls...

All was quiet in Wolverhampton, it was Winter and there was a light dusting of snow upon it and in the distance you could hear the wailing of a lone Spice head as he fought off one eyed demonic slobbering many fingered demons...or West Bromwich Albion fans as we know them better. It was a strange day and night even...

At his desk Nuno went over the team sheet again and again. He was balancing the team and seeing in his minds eye the beautiful forms they would take as he unleashed them on the frantic madness that he would see tomorrow. The heating kicked on and disturbed his concentration for a moment and he stroked his beard in annoyance. Yes, his mind was set and his philosophy was written. There was a knock upon the door and verily it was young Kevin Thelwell (Wolves Director of Football) with his eager face excited and flushed. He was wearing one of those Primark combined fashion disaster 'Jumper shirts' and Nuno felt a bit angry...

'Nuno! Nuno! Ipswich tomorrow, verily have you known better joys than a football match this close to Xmas eve??' Young Thelwell exclaimed. But Nuno was intent and had thoughts, plans and ideas. His anchor would be Neves and the point of his sword the undoubted Jota, ideas of new additions to his idea. The plans he had...

'Begone!' he shouted. His hands large and calloused rubbed his black and silver hair and ran down his face to his beard. Softer now...'begone' almost a whisper and Thelwell with a tearful face ran from the room and slipped on the snow outside...nobody saw and nobody cared and little Thelwell ran back home with Nunos angry words ringing in his ears which were tingling in the frost.

Nuno was angry. He knew as he looked through his reports on Mad Micks Ipswich that the game would be one of those. A tangled mess of football. It was the McCarthy way. There would be six across the back at times and on others the beautiful midfield of Wolves would be negated by balls which would flash across the sky in huge lumps. Thus Neves would get a cricked neck and Saiss would giggle to himself at the whole crazy world of Ipswichian direball. And verily there would be two massive centre forwards with big necks and little intellect.

Nuno threw the reports away and went to bed. He lay for a while and the voices and creaks of Molineux moaned as he tossed and turned thinking about McCarthy, thinking about Thelwell, thinking about everything and at last the ghosts of the Molineux went quieter and quieter until BANG! The door burst open and there stood a ghastly sight to behold and Nuno pulled the bed sheets up to his chin in alarm! Where was security?? Where was the protection from this!!! The sight in front of him was a shambling figure moaning and groaning. Covered in layers of fat it oozed out of a cheap Marks and Spencers suit that had seen too many office chairs and now hung on him like a black shroud. From inside that horrendous suit the muted screams of those players that had sold their souls to him and which he kept eternally.

It's face was wreathed in a ghostly fog that crept across the floor of Nunos bedroom. The figure crept closer until it's hand touched Nunos bare toe and Nuno recognised this ghost, this horrible spectre! For it assumed the shape of a short fat man with greedy probing fingers and an angry countenance that wasn't backed with physicality but with threats and rumours.

'Yay Nuno, do not tremble' the weedy shrill voice said for it was someone Nuno recognised and it was the Ghost of Christmas past. The Ghost of Jez Moxey! He shambled closer to the shivering Nuno and grabbed his hand and Nuno was taken away from his cold room in the Molineux and behold! He was taken to a strange uncomfortable place and he wondered why Moxeys hand was a little sweaty. The place they came to was a strange and horrible place. Here there was no laughter and no joy. The songs that used to be sung here were now just echoes between the glass fronted facades of offices and retail opportunities and Molineux was nowhere to be seen. Nuno was distraught! Where was the Molineux and where was the pitch, the noise, the place where Nuno made beautiful things happen. This place was bereft of Joy for there was no football here just echoes and ghosts. He could still see St Peters Church but where was the South bank?

'Where is the MollyNox' Nuno exclaimed and he wrenched his hand away from Moxey and ran into a central plaza where the odd plastic bag blew aimlessly around and there was a light in the foyer of one of the offices and Nuno ran towards it, his hands scrabbling through the tendrils of ghostly fog that crept around him as Moxey followed. At last he reached the light and Nuno banged on the door until a Security guard bleary eyed answered the door. The face of this man looked familiar to Nuno and then he realised! It was Young Thelwell!! Thelwell looked sad and ill, his security uniform was ill fitting and the enormous torch that hung from his belt threatened to pull his trousers down to his thin ankles.

'Thelwell what are you doing in this strange place? Where is the stadium? Why are you not preparing signings for the team and doing whatever it is you do??' Nuno said and grabbed Thelwell who shook him off angrily.

'The stadium hasn't been here for five or six years, they demolished it soon after Morgan turned down selling the club to Fosun, he built these offices and retail opportunities on the site, he made loads of money' Thelwell said sadly. He waved his arm towards the colossal but emotionless surroundings and said, 'Wolves play in Telford now and are pushing for a league place again and we had 3000 fans last week when we played Torquay.

Nuno was sad and he looked around at the Ghost of Moxey who was stuffing a pie in his face and in his other hand he held a ghostly spectral pint. He grinned at Nuno and Nuno saw in the ghosts black suit there was a slip of paper and Nuno pulled it out and read it. It was a P45 with Moxys name writ large upon it. The atmosphere grew dim and Nuno held out the slip of ghostly paper to Thelwell but the paper dissipated into the cold night and an even colder hand lay on Nunos shoulder as they travelled back to his bedroom at Molineux.

'What is this!' said Nuno to the ghost of Moxey who now had another pint in his hand and another spirit pie, he was chomping noisily upon it and Nuno noticed there were chains wrapped around him and in among those chains were the faces of all the players he had sold to other clubs so he could get his commission.

'Verily' Moxey said through a hail of ghostly pie crumbs. 'This is the way things would be without Fosun and Verily the Scouser hath sold the Molineux ground for development and now you see Nuno Espirito Santos the things that could have been' and the Ghost of Moxey wailed back through the door picking up the odd pound coin that had fell between his chains for verily no money escapes his eye and the room was again plunged into darkness.

It was now 11pm and Nuno shook his head in despair and had a quick look through his bedroom window at the pitch still lit outside. It was still there thank God. Nuno put his wise head back on his pillow and again the face of McCarthy came to him and that face roared his undefined words and his platitudes. Nuno felt his eyes heavy as he moved his players around his head in some pre sleep tactical madness unto… Lo!!

At the foot of his bed was another Ghost and this one was small and demure, it was dressed in a nice suit and had a jolly face and it grabbed Nuno by the toe and took him to another place. This place was Sheffield on a cold Winters night and there upon a football stand at Sheffield Wednesday was a group of men and women watching the Wolves and they were happy and were singing songs loudly. Nuno looked around at the little man and saw that it was Jeff Shi and Jeff was also smiling and happy and he said to Nuno.

'See what happiness we have brought to these people? We have changed the emotionless chains of finance into something of beauty and happiness. Our hard work over the season has brought these people here, who can ill afford the fucking atrocious ticket price Wednesday charge to see our team and more importantly you, yourself. They believe now Nuno and you have a place within their hearts nobody may mar and spoil. For these days are golden' The ghost of Jeff Shi said. They floated over the Wolves fans and looked at the expectation and joy on their faces and Nuno was happy and he too wanted to sing and join in the laughter, but that time was not yet.

'Verily' Jeff said. 'We must continue to build our ideas into an unassailable lead and we must remove ourselves from these places. For have not these fans suffered enough the trials and tribulations of the Championshit? Have they not suffered enough? And in the true spirit of your name will you be the one who has the courage to guide them through these turmoils?' And Jeff Shi floated across the crowd again narrowly avoiding an errant flung coin.

Nuno looked at the fans, he knew they were important, he knew they were passionate but now was the time when doubt was sown and he knew his team and his fans would be a target for the sad and the dejected of other clubs and verily the hearts of those fans were expectant but also fearful and it was his time to placate that fear and to assure them that his heart was within them too and our journey was 'our' journey and not just the abstracted dysfunctionality of those bastards down the road.

Jeff now floated above the crowd and Cavaleiro had just scored and the noise lifted them into the sky above Sheffield and all was murky and misty until again he found himself in the coldness of his room at the Molineux and the ghost of Jeff at the foot of the bed said 'Sleep now Nuno for thou hast seen the past and the present, but what does the future hold?' and Jeff whished away like a bad fart under a duvet and was gone into the mists of Molineux while Nuno again ran to his window to see if the pitch was still there.

Nuno wondered if the whole visit of Ipshit was bothering him on some metaphysical level. Why these dreams? The ghost of Moxey for fucks sake. Why him? This was one of those matches for sure. The virus of Warnock would again be fed upon the romantic beauty of the Molineux pitch and again would be sullied by those who would punch their balls at the football we play. Their would be elbows and off the ball incidents aplenty and when this starts Nuno would know that he has won the game. He knows once the tackles become insane and the referee in his abject and woeful life would not protect Nunos ideas and flow.

He knew the Warnockian diaspora of tacticless madness would slather across that grass tomorrow. He felt his eyes grow heavy again and as he was falling asleep he heard a strange sound. It was the sound of many people singing and shouting. There was joy and there was happiness. He thought there must have been a party going on downstairs and he put on his fluffy slippers and carefully. Quietly he walked down the corridor of the Billy Wright stand until he reached one of the conference rooms which was empty and in front of him the stands were packed with Wolves fans in a delirious state. They were singing and shouting, throwing confetti, there were flags and banners and on the pitch he saw Cavaleiro and Jota, Boly and Coady, there was Ruddy with a child on his shoulders, there wearing a suit was Bennet, Douglas right next to him and they were walking around the stadium in joy and happiness. Nuno placed hs hands on the smoked glass window and smiled himself. He felt a hand upon his shoulder. He turned and there stood Robert Plant in his Godlike stance.

Robert Plant spoke, 'This Nuno is your legacy. You have won the Champions league with Wolves and the City now rejoices at your name, do you see the joy? This indeed is the reason you were brought here and we see that verily it has been done.' Planty walked Nuno to the other end of the suite and onto the pitch floating above the streamers and the party popper strings, he pointed to the Southbank where there were limbs and madness not seen for many a year. We sang and danced all day for we had won the Champions league and on the horizon of the city there were new developments and new business brought to the town by it. Indeed from the Southbank and all the other stands the crowd invaded the pitch and grabbed hold of Nuno and put him onto their shoulders and took him all around the pitch where everybody sang his name and all was good.

You see, Nuno will awake the next day and indeed it was Christmas and Nuno will probably clap Thelwell on the back and whisper a few platitudes to him. Moxy and Morgan will always be ghosts to us now and perhaps we did avoid him selling the land our club has been built on, perhaps we did avoid the car crash that his ownership could have brought us. Maybe.

Yesterday I was as pissed as a fart wandering from pub to pub selling Southbank Resistance stickers. Meeting good people and drinking with them, telling stories and fables, laughing and being joyful. Our team of course will be preparing for the matches to come and the joy of Christmas is tempered by running around at Compton for a few hours before they rest and have recovered. There will still be tactical talks between the backroom staff and Nuno. Minor injuries to sort out. Ipswich of course has gone. The Cavaleiro goal a thing of beauty out of nothing. Our team keep doing this. Plucking out of the mud of the championship these diamond results. Even the stoic McCarthy has been sent from us with his face a bit grumpier. Fare thee well Mad Mick as you traipse back to the netherworld you have made your home. This is what could have been if you and Moxey and Morgan would have had eyes to see beyond the anachronistic dullness of your visions.

This is what you could have had and the journey that Nuno had with the ghosts above could have been yours really but the ghosts that torment you are of your own design. Nearly half way through. The Southbank was quiet yesterday but not in any crux of pain. We are waiting now. This is the intake of breath part of the season when we are waiting for the end. We will erupt and we will define what it means to say 'Limbs'. Our team didn't stretch through the gears yesterday and did what needed to be done. It was surgical and refined. Energy conserving.

We could have done Ipswich 4-0 easy. But here the vision is the fixtures over the next few weeks. Conserve energy. Just do what you need to do to get those three points and another handhold out of this shit pit of a division where the tactical nous displayed by other managers is stick another lanky brick shit house on the pitch to steal a header in the box. It was disgusting Readers Wives football after you had leafed through a few pages of slick models getting to Rita from Huddersfield with a hairbrush stuck up her arse and a big boil on her arse cheek. That! My McCarthy is what your team are. Rita from Huddersfield while we are Angel from California who likes long walks, sky diving and hot sex.

Does this post make sense? I don't know. My heads banging from yesterday and I'm trying to remember the people I spoke to who have disappeared into a fog of alcoholic madness. But I enjoyed it, I loved it and I love my team. Merry Christmas Nuno, I've got a message for you from a little old lady I spoke to while in the Wheatsheaf pub, she said…

'I trust him, I didn't want to but a little voice said I should, and I always trust me little voice'.

But these days are a confused mess now. Games coming on fast. Sometimes I don't know who we are playing until the day before. Sometimes I'm in the ground before I remember who they are. It's Winter, it's grim, but we are ascendant.

Put your coat on over ya Xmas jumper. You've got new socks on. They are fluffy. Your head feels a bit weird. Posh alcohol your body doesn't know how to deal with. On the way out the house put your hand in the Quality street tin and fill your pockets with those little sparkly delights. Then off down South to the ravaged land of London. There is a team there, we know a few of them. Millwall. Jesus Christ, I'm not going.

I have to pick and choose matches and I haven't picked this one. Why? It's a pain in the dick isn't it? I feel like Ipswich was again one of those games where we didn't get out of low gear. Of course if we had lost the match there would be fumes but we didn't look like losing it did we? I think Nuno put the brakes on the team and the whole spectacle was one of 'that'll do' and 'just stick some stuff over it, nobody will see it'. Of course it was all tactical. Nuno won't want to really throw the art shapes at a team like Yampy Micks. There's no point, it would just end up in one massive circle jerk. Ipswich got what they deserved, which wasn't a master class by any means but a sliver of what is to come.

I'm listening to the radio today and have a glass of whisky by the side of me and access to various foodstuffs within reach. What is a Millwall? It's a very angry thing isn't it? I don't quite understand their angst and to be honest I don't care either. Saville again today, he runs like he's got curlers in the hairs of his arse crack. I'm glad to see the back of him to be honest and glad that he's playing 'down there'. There's nothing worse than a player who fails to ignite your own team then we sell him to another and….oh he's a bit shit there too. Plus I actually forgot who Jed Wallace was, I had to go on Twitter and ask. That was after seeing his name on the Millwall web site and it not even registering that he played for us.

Wallace will be huffing those 30 yard pokes at goal today probably and Saville will be puffing around in midfield doing what he does best which is puffing around in midfield. But my days, what a difference in our team now compared to back in the day when Wallace was supposed to be the second coming. I've waxed about it earlier in the season so I'm not going to chat about it now apart from say…Jed Wallace runs like he's forgot to turn the gas off in his burger van and the Plymouth fans who were hanging off his dong when he signed for us can really honestly do one.

Man I was excited at the time. Even Kenny Jackett looked like some emotion was bubbling away but it was probably wind and when he tripped up in the dugout it probably came out and he wondered what the fuck he had done. Jed fucking Wallace. That's him.

Millwall is probably the place for both of them as they now sidle away the money from football, investing maybe, looking at the new Ford Transit they are going to buy for when they are both plasterers again. But my team. Are we in the zone? The Southbank was quiet and I intimated it was an intake of breath before the final push. We don't look jaded. Watching Cavaleiro against Ipswich was a thing of beauty. I loved it. He's just behind Conor Coady in the SBR love in poll. I know Neves and Jota are a thing and I love them, but the progression of Coady and probably Cav too has given me joy and pleasure.

I think, truly that Nuno has put the brakes on for certain matches. He knows we can do teams like this every week. The lack of imagination from visiting Managers makes the whole Wolves V Ipswich/Millwall/Cardiff etc etc not a fixture where you want our Jota and our Neves to stretch themselves. A clean sheet, a moment of brilliance then let the whole event run down through the 90 minutes as we soak pressure, deal with hoofballs and the odd off the ball elbow in the throat. Just this minute I watched England V Tunisia in the World Cup. So I'm having flashbacks. Violent throaty elbowy ones.

Nuno I suspect is holding these players back. Perhaps his intelligence gathering in the close season has paid off. No need to slather the Hugo Boss suit on for a night of bingo down the Royal Legion is there? Throw on a fresh T-shirt, jeans, comfy trainers. No need for slickness against teams like this and your aftershave is £50 for a spit full of smelly in a funky bottle. Do you want to waste it on Piss ya pants Phil down the Legion? His sense of smell stopped when he was hit on the head by a scaffold plank when he was 23. I'd like to say Doherty too has kind of kicked down a gear or two. Whether this is down to tactics or whether he is having a few weeks off I'm not sure. Our attack comes from the back always. I've noticed Boly getting forward a lot more until Coady bollocks him a bit, I think that's a meme that runs through all of the Wolves team at the minute. They want to attack, they want to stretch those passes around and it's only the Will of Nuno that's holding them back. He understands I think that the whole Championshit season is built on gobbling up the points and at the same time trying to keep expectation and desire under wraps while conserving not energy (I think 'energy' is something we have in abundance) but excitement. I think this team just wants to attack constantly. They aren't happy unless they are all swinging their way up the pitch waxing those balls around in intense 30-40 yard passes.

Costa will make an appearance today too. He's been on a slow fizzle that dude. Watching him over the last few games has given me a lil tingle. He looks like he's ready to start twisting up those mans on the by-line again. At Wednesday his cameo left three Wednesday players face down in the grass wondering whether they should have gone into Uncle Nobbys scrap metal business instead of football. He's fizzling just at the right moment. Part Two of the season and I bet any money on it, will be the Costa show.

Bonatini will be rested a little. He's done a brilliant job and deserves five minutes to be honest. Keeping these players fresh will be tantamount in Nunos mind. Not only physically fresh, but as Nuno develops their brains as well as here abilities he is shaping them. These little drops onto the bench will not be done willy nilly without thought. I bet Nuno and his bredrins will have sat down and worked out every last detail in every match to come. They aren't fools this lot. Dropping a player won't be due to angst or some passive aggressive needle, it will be part of the plan for sure. It's all focussed now, not as abstract as previous Managers and Coaches when you needed a Crystal ball to find out what they meant in terms of tactics.

But as is the way the baby Jesus treats us Millwall are having a go aren't they? One nil down and Saiss is getting nibbled by all sorts of madness. He must have the wind too as Wallace and Saville are running things by all accounts. Of course ex Wolves players doing things they never did here is a common thing. Like a scab you keep picking. It keeps happening. Our Xmas Hangover headline memes are looming.

Costa slips past Millwall and puts a shot right on the keeper. It's positive is it not? Millwall have given us the love eye a bit. Radio saying Costa should have wankered the thing instead of brushing it. I don't know man, I'm making up pictures in my head as I listen and type. We will stretch this Millwall team out a bit in the second half. They will be fucked. We need to up the gears a bit. Chances are just dances my friends. That ball has to go in the net. Costa blazes over from 20 yards. We will win this I'm sure.

But chances have been all over the place in every game I think. Lost chances in a game where we won but the scoreline could have been more luxuriant. I'm dipping a biscuit in my coffee and everything does seem laid back in my mind at least. There has to be games where the other team have a pop. They are human too I suppose even though Wallace and Saville can't really step up to that plate.

Mclaughlin nearly kills Douglas in a shite tackle. The Dutch dude on the radio is going mad about it. How many times though? We're always targets especially for players whose names sound like someone being sick. He's in the book any way. Maybe he will keep his clod hoppers to himself now, give Saiss some room maybe.

As soon as I type his name Saiss boots a Millwall player into 2014. Good work brother. Show them that you too can give a little loving back. Total enforcer. I've noticed every time an opposition player goes through one of our team Saiss turns up to set the record straight. He's the big brother that saves you from the scrotes in the playground. He's Denzil Washington in 'The Equaliser'.

Ruddy hoofs a low ball up front to Jota and Jota cuts back to Costa but blah. Millwalls haircuts are harsh council like things aren't they. My mate Charlie has sorted me a stream out. Cav back battling a Millwall cross. I mean I know I love my team but we do look so much better than Millwall at the moment for sure. But Wallace has done more running in this last ten minutes than I ever saw him do at Molineux. Goal?

JOTA!!!! Thank fuck for that. Lovely movement, slick and sexual, stroking, candlelight football. Furry rug in front of the fire football. I'm in an open top car driving down the Californian coast. She is next to me smiling. She has great teeth. The car is a Ferrari Jota. Oooh she's just put her hand on my thigh and laughed…she adjusts her Wolves top a bit as the air con is blasting cold air.

Oh my days.

Coady is being Coady again by being fucking brilliant. He just lets people foul him looking for the free kick but he always has a toe in the grass so in case the Ref doesn't blow he's up again and harrying their attack. Brilliant. Love him to bits. I should write a Coady Part 2 thing. It's half time and I've eaten two slices of Turkey, a fondant fancy, three strawberry cream chocolates, a Beef scotch egg and drank a coffee with brandy in it and a brandy with no coffee in it, another fondant fancy and a Walnut. The dogs are farting loudly and it stinks. Every time I eat something one of them Turkey farts right underneath me and then slink off like it was me that did it. Every sweet mouthful has the scent of dog arse.

It smells like Savilles trim which is fully whack, he looks total speng. Dog fart haircut mate. I wonder what you and your mate Jedward are going to do in the second half. He looked knackered to be honest. These dudes we get rid of from our club are good for 20 minutes or so that's it. I bet Nuno is whispering his magic words to our players.We kick towards our fans next half. That means we can suck the ball into the net with our belief too. How can a player not run for Nuno until he's coughing his heart and lungs up?

Cavaleiro has taken a whack so I guess Bonatini will come on next to score the winner. He's bound to have a bit of ooomph in him now. A bit of that fuel you get when you've been dropped to the bench maybe? He might score two, it's overdue. I love Bonatini too, January will see some flash striker arrive but I think Bonatini will be a face in the next few months.

SAISS!!! From range! The laptop went up, I've spilled something on me leg. The dogs are barking. It's all gone tits up! Hahahahahaha bless his little heart. Enforcer/Saviour maybe? This will take the wind out of Millwalls shrivelled little chests. Quality and brilliance. Chances taken. Costa having his fizzle poured on his dizzle in spades. I told you he was just warming up. Another year on this lads head and he's stellar. Absolute Universe. And at last one of those worldie shots goes in too. This is the point where I'm hugging Horace and shouting in his face but I'm damp with hot tea and for some reason there's a cocktail sausage stuck to me arse. Millwall. Wolves. Boxing day. Saiss thirty yard wonder goal. My nipples are hard. Fat rosey cheeked women in scarves, winter walks along the canal, channelling Bill Hicks. Oh Mar Days.

Big Willy off-Miranda on. Looks like Bolys hamstring. Maybe it's a little tight? I hope so. Miranda is a thing, maybe just what we need here too. He's a lot more flexible and like moving around. I don't know. Do a job son, don't let them in. Get well soon Willy. Boly is a man that blocks the sun out he's that tall and wide.

Spell of Millwallness here. Yes, they've scored. 2-2. Is it going to be one of those days? Balance upset? I'm not sure. It's Xmas for them for sure. Playing and moving. Do we need a bit of madness a bit of Brighty? We don't look very sharp here when really we should be hanging out the back of these freaks. Couple of mistimed passes. A cross that stretches the description…

But then again we are having a sunset moment here. Good crosses, a few decent passes into space but it looks angsty still. Maybe we are half a yard short. Millwall have upped the pace and a few balls are going skywards again. Ping pong ball a bit. All heads and falling over. The eighty year old grey haired bloke who plays for them is doing some running. Quite fast for an old'un. I love the way big Alf wants to get forward, I don't understand why Costa is off but I'm not Nuno so I remain in ignorance about that.

So yeah Millwall. That was weird wasn't it? But then again maybe all these fixtures against these types of team are weird. I'll take a draw. It's cold, you're in London, you're playing against Jed and Sav and company. It's bound to take a mental toll on your abilities and fuck me even a Wizard like Nuno has to be content with that. Millwall are the team that exists even when you stop believing in them and I think this fixture will be one we don't want to see repeated too soon. It was Farmfoods football that makes you scour the inside of your mind for a reason. I don't want to say 'Onward' because everybody says that but I will say 'Ay' and that's all I've got to say. This game was just having ten minutes to look around a bit. Get ya breath back. I feel like Stephen Hawking in this chair. Listening to after thoughts of the match and the radio there are words said about racists chanting at the match today.

Racism eh? Songs and calls from the Millwall fans about the eating habits of some of our players. Big Alf here for the Chicken? Have you been to Dixies? Jesus Christ. Millwall of course were just being Millwall. They have been 'Millwall' for countless years. By Millwall I mean well…It's a bit of a place isn't it? Hemmed in on all sides by the cultural blancmange of whatever London is. They have a siege mentality, a kind of closing off of the mind when it comes to bantering and songs. They aren't stupid, they know the songs and the casual racism will have some effect and they know those songs and 'banter' will identify them as purely Millwall. I've walked out of there with a lock knife stuck in my knee. I know this 'Idea' of Millwall. But fellas, to paraphrase Terrence McKenna 'your culture is your enemy' it stops you opening your eyes, it controls your lives, it filters out the world for you, its a firewall for interesting stuff.

The whole idea of Millwall as a club is solidified by a section of their fans as having that anti-cultural meme that all dystopian populations have. They do it because it winds us up and then there's a whole gamut of threads on social media to peruse and either laugh or cry. Lack of idea from them? Of course. When you have to use somebodies skin shade or country of origin to get banter points then you've pretty much lost the game.

It's rubbish and it's crap. But that's culture for you isn't it? Millwall have their own twisted entrenched and lumpen culture that involves being paranoid about what people think of them. Automatically thinking it's going to be a negative view they are on the attack straight away regardless of what 'we' think. Can I cuss them? Yeah I think so but most of all I'm sad that they lack creativity to define themselves in the madness of their city. They lack the driving force of novelty to decide how their club should be seen by reverting to redundant racial slurs, songs about chicken, vociferous debates on social media about being a 'snowflake' a term probably stolen from the AltRight soy boys of the USA. It's not banter, it's just bollocks isn't it?

I could blame the lead in petrol, the fumes around that place make your eyes sting. The chemicals, the lack of fresh air maybe affects Millwall pre natal mental development who knows.

What bothers me more is the identifiable and glaring casual racism shown by certain club Managers and the Sports Press. It's there isn't it? The odd throw away comment hidden in an article, the comment lost in the fog of a fast paced radio interview, the odd now deleted tweet. This is the arena that pisses me off the most because I know it intimately. I saw it in offices and schools, in meetings, visiting businesses. We get it in slurs about Winter time, whether these Mediterranean footballers can hack a cold North Easterly in Middlesbrough. It's rubbish isn't it? Their ideas about our team are ignorant and lack energy.

We have in our broadcast media a tranche of people who regard casual racism as a way to further agendas. I know a lot of them have an agenda against Wolves. Against our Chinese owners, against foreign players or foreign involvement as a whole. I had a ten minute conversation with Robbie Earle years ago when he was doing a football show, he pretty much agreed with the above but in football in general. The FA I suppose has some blame as well. But Robbie Earle was the best commentator and pundit I've ever seen in the media. I looked forward to him talking, for him to show me new things I had missed during the first half. He indeed grew my football knowledge in leaps and bounds but…we never see him on the TV. Instead…Alan Shearer.

So what's the conspiracy here? The 'establishment' want to know where the cash is going and why it isn't going in their pockets. The English FA and the Press have a great relationship, the English Press and shadowy business interests have an even greater one. It used to be forged with secret handshakes in Masonic lodges and in the corridors of power in Westminster but as you know Jeff the world has changed. Now it's done over expensive coffees and focus groups, in relationship initiatives and friendships made in Oxbridge University clubs. Even though these personalities wax lyrical about global opportunities and the global market they are in essence still deeply routed in the 'old boy network'. It's a white man dominated colossus, it's a house in Buckinghamshire, it's a Jag or two on the drive, it's the weekend cottage, the back slaps, the juicy contracts, kick backs and fucking the PA in Travelodge. It's defunct Jeff. Has been for years.

But under all the snide racist comments there is a method. This method is used as a vehicle to further an agenda and that agenda has to be set by somebody. I wondered, yesterday, who that group of people were. Of course I have some ideas. I intimated a few of them earlier this season when I said as soon as we started to put together a good run of results (which I knew we would) we would start to suffer the little digs and prods from sections of the media. And haven't we half? Having a go at Saint Jack Hayward… we know he was a bit reticent about paying his taxes, we know he was a bit rah when it came to living his life. He loved his country (though he didn't live here) and he loved his town (though he didn't live here). There's a whole thick folder of information about his financial dealings and the rest of the crap all in the public arena. I could write a shit load of blog posts about it to be honest. But…

We have fought these battles for years and years. Walked into meetings and had our accents mimicked and made fun of. Had our teams denigrated in the national press and media. This is what the 'soul' of Molineux is, the ability to withstand the slings and arrows and stay true to our ideas and beliefs even when it seems everybody is against you.

'He's one of our own' part of the song we sing about Sir Jack. I'm quite happy to sweep a lot of his dealings under the carpet because of exactly that. He saved this club, which at the time was rattling around in some serious bad funk before he arrived. But he's a target for sure. A way in which those fucking Lizards in the press can wheedle their filthy fingernails underneath our armour and get reaction, to try and build some sort of proto racist platform to have further digs at our club doesn't amaze me like it does others. But he's one of ours. With all his faults. This is why he is being attacked really and why some half pissed fat gutted shit beard journo fancy having a pop, because it gets a rise out of us, the fans.

Wolverhampton…for you fat press gimps, is a bloody hard and soft place. You prod it and it will bite back as it's doing now on social media. You can't have a pop at us because we are far too strong for you. Far too strong for you spineless free loaders with your double chins and your shit beards you grow to try and hide it. You are the blank men in M&S suits with the shiny arse. You are the 500 soulless words on a website nobody reads. You are the glad handing grease smeared face on the other side of the taped off corridors of power. The FA were also you at some point and you circle and preen each other like arse sniffing dogs. How fucking dare you denigrate my team. How dare you denigrate people at my club.

You bastards never grew up here, never knew what real racism is, never knew the struggles we had. Those years in the wilderness have reforged the whole idea of what we are as a club and Sir Jack himself had a part in that albeit through the filter of Empire and The King. 'Kick out the Jams Motherfuckers' That Detroit band MC5 used to sing, but what was a 'Jive Ass Motherfucker'? It isn't the people that stand at Molineux every week. It isn't even Millwall boneheads for we have discussed how their worldview is filtered by the dystopia they live within. It's 'them' again. The dickheads from the home counties that get into good Universities because Mommy and Daddy have some cash. These people tumble through University on their Journalism degrees or new fangled Social Media digital bullshit degrees. They build contacts through the hazy bar burping up Jaeger bombs at a quid a pop. They forge links with others like them. People that talk like they do, make racial slurs in quiet voices while looking around to make sure there isn't some angry black dude around. It's like Freemasonry all over again but instead of handshakes it's a tweet here and there. The odd weird article about a players background. The endless parade of crap pundits on Match of the Day. Their 'ethnic' friends have anglicised names and will choke back the overheard racism because they have a foot in the door of this world awash with cash. It makes me sick.

Here we are, us Wolverhamptons. For the most part we have embraced this idea of globalism and we are learning fast. That learning was forged in council estates where we had to learn to live with people from Pakistan, from the West Indies, Africa, India, the Middle East. That learning was hard for all of us. New cultures, languages, ways of doing stuff. New foods, smells, ideas. There were hard times when we couldn't look each other in the face and we didn't have the luxury of government cash to assuage the hardships. Sometimes it was so hard there would be battles and fisticuffs and there were things said and done. But on the whole we have come out a lot better than most places in the UK. Forged in the fires of the economic hardships of the post industrial landscape we have come out hardened off. Still with an idea of our own backgrounds and ethnicities but smashed together to form a new culture I suppose. Wolverhamptonism. Where the fellow you knew years ago who abused George Berry for being a 'black bastard' now walks his mixed race kids around West Park to feed the ducks. Don't tell him his Grandkids are 'little Monkeys' He'll probably kill you. In fact thinking about it he would.

That's why we have embraced our Chinese owners. It's not hard, we know this shit off by heart now. You tell us about your ideas and we will tell you about ours. You come from another country? What do you eat there? How do I prepare it? What music do you listen to? What are your ideas? And here of course is the rub. We have a Manager in Nuno who has been forged himself on an island in the Atlantic Ocean that has felt the boot and bare foot of many different cultures and ideas. Indeed he has come through that fire to present to us his own idea and how beautiful is it? How lucky are we? And how lucky is he that he decided to Coach a club that has itself been through a fire or two and come out tempered and stronger?

The media disinformation campaign against the Wolves is kicking in now. The odd article filled with bile and untruths. The Manager quotes (Yes you Steve Bruce) that have all the intellectual nous of a fucking Yoga DVD. Love it, bring it on. You fucking Dinosaurs, how dare you. You haven't got the right to print anything about my club, you haven't earned it. And your team got beat at the Molineux? Tough fucking tit. You're all living in the past, Managers, Journos you have failed to evolve, you are old photographs, sad TV formats, you have failed to create new ways and new systems. We are the media now.....fuck, my biscuit has fell in my tea. Yeah the disinfo, the fake articles, the men in tight suits and tighter expense accounts, the back slappers, the sidlers, idlers, the useless dregs of the old order...picking out a floating half a biscuit in hot tea, shoving it in your face while your fingers burn. Got it all out too. Kwan. Belief. Just say No to Fake Football journalism

Let the fools in the media gloat and preen, present their shit to us, what does any of it mean now? The world is changing fast and they are too fat to drag their arses to the window to watch it as it goes by. What is a Talksport? What is a Broadcasting sidekick? What is all of this shit? My Nan used to say 'if they are having a go at how you look then they have run out of things to say' and that is the God sent truth. Talksport and the general Broadcast and print media have run out of ideas. My advice to all of us is to stop reading their shit. Get your news from fan blogs and web sites. Communicate with people, take in different opinions and utilise them to gain your own ideas of whats happening in football. Talk to people and exchange ideas, learn how to put a blog together so you can share your ideas and news, your points of view. Let everybody know what they are and build up a greater picture of how Wolverhamptonism flows. This is the way we destroy them, this is the way forwards.

'It is only for us' – Nunos post match Interview after Bristol City

Well it is that of which we said it was gonna be. What price this life and this madness? That you can commit your heart to such madness, indeed live it and breath it in with people you love and respect and then right at the end, such an outpouring of love and emotion that all of a sudden it seemed like all the stresses and strains of the last few decades have gone. We stand on our feet for a moment as the limbs thrash and shins get whacked, chaos ensues. Names are writ on the hot flesh of hearts. I'm in Bristol because I've been subsisdised by a few lovely people who clubbed together for a ticket and a few beers. Trust me I'm a few quid off being a tramp and living rough. I don't want to live on somebodies floor, I'd rather freeze to death than do that. But Douglas you absolute star.

Douglas, a man who defines the whole idea of a dead ball master. Bennett who was denigrated so badly by Norwich fans that his heart must have jumped from his chest the way he jumped up and then time kind of stopped didn't it? The winning goal, I was twenty feet from it and my hand stretched out to grab Horace and everything slowed down and there was a silence of sorts. A silence of expectation of everything 'being in it's correct form'. Of course we were going to win it. I watched Bennett connect and it was done. The ball wasn't even in the net and it was over for me and I knew we had at last arrived so I shut my eyes and shout screamed that primordial victory.

'We're going up, they're going down, We're going up, they're going down'

What even is Sambuca? There was a tray of shots and I was invited to partake. I drank one and it was burny and good. I turned around and somebody was talking to me about my writing and I was wrecked and didn't know what they were talking about. I was just a Wolves fan getting rat arsed before the game with my mates. All was wobbly and funny. All was wavy and curly. Outside the pub the people of Bristol did their thing and what a load of weird things they were. I understand the 'idea' of Bristol but I don't understand it. We had a smoke outside and I watched their fans do their thing as they walked past. They were quiet while we were loud. Loud because we are proud? Nah and ar, loud because that's how you talk in a factory where machines grumble and roar and some knobhead always drops a load of metal onto the concrete floor. That's why 'Tea' is always 'Tay'.

I'm in the concourse and I'm dancing around in the middle of Wolverhamptonism, a bundle of beer soaked singing lunatics. Beer is in my eyes and I cant see. Somebody kisses me on the forehead. My glasses fall off. My eyes are stinging. I can feel my wounds aching and I can't feel the tips of my fingers. I put my glasses back on but everything is a swirl of Black and Gold, Stone Island coats, red and white Bristol colours on the walls. Somebody pours beer over my head. I'm laughing, singing. What is this jollity and madness? Consolidation of the fan base. Solidarity in joy. Thank fuck for this.

What was this day? This day of victory? Probably the most important match of the season and still halfway through. It was sweet and it was divine simply because it was the test of ideas, the test of our metal, the discovery that our team are tactile and centered. What do I mean by that? Our shape never wavered. Danny Batth wanders off the pitch after one of those challenges you watch again and again. Was he right to be sent off? Debate and argument over it of course but I'm Wolves enough to back Danny whatever the outcome and I knew going down to 'ten men' wasn't going to be a massive hassle for this team. Play restarts and our shape changed. There was new order and new tactics, new positions and it didn't look as if we were bothered that much.

I'm thinking of what would have happened if Lamberto or Jackett would have been in the same Nuno position. Nuno gets sent to the stands because he puts a foot out of the technical area. I'm not bothered, in fact I like it. Passion, madness, the mind of an artist is never fucking still. Art grabs the passion out of you surely? But on the pitch the art was changed and mastered by every player in that position.

Cavaleiro comes on. Somebody turned the footballing volume up to 11. Play was louder now. Play was sublime. We never looked like anything was much of a hassle. Why? Because behind the team was a weight of intent. A juggernaut of possibilities with a momentum that cannot now be stopped and we saw that in Austria didn't we? Pre-season which seemed that long ago now. Soaking up the rarefied atmosphere of mountain air our new look team marched onto the fields in those mountains, who knew?? Who expected it? Well I did to be honest. The season we had under Lambo was a disgrace, we needed a whole new philosophy and whole new outlook. Lambert was just the scrag end of a succession of club foot Sunday dinner football we have had to endure. Why can't we have a Coach with thoughts of his own?

Saiss amazes me. Nuno had given him a new dogma. To make that role his own as Saiss sees fit. That's the secret of Nunoism. Make the player not believe, because belief is airy fairy elf bollocks. 'Belief' is the death of intelligence. Nuno instigates players to cast away belief about the way they play and instigates 'Knowledge' of football. Belief in the way you play is a one way street when the crassitudes of the daily grind for points wears your team out. Normally around this time of the year as Bristol City has found out. Nuno is sent off again.

They do not know what to make of him and now we are a target for those with a lack of idea. A foot inside the pitch? Outside his technical area? Nuno has a heart that wants to be on that pitch. His bravery is standing inside the area and not running on the pitch. During the first goal celebrations I too was climbing over seats. Love. I wanted to celebrate. I know it's illegal. I was beside myself and emotional again. Thoughts of Nuno standing in the Directors box, all around him the enemy, the former Managers, the hangers on, the defunct Bristolian philosophies, still brave, still El Nuno, he doesn't give a shit, I loved him after a few games and with each game I love him more, what passion what love, he is a Knight of old and that blood of the warrior runs in his veins. Five hundred years ago his phone would have been a sword. Castigate his name to me and I will remove you from my mind. Viva Nuno. Endless victories for this man please.

This match describes that philosophy perfectly. Here was a team that has just beat Mancrusty Disunited. Bristol had a belief going into the match. Their whole existence built on the 'belief' that they were doing something positive and heroic. And that's shit my friends. Because we ourselves have had that belief for years and years. We beat Liverpool, we get arseholed by Burton the next week. We believed everything we were told because that powerful sense of belief is a real tangible thing that teams like Bristol City and us last season held onto tight. It's all we had. But it didn't do us a lot of good. There's an old adage about a group of Fishermen in a life boat being buffeted by waves and in danger of drowning.

'Pray to your Gods, but row towards the shore'. Bristol were praying and believing, our team were rowing that boat towards shore hard and fast for 90+ minutes. On 94 minutes we stepped out of the boat onto dry land and thanked God yes, but we have blisters on our hands and we watch the Bristolians struggle in the crushing waves of our joy and happiness. Costa my little love button. Throw away the beliefs you have in yourself and have knowledge instead. Have the knowledge that you are perhaps one of the greatest footballers to step onto a pitch. Don't believe but know. You have been injured and hurt, you have watched other players come into the team and make positions their own. You have sat on the bench and watched them victorious. This place is yours Costa, if you start knowing you should be there with them. It will come in time Brother be strong, keep rowing towards shore. Last minute, or last second winner, I try to run on the pitch but they have stretched stretchy stuff over the seats and it's like quicksand and I'm shouting and screaming along with everybody else and everything is crazy. A snatch squad tries to grab me. Not today mate, not today.

Outside the ground there were a few words between us and them. Little snidey comments from people who really shouldn't debate with us. Their words lack power. The words they have drop into the crusty potholed roads around the stands. They fall like dead things with a slap and a comment. I'm soaking wet and shivering a little. There's some Bristol fan in a duffel coat shouting at me but I don't care. Fuck off Paddington. Go away.

It's the halfway point really isn't it? We have built up to our current position with creativity and with novelty not belief. In the games to come that stoic inevitability of a good result will continue to get stronger and stronger and then it will be over. What happens happens. I cannot see any team in this division challenging the Philosophy of Nunoism, it's a philosophy that engenders positivist energy on all counts regardless of the situation. You see it in Nunos interviews where any negativity is trod on straight away.

Nuno has built a system were each player is given an academic basis to his play, where each situation and problem has a solution and that solution is drilled into them. But with this quantitative tactical madness there is also a place for a player to grow and to make his own decisions based on the creative component Nuno has also given them. The place where each Wolves player is under the impression that the ball is ours, and if the opposition has the ball then they have stolen it and it is not theirs and must be taken back. Saiss never let that ball get away from him. What a wonder he is. Constantly chasing 'his' ball, getting 'his' ball back so he can give it away to another Wolves player. Another attack. Another foundation stone in the great edifice that Jeff Shi and Nuno are building.

I'm emotional and tired. Wolves always do this to me. I'm sitting typing and smelling the stale beer from my jeans. I watch Nuno celebrating our winner and I'm emotional again. We have to play our part in this madness now. Get onboard this crazy train and hang out of the windows shouting at every passing City and Town on our way.

We have to get out of this division and it's lacklustre bullshit football where other teams have this vapid and spiritual belief in their club and their players. Even the Premier league will have it's own ideologies and madness but again we must gather the momentum to break through that ceiling, smash the windows of football conformity and continue to grow and decimate our opponents. The Champions League, the epitome of beautiful creative football. That is where we must be. Look at the potholed roads surrounding these stadiums but keep your eye fixed on the lights at the end of them.

Those were the days my friend, we thought they would never end, we would sing and dance, forever and a day. It was funny coming out of Ashton gate with that feeling and it was familiar of course. Somewhere deep in the belly you remembered it and it kind of put a spring in your step and even the banterous bullshit City fans outside the ground were a bit taken aback with the vehement replies to their crap bars. Shaky Jake came round the next day laughing in his new groove. He's been off Heroin now for eight weeks with my help and we are coming to a point in our relationship where he needs to know about the Wolves and what happened in Bristol. The fog is clearing a little and it's the same with Wolves. Nuno is getting his shake on. Going mad in the Directors box. I point Jake to the Gif and I point him to his own victories. In my mind alone they go hand in hand. Both of them surmounting the odds to achieve some sort of relevance in a world that can crush and annihilate you in a second. A bad game would change Nunos zeitgeist and a visit from the Bailiffs did indeed change Jakes.

My cash supplies are down to £2.47p as I spent £8 in Bristol and Jake needed to get milk so now that last few vestiges of the cash society have withered away and gone but all is good and all is positive. If Nuno can survive this shit, if Jake can hide away his shakes then yeah. All is good.

Brentford I can truly say, 'What is a Brentford?'. Do I have to castigate every team I write about? I had a great email from a Bristol City fan berating me for not mentioning one of their players in my match write up. I didn't even mention Lee Johnson either. But he was a bit confused as to why. It's because I'm not interested in them as individuals or as a team. You truly are just another stop on the journey. Barrelling through these towns I can see the fog of faces standing on the platforms but you all just blur into one and often I don't even look at you, I'm staring at my own reflection in the glass, wondering and pondering. Your journey doesn't interest me. I'm done with forensically analysing team form and shape, how they have done over the past few weeks. Ignoring all the 'they have done well this month' talk. I couldn't give a shit. You are a number and three points maybe. My heart has hardened.

I'm driving past Jakes and I see two arseholes in quasi military stab proof combat booted horribleness and I block their car in and get out. One of them has a shit beard and soy protein tits. Jake is nowhere to be seen but his woman is in tears and I am angry. I want to kick these doughnuts around but they are recording me up with funky Go-Pros with the velcro on the stab vest. I ask one to take it off and come around the corner for a proper chat. Angry and stoic I suppose. Don't be afraid. Nothing is won in anger I know but the season is now at that point where anger is palpable in the air and solid. But it's time to think properly and be academic about things. I'm ready to kick off but afterwards when these doughnuts do get their money and after a load of abuse from me and the lads they go off into their little bitter existences. I find out afterwards there were things I could have done to alleviate the situation but I lost it.

So I stand with the dogs down the canal in the cold rain under Devils Elbow bridge and the dogs are sniffing invisible scents and the cold canal is clear and I can see beer cans, bottles, a bike frame, a microwave, a lone Perch and a dead Jack Pike. I see Brentford tonight and I don't know who they are and I don't care either. That rain is cold and we have to reign in our fire too. Not on the pitch. Our team are too professional to let the next few months bother them, maybe. Jota is becoming a machine. Saiss a leader. Boly a monument. Doherty grows with each game I see him. Bennett, how they castigated you at Norwich, how you have instilled new belief in yourself. Douglas a vision of the dead ball art. Neves unstoppable, dynamic, sensuous, a delight, a constant threat. Ruddy again believing, commanding. lithe and bald is indeed beautiful. Coady on that stairway to legendary status. I go through the whole team and I see no negativity in it, no angst. What will Brentford bring to this concept tonight? I'm not sure. How would you play against Wolves? Bristol City relegated all ideas at one point and brough a hulking tower on for snotting. The ball arced over the midfield again and again. Lost ideas. Lee Johnsons concepts were lacking. 94th Minute and I still can't talk now, a few days later.

One game blends into another but I will not waiver and lose it. My mind was set on the positive from the start of the season. I just chose to believe for once but not just that errant belief you have at the start of every season but a new belief. Always be positive. Never cuss a player. Never criticise during battle. Give your all every game. At Ashton Gate the Wolves fans behind that goal sucked the ball in with belief. If that ball was just placed on the centre spot with no players there our energy would have sucked that ball right into the netting. We must do the same every match we play. Are we the proverbial 12th man? No, we are the soul of the whole edifice of Wolverhampton Wanderers. What is our bonus for promotion? Zilch in monetary terms, it's not going to pay that gas bill, the Virgin media bill, the demands from Severn Trent, but in emotional release? Everything. Why do our emotions tangle up with Nunos celebrations? Because he is us, he is our edifice and our monument too, for now at least. Our empathy is complete with him now, his journey is also our journey, our footballing DNA wrapped up with his. Did you see Jeff? Do you understand the courage and bravery he showed in running up those steps to Nuno. to stand by him as if Nuno was going to be attacked? Do you realise he broke one of the central tenets of Chinese business ethics in an outpouring of emotion?

Do not listen to negativity I plead with you all. Don't worry about anything. This whole concept of the Nuno-Jeff-Us merry-go-round is starting to enter it's last conclusions whatever anybody says. Nuno is right, nothing is won in January but we have won one thing already and that's the belief that we can actually do it and that my friends is a priceless thing in the months to come. Hang in there Brothers and Sisters and those that aren't sure. Be strong and carry on believing. Oh yeah. Fuck Brentford.

I don't know what to write about the match. I have stories and angles but none of them fit what I witnessed. I haven't a clue. I've never watched a more complete game of football than that. I can't cuss Brentford, whoever they are. Played well. We did esoteric things. Other worldy. If a UFO would have landed in the fucking centre circle and Elvis strolled out I wouldn't have been more gobsmacked. Jess Christ. I don't watch other teams. I don't watch them because

I don't have any affinity to the end result of their matches. I don't care. Elvis in his Vegas suit stepping out of a Flying Saucer. Fangyooverymurch Wolves. Amazed. Then the day after…

I do know the invertebrates at the FA have decided to throw their fat arses around in regard to charging Nuno over the Bristol shoe shuffling out the technical area. You bastards, how dare you…I'm reminded of Bill Hicks

"Shut him up! I've got a lot invested in this ride, shut him up! Look at my furrows of worry, look at my big bank account, and my family. This has to be real." It's just a ride. But we always kill the good guys who try and tell us that, you ever notice that? And let the demons run amok …

Well the War pigs and the demons are running amok. The demons at the FA the psychic vampires of joy, a scourge and uncreative listless policy circle jerk. They disgust me…I know Nuno will get a fine and a slap on the wrist. He should tell them to piss off or pay the fine in ten pence pieces. Cheeky bastards. What it is of course is a similar thing to a load of gangland beef. Nuno is the new face who's making a name for himself but he doesn't care much for the fat men sitting in their expensive shirts driving big shit cars. He couldn't give a shit.

Where Nuno comes from is a fucking harsh place to grow up. You see it in Nunos face. It's years of thinking fast on the edge of shit, kerbside lunacy with the traffic. He's edgy Nuno is because he's driven and intent. But he knows that shit could come to an end at anytime he takes his eye off the road. He's seen it so many times before. His passion and his absolute dedication to his art borders on the metaphysical and the realms of the eternal fight against the light and the dark. That's probably why this whole Wolverhampton thing attracted him. He knew it was the right thing. Deep down he knew it. On the western side of his island I bet he would have spent a lot of time looking at those Atlantic storms smashing onto those rocks and feeling that awful power through the rocks under his feet. Yes, he has passion and knowledge. They are afraid of him. He scares them. They are knocking his door. Fucking around with his car. The FA are the person on the other end of the telephone at 3am and they aren't saying anything just breathing heavily. So he gets the fucking message.

Helder my little pudding. It's one of those times isn't it? Everything seems to be going to shit. Every ball that comes to you has the wrong spin or is just off centre for you to collect. You run, you dink past a player and he gets the merest of toes on it, a taste that's all and its lost. Maybe you feel the ankle tweak a little, maybe some other turn of the great wheel of the universe bobbles over a metaphysical pothole. A lost pre-season, maybe Lambert playing you through an injury. Who knows? I know my heart is bleeding for him a little. I feel a connection with my team. That's why I can't denigrate them too much. The same reason you don't cuss your kids.

I do know what it's like to try and regain some kind of movement after injury and I know it's tough and I was nowhere near the athlete you are. But I know it was a bloody grind trying to do the same things I did pre injury. I know it's shit looking at all these fresh faced new recruits who seem to be able to twist and confuse the opposition as you do. Watching them receive the love. I love you Helder and I'm thinking about you every match, I look for your name on the team sheet, I sing your name loud and proud, you…Helder are 'my' Helder Costa.

I know it can cause a bit of depression and a feeling of isolation maybe too. We used to call it 'The Clutch' in skateboarding. You see we would often have almighty fractures and concussions that took months and in some cases years of rehabilitation to get somewhere near full flexibility but then the Clutch gets ya. What is the Clutch? It's the fear Helda and the pressure. The injury is done and dusted but the fear is still there. In your case it's maybe the fear of getting a further injury, a long lay off, it could be the fear of not being able to do what you did before the injury. Strange that in a few months I'll have my own and I will read these words again nodding to myself sagely. Oh Helder.

Last night when you were subbed in the Brentford game my heart dropped because I knew the Clutch had you. You were upset about being subbed as all good pros will be but you came off after doing a sterling job. You decimated Brentfords left back. He was fucked. You ran him all over the place. Your movement off the ball was sublime. I know we were getting our Jota and Neves love bone going. I know most people were watching them, but I was watching you Helder. I was watching you because I understand what you were doing and what the whole game play was. Now I could wax about how great it was to watch the game last night. It was brilliant and it was entertaining and to be honest it was that beautiful I sat with my keyboard on my lap ready to write the 'ab'normal match report I do every game and all I could think about was you walking off the pitch.

I don't think you have found your 'place' or know how valuable you are within the team, I don't think your Kwan is flowing brother. There's a blockage there that makes those potholes appear all over the pitch. Get that Kwan back Helder, have some time to get your head straight as you above all people in that team deserve to walk onto the pitch with your head held high. Remember last season? Remember how you settled into your rhythm? Remember how you ripped apart defences with your runs? You alone fought through the bullshit Lambert months while others sat and fiddled.

You alone stood up and puffed out your chest and ran those channels with aplomb. You Helder, little Helder had the whole world of Wolves on your shoulders and you did fucking brilliant. Now is the time little brother, to castigate the naysayers, to throw caution to the wind and let your footballing soul burst through these dark clouds we have had in the skies above and state your claim again. Get that Kwan back, listen to Nuno, listen to us. Believe in yourself little brother, believe in yourself like we believe in you. Don't listen to the Lizards little Helder. They survive on strife and pain. They feed on you if you let them. The shadows are always banished my hard work and laughter.

But the Invertebrates are coming aren't they? The Lizards. The men that have no soul. The War Pigs. I'm walking the dogs down the road to the canal and a van goes past and some comedian shouts something about Wolves with Fuck words and hand signals and he nearly fell out of his van. I had my wolves scarf on. The Lizards. We've got a stick and we are poking their shitty little nests of cash they hide in. Allo? Allo? It's us…..Wolves…poke poke poke.

Now these mother fuckers are starting to show their horrible little faces. The Coaches from other teams have things to say, things to do with us. We occupy their minds now and they are threatened. They are starting to make contingency plans for us. There in their little pea heads the plans stew and cook like bitter flavour for their bitter little lives. I am happy. What's the remedy troops? How do we respond to this in the interwebz. We inform these mother fuckers of the truth thats all. Define your arguments, research your facts and bombard the ignorant with our thought and our intelligence regardless of the insult and the cack gif warfare. We must respond in the way our team does in matches, with skill and with reasoned debate…kind of, well not debate but maybe…I dunno. You know what I mean. I'm angry and it shows I know. I'm sorry.

Cheeky bastards. 'Let them have their day in the sun' one said. A Cockney Red. Two words that make your throat feel like it's got a fucking frozen fish finger in it. They make you look at your kids wondering if they are really yours, like walking past a cemetery while there's a funeral going on. Day in the sun my arse, who the fuck do you think you are? You've had your day in the sun pal, spunk 90 million squid on a player. Oh God I can't even talk about them and I know 'fans' who used to drive up to Old Trafford to watch Manchester United from Wolverhampton. They were 'Wolves fans who just liked to watch good football' they said, The fucking animals. Now they keep popping up talking about Wolves a fucking lot. Lizards man, they could be standing next to you right now. I'm feeling paranoid.

It's going to keep happening as well and I'm not looking forwards to it. It's going to be intense on a packed train and some lollipop having 'banter' says 'yer well you've bought the title haven't you?' and there's no red mist, no getting your skin ready and thinking about where you are going to chop him.

It's cool man. Because we are the fucking big monkey now. We are the big rich smelly ape on the squashiest, comfiest bit of the shitty jungle. We are the ones that are sitting in the sun while some underling Championship side picks the fleas off our ball sack. Being the Big Fucking Monkey or the B.F.M feels good and positive to me. Yeah it was dark in the jungle with the rest of the mange ridden outcasts trying to get a shag before Big Fucking Monkey saw us….well F.B.F.M (Former big fucking monkey) ie the current Premier sides, their fans aren't happy. The little monkeys are gibbering in fact and it's disturbing our happy time in the sunlight chilling. Their gibbering is loud and soon the Big Monkey is going to get pissed off and he'll make sure the little monkeys never get a chance to pick his ball sack ever again.

The JAMS and their little monkeys eh. I can't wait to smash them in their own grounds. Watch their sad little faces file out all glum and miserable while I'm laughing half pissed with two hookers in an executive box because I sold loads of t-shirts and books and stickers and now I'm rich and lads and lasses I swear I'm not going to waste a penny. My life.

Tramodol 50mg sort to control the spirals of ache I have and I'm up town walking around and in pubs with people and we are chatting and laughing and all is good. But I have filters. What is a Swansea? But I'm that tranquillised it takes me twenty minutes to work out that they are in the Northbank. We have the other incarnation of Nunos mind today. The players he keeps hidden away from us. The Home grown Morgan Gibbs-White thing. He's a handful isn't he? Head up searching for a pass. His movement more refined from when the last time I saw him. I don't remember when that was but my addled head works out, yes, he's improved a lot. Especially the way he moves into space, the way he blocks and moves. His runs are a thing for me. I see him in all sorts of roles in the future.

'Fucking hell Ruben you fucking wanker'

People hate the our stand the Southbank don't they? Little snide remarks about it, much fume in Social media. It's reptilian and the Lizards are scurrying around again. Up and down Molineux alley. In the executive boxes, in the seats among the woollen clad Billy Quiets, blankets over knees, their families have had them seats for years and their fat arses are welded to them. Ruben Vinagre wanders off after a red card. Was it deserved? Some say yeah some say no, some say I dunno. It's done any way and Ruben is now about to enter that part of his career known as 'A Pain In The Fucking Arse'.

Three games out and who knows what Nuno will think of the incident. I know sometimes these trials Pro Players face will either harden him up and centre his kwan or he will wilt and be sent out on loan to Le Loco's on the Iberian Peninsula. I loved him at the start of the season. I like the way he runs down the wing, I like his crosses too and now he's carrying one. Ruben I can't help you out man but have strength and let this make you strong.

Filters. We all have them, and they slide into place when we go somewhere or do something. It's what we use to protect ourselves from the vigour's and the madness. Some use their filters as a shroud to hide their vehement and horrible opinions on how a particular player is doing. Others like me just grin and try to be happy as I hear the doughnut behind me cussing Brighty again and again. This is his stage, old misery guts is the central character in his own play 'Miserable Cunts Who Think They Know About Football' a play in two parts with an intermission. The play lasts roughly 90 minutes. 'Gary Safttwat' works in a factory making parts for things nobody wants to talk about because it's dull as fuck. So he can't wax about how he hates it, but because the dull man has turned up on time for the last 30 years and doesn't like taking holidays he's been promoted Sales and Technical manager of 'the place that makes boring things'. His office window looks out onto another factory in Ettingshall. All he sees is this factory. Sometimes he sits in his car and cries before he goes home. His Phil Collins CD is skipping as he sits in traffic on the Birmingham new Road.

He a Wolves fan. He's got a Wolves mug at work. Saturdays are his days when Wolves play at home. But he has filters. You see people like Gary have a deep seated problem with themselves and that problem is self hate.

'Fucking Hell Brighty you fucking cunt'

Molineux is a stage with around 30,000 actors all vying for the audiences attention. All thinking they are the stars of the whole show and of course they are. But there are a few voices all shouting and a lot of it is negative crap. Gary is doing it. His mate does it a few rows over. Every now and again you hear it through the cheers and the groans. Solitary filter-less actors letting that negativity they have harboured and grown throughout the week grow into a mass of bubbling angry moods they keep hidden under their scarves until an errant shot or a misplaced pass makes them erupt into madness. The Referee is one of those actors. His resilience to common sense is majestic. At times he choked the game at others it lost control careering across the filters and becoming confusing. Their goalie looks like he forgot his kit and has had to get stuff 'Out of the kit box'. Scruffy bastard. Swansea are singing something I can't hear.

'What the fucking hell are you doing Costa you useless twat'

Every time I hear it my own happy mood starts to dissolve and run away down the concrete steps like hot piss. For fucks sake. The back of my neck crawls every time I hear it and another filter goes down and my head starts to ache again. These solitary and sometimes numerous voices leach energy from me. They are the vampires of joy and happiness. Throughout the match he does this.

Each time my head sinks further into my coat and my back gets hunched and I too see every shitty pass and mad attempt to score. I too start to build my own filters up and they are dark ones, I see dysfunction in the team, it's not going right, he should have shot, he should have done this. And each mental node is stinging with negative vibes.

I see him at half time in the concourse drinking and laughing and I want to punch him in the throat. That's how his negativity has affected me. He doesn't give a shit about the match. It's his moment to shine. It's a day when nobody is going to ring him up moaning about the parts nobody wants to talk about. His Missus turns her back on him in bed and he's horny and it's doing his nut in. But that new secretary at work, he tries to suck his gut in a bit. Tries to wedge his thinning fringe a little with hair product that makes his head smell like pot pourri. This is where he pours out his bile. It's not the team. It's him. He was a Champion table tennis player for Birmingham under 15's. It was his zenith. Now he is on the darker slopes.

Big Alf is having a great game. Everything that moves towards him is broken under the will of his intent. I like him, he's a bloody useful addition. One day Nuno is going to let him attack and that day will be one to make Big Alf his own legendary part in the play. We didn't play too bad I thought. Doherty looked a bit knackered. Defence did OK, Coady didn't look hassled by anything at all really seeing as the team made a load of changes. There is negativity here and it's reflected in the play on the pitch. No matter how Costa and Cavaleiro tried to jump start some movement I suspect the negativity in the stand is being felt on the pitch. We should have done Swansea. They were fucking lucky. Rafa comes on. Debut, he's massive, all elbows and angular bits, getting the ball off him would be like trying to fuck a shopping trolley. Few glancing headers which made me feel weird and happy. Few moves, he's strong, you could tell a bit stale too, nothing a week with Nuno wont sort out. The next time we see him he will be treading players into the mud and scoring goals.

Yes the Southbank is a bit quiet. Funny isn't it? Most of the people in the Southbank probably haven't had many days off over Xmas. Most of them work in hospitals, factories, building sites, places where you 'work' instead of sitting on your arse updating Facebook about how much you hate Bright Enkobahare. Probably slagging off the Southbank for not singing loud enough. Yes. But we do what we want, that's the whole point. Here in the Southbank we are a tribal lot. Not everybody in the Southbank truly understands what it is and these people enjoy it but they don't understand it. You don't like the Southbank? Tough tit.

During my half time fag break I had to go into the right side of the stand. It was quite unfamiliar to me and I was lost in thought for a while while I smoked, looking at the memorial bricks. I think all those names on the bricks would love to be there right now looking at these players and loving the whole excitement of it. I bet those names on those bricks, the Sandras, the Stans, the Steves, the Alberts etc would fucking love to be stood there now watching our team. Wrapped up with a big scarf on having a laugh and a sing, a beer and a chat. I wonder what they would make of Gary Moanarse? I think they would do what I did and just filtered them out. Because at the end of the day every time I walk in that ground I'm happy to be there regardless of the score or the match itself. Winning is just Cherry time, plop on top of the lush triflely feeling of standing in there, watching and loving it. Ah I dunno. 0-0 and me and Horace are off to Swansea to watch the replay next week. I don't give a shit about your negativity, I enjoyed it, I thought we were brilliant but unlucky.

I love every game I go to. I stay till the end. I sing songs by myself. I clap so much I cant feel my hands. The next day I can't talk. I love watching my team. I only see the good positive things. I only want to say positive things about my team. I only want to encourage performance. Those are my filters.

Way back in 1977-78 I only had a ghostly grip on what I was actually doing when going to Molineux to watch a match. Me and a few mates would be up town walking around maybe doing a bit of shoplifting or just being a nuisance. Manchester United were in town and they always brought a lot of bodies with them. It was a definite thing and throughout the day we would bump into a load of them and get chased through the old bus station by what seemed like a horde of them. Thousands of them. I remember that day like anything because it was the first time I got a kicking. Now don't get me wrong here, this isn't one of those Hooligan Glory posts where I wax lyrical about famous punch ups. In those days it was horrible going to a match, but it was also exciting too. At that young age (10 or so) we shouldn't have been up town at all, especially during a Wolves-Manchester match. But we were there and that counts for something

At the rear of the Southbank was a wall from a building, an old workshop I think, that looked over the right side of the Southbank. You could climb the crumbling brickwork and watch some of the match from there, we had 70% of the pitch in view. You could get an idea of the match anyway. Bits and bobs. Plus you were right over the open air toilets for the visiting fans and it was funny to drop the occasional rock or bottle at them while they were having a slash. Sometimes the cops would come and throw you off. Sometimes you would get a punch in the mouth off one. But we would be there. Four kids hanging on for grim death in a space for one, a toe wedged in a mortar crack. Fingers slowly going dead as you clung on.

There were loads of United in town though. They were everywhere. five minutes before the final whistle they would open the gates to the Wolves end of the Southbank. I can't remember if there was a line of cops between the fans inside, but when we all poured out at the final whistle. Things got hairy fast. You see United were coming out too and we met, right by the subway. It kicked off big time. United were filling the slope up to the Uni art block and they poured down when we arrived.

They couldn't care less these United fans and just flowed in this mass towards Wolves who were flowing down from the Hotel car park. Wolves were backed off. There were too many of them. Red and White bollocks everywhere. As is always the case the Wolves at the rear legged it back up the slope. United pushed on booting and punching. I was only little and got a few whacks. But it was mad, we were trying to escape back up the hill to the hotel. I remember this dude just standing there. Wolves fan, big belly, half his shirt ripped off, hair everywhere, blood pouring from his nose looking back up the hill.

'What the fuck are ya doing? Fucking Wolves ay we'

We turned back, poured down in fact. Everybody. Kids, adults, few women too. Rocks, bits of slab, bottles flew towards the United fans and they were off, chased back up the slope onto the ring road. Monsters man. He was a monster this dude. Moustache, a few teeth. Big rough hands, fingers like Cumberland sausages. Fucking Wolves ay we. There isn't a question mark. It's a statement. What the fuck are you doing running off, haven't you any shame? Your Towns honour at stake mate. Stand your fucking ground. And we did. Me with sticky boy arms nine stone wringing wet. But I'd never thought of this concept of 'us' before then. Now I realised that yes, there was a 'them' and there were an 'us'. My vision of my place within the universe was stamped firmly on my consciousness right there as I looked up at this beautiful blood soaked bloke who wasn't fucking moving anywhere. So I stood by him, he fought, he dropped somebody with a punch then I ran in and kicked the fella in the nose and backed off quick. A kid, playing adult games.

It was funny watching Rafa Mir doing the 'Wolves ay we' video thing. It made me laugh. It made the stand laugh at Swansea when he appeared on the big screen doing his thing. Hilarious in fact for some. But then I wasn't laughing. I had a horrible feeling standing there. Most of these people standing around me wouldn't have had a clue. Identity. A sense of belonging. History that you wont see in the club museum. 'Wolves ay we' has become abstracted and a buzzword far removed from it's snot and blood origins.

I'm not glorifying any of the violence, I didn't revel in it at the time but it was the zeitgeist of our anger I suppose. A way to come to terms with the big changes that were happening in the world and the town.

Have we got a part to play in the next ten years of our clubs development? Has this blog got a part to play? I'm not sure. The club is definitely not losing it's soul, not yet any way. When it does it won't be the global entities that have shoved the soul away but ourselves I suppose. What changes will come? How will the ticket prices change next year? Season tickets, a few drinks before the match, a beefburger, a pie, taking one of your kids to meet Benito Bronzegod our new signing wandering around shell shocked under the glare of a few lights. Mumbling 'Wolves ay we' and not having a fucking clue. I know I'm going to struggle to get a season ticket for next season whatever happens. Already I'm cutting corners on other payouts and bills.

So what happens to the being creative thing? Does it become a stale repetitive medium for old school tales and memories or do we strike ahead and make sure we become part of the narrative? I think the latter. We resist I suppose, we resist them using 'Wolves ay we' as some sort of marketing bullshit. It's not theirs to use, it's ours and sealed in the drops of blood coming from that monsters nose and dripping on the slabs by the subway. We resist changes that will affect us negatively. It's time we were able to have a cheap nourishing pie or burger instead of something that's been kicked around the floor. I want to resist expensive bottles of beer at half time. I want to resist being treated like a number. I want to resist having to buy a ticket for a game without being on the phone for half an hour or sitting in front of the lap top refreshing the screen every ten seconds. I want to resist being charged a booking fee.

You see 'resisting' is part and parcel of the whole experience here. This particular thought isn't about being negative. My teams results are of paramount importance, my team is everything to me and if I had to crawl over broken glass to see them play then I would. But we mustn't forget the past and what the club is to all of us that stand or sit every week watching it. Is this why the Southbank has been quiet over the last few matches? The lack of opposition fans to wind up, that feeling of disconnection? I'm resisting it of course. I have to. We've invested more than cash into this whole experience of Wolves. We've invested blood. I've watched Wolves holding my colostomy bag on because the skin around my stoma was infected and the gasket wouldn't stick. I held the fucker on and clapped by smacking my hand on my forehead. Investment, yeah. We've invested everything, some of us.

We're in a battle here. We have to get out of this division, it's an imagination killer for sure filled with the boring and the unimaginative coaches who snot for a living, who denigrate us with lacklustre bars of their madness and their stress. Enough moaning. I apologise for being a little negative and unsure, a little angsty. Support for the club is everything to us. Positivity, constant support for our ideas, our coach, our owners and our team. But don't forget us Fosun. Don't forget those that spend nearly all their disposable income on supporting the team, don't forget us when we are chugging stale out of date beers, half frozen pies and still find the energy to shout and sing until our voices just stop.

Because what will happen is those stands will be filled with grey faces and moaners instead of us and the world will continue turning of course, the wheels oiled by the sad and the depressing onslaught of global dullness where 'Wolves ay we' is just another corporate buzzword. I'm a bit angry again I suppose. It's Barnsley next week and I don't like it there. I'm thinking of the ghost of Warnock again and that always winds me up.

Barnsley is a strange place. The people there look like they grow their clothes on their allotments and the whole aura and reason for the place is one unknown to me. It was senseless of course 0-0. All the noughts, noughty nought. Of course we won. We scored, which means we've won regardless of the Referee who was tripping his tits off on some strange chemistry or he was super turned on by the sexiness of our football. Who knows? Disallowed goal? There's probably a good reason for it and someone will of course know what that reason is but, fuck. Ref? You're another fucking midget, another obstacle to our journey, another fucking red light, another contra flow system. The feeling when we score. Addicted I am.

We were in a working mens club by the ground and having a couple of pints. They had a 'home' bar next to the 'big room' where we were having a drink. I say we. You had to stand outside as a line of Wolves fans came out a bit red faced, swaying a bit to get some air. It was a bit humid in there and you had to peel some layers off before the sweat started to break out and you felt a bit faint. Barnsley fans kept walking through this sweaty mass to get to their part of the club. They looked normal I suppose, a bit like us, But not as tall, and not as good looking either. Wolves fans are a handsome and beautiful lot....well most of us. But Horace is not here and we are feeling that absence strongly.

What did we think of the game? My friends?…we have to get out of this place. In the ground we noticed the ball boys had been relegated to the stands where they sat with their hoodys pulled up, curled up, put there by their club and told to slow shit down. This is their idea really, before a ball has even been kicked. A directive to smother and slow down the play. This was the tactic. In surviving the roaring tempest of the bottom of the Championship you have to swim hard and as Barnsley are getting lungfuls of water in them, they thrash the stinking waters to a foam in fear and maybe even terror. It is known that these poor souls who are drowning will grab and pull a potential rescuer down with them. This is what happened.

I'll be honest, I did mention to my eldest lad these Barnsley players looked tiny until he said they were the mascots.

It wasn't Warnockian madness, well not as bad any way. As soon as the referee came out you knew what was going to happen. Breaks in play. Weird decisions. The bitter Hobbit of a Ref strutting around like a prize prick without any real idea of what constitutes a game of football, So there were breaks in play. Barnsley would often forget themselves and roll the ball around quite well. In moments any way. Until Jota got hacked down again and… again. Which made things lumpen and grey like the sky over that place. Their team looked like it needed a lick of paint, like everything else but they lacked even the idea of Warnockism. The angst was uncoordinated and clumsy and I suppose we were too at times.

I thought Saiss had aged terribly over the past week with his blonde hair that looked grey from where I was. But he ran a great game again. In fact we did play ok, we made chances, took positions, looked like this years Wolves but it was a 'bobbler'. Going after the second ball was a bit fruitless like Caffeine free Coffee. It looked like great football but there was something missing for sure. The ball wouldn't fall right for us. There was some metaphysical blockage going on. A few Gremlins in the engine making themselves a nuisance. Costa is getting faster and his Kwan is increasing in power, slowly yes, but it's coming. Some of his twisty runs were lovely to watch and of course I had Costas mortal enemy standing somewhere behind me and he was quite vocal in his cussing. But last week it annoyed me and I waxed about it in the last post. But today I can't say anything. He's improving that lad, and I like it. People should have different opinions and that's cool. But you should encourage your team.

So it was bobble ball. A lot of our passing was straight at the knees. But some of our touches. Neves flicking the ball off the edge of his foot, caressing it. Boly, what a thing he is. Like a midfielder when hooking the ball from the morass of a Barnsley attack to spread it wide, or to Saiss/Neves. Coady being Coady again, marshalling, constantly directing the play. What a player he is. Of course we are going to have these games. Manchester City lost at Palace? There you go. There's a benchmark for yesterday, there's an indication of the day. But nothing went right. A disallowed goal, a booking, Jota on the floor again after a tackle that last weeks Ref would have got a card out for. Unfair decisions, snotty play from Barnsley who choked the shit out of everything in large periods. The Barnsley players were knackered at the end of the game and they went around congratulating each other for their display. It was a point for them. Maybe a precious one as they choke on the swirling tides of shite that this division offers us.

But wow there were loads of us there. Over four thousand, singing, dancing, half pissed, fully pissed, angry, happy, grumpy, laughing or crying. It was all there on offer. Then ten minutes into the game we saw at the side of the stand another load of Wolves coming down the hill from the coach park. The late arrivals. It could have had Bristol City levels of limbs for sure. But this was a snotty game from the start. This is Yorkshire for Gods sake. Suffocating where Bristol City was vibrant. The ground was small but not intense. I don't think people are enjoying the Barnsley ideas at the moment. But how can you have ideas when it feels like your being suffocated in an Asda carrier bag?

Cavaleiro comes on and it looks like somebody has mixed his legs up and he's cross threaded his ankles. He probably thought what the fuck is this place? He tackles himself at one point and Douglas just ten yards away falls over onto the grass for no reason while Saiss looks on puzzled. Air was sodden with dysfunction at times. It must be the horror of that place, an effect that gets in the turbos of our players. Chokes the carbs.

Leo needs a holiday. He looked like poor old Dicko at times running around after the odd ball in the box. Running around a lot but the 'feel' was lacking a bit. He's getting a furrowed brow our Leo. He's thinking too much about the game. I think everybody was thinking too much about football. But it's that time of year isn't it? I think we are going to have a few more games like this for sure, before everything starts to get really fucking real in April and March. But that's also the time when the weather starts to get warmer, we see a bit of sun, our sap begins to rise. This is the calm before the storm for sure. May I prod the great mind of Nuno in my ignorance? I would have started Cavaleiro for Costa, played Mir instead of Bonatini. Swap Cav for Costa on 70 minutes, do the same with Leo and Rafa…but what do I know?

I don't 'expect' anything at all when I turn up to watch my team. It's dynamic and beautiful football that we play. There are so many abilities and temperaments in this team that Nuno must be cracking his coconuts trying to make sense out of it all. And he did I suppose, in a way. This really was a game Barnsley had set up well for. Those ballboys in the stands an indictment of their mindset. They were well set up to annihilate ideas we had. They again smothered the flames of our intent by needling at the second ball, a few elbows, a few words. Add the dystopic miasma of Yorkshire and you have a perfect storm of 'non possibility' of abstract relentless football which you find in this division. It's bloody horrible. Like going around somebody else's house for tea every night. It's food yeah, but they cook it weird and you eat it out of politeness.

We parked the car in a side street. I had given a couple of kids a few quid to look after it as it was brand new. It had screens, and sensors, a turbo that was slick and progressive, it drove us beautifully and it was filled with good beautiful people too and I didn't want to return to it with a scratch on it, even though it wasn't my motor. But as it sat their among the grime infested terraced houses and the shitty transit vans it looked lonely and I felt like it had got us here, but it didn't want to stay. I think again. We have to get out of here man. We are banging our heads against the other teams in this division. I can pick apart the play and the tactics like everybody else. Being forensic and empirical but there is a bigger idea at play here. These games are hard for us because this division plays a football that we have no affinity to. Plus we have a Ferrari like team that are only used to pick up a few bags of cat litter from Aldi because they are on offer. It's beautiful and fast of course but the cat still needs somewhere to shit and even if we have a fast sleek red sports car you are still only as fast as the old fella in the Nissan Micra in front of you.

In March and April we will see the sunshine. In those months we will enter a dual carriageway and ease the throttle of our Ferrari and slip past the old bloke with his face inches away from the windscreen concentrating. Maybe his air freshener is bumping his head too. We will look at him as our engine roars past his 27.5 mph Micra. The roar will shock him a bit and he may look around as he sees us glide past. He may even grumble a little. But set your eyes on that open road my friends, set your eyes on that destination in front of us. We are coming. Put the kettle on.

But strange as these lyrics are I still have some joy left for strange towns. I hadn't been to Swansea for ages and ages. I was looking forward to it even if Horace was crying about his flu. He couldn't come and I was sad. He's my mucker he is. Instead he's sorted a lift with Tonka. Good lad Tonka is.

At one point the wind and rain blew a crisp packet into my face and I thought it was funny and I turned around to Tonka to tell him and it blew back again. Slap. Right in the mush. Now I had rain in my eye and my open mouth had rain in it with a slight cheesy oniony flavour maybe. So I just shut up and narrowed me eyes and navigated myself back the the Landrover by touch. They were Cheese and Onion crisps. The packet was following me.

Around the Swansea ground there were humps of hills that looked like some great prehistoric gargantuan animal had just reached Swansea and decided to lie down and die. Then some humourless council planning staff decided to open a catalogue of 'Cack Dystopian Street furniture' and went pointing with a snotty finger 'I'll have that, and that, and that, one of them, two of those and yes. We want a fucking ruck of those'. I'd like to think, as we walked into the ground, that maybe one day we can visit somewhere that takes your breath away with stunning footballing vistas, beautiful cities. But now these visits are becoming blurred and melting into one great war, one great series of battles, one endless great grey landscape of trying to find somewhere to park and I think, although our bodies are not tired, our minds are becoming infected by them.

Leo Bonatini is definitely affected. He has a heart this lad, he runs and he jinks and he's deep again. Too deep to collect a ball, poke it into the net. Four times the ball went across the face of goal waiting for the foot of a poacher. Four times Leo was a few yards away. The second incarnation of Nunos mind and idea was a whole different beast to Barnsley. It was Kerplunkian dynamics.

Take out the colossus that is Boly and Coady and the marbles rattled deeper down the pitch. Batth and Hause did a job of sorts but the ghosts of Lambert and Jackett were wailing down the touchline clanking their chains of despondent negative potentials. The team played deeper with them and inertia set in fast. Swansea showed at least why they are in the Premier league. Moving was lovely at times, the ball zipping over a pitch that was uneven and Welsh. Like they had turfed over a hastily raked flat slag heap. But Swansea don't believe anything at all. They are resigned.

Morgan Gibbs-White is a thing for me. His slight figure twisting and turning in midfield. So young and yet so full of promise. I watched him the most and even grew to love him a little. He needs anger and intent too. He needs to channel that look Nuno gives stupid interviewers and mold that into his intent in that midfield. Less tactical nous and more emotive expression when he has the ball. He needs to tell those expensive players around him where they should be to collect a pass or where he will be to receive theirs

We were deep and we were sometimes under the cosh. But when we did get hold of the ball, we flowed too and we had chance after chance. You see this was the League one team with a few additions. The base of the whole idea was our second incarnation of the partnership between Batth and Hause. Now I was ready to start slagging the pair off last night. I know, it's silly. But the psycho-geography of South Wales is a hard fucking porridge to chew, mentally at least. It gets in your mind fast and starts eating away. The rain and the wind, The damp cold. The lack of anything to see except the generic architecture of the ground, the dotted around fast food places full of disinterested staff, stewards with faces like they had been used to beat out a skip fire. Skin like an old football weathering away to dust on a garage roof, a single shoe dangling by a lace from a telephone wire above, and a wind that was relentless.

But we are getting to know each other aren't we? Us in the stands and them on the pitch. I know it's a difficult time, it's fumbly and a bit leggy. Our conversations between the fans and the players are going to be a little mistranslated sometimes and that goes for the fellas on the pitch too. Yes, last night had a few errant passes and confused moments where the language of football was blown away across the pitch in that black miserable wind.

Saiss found it hard to understand the pitch for sure and the interplay between him and the team was like jumping barrels for sure. Add the 'Bastard in the Black' to the mix and stuff did get blocky and pixellated with confusion. A game of football did threaten to break out until he disrupted the rhythm with his play acting decisions. When ever a Referee tweaks his body into some vogue-ish contortion while making a decision, well it makes me want to run on the pitch and kick his head off. Don't forget mush we paid money to watch football, not some jumped up prick who gets his fun out of taking pictures of his little acorn dong to send to bored housewives on Tinder.

Swansea fandom made strides in my mind today. Who plays crowd noises on their PA? Is this a thing? They are a dour lot in South Wales. Every Steward seems to have a bald or shaved head and a broken nose. One of the women stewards actually scared me, she looked like she huffed deodorant, hair like Lucas electrics, dyed angry brown/red/grey. But look don't hassle me about it, just observations.

Leo played well. I'm liking him more and more as I watch him. Fair enough the goals have kind of dried up but is that Leo? Has he been told to play deeper? Link the play more for Jota and Cav (when he plays?) Maybe. I don't know. It certainly worked at times last night but I'm still thinking that they need a little more time together, a few dark periods to gel and become a complete team. The German Psychoanalyst Jung said that to be the complete man you have to embrace the dark side of your personality. Maybe our team needs nights like this. A tempest of football darkness to roll around in. Some chaos maybe? An instigation of intent borne from disaster and murderous footballing intent. There would be no greater place than this to investigate the darkness inside them. The sky was black and the raindrops as flung stars in the light from the floodlights. There is another Swansea rally call on the PA system and I felt like weeping again.

But the rain swirled and rolled over the stand and the storm grew more prevalent as the match progressed. Jota did a 'Jota' again and showed us why he is the 'Jota'. I love him more I watch him. Only a little fella but I've talked about that before. But he has a strong mind. Who else could delve into thine bag of tricks and pull that goal out? Sublime and gorgeous for sure. I did erupt. The stewards were watching me closely and I threw a few swear words into the wind to provoke them. Why? I don't know. I get angry sometimes and those fans in the stand, the moaners and the naysayers, the jolly, the half pissed, the fully pissed were my mates. I don't like the hands of stewards on them.

Big Alf has the ball and he looks for a pass or a run but there is nobody there. The rain blocks thoughts when thrown stinging into your face and he wipes a hand across his eyes and the chance has gone, blasted into the black hills around this place. The Swansea fans are singing something but I don't know what it is. A dollop of rain gets me right in the ear and I shiver. What is football but this? Wet feet, rain blowing around the stand, hungry, needing a piss, but you don't want to miss a chance or one of those pinging cross field balls that slither out of touch. The ball goes into the Swansea stands and they don't want to give it back. That sums them up for me. Stragglers and defunct of idea. The PCSO in front of me looks like an old Nuno and I want to throw him down the stairs when he points out a fan who has covered his face. The young lad gets escorted out. But lad? If you had kicked up a fuss I would have kicked off too. I'm a blogger but I was a fighter first.

Is this post 'Pretentious'? I don't know. Maybe. Or maybe the whole idea of writing about your team is pretentious maybe. I stand, there in opposition stadiums and all I do is support my team. That's what I do, then I write about them as best I can. I see Wayne has stuck another 'Southbank Resistance' sticker on another opposition stand. He watches Wolves where ever and when ever he can and he supports the team. That's what's important to me. The drama on the pitch reflected in the dramas we have as fans and supporters. We were quiet yes. Maybe the landscape leaked the joy out of us. Maybe we looked at Swansea and thought 'is this the quality of what we seek to attain next season?' and found it lacking a little. The plastic stadiums and the plastic cups of beer, the shit food, the relentless dystopian landscapes we travel to week after week, the deleting of comments on here from other teams fans who don't like what I've written. Well honestly you can gargle one of my balls. What the fuck do I care about your team and your town? Shall I do a podcast where I interview you and we laugh about our teams and it's all jolly and friendly? Shall I add you on Social Media and wax about the state of football today? No. I hate your towns to be honest and I hate your teams, I hate your strips and I hate your players, I hate your songs and I hate your fans. When I walk out of your stadiums I just want to punch you in the face but it seems that I'm stuck in some weird future where we don't do that any more. I think it's a shame. Now you just 'block them' Jesus Christ what have we become?

I don't give a fuck. You've all had your days in the sun. I've become stoical and malevolent as I watch my team. This is the part of the season now when you have to dig in. When I used to box our trainer made us use the last twenty seconds of a round to fling combo after combo at the opponent in rapid fire lung bursting effort. We must do the same now. This is a critical point. I suspected at the turn of the year that it would be all plain sailing now as we batter teams into submission. But you know. Even though we are flinging these punches willy nilly towards the lumps in front of us there's still time to get caught by an errant punch or two. Right on the chin, on the nose maybe and your eyes start to water and blood-snot fills your nose. But sometimes you connect and he falls to the canvas and you want to kick him in the face too, but you can't. Ah who knows. Forest on Saturday. I hope Horace is better because I'm missing his big grumpy face.

Has the atmosphere been bad at away games and at the Molineux? Is it the Southbanks fault again? I know it's been quiet and I'm sure the diaspora of Swansea and Barnsley has added to that grief somewhat. At the Molineux for certain if you take out the gibbering opposition fans from the Steve Bull lower then your ire and your localism tends to dissipate into the cavernous environs of the ground. It's a big ground Molineux and it takes a lot to fill it with noise for sure. In the 70s we knew the score from the sound from the stands. We would stand in Reans (an inner city area of Wolverhampton) a few hundred yards from the stadium, anywhere in Reans and you could hear it. It rumbled through the geology underneath your feet. In fact we would dance around under the stree tlights cheering then inevitably start kicking the shit out of each other with joy. Lads eh?

Yes, I suspect it has been quiet. I think the Steve Bull having a sing and 'shaming' the Southbank is hilarious. Of course it sounds loud to you singing in your stand. That's cool, it gives you an identity I suppose. But really it just sounds like a few blokes singing in the gaps between our songs. Of course when we start the fucking ground shakes. In full voice the Southbank is relentless with it's dishing out of decibels and limbs. We are brilliant really.

But what's the zeitgeist here? Why is the atmosphere a bit shit? We are doing excellent in the league, beautiful football, everything is tanned and sexy, healthy, big white teeth time ay it? Well yes, it is for some.

Winter is a dodgy time for supporters, especially January. Nobody has been paid yet (if they get paid monthly). We've just fought through Xmas and the splodging out of large amounts of wodge so our Princes and Princesses can get their sticky ungrateful hands on the latest bit of tech from Father Xmas. Half the Southbank is probably into their overdrafts by a good amount. I see a lot of blokes and women I know didn't have much time off over Xmas. Getting to the games still in their work clothes and boots. It's a thing and I can wax all day about how tough it is for some people but is this the reason? It's definitely one of them. But I suspect that it's a problem that is circling around all football like Vultures in the skies above.

I suspect at least in our case the 'problem' with atmosphere is one with many variables. Not least the edgy feeling we have about the football we are watching. It is beautiful and it is sexy but we are here sitting on the edge of our seats. Trembling probably, with the fear that we don't really understand what is going on. It's information you see. Wolves have decided that the Express and Star isn't really a partner in the information merry go round. This is where most Wolves fans go for their information about the team and it's there in bite sized digestible chunks for your perusal. It's generic and it's a bit dull but it's there for you. Online or in the paper we can check up on the scraps that Nuno and Fosun have decided to chuck at the media but its sterile and meaningless most of it.

There is a bit of a gap here between what we want to hear and what we are being told. Fair enough Fosun like to gather their information resources and let them out a dribble out a bit at a time. Information is a resource and it's a valuable one and globally it's the way big corporations tend to utilise the stories of their goings on. So that means we have to deal with these little morsels on a timescale of a few days or a week at the most. I realise signings both real and prospective have some element of secrecy and have to be kept quiet. But having to pick over these little bite size chunks doesn't really give us, the fans, any great picture of what the club are doing in the wider informational spaces. We are ignorant in fact. There is a problem folks. I call it the 'trailer' effect. Every Saturday and maybe a game in the week we are watching what amounts to a trailer to a blockbuster film. We are offered glimpses of the vision Fosun and the club have but we aren't seeing the wider full scale warts and all vision they have.

This means we are pretty much bystanders to the relentless juggernaut that the club is slowly becoming. We've heard the stories of the new stadium, the plans, the players, the ideas but they are just stories. Nobody has really told us anything at all. We are having to exist on what amounts to gossip and hearsay and that makes us a bit sad maybe. Perhaps we don't really feel engaged at all with what's going on. Maybe we feel a bit left out? Maybe we feel that this sexiness and virility within the club isn't really anything to do with us as we are herded into another concrete away game dystopia and shoved around by stewards and dickheads into our seats. We watch the team, they win, a lot of the time, we get limbs and sore throats and we are proud….but we are still ignorant really.

Bristol City away was a limb fest. So what was the difference between that match and Swansea away say? Maybe it was the fact that Nuno had some needle, some aggravations about that match, he wanted to win it and his interview before the game with Mike Burrows…well you could see Nuno had a hard on for it. That made the game meaningful in an emotional sense. We had to get behind him no matter what. We were loud, proud and joyful all through the match. But after that the flow of emotional information stopped. We didn't really have anything to pin our angst on at Swansea. Maybe with a few of the latter games at Molineux we felt the same?

Of course who am I to wax lyrical about the ins and outs of how the Molineux hierarchy perform their information war. Perhaps the propaganda from the grey faces and the lizards in the FA and the national press have made the voices within the club, who have access to information, reticent to share it? I suppose we turn up at the Molineux like 'customers' and 'clients' and are expected to just cheer and buy the cack from the concourse and shut up. Maybe, I dunno. I just feel that we are fumbling around in the dark eating the shit the Express and Star throw at us and when you are stubbing your toe in the dim light you don't really feel like singing much. Perhaps that overdraft is really the most important thing on your mind. Perhaps we would like to know whats going on.

You see clubs always have a philosophy to underpin their intentions in any future. That philosophy is here to see. The magic of Jota and Neves, Cavaleiro, Costa so beautiful, so refined, so effective. We see the club being connected to this player and that player, rumours of war, rumours of the philosophy. But you see if a supporter hasn't got a firm idea of future intent, planning or a discussion of a concrete philosophy then we are basically a customer and not anything to do with the clubs vision. This leaves a gap between us that is empty and that gap is then filled with hearsay and rumour, nobody knows what's going on really and once a rumour starts then it's hard to shake off.

It's just a few things to think about anyway, a couple of points to talk about but personally I would like some more information thanks. A few morsels to underpin the season so far. I'd like to know more about this Nuno bloke for one. I'd like to know more about what Fosun have planned (as much as they can say of course) and I would like to see some funky artists impressions of the new stadium which to be fair everybody knows it's going to be built but we would like a look at it. It's our home you see and nobody has asked us what we would like seeing as we are the ones who are going to pay a lot of cash to actually be there. A model of it would be nice, so we can walk around it and look where we would like to sit for the best view. Maybe we would like to hear from Fosun about what they actually have planned for the next few years as they unload more investment and more ideas upon our club. Maybe if we feel a lot more involved with what's going on we could better feel a part of it? The soul hasn't gone for sure. We see the emotions laid bare every match in the faces of the people around us. It's a battle for sure this season but we only have a vapid spectral idea of what we are doing. Promotion yeah, but then what? What's the vision? What's the philosophy you want us to pin our colours to?

Hey you! You Nuno Espirito Santos! Who are you?

12 Minutes and 54 seconds the Southbank sang the same song over and over again. It was a mantra really. Nuno had a dream, to build a football team….and it carried on and on. We sang our hearts out really. 'The Steve Bull' song from the new stand lasted 12 seconds. I didn't hear the Northbank. The Billy Wright stand are wondering how much of their pension fund was in Carillion shares. 12 minutes and 54 seconds my friends. Never castigate my stand to me again. Nuno is remonstrating with the Referee…who is this Nuno?

This man who has decided to pull this club from the nether regions of the Championship, who is he? We see him on the touchline, mobile, passionate, animated but also at times refined, magnanimous sometimes and sensitive. All these facets wrapped up in this man and yet to us he is unknown in many respects. We know his football, total football at times and yet he has not been here a year and this team is his. They belong to him. Saiss has been emasculated by his new blonde hair do. He should dye it black again. It's cost him half a yard of pace. Another bow legged Forest player skips past him and he falls over like the kids trampoline into next doors garden. Confused, wondering what happened. Looking a little out of place. Nuno.

São Tomé is his place of birth and it bears the psychological scars of hardship. The boot of foreign invaders, the bare feet of the slaves that were brought to work on the sugar plantations around the island. Now looking at it you may see it's beauty and it's elegance but you also see the rage of rebellion, the cords of harsh work in tropical conditions, the resentment against authority too, independence and fortitude. I am a firm believer in the effect that a persons home town has upon them. Do we not know? Us in Wolverhampton, how a place can instigate a certain character and vision of the world?

I think this place São Tomé is indeed a place where Nuno or a person like him would be born. It is situated on an island, so yes, Nuno will understand the island mentality of us British. And I suppose in a way Wolverhampton is a proverbial island, surrounded by 'others' in a sea of conurbations and clouds of petrol fumes.

But I think these things have condensed somewhat into a Philosopher now rather than a warrior. I suspect that his presence within the system of young men at the club has had a galvanising effect. I suspect that he has given them a new purpose borne from the sun blasted Island on the Earths equator. Maybe he has given these young men not only an arena to perform to the best of their abilities utilising all their creative aspects too, even the ones they thought they didn't possess, and offered them a respect and an opportunity too maybe. These young men at our club have had varied careers and seen others places before them in the team. They have been farmed out to other clubs where they were a minor success or failed to spark. They were perhaps young men short on confidence possibly.

Now they have the space and the philosophy to grow and develop into the players we as fans would expect them to be. We must forgive them for today. Forgive them completely and instigate them to pick themselves up and forge ahead again. Pick the sword back up and stand straight. Morgan Gibbs White, you too may stand with your brothers and be equal to them. You are growing and learning young man. Talk well with Bright Enkobahare and know each others minds.

I am comfortable to regard Nuno as Philosopher/Coach. I think there is a hint of Jedi about him. Recognising that 'us' the crowd, the great unwashed demand the most excellent football but alas. Dark paths in front of us. Through one reason or another I had to walk home from town to Ashmore Park. Along the canal as soon as I got to Bentley Bridge. In the mud and the dog shit, the snow and the freezing puddles. Sometimes it was pitch black and all I had to see by was the lights from the houses that backed onto it. What happened today? I'm not quite sure. It didn't fucking click did it. The gears of the universe that is Nunos intent lost some fucking teeth and slipped a little. We were slow off the mark again. A Forest team full of those grotty little bow legged boys with the 30 quid trims and the shitty beards. Probably on 300 quid a week, coming here and roundly taking the piss against us.

We were firing blanks. I wrote about atmosphere and totally lost the plot didn't I? Moaning about Fosun not telling us everything. Communicating little to us but it was never that was it? It was always going to be that shiver that starts in your feet and works it's way up your cold legs, up your spine to your neck, then around the top of your head to your eyebrows, then your brows furrow and you get that gold and black angst again.

A dropped glass or plate in the pub would make my Squaddie mate Ian jump and grab onto me, then he would go for a piss and hide in the bogs for ten minutes until he sorted himself out. Stress. We knew didn't we? It was coming. It was great getting those wins but pessimists that we are we knew it wouldn't last and that's why it's been quiet. We knew what everybody else didn't know. We saw it in Saiss. We saw it in Bennet and we saw it in Doherty too. It was creeping in and the light from the floodlights got a little dimmer as our brows furrowed and those thoughts, those black dark canal paths disappeared into the gloom. Another puddle another fucking splash of mud on the back of your leg.

It wasn't even that Forest were any good. They were just as good as Brentford who we bollocked 3-0. Same looking side, set up the same. Moving the ball lovely. But here we are and we are too fucking slow off the starting block. Fair enough the building of momentum throughout the match is a beautiful tactic. But these bow legged bastards need to be put under the cosh from the starting whistle. We need to destroy these teams from the get go. Instead we allowed them space to grow, space to move while we stepped over the ball, jinked a tasty pass into nothingness, ran.....somewhere, to do....something. I don't know what.

The Crazy Train has pulled up at 'Dysfunction Junction' and the music has gone a little quieter on that train as we stare out of the windows at the gloom. It was bound to stop somewhere along the track so a few people could get off moaning and a few people could get on. We knew the party would get a little quiet around this time. It's a fucking long train ride isn't it? There may be a few more of these towns too. Dotted through the last half of the journey before we pull into the Premiership or crash off a bridge into a rain gorged river. I haven't got a fucking clue to be honest.

Leo looked knackered. Jota got a kicking again. Another useless fuckwit of a referee. Another long trudge back through the wet dark streets home. I'm sure somebody is following me at one point then see it's my own shadow. I'm counting canal bridges, three more to go, counting matches left to play but all I count is months. 2 fucking 0. For fucks sake Wolves. I'm thinking of throwing myself in the canal, then laugh at this foolish though, then realise it's dark, I'm walking down a dark canal laughing to myself. Jeff? Nuno? Laurie? This is what it means to love the Wolves. Half insane men down dark canals laughing at their own jokes.

But I'm not going to be sad. You see Nuno was born in a place that looked like paradise but had blood soaked into it's soil through struggle. That struggle was for freedom from bondage. This division is fucking bondage to me. Do we have a right to say how shit it is? Forest fans sing 'Champions of Europe, you'll never sing that'. We fucking invented the European cup you fools. Nuno will know how to deal with this place, this Dysfunction Junction'. He now has to motivate a team that are demoralised by it. Who think their pretty little jinks around the pitch will shine a bright light in the snotball of this division. Sometimes it does. But poems don't win wars. Pretty faces still get punched. Brand new cars break down. Wolves will sometimes lose games. Nuno will know what to do. But now they are off on a mid season break. Sun and sand? Nah not really. If there is anything I have learned from Nuno this season it's that our players wont be in nightclubs at 4am preparing to nick a taxi back to the hotel.

Amazing what you can actually buy from Aldi with two quid. It's like a Mediterranean breakfast or something. Four croissants, soft cheese, butter and a funky coffee. Two quid! So I eat like an Italian Prince as the rain and wind beats on the window outside. Beautiful Wednesfield. I'd swap it for a gentle bike ride around some Spanish island for sure. Wonder how the lads are getting on in Marbella? They look happy. Hause and Graham doing the Instagram strategy very well. They believe in themselves I suppose and that's good. These times don't last forever though do they? Now is the time to be working on your game and getting focused I suppose.

I did intimate to a few people that this trip may well be a smokescreen of sorts. What a beautiful place to meet 'certain' people who may join the club. Somewhere quiet in a small bistro. Perhaps Nuno will be there, maybe Uncle Mendes too. Probably some Spanish or Portuguese starlet who isn't feeling the love at the club he's with at the moment. I bet there is a DVD somewhere of Compton and the Molineux looming large on the 4k TV back at this young lads Hotel. I mean you can't drag the poor bastard to Compton in weather like this. He'd be like 'fuck off' in some Latin lilt and he'd be off quicker than a rat in a skip fire.

Add to that a leak from the Compton staff that 'Boberto Sexylegs' is at the ground and the Wolves Social Media army would be chewing their fucking fingers off. So is it all a smokescreen? That Vitamin D comment from Nuno sounds like a massive laugh. Perhaps his humour has levels, I suspect it does. Especially when you see the team loving their break. I think it's a sterling move for sure. Of course Gaz Mastic wasn't happy.

'Eh fucking off to Marbella for a week Eh? Eh?'

As I'm trying to get through the front gate. The wind is trying to get into my coat and I'm holding my Croissants tight in case they blow away. It was writing about them the other day. These delicious French curly things. I fancies one. I had two quid. I dare not show Gaz what's in there but he's hanging onto his Staffy as she noses the bag. Gaz wouldn't like a Croissant. I know he has Margarine on his toast. He can't tell the difference between butter and Margarine you see and we've had a long conversation about it in the summer which I wont bore you with.

Of course the break will do them all good. It's a working holiday after all. Now they can train and groove along by the pool for a bit. Have a sunbathe and a chill out. This season is long isn't it? It seems longer than the ones in the past anyway. For certain. I think that's because we have had so much to cram into our little minds about how the team do their thing. New members of the squad, the emotions and the madness of the start of the season. That loss to Swansea and to be fair that rain coming back from there was a nightmare. I fancied a holiday after it. Fosun should have chartered a few planes to take every supporter to Marbella for a week or two. Yes, I see it as a positive for sure.

Our momentum had declined somewhat over the past few weeks. These are young lads after all. The incessant grey skies above us are a hefty mind bomb for kids that have spent their lives cavorting on sun drenched pitches. Now there is mud, and rain, and grey. As much as we British can huff and sneer at the weather you have to remember we are used to it. We have the skills to deal with it. We enclose ourselves in layers and get out there in it. I think we actually enjoy it sometimes. That's why we go insane in the sun. Have a riot or two. We are just happy that we have one layer on instead of six. Perhaps these lads will redefine their game at Ipshit maybe?

'I've always said we needed a striker, I said it last season and the season before that, there's no difference between Moxley and Jeff Lee'

Gaz is apoplectic with eye bulge and the odd spray of spit. He is getting his rage on. He is Molineux Mix made large and organic. He is 'Dingles Ay We' there, right in front of me and there is definite rage for sure. His thin legs are trembling again. In my pocket I have a lone crumpled Southbank Resistance sticker and I give it him to try and stop the rage before he gets on to Afobe.

'What the fuck am I going to do with that? I'll put it on me tackle box ta'

I had been told that Afobe didn't want to go, didn't want to leave the club. Good sources too. He loved it at Wolves. Loved the stadium. Didn't much love the ball being hoofed up field for him to chase. But I can't say anything to Gaz because he has his own ideas about Afobe and they pour out. I wonder if his rage will turn my cheese into mush. I suppose that will be Moxeys fault. He rages. That's what he does and I do love him for it because that's what you do when you love something. He shouts at his dog who rarely listens but that dog eats steak and Liver that Gaz buys and cooks for her. His rage is just the way he filters the world out. Do we actually need a striker? Leo may come back a different man. Ready to start smashing things. Perhaps that mystery Striker will come in the close season after he has perused the DVD and Nunos magic words start to entwine with his own Kwan and becomes a thing. Who knows. Would Benik fit into this team? Is he even a thing?

What interests me is that I suspect Nuno has the knowledge that despite a couple of losses he understands that we have won this thing. He's not an idiot. He's looked at the teams around us and I suspect he sees them lacking. Doesn't quite see how these teams are going to challenge the quality he has at his disposal. I think he's confident and this sunshine break is perhaps the perfect coda for the first part of the climb out of this division. The players wont understand of course, but I think Nuno does. I see this break as a perfect example of how Nuno works on the minds of these players. He has segmented and parcelled away the previous months and now there's a chance for a new start and a new opportunity for the players to really start to impose themselves.

'Are you going on Holiday Gaz?' I ask him. 'Ar Skeggy in June same as always, Love Skeggy' he says as he wanders off. That's fair enough. I have the idea Ipswich is near Skegness. I'm having a geography moment again where up is down etc. Ipswich Town FC. Ipswich and old big Nose eh? The last time I went to Ipswich was in the 90s and that was bad enough. Micks teams are a bit like the town really. A mix of Brexit leaflets, shit graffiti tattoos, crustiness, gritty, a bit boring, a bit sad maybe. Has it changed at all? Perhaps one of our travelling fans will illuminate me when they get back.

Our lads have come back from Spain now. It's been sunny here the past few days and I was hoping that it would ease them back into some sort of 'warm' football love thing. The game will be a weird one for sure. Ballardesque. I keep harping on at people to read JG Ballard. He explains these places very well. Of course I'm not putting Wolvo above Ipswich in any way. Same thoughtless post modernist landscape filled with greyness. But we have an ace in the hole us Wolverhamptonians. We are funny, they ay. I can castigate them because they are the enemy today and of course they must be hated fully, that is the way.

Big Nose Mick is out of contract in the summer and there have been rumours of his possible exit. Well. there's only so long a guest is made welcome in your house before his underwear drying on the bathroom towel radiator becomes a pain. Those faded skid marks of past shits gone wrong, the faded cotton, the elastic half hanging out, the comedy pants he got at Xmas 2007 with the minions on. It's all there for Mick. He hung on a long time fair play to him. But that's Yorkshire for you. Temerity, stubborn stains that don't go even when you scrub the bloody things. But he is history, and will soon be just footnotes in a book somewhere or a few lines on Wikipedia.

Mick wont be happy if they lose today and Jota & company are in for a wake up call from that sun warm lounger by the pool and the instagram lolz, Tyson Fury, sun. Jesus Christ the poor sods. Now they have to face an 'injured wild Mick' fighting for his job. The pitch will be a mud fest. He acts all nonchalant of course but we know the seething mass of anger and bitterness that lies beneath the surface of his persona. It's his job on the line, his pennies are under threat, He wants to take McGlodbrick or whatever his face is with him to where ever he may be forced to go. So this will be trench warfare with a bit of dancing.

I hope the sun remains in our lads hearts as they walk out there to play. We need to make a statement today and there is no better team to do it against than the void of ideas snotball that Mick is playing down there. It's black and white telly ball. Dickie Davis ball. Pans People on Top of the Pops looking like they have snorted a couple of keys of Ketamine, moving around like slack jawed robots. I can't help being critical of him but I liked him, he was funny at times especially in his team selections. In the grand scheme of things he wasn't what we needed at the time. Morgan and Moxey kept him too long. They didn't mind the underpants on the radiator and the way he flicked his fag ash in the tea cups as they really didn't have to live with him, but we did.

But what of Nuno? It wasn't a holiday for sure. Certainly time for squad bonding and getting to know each other, maybe to work on some ideas he had now that a big chunk of the season is gone. Perhaps he has time now to try some new things out, new ideas. I think we may well see that today. Ipswich are certainly a blank canvas, no pushovers don't get me wrong. I have actually watched two of their games this season and although not impressed with their play I was appreciative of the way they moved he ball for certain periods. I think even Mick knows that sometimes you have to be a little delicate and clever at times. Nuno will love that now that he has 'reflected' on the previous few games. He's a Chess master and he knows that time is getting shorter, already the snowdrops and crocuses are sticking their heads above the wet soil looking for the sun. I think we are too. Ready to unfold our leaves and get some of that solar love. I think then that we will expand our capabilities, not with new signings but for sure a new intent, the final few seconds of the round is where stuff is won.

So we unfurled our leaves for sure 0-1. Away win against the madness of King Mick. I bet he is in a right mood now. He's been there himself, winning games like this, enjoying the adrenaline and the buzz, going home and doing a bottle of wine, King for the week. Watching Nuno celebrate with players in the golden shirts must have made him curl up a little over what could have been I suppose. But man, we lose or draw these kinds of games. This one last season would have had a 2-1 home win for Ipswich all over it, probably a draw. If they had done us for a draw at Molineux they would have clapped themselves off the pitch quite happy. But this? We won, one goal fair enough but it's points that win prizes not goals, but goals help….I dunno, anyway.

Doherty got his head on one from a Duggo cross no less. Our front three moving about must have made the Ipswich defence feel like they have been sniffing glue. How insane did it look? Now things are picking up and getting weird. 12 points in front. Dare we? Just a little bit? Run away down the bottom of the garden where even the dog can't shit and crouch down in the dark, cup your hands over your mouth and go, really quietly…'fucking hell' into the dark so nobody else can hear. It looks good doesn't it? 12 fucking points. I wonder what effect that break had, wonder how it affected them and then you see it all laid down in front of you in the form of three sexy points.

Last year I was woken up by one of my lads who said 'We've signed a new manager Dad, Nuno or something' and I was half asleep trying to raise myself through the different levels of waking. I had a weird feeling that I knew who this Nuno was because I had already stood in Queens square as an open top bus came past, there were players who I didn't know on that bus. There were a few Chinese fellas, and this dude with a grey and black beard smiling and singing. At some time while I was dreaming I had already stood with my mates who I love, it was all a crazy day.

We had been promoted already. We were going to the pub after the procession. Somebody had put a scarf on the man on the horse. People were hanging out of windows around town. The sun was shining. A few people were half pissed already. PremierLand. Europe on the horizon. Belief and madness. And there was me trying to shake these mad dreams off and try to find out who this Nuno was on a phone that I couldn't focus on. But the songs were still reverberating through my consciousness, but I knew already. The feeling was that strong I knew I had to write about it. Get everything down on the internet so I could make sense out of it all.

I'm still going to go to the top of the garden to whisper swear words and excited things into my cupped hands so nobody can hear. Still tut when people talk about next season and smile. Still try and stop my eyes from stinging with tears when we win. Tread on that big butterfly that flaps around in my belly when I look at the Championship table. Still close my ears off to 'that kind of talk'. But it's coming isn't it? It's nearly here. Those long dark roads to away games, the storms, the getting thrown out of pubs, the feeling that you shouldn't have come because you are ill, the trying to park the car, the trains, the tubes, the walking to the Southbank from town after a few beers, singing in the subway, checking your pocket for your season ticket again. Thinking about the ghosts. I'm emotional again. Ipswich for fucks sake and all of a sudden the dark black clouds have parted for a second and there is a glint of light right in the center of that blackness and fuck, have we not had enough of that darkness to see the light for what it is?

Jota. We are going to sign him on a permanent deal from Atletico Madrid. Young Jota my dear friend how I have been worried. Watching you slide and tickle the delights right up from the depths of my belly and into my heart. How I was worried you would be gone. That you would look at our little City and wonder what delights may be provided elsewhere. Little Jota how you have made me happy that you can see your way forward into the golden light ahead and choose to do it with us. How happy I am.

I saw you. I watched you play in Austria through the delights of a shit camera and a dodgy WiFi connection. Jinking and running around. Moving with a mind that seemed to be three moves ahead of everybody else. Then those around me had denigrated your presence but I was confident. I was sure that this beautiful football would be in your heart forever. You sweated and you fought. You did everything right for me then and you do now. What courage you have. What bravery. Then in dark places we have travelled to this season. The wind and the driving cold rain bothered you not. You still fought. Still out thought the opposition. Your blood runs hot with the fire my brother. That golden fire that drives it's enemies into the dystopias they have dared raised their heads from.

I was of course reticent to show my love early this season. How can something as beautiful as you play love something as unbeautiful as us? Of course the love was conditional. That you would stay here and weld your vision with that of Nuno. Now I can see that there is a place in the future for both of us. Now can I love you properly? I think so. I would cast a glance at you as you played and my heart would skip a beat as you moved across the pitch cutting apart the enemy with your love for proper football. That you would often in your skill pass a ball into the maelstrom of the Championship and feel that this place was not for you and then we wouldn't be loved by you either. I would hold my breath and believe that one day you would sign and that day has come. Now I can look into the skies and love being alive again. That you Jota would cast your signature on a document that bonds us all. It is a blood oath of sorts and now we have mixed our blood with yours and now your fights are our fights.

Jota my sweetheart. What will become of us? In a few years we will be skipping across the tram lines of some European City half drunk, singing and shouting. You will be in those songs. You will be in our hearts and in our souls even. We have cast our love to the mast and nailed it on with forged iron spikes so the wind will not cast it away.

Brave Jota. Our dogs are Staffordshire Bull Terriers. They are small and ferocious when attacked. They show no pain but have endless capacity to suffer the slings and the arrows. As you have this season. How I was angered by every misplaced tackle, every offer of violence to you. I would have ran upon that pitch and sorted it out myself if I wasn't grabbed by others. But every time you picked yourself up like the warrior you are and I realised that you didn't need me at all did you? You had the courage of a Lion and the heart of a Wolf and seconds later after another crushing stud ridden challenge you would answer that discordant football with your own notes, your own music. That music does flow across that green grass like a symphony and Jota? I could cry at the beauty of it. I could weep at your bravery.

Now a new dawn. A new beginning. We will worship you of course. You will never be loved as much by others as you will be by us. Bring us the victories we deserve Jota and we will set aside a part of our hearts and it will be forever a sun drenched beautiful place we call 'Jotas place'. It will be next to Steve Bull maybe. Hibbit possibly. Derek Parkin too. Derek Dougan as well. And even if these players from the past that nestle in our hearts seem a little tall and tend to block out some of our love stand straight Brother, and push your way to the front.

The Premier League calls us and there is nothing to fear here brother. No darkness to sidle away at your heart. You may stand among them too, those teams that once left our mighty stadium sad and said the name 'Wolverhampton Wanderers' with fear and respect. Bring us that respect back Jota. Make them fear us again under the tutelage of Nuno. See his vision and tangle your own within it. Little Wolf you are and you will make the Lions of the world tremble. Now of course we are consolidating the whole 'thing'. The whole Wolverhampton Wanderers team is being strengthened. Benik Afobe on the radar. I drink tea, I eat biscuits. I watch Sky Sports news avidly. Will it happen?

Well it happened. Not Benik Afobe grinning on his signing video. not us feeling the love 'again'. We loved Benik any way. He's just been on holiday to Bournemouth as far as I'm concerned. Not the excitement of seeing him playing the Athenian Harp in the Emerald club either. What's happened? Healing. The wounds have been covered up by the wonders of Chinese medicine. The last infection of the Scouse Virus has been given a killer dose of

Antibiotics.

Benik? Horace has been round. He was having dinner with me and bought some French Fancies and some sexy Baguettes while we waxed some bars down about you. While I made the tea we talked about you, Dan O'Hagan (a 'sports journalist')and some other doughnuts. We had to get you straight in our minds, we had to talk about it because we are happy you are back. We both loved you man. Now everything is good and positive again... what the hell you are going to think of the passes you are going to get is anybodies business. Dude these balls are going to fall at your feet, we have magicians not footballers. We have a Coach that is metaphysical as well as physical. You are going to love this stuff.

Those wounds that Moxey and Morgan opened up when Benik waved goodbye have been open and festering for me at least. They stunk the whole place up. I couldn't talk about it to anybody. Even when I started this blog the whole Afobe thing was one I couldn't touch. What was the crux of the whole matter? Benik didn't want to play for us they said. Thelwell in particular, probably instigated by Moxey. But these political machinations are far above my head but I took those words to bed with me while they festered and wormed their way into games I watched and conversations in the pub too. I was lost. Who wouldn't want to play for us? Who would want to go to fucking Bournemouth of all places? That's where people go to die. Thelwell will be big enough to go up to Benik and shake his hand and welcome him back but I bet the first goal Benik scores for us he will point up to the Billy Quiet and point right at Thelwell and wink. Gun fingaz. Boom. Have that. Bludclaat.

Healing. Jeff has bandaged my angst up. He has metaphysically demolished probably the last damaging thing Morgan and Moxey did to this club. Broke up the old school Holy Trinity we had. Sako/Dicko/Afobe smashed against the rocks and thrown to the lions. And yet we were so close with them. They had a telepathy that was spooky almost. Every cross and every pass falling onto the feet of their mate. We know how that goes though don't we? We know the people closest to us, have some kind of telepathy and that feeling is golden and new. Until it was disrupted by hearsay and destruction.

I was angry when Benik went of course. All the missives coming out of Castle Molineux were dismissive of Benik. I know that's the propaganda via the fog of footballing wars. But I'm one of those truthful, honest fellas. I took the rumours coming out of Molineux under the tutelage of Moxey with a fair and open heart. I actually believed it. You see, even at that point I still believed that Morgan and Moxey would be working for the benefit of the club and the City (in the wider scheme of things). Maybe at points they were doing some good. But that 5,000,000 in the Molineux coffers after Benik got sold certainly went some way in making the transition to Fosun a lot more attractive for certain. So it's swings and roundabouts I suppose. I'm just a dull and simple lad who can't figure out how these things work and to be honest I don't want my Kwan contaminated with that stuff. I see it as it is and that's it. Morgan and Moxey. They cost us a year those mother fuckers did. They condemned us to another Championship season. This was their legacy and it stinks.

In other news I see that the rats are chewing away at our ideas again. Mr Dan O'Hagan has suffered some pelters lately. I do actually feel sorry for him for even this humble scribe has suffered a few digs on Social media after having a go at Barnsley or Swansea. Thing is, the difference between me and him in one respect is that I got a ban, a hack and threw a few threats around too. He can't do that. But then again it's obvious that us 'fans' are a bloody vehement lot. Other clubs can crow and get high and mighty about their successes but are we not allowed? Do we have to shut up and buy our clappers, foam hands and just gobble up the bullshit the media ladles out? They can go and bollocks. You see if I was in a Pub and Dan started having a go at our owners and management etc. He would get pulled away to one side and told to shut the fuck up. You can do that in wine bars and trendy gastro pubs. Don't do it in a shithole pub next to the ground full of angry tired excited Wolves fans who have just done a Saturday morning. Because that is basically what Social Media is. A shit pub full of lunatics.

Yes, it is strange that we can crow about the success we are having but fucking hell, we deserve to be able to. These Journalists have that passive aggressive banter, office wanker level stuff. Where they bet each other over some result and the loser has to wear their rivals shirt. It's geek bollocks. I could never even touch an Albion shirt yet alone put one on. Banter to us leads to swapping blows on the factory car park behind the containers so the cameras don't see you. It leads to splits in families and friendships. I know it's daft and I know it's stupid but thats simply the way it is. These pundits concerns in life are their mortgage, their exposure and their careers. We don't have careers, or mortgages half the time so our football club takes up a lot more love than we can handle. That's why you get the piss ripped out of you and this battleground is full of half insane people who love their club a little more than is good for them.

That's why these doughnuts are a bit shocked that the reaction to their piss ant depressing posts about Wolves are being met with such disdain. They operate within a sterile passionless environment where sound bites and not succinct analysis are the cloth from which their careers are cut. But because their missives are short and defunct most of the time so is their emotive styles that they cast on Social Media. To them it's a passive aggressive sound bite. To us it's a fucking declaration of war. How fucking dare they.

This is why those emotions lack context and background information. It just sounds like babbies throwing their dummies out of the pram. And I know why that is. Nobody fucking talks to them any more. The broadcast and print media are seeing the powers they once had fritter away like their hair. They are pissed off. Now they have to utilise Social Media like never before and they don't fucking like it. They don't like being pulled up about some 'fact' by Reg Bollockrash from Gornal about the intricacies of the transfer market or over past tweets. Social Media has made 'them' have to interact with 'us'. They don't like it. No more Press buffet warmness, no more back slaps off Managers, no more quaffing a clubs wine with the rest of the Lizards, no more first name terms with star players. They, like us, are just passers-by now.

So take any news off these pundits and Social Media lizards with a pinch of salt. Don't get too annoyed by the depressing comments and the snidey bollocks they tweet. They aren't important any more. The club has never been important to them either. They always bow to their job and career before the Club and that's the way they will always be. Them chatting up the sexy lady friends in their plush office and us fighting two Albion fans behind the containers…remember it's always their right to pull you up over insults forgetting they started it in the first place. By all means define your arguments empirically and quantitatively but when the information you are getting is half researched 'points of view' quality shit then it's time to steam in fists flailing. It's opening these presents your rich Uncle has brought from Europe and moaning because your presents are better than everybody elses. It doesn't make sense and neither do their trims.

Benik man. I always loved you even when the propaganda machine went into overdrive. I loved you even more when somebody told me what your Dad said the day before you went to Bournemouth. The real story. Out of respect for the person that told me I'm not going to repeat it. I suppose we needed the black ink in the books to get us sold and out of the hands of the 'Double M' mafia. I suppose in a way we just 'pawned' you for a while. Somewhere nice too, the seaside, playing for a team that had all the attraction of a dusty Pawn Shop window too. Now we have the ready cash we can buy you back and put you back in the team again. So the whole sorry saga can be put to bed and we don't have to talk about it any more just 'Yo Benik, what ya sayin?' when we see you. Nuno is here now, and you can talk to him about your ideas safe in the knowledge that we have an intellectual in charge of footballing matters. Listen to him and learn Benik. Listen to him and learn to love him like we do. When you score you can run up to us in the Southbank and remember us. You're home now mate, everything is good again. Sheffield United next.

How do you write about that match against Sheffield United? How do you sit down with a cup of tea and try to put this four dimensional football onto a two dimensional medium like a book page? Standing behind the Wheat sheaf pub after the game I was struggling to understand anything about it. I was standing up straighter I know that and we were all louder than normal. The sounds of our laughter bouncing off the walls around us. I had another sip of beer and actually felt like sobbing. Why? It was an emotional game. No ghosts, no departed souls in mind but the beauty of what I had just witnessed drove me to the edge. My normal miserable view of the world had been shattered by that football. Now the world had turned into a weird blend of 60 yard passes, of Neves, of Jota, of Cavaleiro, of Coady, Boly and Bennett. The whole drama was running like a film in my head now. It was cold and my fingers were numb. The night was dark but…I don't know man.

But four dimensional? Sweet football. It transformed from the edgy sometimes clumsy 'getting to know you' vibe of some of the last few matches into a feast of effortless and trans-mutated football that inspired me and also left me speechless. All I could think about as we talked about what had happened was 'what the fuck am I going to say about that?'. I'm fucked. It has destroyed me. Can one man be so filled with awe at what he just watched that all he can do is sit and stare at a screen and all he sees is that pass from Coady to Cavaleiro, the sublime manipulation of the ball to Neves and my heart stops, Neves looks up for a split second and then he puts the ball into the air. I see it floating and the time had stopped, relativity my friends. That ball took at least twenty seconds in my mind, until it hit the inside of the post and went in. I didn't even shout as the Molineux exploded into a noise I had not heard for a long time.

Was this the point in which our voices unleashed that anger and passion we had been holding back? I'm not sure. But I turned to Horace and we both just stared at each other in absolute magnificent respect for that absolute pearler of a goal. It transgressed the idea of 'goal', it twisted and turned the definition of the word and I can't say 'wonder goal' because it wasn't that either. Relativity I suppose. Some people saw an excellent goal, perhaps it was 'fantastic' maybe even 'sublime'. I don't know. But I have to be a good loser here and say in all honesty that I cannot truly find words to describe it. Lets just say it was 1-0 to us and Sheffield United were already fucked.

Deane and Agana eh? Those battles we used to have in the lower divisions when we were battling for top spot and promotion. They were always a noisy lot these Yorkshire bastards. But today. Nothing. Their ideas were unforged and lacklustre. They stunk. Lee Evans boots the ball into the family enclosure. The petulant little bastard. He's put on weight, he looked slow, he was a pondering kind of player for us. He lacked quality here even under the tutelage of a decent Coach in Jackett. But now his career is sliding back into the abyss with his cohort Leon Clarke. We all knew that Leons time as a goal scorer of worth would end. We saw that yesterday evening as he threw himself at Coady and

Boly time and time again with no result. His runs were short and aimless. There was nothing the United midfield could give him. At one point he held Jota by the throat and Jota just laughed at him. Don't fuck with the Little Wolf Leon, he'll bite your fucking hand off.

This Sheffield United thing. They too had lacked any real focus pinging balls at each other on the rare occasions they had possession. It seemed like nobody wanted the ball. Big Alf did. Rumbling across the pitch. If Jota is the Little Wolf then Alf is the Big Bad Wolf. Slathering passes, holding the ball, getting into that twenty yard space in their half and blowing the fucking door off the little piggies house and eating him in one bite.

Beautiful. Coady again massive. I told you he would be England Captain one day and he will. Effortless defence, vision and thought. Here is the class that this lad shows, here on the pitch in front of us. The whole edifice of the Nunoist philosophy is built upon the foundation of the Boly and Coady nexus. Of that rock solid partnership. They understand each other because they have the intellectual nous to be a companion to their physicality.

This is Nuno, this is what he has built here and again watching them I am fraught with fear. Am I a good enough fan and supporter to appreciate this? Am I able to understand it? Am I worthy of watching it? I'm not sure. I can't look sometimes during the game and I shout abuse at the Sheffield fans instead for something to do. I can't stand the utter beauty of it. I am ignorant and ugly, my language is course and gutter ridden, my boots are stained with mud, I have nicotine stained fingers and bad teeth, my hair looks shit. I am shit. I really am not worthy to watch this.

The Holy Trinity of Jota, Cavaleiro and Costa. Helder, I knew you would stop 'believing' and start 'doing'. How happy I was to see the movements you presented to us. How many times was another Sheffield player left tackling empty space? Loads. Every time you did it I laughed. This wasn't entertainment, this was art in it's purest form. The play smashing the whole abstract ideas of football into a coherent and tangible beauty. You Helder, you little treasure. I told you it would come, he skips past two United defenders who might as well have just seen the Holy Ghost wafting between them It was like he wasn't really there as his movements are ethereal and unreal. A dip of the shoulder and a twist of the hips, accelerate, move, pass, collect the ball back, twist and he's gone again. I never stopped believing in you Costa.

Cavaleiro. What can I say about you? Again, words fail me. They aren't sufficient a medium for you, there is a famine of superlatives for your play. I think a piece of music or maybe a big canvas would. Darting between players he swapped places again and again. Appearing here, then there, then again over there until it seemed as if there were two Cavaleiros playing. Sheffield United were dizzy now and their Kwan was non existent. Their fans were stunned into a silence that is typical of many opposition fans we have seen this season. They are quiet because they are sad. They will never have this. For as long as we watch this passion from this Holy Trinity we will see again and again the sad long faces of the sticky headed opposition fan bobbling in disbelief. Watching Lee Evans comedy football and then looking at Neves. Lee Evans is the Austin Allegro compared to the sleek Maserati of Neves. Even Evans haircut looked like it had been done by gerbils gnawing on his head, his whole countenance lacked anything of value. What a disgrace he is.

Their Goalkeeper tries to decapitate Jota. He is sent off. This is their reply to us. Violence and physical reaction to things they will never understand. Cavaleiro takes the freekick and a deflection, a bobble, their sub keeper disconsolately picks the ball out of the net. His first touch of that ball and the ball was probably still vibrating with excitement and intent. It was 2-0 now and I honestly thought the Referee might as well blow the whistle and save Sheffield United blushes. Things will go two ways with that Sheffield Team now. They will be sitting in their cars outside the training ground silent. Staring out of the window of their slick luxurious cars, just looking at the sky maybe. The radio is off. They grip the steering wheels tight as they replay what had just happened. Afobe comes on for Cavaleiro and the whole stadium erupts. Healing. We have ripped off the bandages and see pure flesh, unmarked and unsullied.

The ghosts of Morgan and Moxey are silent in their tombs with just the gentle tinkle of a chain as the wind that Nuno has wrought blows the doors of their tombs. He came close too. He was a handful. We know that just being in this place will give Benik another half a yard of speed. Another phase to his game. Benik Afobes back home and it is actually magic, the whole crazy thing is esoteric and spiritual. This feeling that we are bound for glory is tangible and real now. Benik slaps the badge on his chest and my heart skips a beat or two and I fill up again. What is wrong with me?

Jotas goal was beautifully taken. The whole aspect of the game for me was metaphysical. In the pub before the game I was with people I love, in the ground I love watching the team I love. What madness this whole season is. Nuno smiling on the touchline, Cavaleiro grinning, Coady slapping somebody on the head again. Beer thrown in the air, singing in the subway. Me searching out people like Stan who I have known for years, asking him…'What are we watching Stan?' and him replying 'I don't know'. I don't think we will come to terms with this season until we are sitting in the garden one day in the summer, watching the Bees fly around the plants. We will be wondering whether to have a can of beer maybe then it will hit us like a delayed reaction and we will fall face first onto the lawn in shock. A mouthful of grass as we suddenly understand it all. And this is just the start of the whole fucking show. This is just the beginning my friends. And if this is the beginning what will the end look like?

I do like Holloway. There I've said it. His little turns on camera where he ladled out these superlatives were funny…but they are funny at a distance. When you have YouTube cranked up and feel like a warm giggle. But earlier this season Horace made me have my photo took with the QPR Mascot and I thought that was funny too, until we watched the match and were trooping out with faces like we'd just snorted somebodies eczema dust. Now I wish I'd have set the Lion or Tiger whatever it was on fire.

Holloway. He's got a face like he's been sucking goat piss through a tramps sock while he's being beaten with nettles. Like he'd forgot to finish his shit. Like the dude on the stag do that quietly packs away the blow up doll 'for later'. A bloke that has all the Managerial football nous of a canal walk in Darlo. But I still like him, but I want him on that coach back to Shepherds Bush sitting there in the dim orange light of the overhead lamp crying that much strings of snot are leaking from his little peanut sized Gollum head. He's got a flat cap on. 'You're just a shit Peaky Blinder'…your actually a shit Ian Holloway to be honest. And I don't even watch Peaky Blinders because the Birmingham accent makes me feel violent and angry.

We need revenge for sure. I had a lovely day down at QPR apart from the football, where Holloway used his one football idea to stick the knife in a Wolves Team that were squashed by the horror of that ground. Fair enough we were just getting to know each other then, our team. And somebody has to have a crack sometimes. Somebody had to throw caution to the wind and have a poke, and they did. Although it wasn't quite football as we knew it. The same old tackles on Jota and the odd thrown elbow to the throat. But we have learned a lot since then and our idea box is full of jangly fangled sexy things that Nuno can pull out. Now we have an Afobe. But we also have a Neves and a Big Alf. I hope he plays today. I hope we show Cider Gollum what we have learned since we last played his team.

You see this is the beginning of the end now. The season will be speeding up both in our minds and on the football pitch. This morning was sunny and I opened the curtains and it was like memories of summer (apart from the odd snowflake). The birds were noshing from their feeders in the garden getting fat ready to make baby birds. I hope they are a success as this food costs 3 quid a bag and they are noshing a bag a week. But yeah speed. Momentum of ideas has certainly pushed our team up the table to the heady heights and the top spot. More importantly than that it's woken up some right trolls in the media and social media. Radio phone ins are now stuffed with prongs from Albion and Villa who sit around in their piss stained joggers all day waiting to phone Radio

Birmingham with their latest rant about Wolves. I love it. I want their anger to blow a blood vessel in their head. Live too, that would be good. And all you would hear is a dull thud halfway through 'yeah well Wolves will blah blah blah' and through the radio you will hear a tinkling and a crash as they fall through the safety glass on their 'DONG' coffee table from Ikea. Radio Birmingham my arse. I can't wait for Villa and I may even tune into whatever show it is that has these prongs on so I can laugh my balls off when we destroy them. Aston Villa, Jesus Christ.

It will spoil a lot of football fans Summers for sure if we get promoted as Champions and this should be our target. We have big matches coming up and now that momentum should not take us that fast that our legs fall from underneath us and we go crashing on our face. Now is the time for Nunos ideas to shine as Spring starts to raise its pretty little head through the winter mush. Now is the time to take that slice of early morning sun and utilise it to galvanise and inspire our last few steps to glory and the madness of a promotion piss up where we will tell tales of Swansea away and Barnsley, all those insipid horrible shit holes we trekked through to watch our team. This is our time too you see, this is where we get to slap each other on the back too before we have to scrimp and save, sell our belongings and maybe even do away with a holiday this year to watch our team play some Premier league football. But it's not here yet. We have some more work to do and Holloway, his team, and that defeat he subjected us to will be banished forever and that little Gollum head will wax bitter missives while we laugh and dance a little.

Fucking London. The thing is…it was bound to happen wasn't it? Of course the hangover from Manchester was a pumper, one of those bone deep hurting ones and it was accompanied by that Cider Gollum of the West Country Ian Holloway himself, a man that epitomises the tight knot in your shoelaces you can't tease apart. It hurts your fingernails, frustration, complication, exasperation. The train screams and squeaks to a halt at Shepherds Bush tube station and I imagine for a moment that's exactly what the toilet in the Holloway household sounds like when he's having a shit.

But it's that weather again. Coat choices. This morning is cold I know but it's time to sweat a little or freeze a bit due to the wrong choice. That's why Nuno is a Philosopher Coach. He has a myriad of choices to make for his team and here's me wondering what coat to put on. I would like Big Alf to play, I think he has given us some much needed Yin to Neves Yang. Everything looks more balanced and more dynamic. I love Saiss but maybe he needed some time off, a few games to re-center his groove. That blonde hair do is a thing. He's been shit since he had it done. It's affected him those toxins from the hair dye probably. Made him a bit addled. There's a few addled souls in the pub too.

Match wise I'm totally loving the Morgan Gibbs White thing again. How secure is he? I don't know if secure is the right word but he harried the QPR midfield like a Don splashing out a few angelic balls to feet. Moving around well, shutting down players, moving players away from danger areas with his movement. I like him. Especially as he looks like Nuno has grown him in a little soil and watered him with Nuno skills and now he unleashes him. The stamp of Nuno is on everybody in this team. Eloquent and civilised reactions to every situation in that first half. Two beautiful goals. Holloway was getting angsty on the touchline and you could feel his comedic malevolence threatening to boil over a few times.

Nuno reacts to Holloways touchline antics with a few of his own enraged shapes. It was like a dance off at some points, but it's that time of the year isn't it. February is a funny old month for football. We are starting to see other teams going for the ugly sister instead of thrashing out the moves for the sexier more lush football we see from our team. QPR banged it about. Their fat striker who's name I forget was a bit of a handful at times. They are a team in the Holloway mold for sure.

They have a good pop. Like Uncle Nobby at the disco, he doesn't quite get the 'agadoo' song and it's moves but he has a go….while people laugh. So weird darting runs at our defence are met with confusion most of the time by our back three, or four, or five. They move well these QPR's but blah. What can I say about them? At Loftus road I watched them play the same game which at the time was quite effective for them at least . They won. We trotted off back to the tube with big sad faces. But here's the bit I don't understand. QPR played the same game as the previous meeting with us this season. Kerplunk football. While we were a completely different looking team to that day last year. We had progression and they had…oh look…that big fella is coming on.

Now we were in for some ping pong football as Holloway dusts off his one tactic again. He goes in the cupboard and there at the back it's right where he left it. Bit of dust on it. Nothing that a squirt of Pledge and a duster wont shift. So Big Neck comes on the second half I think. I notice him because at one point he's standing next to Jota and he towers over Little Wolf. Not that little Wolf cares. Jota gets a punch in the face off one of QPRs defenders later on and to be honest Jota doesn't give a shit. Neither does the linesman who has obviously seen it but ignores it. What a shower of shite these 'officials' are.

Of course the last twenty minutes is an Afobe cameo really. It will come Benik trust me. I'm right most of the time. I can feel your desire in the middle of the Southbank as you moved towards goal, a chance, header but it's over or past whatever…I can feel the energy you have and it will come Brother. Your day in the sun at Molineux will bear fruit. It will bear waves of love too because nobody wants you to score as much as us. Our goal is getting battered. It's now route 666 to our box as balls get lumped in. Willy Boly really doesn't care about their strategies. He knows it's defunct. Boly has an intellectual basis to his play and moves with a certain grace that belies his size. His temper too is level and controlled. He's been booted and pulled around everytime he goes up the pitch for a corner. He has some beef with their defender, a unit, but not as 'Unitty' as Boly. At one point Boly is pulled from behind and he trails the defender along with him like tissue paper stuck up a beer monsters arse crack. They've scored a goal. Oooooh you're hard.

Ruddy has problems with those kind of crosses. Always from that side too but hey, it was an onslaught. Captain Coady is kicked in the face, there's a goal line clearance from him or Bennett I couldn't see, I was hiding like a coward in my seat biting somebodies fingernails.

Walking back up to town I've got to the pub without any real idea how I got there as when I'm walking by myself I go off into a kind of trance state where I'm fitting together what happened. All those incidents and goals into some sore of coherent narrative again. It's building up this whole idea. You can feel it like electricity through the crowds as they move around outside the ground. It's a tangible thing this static electricity of possibilities for the future. What is it going to hold? Dare we even think about what the fuck is going to happen during the Summer?

I'm trying to juggle the expectations of us all with some sort of inner peace. I want to wave flags and let off smoke bombs now. We've been waiting too fucking long for this. Cider Gollum will be back down the M6 waxing his Holloway Lyrics to anybody that will listen. They are funny, like your dopey flat cap but jokes don't win things Mr Holloway, neither does 'belief'. A bus nearly runs me over outside the art gallery and some dude grabs my arm and pulls me out of the way. 'Cheers ahk' I say and he just smiles and winks. He knows that I know and I know that he knows what we all know but nobody wants to say it yet. But we know don't we? We know. But we can't talk about it now we just have to look at each other over the empty pint glasses in noisy pubs, when the conversation gets a bit quiet, there's a lull. We catch each others eye and just wink or have a little half smile. The thing we don't want to talk about is coming. The thing we have been dreaming about for years is coming. The thing is about to explode onto this town like a gold and black nuclear explosion. The thing we don't want to talk about is coming. A trip to Preston? Or the thing we are not thinking about?

Preston. What is a Preston? Parking the motor in a post industrial landscape I looked around. We were parked on another 'Tile' warehouse showroom thing. Everywhere around us were the dystopic builders merchants, flooring companies and home improvement shops and yet there was no evidence of any improvement to the area since I last came here. The area reflected perfectly the names of their players. Robert Scrotenugget, Brian Gruntworth, Neil Shudderflange…the list went on and they are coached by Alex Neil a man that tight he's in danger of collapsing in on himself and forming a Black Hole which sucks the joy out of anything that comes within his envious and bitter gravity. I'm having a cigarette outside the Moorhouse real ale pub and watching the detectives. The locals mill around with that patina I have seen before in Barnsley. Unironed shirts, front hair flicked up with lard, they have a layer of dust on them from the filth that flows around their stadium. The Cops have been told to rein in their aggression today and be nice. People are happy with that, there is a lot of love for Preston old bill. I stand and take no notice. But I'm thinking of kicking off to be honest.

We knew it was going to be one of those matches didn't we? We expected it. Preston sit high at the table of horribleness. The tackles and the aggression, the anti football, the pulls on the shirt all testament to the lack of real ideas they had. They were good don't get me wrong. In the first half they wanged the ball around like pros. Good football peppered with flannelly late tackles and aggravations but it's what we expected, what we knew would happen. But it's still shit. I never know why these teams have two ideas and two ideas only. It's a game of football. Play it properly and with a modicum of skill and you will reap the benefits of a decent points haul and maybe even a pop at the play offs.

This 'football' is great because we can only play well against teams that actually play football. Of course when we do start to get some passes flowing along the grass the second idea comes to the fore. We saw it with Cardiff and Barnsley, to an extent with other teams as well. The dragging foot. The shitty pulls on the arm and the shirt. I forgot how many times Cavaleiro burst into action having two Preston players hanging off him like a shit shirt. Helder too, little Helder darting between two Preston defenders got a whack across the face from a directed flailing hand. Jota goes down after a tackle from behind (again) that rakes the back of his knees. He shouts out in pain. The referee waves play on…

The Ref was an awful thing. Pumped up on Soy protein that made his arse look like a Moms smoking a fag outside school in her Primark leggings. His soy titties bounced while he ran, It was all about him. He was the star of this show. He will video it so he can show some disinterested woman he has enticed into his Travelodge room. 'Look that's when I showed that overpriced Portuguese bastard who was the Boss' and she's not looking really, she pours another Prossecco and gulps half of the glass down to deaden the next few seconds of him humping her and grunting like a pig before she slides out of the room and gets a taxi home to expunge the memory from her mind under the needle sharp hot shower.

To the left of us the Preston Doughnut squad. The scruffiest load of fooligans I have ever set eyes on. When they score some prong throws his shoes on the pitch. He'll be in the clothing recycling skip later looking for a new pair. They are angry but pointless, grey faced, the only tan they get is from the Ultra Violet fly killer lamp in the local chip shop. The dust doesn't allow them to get their vitamin D from the sun. The only vitamins they leach is from the Doner Kebab and the dirt burger cuisine.

I knew we were going to score. It was obvious what kind of game was being played. The ball goes out of play and the ball boy holds onto it while their goalie 'Fudd' runs over to collect it wasting precious seconds. In the pub I collect a pint of beer from the crushed bar and some of it drips onto the head of a Preston fan and he looks around as if he's about to say something and then decides not to. Good choice mate. So the Ball boys have been coached to hold onto the ball so they get their point. What a fucking disgrace that is. It means some adult has got them together at some point and said 'Lads. don't give the ball back quickly, hold onto it' and these poor little half starved bastards looking for direction and inspiration in life are given the hardest lesson of all. No wonder the dystopia is in their hearts as well as their ends.

Neves has three players around him every time he gets the ball. But still he manages the odd crisp pass and slide. He plays well even if he is concerned about a booking. I don't want to lose him for one single game thank you. Preston however can't even get close to him to stick a foot in his ankle. Holy Spirit he is. He's there and you don't always see him until he has something to say..

Cavaleiro knocks past the encumbered and static Preston players and sets Helder up. Bang, goal. I run down to the hoardings to celebrate much to the humour of Horace who says I ran like a Rat up a drain pipe. I was happy for Helder. I have sat and stood most of the season listening to people slate him. Now he is ascendant. He is Helder of course, always has been but now? Maybe he has something else. He has traversed the negative slopes of the mountain to gain a hand hold in the next route upwards. He is my Helder. Of course he was going to make his way back. Knowledge not belief. Cavaleiro is busier than a one legged firewalker. Busting extreme football shapes here, then over there, then he pops up again and throws down another dinky pass, another sublime shuffle of the footballing latin jazz he espouses.

We are drawing the game and they have shut up shop but it's still beautiful to watch. This my friends is the greatest entertainment I have ever witnessed. It's lovely to watch. We are entertained. I suspect the venom of Preston fans to the alleged play acting of our players is just jealousy and bitterness. They will never have this, they will never watch a team like this again this season. Alex Neil is threatening to implode on the touchline, his little weedy arms going like a wind up monkey with a pair of cymbals. It's obvious he has given his players the Dunkirk speech at half time. He has filled their hearts with darkness instead of inspiration. He has dragged them to the cusp of half hidden violence. The footballing abyss where Colin Wanker makes his home. They are filled with belief from his anger, but that anger is void and hollow.

Cavaliero goes down again from a fateful errant leg raking his ankle. He falls and crunches himself up in pain. I watch his face and it's real pain but he centers himself, uses his powers to shuffle that pain off and he's back on his feet in seconds. Preston fans think he is play acting but I know better. Cavaleiro wants the ball back so he can have his revenge, not in a reprisal tackle but in a perfectly weighted pass, or a swivel of those Elvis hips as he glides past the anathema ball of Prestonite hollowness.

Saiss is on. His hair looks weird. I guess he's toning it down now into some sort of ashen grey madness. Certainly mad, he gives the ball away twice on the trot but that's OK too. He's been out of the side. He's trying to get on the Waltzers while they whizz around disco music blaring, lights flashing on and off. It will take a few minutes for him to center himself and get into the groove again.

Nuno wasn't happy when he came onto the pitch to applaud the travelling fans. You could see he had the furrowed brow, a hypothesis about a lost opportunity to extend our lead, to make the idea more concrete and palpable. Of course Nuno in his absolute gentlemanly way he conducts himself will never denigrate the opposition, never lay bare the cables and conduits of these teams inability to play against us.

I may be wrong I suppose, perhaps I see this team we have as one of the greatest teams I have ever seen and to be honest I cannot be forensic enough when caught in the moments that have slathered their way across my mind over the past season. Of course beauty deserves to rise unhindered by ugliness but I know too that beauty is often marred by a scar here or there or an errant stray hair across a beautiful face. I'm aware of that. Perhaps I can give this to Preston and Barnsley and all those other towns and cities we have travelled to, perhaps their ugliness has made our football at times a little too beautiful and makes us want to entwine and blind ourselves with it so we only see other teams offensive blartball in contrast to out own ineffable ideas…maybe. But Nuno is both angry and Saintly in equal doses and I am reminded of St Augustus.. 'for when I was angered thou would never pull thy thoughts from me but let that anger be formless and vapid and mean nothing'.

After the match myself and Horace sauntered around the ground and we found ourselves by the players entrance and a small crowd of autograph hunters waiting for them. We stood talking to three young lads from County Cork who had flown over to England to watch Preston and a few of their Irish players. They were young and fresh faced, I was amazed that they had travelled so far to watch something they loved and I had an epiphany of sorts. Beauty is in the eye of the beholder I suppose. They see their teams beauty and I see mine. I'm standing there swaying slightly as Conor Coady comes out to sign some autographs. I want a photo with my hero too. I'm 53 years old in May and I still get the shakes when I meet my heroes. I mean heroes in the fullest sense of the word. Conor is lovely and polite, you can see he has that humour and scalliness of his ends. I get my photo and we walk back to the pub through the long featureless streets of little boxy terrace houses where people sit and engorge themselves on idiotic TV. We pass a few lamp posts and cars with lovely Southbank Resistance stickers on them. Gold and Black. Nuno is always centered on the next match. He doesn't want to pontificate on how we draw matches or even on how we win them. It's gone and dusted. How many points? Just the one. Two points lost. These points he will not ruminate about at all and that's good. He has a Zen about him. The realisation that this season is indeed a struggle, not in terms of physicality and snot but in idea and foundation building and these two tenets of Nunoism are the cornerstones of his philosophy. The points are the mortar between those blocks surely?

We walk back to the pub and find ourselves among twenty or so grey faced scruffy Preston Hooligans but it's OK because nobody can touch us, nobody can dent the shellac of success we have already coated ourselves with ready to unveil the real madness we are holding within ourselves. There are no furrowed brows here, no fumbling quick bitten fingers and no tallying of possible points hauls. This is our time and our place. The Fooligans part as we walk straight through them. Like our team really. We've stopped believing and started knowing.

There's a definite feeling I have that wanders in and out of my mind. We are watching Norwich and the dichotomy of success and failure is one that is boinging around my mind for the full extent of the match. Will we wont we? Is it happening or not? Do I trust Nuno? Yes. Regardless of results.

I got back last night after Carls lad had dropped me off. I was a bit worse for wear. A little miffed, a little sad and all the emotions we have were running around my little peanut head like demons jabbering and moaning, pulling out all the old grievances and scenarios. I tried to lift the latch and it was stuck. It's bent you see, from people kicking open the gate instead of lifting the latch properly. Amazon delivery drivers, pizza leaflets, Postmen and women, drongos and basic wet wipes. I tried to lift it again but it was stuck solid. So I just ripped the fucking thing off and threw it on the front garden. Fucking shitty thing. I shout 'fuck off' to the sky and I couldn't care less what the neighbours think. Fuck 'em.

So the night went and so we feel the last minute Norwich equaliser deep in our hearts and we suffer. Everybody else around us suffers too. Walking back into town there was hardly any match analysis at all. No laughing and no cheery hugs and back slaps and it was ridiculous but you can't help it you know. We still get the pangs as a team pisses on our Parsnips when they play uncompromising pressing football. I'd like to write a few paragraphs about the Referee like I always do but now I'm resigned to these talent-less gonads constantly making weird LSD laced decisions about incidents. He is what he is. Redolent of the whole Championship experience really.

We destroyed Norwich in the first half that much is true. But the weight of the season is now pressing down on the team. Individual brilliance mixed with that dysfunctional team ethic where the metaphysics of the passing and pressing play we have been used to over the season seemed weighty and cumbersome a times. But of course as Wolves fans we jump in the air like an ex squaddie at a back firing car. It's stress for sure. A last minute equaliser for fucks sake. They always hurt and we jump at it. I suspect our team was a bit like that tonight. No cracks but we are flexing for sure, it's been a long season man, you know this.

This is the legacy Morgan and Moxey left us with of course. That feeling that it could all go to shit again. It's disgraceful really. I'd really like to blame everything in the past for what we feel this morning but fucking hell, just look at what we've done. We have decimated good teams this season week after week. Played such beautiful football that we have indeed walked out of grounds, me and you, gobsmacked. Now I thought the arse end of this season would be a downhill jog where we look back behind us and laugh at the Cardiffs and the Villas, we laugh and stick two fingers up to them as we watch their dysfunctional teams become a thing to giggle over. But it never turns out like that. There's always some bubblehead behind us moaning. Always somebody booing and crying as we stand there and do our best to fire our positivity at the team through our thoughts.

But we don't have anything to complain about really. Last night we still played beautiful football but it's the Yin and the Yang of this football madness that has made us walk out of Molineux with our faces like they need a shit and it's ridiculous isn't it? Morgan Gibbs White for fucks sake. How he moved that ball around was a pure delight wasn't it? His football is indeed arty and sexual, creative and dynamic. And he plays for us for Gods sake. That makes me happy. There were a lot of things that made me happy last night.

We scored two goals, fair enough we let two in as well. But these doughnut teams that come here to Molineux are playing for their lives, in front of a Molineux crowd, under the lights, the hallowed turf. They pull an extra 20% out of their weedy little legs to take the piss out of us if they can. We play teams that aren't demoralised like they normally are. These are teams galvanised by the way we play football. And it makes it tough, like it was during the second half last night. I had Jackett flashbacks and could see Lamberts Trainer shoes, Dean fucking Saunders weird perm. All these things like Wolverhampton Schizophrenia really. On the one hand the voice of reason and academic football (Nuno) and on the other a baying pack of pundit managers, slack arses and prongs.

Of course sitting down afterwards in my chair nursing a lovely glass of Jack Daniels (straight no water or coke) I ruminated on the game kick by kick. It was good, that's what we do don't we I suppose? The negativity always rises up when we have a few minutes of quiet reflection. It's the Wolves way. We have to blame something. We blame because we lack real vision and that's why we work in the places we do and wear the clothes that we do too. We lack the vision and the skills that Nuno and his staff have. Things are indeed good and positive. We still sit at the top of the hill. We are still kicking the other teams in the face that are scrambling their way further up the muddy slope of the championship. We are indeed a target. We are the King of the Hill. We have Neves and Jota, MGW and Saiss. Doherty, Coady (I love you Coady) Douglas, Bennett and we even have Ruddy the big bald headed knob and don't forget he IS one of us with all his faults and flapping.

I know he's a tit for not doing some of the things we would have done (in hindsight mind) and I know some of the team should have done this or that. Benik had a weird one again and at the moment he's a Toblerone of a player in this squad. Angular and bitty, the foil sticks to him when all you want to do is chomp it.

Benik will come good I hope but when you look at the bench. Bonatini, Mir, Enkobahare…I wonder what they have to say about coming back into the team and having a go. Le Fondre and Joe Mason are in my mind now and I think fucking hell, how we have progressed. The things Nuno has done here gives me a feeling that yes, everything is OK. Everything is a lot fucking better than the past few years.

What are we to do? Pick ourselves up and roll our fucking sleeves up. Plant your feet firmly into the ground and say we ain't gonna be fucking budged. This game now history, gone into the annals of the record books where it will sit and gather dust and in 20 years time we will look back as we peruse some funky Wolves book we had for Christmas and hardly remember it at all. It's time to really take on the Philosophy of what Nuno is doing here and entwine it with what we are as supporters.

We have to support as we always have done. We have to turn up at the games and sing, shout, scream and support. We have to come together now because us lot, us in all the stands at the game who live all over the UK are under attack. This is what supporting your team is. And fucking hell isn't it a ride Horace? Isn't it totally mental the way it makes us feel? And it is pure living as Jota slides a goal in or Neves curls one on the outside of his foot. Oh my days what beauty and brilliance, what a fucking change compared to the last few seasons.

Bon Scott the lead singer of AC/DC God rest his soul once sang 'It's a long way to the top if you wanna rock and roll' and I never truly understood it before last night. But walking through that subway again looking at the smooth polished floor I understand it fully. It is fucking tough, probably tougher on us than our players. A long way to the top…Preston, Barnsley, Sheffield, Reading, QPR…the Holloways, the Warnocks, Alex Neils, the bullshit and the banter, the cold leaching through the wrong coat choice, aching feet, hungry and pissed off. But fucking hell what delights when we do well and we walk out of those places with another three points. What entertainment and last night, disappointment. All gristle for the mills Horace. all training for what awaits us when we finally shuffle off the hill as Kings and we have another loftier hill to try and get on top of in the form of Premiership football. Now is the time for courage and strength brother. One day we WILL be carousing across some European City, maybe Barcelona, Madrid, Berlin, Paris maybe. Half pissed and singing and that's the way we have to be and it's only right and there is no better person than you to do it with my friend.

Nuno will throw a few thoughts at Mikey Burrows, looking at him like he just turned up for a family wedding with no clothes on. But Nuno will be focused on Fulham. That great juggernaut of Nunos intent will be redolent and raw and there is not another Manager or Coach I would rather stand behind than him. It will be OK ya know. It's a long grinding road to the top if we wanna rock and roll brother. and I have a gate to fix.

But...In essence you have to know the darker and more shadowy parts of your personality to grow as a person. You have to know those darker aspects intimately of course in order to fully understand the whole of your psyche, you have to know it to develop fully. I'm not even looking at the points gap between us in top position and the others underneath. I don't care about how many points they need to catch us. I only care about us and what we are doing. I'm not doing the math and I'm not sitting here nibbling fingernails at the horror of being caught. Now I think I do trust Nuno. He knows best.

Walking through the park next to Craven Cottage yesterday there was a darkness I suppose. It was where they filmed parts of the 'Omen' Trilogy of films, Bishops Park? I don't know, but it certainly added to the pathos of the whole moment. I was shocked at the amount of Police around. These Hipster

Fulham fans are a thing then? Do they batter people with their Clappers or something? Maybe run up behind visiting fans and style their hair with Goat musk gel before running off? Beautiful pubs though. We waxed in a few of them. Builders arms, great pub. Neck Oil IPA. tasty beer. There was money in that place. You could see it dripping out of the funky pretend decor of the pubs you could see it in the £80 rounds locals were buying. All surface, all patina, all fake...or most of it. But the only thing that wasn't fake were us within them. The Black Cab driver said people from the Black Country were some of the best he had met. This was weird because the discussions in it were about the best swords to use in a gang fight, blah.

I have said in past postings when I have denigrated the opposing teams, that when teams play against us they play snotball and we don't know how to play against them. Like we don't have any idea to play against he absence of creative dynamic blah...you know how it goes, you've read it enough. But...today here we had a Fulham team that did have ideas and did indeed lather them all over the pitch as we stuttered and farted around like we didn't have anything ourselves...Fulham were pretty but they didn't really have anything to say with their footy. Only two goals and some pretty effortless dinking around our players.

I don't know why this happened and to be honest it wasn't the loss that bothered me so much but probably the sadness of why it happened at all. Isn't this our party? Don't we get all the presents and the love, it's our time surely? But no. There always comes a time when you have a moment or two when somebody has to spoil it. When we start to throw a wobbler and stamp our feet, have a tantrum. Chuck something. Have a good moan and blame some poor bastard for your woes.

We can easily find a villain to blame too because thats the fucking knee jerk reaction isn't it? So the voices that lilted around the stadium after the game had a variety of names. Ruddy, Costa, Coady, N'Diaye, Saiss, Bennett, Doherty, and Douglas were the most regular names to pop up. So now we have to 'sell' those fuckers, drop them or do something that denigrates the team even more after this defeat as if they don't suffer enough walking out of there with a total demolition job done on them. But we have to look at the facts here, get some of the more fantastic reasons out of the way.

We have played three tough games in a week. I know, other teams have too. We have lost our midfield magician to a suspension. We have a Jota that looks a bit like a shadow at the moment too, nothing seems to be going right for him at all over the past few games. Cavaleiro still charges around like a man possessed. Costa looks like he's still getting into the groove too, fumbly sometimes, not really wanting to take on his man, not really physical enough to grab hold of a move and get past a few players to put a cross in. In the second half yesterday as Coady got pushed up into midfield Conor put the two best crosses into the box I saw all game. That was interesting for sure. I remarked that in the last few games it seemed like Douglas and Doherty were being put under pressure and forced deeper and deeper into our own half. Add to that mix (over the last few games at least) we have had opposition teams putting pressure on our midfield too. Neves of course couldn't give a shit, he's a ghost to these teams. He's here and there, every push forward all dangerous ball to the feet come from him. We have missed him today for sure.

There was a lack of anything that moved with the sure footed excitement of many games this season. There was a lack of anything really. We just looked tired as fuck. Tough last three games and I think the memory of that sunlit mid Winter break is started to dissipate just like our hopes did as we fended off the shitty arsed little Hitler Stewards that swarmed over anybody they didn't like. By halftime I could hear the Omen soundtrack playing through my mind as Saiss fluffed another ball to a Fulham player. It was going to be one of those fucking days again.

There were meltdowns of course. You could feel and hear it at half time. A Steward told me to put my cigarette out and I told him to fuck off. He said he would have me removed if I didn't and I didn't really care as the stage had been set really. I knew Afobe would be on at some point and I didn't really want to watch him. I didn't want to watch any of it. But you do don't you? You have to stay, but I did finish my roll up in front of two Cops who were giving me the hairy eyeball.

But I'm not panicking. Yes, there should have been a reaction after Preston and Norwich. Yes we should have taken the game to Fulham from the off. Yes, this reaction should have galvanised our support. But you can't always get what you want the Rolling Stones once sang. We were half a yard behind everything. Our defense started making errors from the off. All of a sudden this 'in form' Fulham side had an extra second on the ball to define what they wanted to do with it, without any real input from our midfield. Half a fucking yard that's all. We did move the ball around well. If we had taken our chances we could have been 3 or 4 goals in front. But players arriving late 'half a yard late' or the ball bobbling luckily onto the foot of a Fulham defender. For Ruddy it wasn't half a yard it was more like half a foot as the ball swung past him for their second goal. We just weren't there. It was like we were knackered or something.

I think this was the crux of the whole result. Fulham on top, they have a hard on for the game, the division leaders, Wolves, everybody hates us. I don't know why we don't sing about it like Millwall. That half a yard we lacked was slack taken up by a Fulham team that didn't exactly believe their own ideas but had a good idea of ours. They knew we liked to play, they knew we liked to pass the ball through the box in pretty little short passes until we poked the ball past the goal line. It was football we shouldn't have played here. It's just too pretty and when we lacked that energy to grab back that half a yard we really should have gone back to the basics.

Saiss fluffed a shot twenty yards over the bar and he hit it like he really didn't believe in himself which is a great shame. Get the ball any where near the edge of the box and somebody should have been there to toe bunt the fucking thing towards goal and there were maybe 8 or 9 chances in the game where I suspect we would have scored a goal that would have changed the game. We lack the energy to dictate beautiful football in midfield then bypass it. Put the ball over the midfield maybe, negate it. Get Afobe running off the shoulder of their last man. Get a chance or two in. Grab a sleeve or two maybe….ah fuck I dunno. I'd just like us to whack a few low angled fast shots towards goal through a knot of players some times…it works for them, why not for us?

I do know that this season seems to be a fucking long one. That training session and pre season warm up in the Swiss Alps seems like twenty years ago to me. Jota the poor little sod has been kicked all over the grounds of the English Championships for months. There was definitely less of that yesterday and fair play to Fulham for not going down that route. But I think it's starting to effect him maybe. I think mentally he is shattered and wary. His almost telepathic ability to communicate with Neves was laid bare yesterday as everything he did when he came on was dark and had that Omen groove to it. Costa dillied and dallied over a simple ball, lost possession and disconsolately crept back to play. But I'm not losing hope.

We will only become a force in football by analysing these games philosophically. We do have to have moments like this to grow. We have to have the pain of it to know how we will repair and grow ourselves for the next game. The dark shadow team. That was what I saw yesterday, the team that had no idea and no hope either but that can also be positive. They will be bitter and angry. Nuno looked pissed off and angry too. The darkness is something we should experience because what doesn't kill us makes us stronger. We weren't killed off by Fulham by any means but our ideas were certainly dragged out into the cold streets around Craven Cottage and given a good fucking kicking. Now we have the ability to know pain and in a certain way agony too. I think we need this, I think it was good it happened. Positivity can lead to a sense of invulnerability for sure and I think the games we have had over the last few months and at times been to beautiful to watch and I at least have fallen into the trap of believing my own propaganda where everything was sunny and Portuguese, beach days, blue sky and flat stomachs, cocktails, promotion parties etc.

I think it still will be that if I'm honest. This result (I hope) will pull our players and staff together more firmly as their is nothing stronger for pulling together a family than adversity. This is it folks. This is the turning point of the season for me and I know it's fucking late on. This is the time when we have to pull ourselves in and link arms, stop over analysing this mistake and that one. Stop naming names as to who was to blame and who needs to be fucked off. We have Reading to come, they will smell blood. They will have a hard on for us. We must link arms…

At the train station after the game a group of lads tried to bully a Wolves fan. In seconds there were a group of us pushing them back. Wolves, in a pack, where we find our strength. The errant opposition melted away. This is the dogma of Wolves, in adversity the strength really is in the pack not just the 11 players on the pitch but everybody. I know that 'strength in the pack' is an oft used phrase but it still is the most important tenet that runs through the whole ethos of this football club but here's another one 'Trust in the pack' and that means planting your feet on the concourse and not giving an inch and if you get battered then regrouping and come back fucking stronger. It's knowing that somebody somewhere will have your back. I think we will do this, I don't think battles like yesterday will stop. Every game for the rest of this season will see the same battling, the same weird half chances, the same dysfunctionality as our players force their tired bodies and brains towards the final hurdles and the end of the season. We must stand with them, we must support 100% during this war. Make decisions and castigate at the end of it when the smoke clears but now, here, on those dark roads outside these shit holes as we make our ways back to Wolvo we must embrace the pain and the shadows. We can do this, you just have to trust.

But there is always the Canal. It's where the thinking goes on and I can finally put everything into some kind of order and sense. Sometimes.

I enjoy a stroll down the cut. The fact it's cut into the geology around here tends to muffle the ambulances, fire engines and Feds that scream up and down the Lichfield Road 24 hours a day. I enjoy the bird life and the ducks. In the summer you can see Perch and shoals of Roach, the occasional trio of Bream chilling out in the sun dappled puke green canal water. After the recent postponement of the Reading match and the rigours of a day on the piss regardless it was good to be out with the dogs. Alcohol was nearly expunged from the system, I still felt positive and there, poking their little heads above the rapidly thawing snow was a bunch of Snowdrops. Beautiful delicate things. I stooped down to look at them and even the dogs stopped pulling for a few moments. Beauty and delicacy, simple stems, those drooping white flowers nodding as if they are ashamed at being so beautiful.

Suddenly I was jerked out of my Spring reveries as a steel toe capped boot appeared and crushed the delicate plant. The boot was a paint splattered thing. The leather that old it looked like mummy skin, brown, split in places. A work boot from the past. No breathable textile upper here. This was War-boot shit. It was attached to a thin ankle. Flapping Umbro tracksuit bottoms flapping around those spindly fucking legs. The trackie bottoms were covered it idly wiped mastic and yes. There on top of that body that even a crackhead would be ashamed to own was Gaz himself. For the love of Christ that face. Those missing teeth. Skin like a tourist camels hump. What teeth he did have left reminded me of an old graveyard in a Western flick. The lips were moving but I was still in the moment. The dogs looked at him as if he was some errant happening.

'…Nuno you see? I don't even know where to start Mikey but...' he said. Hello Gaz. For it is you is it not? Fucking hell, here we go. Yes, Nuno. What about him? Some more angst to pour on the fire Gaz? Some of that Northbank ire maybe? Gaz has transferred from the Southbank to the Northbank you see. He liked to check his bets and sit down after being on his feet all day. Now the Northbank was the best thing since sliced bread or roll your own fags. That cheap Polish tobacco he bought. Those nicotine lips that yammered. His hat looked like misshapen black fungus, a fucking toadstool of a woolly hat…

…' I knew Benik would be shit back here and I said to me mate ya see, I knew it. If I knew it why day Nuno? He's paid a lot more fucking money than me ay he? All that skill and it means fuck all. It's a great view up there in the Northbank ahk, you can see everything. I saw him mate he was shit. Fucking Costa as well the knobhead. What the fuck is he about?' Gaz pontificated. I hadn't even said hello to him yet.

'Mar fucking dog 'ud knock Costa over, and I said to mar mate he should be fucked off and Doherty and fucking Ruddy, he ay done anything of value 'as he Mikey? He ay done anything. Lambert wouldn't have put up with that shit..'

Gaz is the black cloud of despondency and of misery. He talks and he waved his little spindly arms around. On the one wrist 'Wednesfield Skins' done in Indian ink and a needle wrapped in cotton, probably done over the Sneyd or Rough Wood., names of some of his kids too, a Wolves wolf head that looked like it had a stroke and not in a good way. Ah Gaz. He had moved out of the way a little as he went mad and I reached down and tried to straighten the bent stems of the Snowdrops. One was ok just a little mangled but three of them were fucked. I had felt bad about the Reading game being abandoned but hey ho. The weather was awful and I had seen a few old 'uns tumbling over. Why do old people go out in the snow? One of them had a carrier bag that had nothing but Jaffa cakes and a pack of butter in it. Couldn't they just chill for a moment? How fucking bad do you need a pack of Jaffa cakes? I know a lot of oldies go to the match and I had a gnawing pain of worry that Saturday morning as I looked out of the window at the weather. I was thinking about fractured hips and pneumonia. Flowers spelling out 'Grandad' up Bushbury Crematorium. All for a fucking football match. For fucks sake what's wrong with me? A day in the pub would be better. I was thinking about doing a podcast in there but there was too much noise and too much angst. And it was a bitter wind that blew around town that day I'll tell you.

Gaz was spitting a bit'…Fucking Chinesers mate, wim going the same way as Blues trust me, fucking Norwich was an eye opener for me ahk, I knew it was all going bad ten matches ago, bloody Swansea, I got a stream day I? Crystal clear, the son in law bought us one of the them Firebox sticks ya plug in, fucking brilliant, all the channels mate all the films, I watched Predator and…'

It has all been a little too much lately I suppose. I have logged off Twitter and Facebook. I didn't want to read the bullshit and the bile about the team. I wanted to keep a positive mindset, I wanted everything to be under control and the best way I knew how to do that would be to 'trust in Nuno' and self censor the opinions that were rife on there. I can't deal with it at the moment. Turn it off. It's all I can do. This season has exhausted me. The beautiful football. The crushing defeat at Fulham. The away days. The drinking. The drugs. The dynamics, Neves curling passes, Benik trying hard, Leo seeming as if he was the world on his shoulders, Jota looking more like a punchbag as the games carry on….all of it was making me tired and I daresay it's making everybody else tired too. Judging by the social media madness it was doing a little more than that. You see Gaz only has a Facebook page so he can keep up with what his Missus is doing probably. I know it's on his phone because I was behind him in the queue at Tescos 24 hour One-Stop the other day as he was buying a fucking Easter egg for Gods sake.

'The assistant at the till asked him, 'Would you like to donate an Egg to a Childrens charity you see…' He cut her off. 'No I fucking dow' and paid for his egg and fucked off without noticing me thank God. But he was checking his Facebook for sure and it looked like a Fart porn page. His missus messaged me on it once and said she was settling down with a few cans of dark fruits and had a pizza on dial up. I knew his dog would be prone on the floor fast asleep, till the pizza came and I knew the can of dark fruits would soon be kicked over and that sticky liquid would join the Pollock inspired fast food and tea stained canvas that was his £3.99 a square yard cord carpet from Mr Carpet. I deleted her from my friends list. I haven't got time for that shit. I'd rather read 'Dingles ay we'. The Tesco check out girl said 'It's like the Walking Dead in here sometimes'. I nodded and smiled.

Yes, the season feels like the siege of Stalingrad to me. Endless and cold. I've forgotten what it's like to feel the sun on my face. I've forgotten what it's like to win a game. Walking out down the subway singing. Lately its been walking down the subway looking at the condensation dripping off the ceiling and tripping over the homeless and the ubiquitous Staffy looking pissed off and fat. Standing in the pub listening to people tell me about positivity even if they don't believe it themselves, they know that's what I want to hear. Thank fuck these players have a good coach and a professional mindset. I hope they do any way. I'm glad the sun is starting to feel warm on my head as I still kneel looking at the crushed Snowdrops. I think my knee is soaked from the slush and I want to cry a little I think as Gaz Mastic waxes his bitter lyrics.

But that sun does feel warm for sure and it's the first time I've felt it this year and I'm a bit shocked if I'm honest. I look up into the sky and Gaz is in silhouette looking like a shadow puppet of a fucking deranged scarecrow and yes, it's there for sure. Definitely and it is hot on my face. That sunlight. Peeking through the grey clouds.

Maybe the season is about to turn for us. Maybe the solar magic will do something to the team. Steve Bruce said 'wait till the winter' and at the time I felt he was a total deranged fucking fool. But now at the arse end of it I feel like old Brucey needs at least a nod of agreement. We haven't been firing it's true. Swansea. That fucking storm. The bitter cold of Barnsley and Sheffield. Am I moaning too much? We have big games to come. Villa and Leeds. Teams that will regard our position, strong as it may be, as not unassailable at least. Teams now have scented blood and regard every game against us as a 'cup final' for sure. No Neves for Leeds but that's cool isn't it? We aren't a one man team for sure…are we?. But I thank fuck I'm not Nuno. Thank fuck I'm not part of the whole merry-go-round that is the Wolves experience. I'm not strong enough to deal with this angst. All I can do is support the team. Be positive. Stand outside the pub trying to keep my roll up lit in the bitter East wind that always blows through Town, up Broad street, past the Hogshead, past the Royal London, past the University, getting through every hole in your clothing.

We aren't the greatest fans ever I suppose. We have our moments of madness when the team isn't doing too well…if you can say nine points clear on top as not doing well maybe. But I have to stay out of the arguments and the angst, the tweets and the statuses, the forensic analysis of who is doing shit and why, the graphics of the team selections, the targeting of a certain player. You look at who posted it and it's an account that has no face, maybe a Wolves head or a player, or a foggy out of focus phone shoot of a bald headed fat bastard on Holiday with his weird looking kids and he's called 'Where I Live Wolf' insert area. And he looks the same as everybody else and the faces and accounts all blur into one and it's sad and I feel a little weird for stalking those accounts whose bile exceeds their wit.

'...Fulham were great, I watched it on a stream, I've got one of those Firebox sticks our Wayne bought it for us for Christmas, crystal clear, all the channels mate, fifty quid a year and...' Gaz goes on. Gaz always goes on. I stand up straight and my knees crack and my back is killing me. My kidneys are hurting from too much beer the previous weekend. The sun shines. It always gets better some how. Everything comes out in the wash. Out of darkness cometh light and I'm smiling to myself a little bit. The son of Gaz is called Wayne then? I've been calling him Shane for years. Now Leeds away? Shane? Wayne?

Benik scores at Leeds. I'm beside myself, I've never wanted anything so much as this beautiful touch from my Prince. That strength, every sinew of his body twisted and resolute as he fought off the ministrations of a Leeds defender. The onrushing goalkeeper. The gap narrowed as they closed in on him and he saw the abyss of the goal narrow as the geometry closed in, became acute, the Wolves fans around me drew in breath. We never wanted as much as this. Air filled our lungs and were held inside, the rush of blood now drowning out the noise and the cacophony on Elland Road.

The twirling of Leeds scarves stopped as if a new wind had taken the air from them too. Right leg extended. The simplest of touches and it seemed the boot of Benik hardly touched the ball. It was a lovers touch, the simple subtle touch versus physicality and there were now only three players on that pitch as the Goalkeeper flapped his arms in the face of this intent, of this assured moment. It was your time Benik, and your boot did indeed touch lovingly that ball and it arced into the air. Time had stopped but flowed nonetheless. Geometry and art as it flew into the air. Desolate, the Leeds defender had a look of anguish on his face, the goalie vibrated with a loss, a disaster for him, twenty five yards out from his line.

They knew where that ball was to settle and so did Benik. The ball hadn't even crossed the line and the tableau of these three men was frozen like a Renaissance masterpiece. The Salvation of Benik by Michaelangelo. In primitive oils it could have graced the stucco plaster of some dimly lit altar in a small church in Rome. The ball crossed the line and the lungs of us, these acolytes of this belief, these disciples of Nuno erupted. 3 fucking 0. Have that Leeds. My knees hit the seat in front. I fell forwards. My glasses half came off, I couldn't see. I fell back. Somebody was hugging me. I held my gaze on the top of the stand roof as if calling out to God himself as I have done so many times over the past season. I looked for Horace and his face was a delight. I fought past bodies to reach him and celebrate. Fucking hell, what a team...and then a little tear came out of my eye. A relief, a victory. After these past weeks of Fulham and other senseless matches, this. We always believed and we were always resolute and our courage was rewarded, our belief and knowledge scoured the furrows of these barren Championship fields and we were harvesting. Emotional Benik.

But...

They hate us. They always have. Now the angst mafia are in overdrive. Steve Bruce can't keep his fat head shut. Now his superiors are joining in with the peasants as they storm the gates of Molineux with their flaming torches of hate and murmurs about Mendes, of Financial Fair Play that they don't have the fucking wit or intelligence to understand, of Gefistute or whatever it is, of Nuno our Saviour, our Moses and our Prophet. Broadcast media bite their knuckles in anger and they pontificate and promote their false heresies and their bile right now in ever increasing amounts.

This gives me belief, this gives me courage. Because when the most dynamic and creative business ideas encroach upon the sordid desolate landscape of English Championship football and suffers the ignominy of half researched facts and ball punching articles then we have won. We have won the battle of ideas. We have emerged from the doldrums of the past with new ideas and have grasped them with both hands. Us the fans have always believed. We only wanted belief. We only wanted somebody with a set of ideas that weren't borne on the backs of a cigarette packet in shitty betting shop biro.

Boly scores from a Douglas corner. Saiss scores, again from a Douglas corner. What misfits these players were. Left out in the deserts of their former clubs intent. Outcasts. Not wanted, not needed. They could have gone anywhere these players. They probably would have had good careers somewhere else, maybe they would have faded and gone somewhere else but...

Nuno. Our players have cost some cash ably provided by our owners who have had a vision much lacking in previous regimes. A global vision of movements of talent, where the football landscape is one not of passion and love but of hard hearted decision making, investments and return. They look to the fertile football grounds of Europe and possibly beyond to glean prospects and the disenchanted. The possibility of making money. But if this is the hard battleground of money then they had to offer a balance. A philosophy also in order to attract these disenchanted warriors kicking their heels at other clubs training grounds. These men needed a pure and non dogmatic theory of football ably provided by Nuno himself. We have bought talent in? Yes. But the most important signing was Nuno himself. Only here could we expect that the previous games would be annihilated by this purest form of football led by a man who will be the greatest football Manager the world has ever seen.

The beasts are charging us down and we twist and turn through the landscape of points and goals, of winning matches, of losing them, of weather and rumour.

Of the EFL 'investigating' our relationships and our investments. These men reflect everything evil and sad about football. They lack vision and they lack moral fibre, they are the whisperers and use the media platforms they have ensconsed themselves within to forge attacks on our pack. Chairmen, Chief executives, pundits, popular social media accounts slather and snarl at us. They are dogs and we are Wolves. Lies and untruths are reported as rote. These disgusting creatures twist and turn on the bloodstained stakes of their own lies. Their untruths are the groans of pain as they see us transform in front of their eyes and they die every time we forge our Nunos philosophies on these godforsaken away grounds on cold nights and colder days.

We played without fault. The pack under attack is a fearsome thing isn't it? Boly and Batth operate with precision and intent. Hunting down any attacks on our half like missiles. Boom. Neutralise this threat and decimate an attack here. Leeds players wander the pitch in confusion. Their ideas gone in the swirling winds that Jota and Cavaleiro leave behind in their wake. Ideas, new tactics that almost come weekly, every match something different forged on the training grounds of Compton and then forged on these games.

New things, new ways. Constant improvement and more importantly the demands from Nuno that they must improve, must work harder and harder. To present what beauty Nuno has in mind to face down the ugliness of other teams. To improve constantly is the liturgy of this new philosophy. To work harder and harder until they have performed as they should, as he expects and as he demands. Bonatini holds the ball and waits for the Gold and Black attack as waves of Wolves players swarm forward to attack. With speed and with absolute concentration. The attack thwarted for a second Cavaleiro rebounds from attacker to enforcer. He slides and plucks the ball from the feet of a Leeds midfilder who spendsa fraction of a second too long in trying to see an opening.

This is the difference between these two sides. This fraction exposed and Cavaleiro plunges in a knife attack of such forensic precision I gasp and am lost in it for a minute. Ball to Bonatini and the swarm attacks again, Jota now the little Wolf ghosts around the centre circle like a wind. He collects. Cavaleiro collects, boom the passing has it's own rhythm and the importance of the collection of the ball is between the spaces and the movements. Attack, defend, this route and that route. Changing from one position to another this team has been drilled like an army of assassins.

Danny Batth, his courage is beautiful, his capacity to grow and develop still amazes me but there is a dark side to him. A weird feeling in the depths of my stomach. Is he really ours?

Coady never put a foot wrong for me and I whispered months ago he would be an England Captain one day as every game he commands more and more respect from me and I delight in him, and in him the threads of Nunos philosophies entwine with his own ideas and he is a giant for me. An instigator and a leader and how England lack a man such as him, how it cries out for him..and I will be honest and say this, there will be a time when we will say that we saw him play, and we saw him grow and we will wax lyrical to people who will never understand really, what he means to us and what he has done.

I love everything about walking out of this ground in Leeds. I hardly remember walking back. Young Kate had hurt her knee celebrating and I linked arms with her on the long walk back to the car. Limbs. Scars of our joy I suppose, and there were some songs sung for sure, some shouts of joy outside as various groups of Leeds fans watched us move through those dark tunnels and desolate streets. But we could not be touched. They knew in their hearts they had witnessed a spectacle of beauty they themselves did not possess today. But they knew that feeling. They still remembered their glory days and it was this memory I think that stopped their own anger solid in their throats. We talked and we laughed and we were resolute again. Our systems were alive, our throats sore, our knees and shins were bruised, we had a long journey back but that journey like our teams would be aloft and airy and that hollow feeling within our bellies after Fulham and Norwich was gone into the shadows around that ground. I gave a homeless dude my last £1.50 and rubbed his matted hair on his head because we too were lost like him once, but now we are found again.

Villa Saturday. We will have our Revenge for your untruths maybe. Will the Gods smile on us? Will we come out of the whole match unscathed? I have never known such darkness there and that visit even now makes me suffer.

A Villa fan tries to pull the scarf off an elderly Wolves fan. The Villa fan spits in his face. I pull the old fella back and push the Villa fan away. It is getting darker here now and there is malevolence and hate. Crushing it is. Senseless. Pointless. I'm on the ground and my lower leg has four fractures. It looks like spaghetti. There are Police and an ambulance. A paramedic shoves painkiller gas at me and I breath deep and the malevolence is tempered by warm clouds and damp streets.

On Tuesday night I was at my Moms being spoiled. Leg is in plaster and the pain is delicious and sharp. I had a packet of sweets and a cup of tea and she had opened the window so I could listen to the Wolves fans singing and talking going up Molineux alley. It was cold and the delicious frigid breeze was refreshing. It was glorious, the memories were smashing into my painkiller sodden brain like punches, as I poked my head out of the window I could see the ghosts of the old floodlight towers against a violet tungsten blurred sky purple sky. The Reading game. Tuesday night matches. When we were kids we would gather together trying to work out what was going on via the roar of the crowds.

A goal would shake Whitmore Reans and we would jump around like lunatics. But now even if the memories were thick so was the pain from my leg and I limped back to my comfy chair laughing and grimacing and laughing again. Fucking have that Villa, losing to QPR. Still I think about them…For even if it was two days before tonight, I was still there, I had left something on those cold roads surrounding it but had also taken some things away too. A new love for us, new friends and a new/old friendship that was reinforced by a new love and respect, an awe in fact. I watched Horace hold back the madness of violence and the ignorance of the Police with his intent. Is he a fan of Wolves this Horace bloke? No, he is Wolves for me. All the songs I sing are for him. So I lie still as the kicks fly and the anger flows and Horace is a mighty thing and so are we.

My Mom has found out an old Wolves Diary 1981-82 season. £30 for a season ticket and I'm laughing again.

It is violent and black out of the stadium. I fall and suffer but I have no hate left for things as formless and vacuous as Villa. Where Birmingham City have tenets of their own hate they are borne from experience and misplaced love for their team. This Villa thing is a nothingness. This is an abyss. A cop tries to shift me out of the road where I have fallen. I think I've broken my cheekbone too, it moves under my fingers. All I see are feet. I have a tank of painkiller gas and I share it with another fan who just needs a hit. There are feet and there is Horace arguing and debating with the cops. I am safe with him. Villa could put out rows of hard faced fools to attack me and his eyes would have them back down in fear. My leg is a mess. Multiple fractures, it's in pieces. I laugh on the cold floor surrounded by Feds.

I mentioned it was hard to write about a football match days after I watched it when inside, mentally you are still there watching it, every kick of the ball and every song we sang still reverberating through the thick viscous vapour of the ether. It's like that for sure. It was a swan song of games for sure. Goodbye to a functioning right leg for a few weeks and goodbye to the Batth enigma too, for me at least. I suspect Danny has had his moment and he will slip away somewhere in the close season and make a name for himself somewhere else, maybe.

What went wrong at Villa? In the grand scheme of Nunoism it's a subtle blip on the heart monitor or the tremble of a muscle maybe. The game was hyped and the propaganda was in full flow…it was like that prematch. The hate had been stoked up and the vitriol was thick as the clouds that kept Gods eyes away from the diaspora of Villa park, the semi deserted streets of the jewellery quarter, the trains there from Stourbridge were full of fans going to the Hawthorns and other places.

It was weird and strange. Steve Bruce had things to say before the match as did his 'superiors'. Dr Tony Xia had waxed mutterings and obtuse crap for days. Villa fans were being put under a deluge of semi intelligible propaganda and 'thoughts' from their army of media darlings at Radio Birmingham and their own staff. This torrent of formless accusation and spin affected the day. We indeed had a new enemy that day and that enemy was not the rabid affected hate of Warnock or Holloway which in their own bitter way was at least concrete and emotive, but instead half formed bitterness, choked accusation over FFP and the involvement of Jorge Mendes at Wolves. There was other shit for sure but the formless 'banter' and mists of this war of words from Villa park was laughable, at least sitting at home on the lap top or looking at your phone. It was a landscape of funny gifs and banter at least from us.

But for them in Birmingham it was different. This was their dogma. Brucism, the malignant relentless symphonies of their angst and fears. It clouded their minds and brought their team out onto the pitch unsmiling and choked, emotionally at least. To the right of us at the Trinity road end their fans hardly watched the game. This was all about us, not football at all. It was about the simple tribalism of these ends, the songs, the cut throat gestures, the unbearable tightness of their horrors. The Stone Island stare, the fucking hateful glare, the rhythm of the violence had no end.

At one point in the game their 'wonderkid' or 'Lurpack Jack' Grealish stopped to run his fingers through his hair, he looked as if he was searching for a mirror. His performance wasn't for the team, it was for the trendy bars and expensive nightclubs of Birmingham and his coterie of hangers on. It was pure Brucism of course. On paper at least the whole game ticked all the boxes for what should have been a season defining point for Aston Villa but of course we know it wasn't that at all and even their team knew it. A victory, 4-1 to them but as they applauded their own fans as they walked around the stadium the Villa team looked as if they were going to burst into tears. This was Brucism, this was the result of their ideas. A victory in name only and ultimately it did define their season. It defined it as a twitch of a hanged mans leg, freshly dropped form the scaffold, it beheld an idea of a former existence, the corpse moved for sure. Four shots and four goals. But there wasn't any life left within it just a resemblance of one.

We of course were the superior team and there isn't any doubt in my mind at all. An artist always needs a Muse of sorts, a channel to let flow the artistry of football we have displayed this season and today our Muse had retreated to the shadows between those stands and seats. She had decided to retreat and let the foul odours of Villa Park settle into the hearts of our team so that we became simply a team for sure. There was no delicate flourish and incisive decision making. Every pass sound like a minor key, every ball through midfield had an inkling of dour and unexpressive love in the face of this Brucist style of football Villa played, where every pass had to have a paragraph of hate or a tweet of bitterness. Villa are a wounded animal at least in policy and hope and in that forlorn way these megacity teams play we had sucked up that virus too. There was a fever for sure. We commanded and we lead at times. But they had an extra dose of the virus, a few degrees more fever. Where we mourned the abandonment of the Muse, they revelled in their dysfunctionality and for a moment or two during the game they actually enjoyed the terminality and inevitability of their fall. The four goals were not delightful events they expected them to be, but were the codas to their decline if they can't navigate the play offs, the end of this game is the cracking of the veneer.

Before the game of course we did as we did. Our team had just won at Leeds and we were ascendant again. Stuck in the arms of our lovers, delightful. We laughed and we sand and were proud. But the closer we got to the game the more heavy the air seemed and the more dull and listless the metaphysics seemed. Claret and blue is such a sickly death like colour scheme. It was dull and formless to me, as was the whole sacred idea of the match. If we had won of course it would have been a victory of delights and 'rightness'. Good against evil so to speak. And fucking hell God, you can throw the odd spanner in the works for sure. By half time I had lost my voice nearly. It seemed to sing and to shout but the sound waves from my vocal chords were just falling to my feet on the grey concourse of that cursed hole. Are we not rivals? No, we are fellow travellers for sure but to rival is to set oneself on a similar plane vying for the same illustrious victory but the difference between us and them is an abyss for sure. A void. Nearly as big as the ten point gap we set back in place after the Reading game.

It's relentless isn't it, this season. Never in all my years of following Wolves have I laughed and cried so much. It's intensity and it's beauty have dragged me to the edge of despair and to the rarified heights of crystal clear orgasmic delights. 'Are you Wolves fans then?' the Nurse in the Accident and Emergency department of Sandwell Hospital asks us. Horace is still with me and he nods with his brow furrowed and worried and I do love him, and I laugh. I have had too much painkiller gas and I'm stoned, I'm looking at my leg bent in all sorts of weird ways, there is bone sticking out somewhere, and blood, and pain. Of course we are Wolves fans.

Are we not beautiful and handsome, are our threads not slick and delightful, casual and rare? Are we Wolves fans? Fans? I'm a fan of Sun Kil Moon, delicious acoustic songs of loss and beauty, love and loss. Sun Kil Moon never made me cry like this. Are we fans? No, we are not Wolves 'fans' we are what

Wolves are and as the threads of Fosuns belief are strong and tenable, ductile, ever dynamic and resolute under the hate we ourselves have those threads that entwine around everything we are. Our loves and hate reflected in feeling and emotion over the hard arse spreadsheet and the figures that roll across them. We lose and we die a little, for a few days at least. I sit in a hospital bed and watch a man struggle to breathe, I watch a young Nurse on the 15th hour of her shift still smile and still rush to placate and reassure him. I watch everything and feel everything. The pain is unbearable now but it's OK. In a few days little Helder, my Helder will slip a ball between his own legs to twist up a Reading defender and forensically slips the ball to Benik who slots home. They have brought me Morphine and I click the button which sends me into a fog of pain free minutes. I love you Coady. I love you Helder. I love you Benik. I love you Nuno. I'm laughing again.

My Helder got the pelters at Fulham. Couple of balloons who were behind us started the rhetoric and I'm shutting them out, filtering them, getting them as far away as my mind could while concentrating on that awful game. Horace has taken his gloves off and he's debating whether or not to pull them over the seats and start that funky 'in stand' violence thing. I'm wearing a boating blazer under my crombie. It ay right is it? We aren't the greatest fans but we don't cuss the team. Ever. Happy clappers? Probably yes.

Helder scores and is gliding across the snow flecked inhuman coldness of Molineux. Wulfrun Heantun or something. Wulfruna High Town. The wind whips around like Neves and those balls he threads and weaves. It's microsurgery, it's brain football, it's holy and beautiful and the wind carries the sounds of Molineux down the alley to me on the doorstep of me moms where I'm smoking a roll up and listening, watching, leaning on me crutches. Helder has seconds to decide who and when to twist up. Neves has three seconds to decide how much back spin, curve, aerodynamic magic to put on that ball. Boly could write a blog post he has the ball that long at one point. Saiss grows his hair at one point he has that long.

I watched the Wolves fans huddled up, walking up, wrapped up and happy regardless of the Villa result last week. It shows how much Villa affected us as we have seen so many times this season, a defeat means nothing to these men. These young men. It means nothing to these people walking up and I watch them and love them too. We weren't worried because that defeat didn't really mean anything in the wider scale of things. It didn't mean anything because the ministrations of the fat headed egotistical bastard who coaches Villa had nothing. His team had nothing. We have everything and in everything there is an infinite amount of possibilities, an infinite amount of emotions too. I juxtapose Nuno with Lambert for a second and wonder.

I try to juxtapose Nuno and Bruce but I might as well compare a Ferrari to a Shopping trolley and I fail. I want to kick Bruce in the face (with my good leg). Maybe my bad one too. Later that evening I watch Karl Henry in the face of some Villa player while Bruce is telling him to 'fuck off'. Oh my days Bruce you total lollipop. This isn't 1981 any more. Could I see Nuno doing that? No…maybe not, I hope not. Thus the columns of the architecture Brucism has cast up in Witton crumble and fall as we knew they would and I laugh again. At the end of this season I can see them having a mighty tumble and I am happy at this state of affairs. There is always Justice however it comes.

I always thought that Lambert won his games despite the lack of belief, that some how he ground out a win here and there through his stoic philosophy of 'shift' football. Journalists write 'shift' articles. I have read one this morning from the Daily Mail again. Some prong waxing about the Wolves when it's obvious they don't understand a thing about what is actually happening here. They don't have the capacity to understand this. They never will. They crouch over their IMacs in first class carriages tapping out their crap. Coughing up their prejudices over a Costa coffee and a shit sandwich. God help these people. Is this football something other than that? I think it is. But I can only understand this Nuno in the context of his predecessors, it's the only way.

Helder glides over the snow flecked wind whipped hallowed ground. The ball is just an afterthought to him. This is more than football. Yes, it still needs the academic tactical analysis and the unlocking of opposition offence. It still needs the days at Compton, going through those gates and parking the funky expensive motor and razzing around on the training pitches. I see that. But I can't extrapolate 'training' and as Nuno says 'Hard work' with what I see on the pitch, where everything all of a sudden takes on a different groove entirely I suppose. Costa has scored. Down Molineux alley the sound of the crowd roars past discarded settees and the rubbish, the makes little tornadoes in the vicious wind but that sound is unstoppable. Helder, my little ghost. They think they fasten you with their eyes but they are deceived, you are gone, you glide and are lost to them. Boom. Fucking have that. Burton, a desolate place I can't even be arsed to denigrate. My crutch slips a little off the step and my broken leg hits the step but I don't care. Hahahahaha I laugh and some refugee looks at me strangely. You don't understand my travelling friend. Not yet. But stay awhile and maybe your children will.

Helder was given my love when he first came here and not an ounce of that love have I lost for him and there are I go again, it's nothing about position and strength, completed passes, assists, goals. It's never been like that. It was always that unstoppable Kwan as I said in one of my first posts on this site. Kwan. It was supporting these players through anything 100%. Forget the displays when things seemed a little slow and confused, when things were never going quite right. As Helders season stuttered over many months then Benik was perhaps a microcosm of his. A short time, two games, people were crying for his body to be dragged behind the team coach. I heard it at away games and I heard it to a lesser extent at home games. But this isn't a statement of how my own personal dogmas are more correct. Benik flies in for two goals yesterday against Burton and Helder still ghosts around adding to the tally. It's what it is because there is something else at work at out club that transcends results and work. Benik is learning and other teams should fear this. We have not seen everything yet, but we will. Benik. Dude.

John Ruddy lets one in for Burton. It was toe bunted through a mess of bodies. Unsighted, may be a few deflections. Ruddy is a big fellow, he is fast though but not really fast. He's our goal keeper, drafted in to replace an ill and much loved goalie for the season. Has he done well? I think he has. It's an indicator of how well the team has performed that we have to look at the position of least effect tactically but the final defender of our intent. John Ruddy for me has also been a wake up call. He does prowl the box. He has made saves, not stunning stretched panther like swoops across the face of goal but workmanlike, foundation goalkeeping. At the beginning of the season I suspect it was his intent that the defenders in front of him were cajoled, ordered and seduced by his commands. He is a presence. His shiny head darting here and there, does he flap? I'm not entirely sure to be honest. I know when he is in the box ready for a rare attack from another team he is resolute and dynamic too. In the air there are again an infinite number of possibilities over where the ball will end up. He is the one that has to try and define the physical variables of leaping and either collecting the ball, or punching it away from the head of the big oaf attacking it. Do we mark zonally? There are spaces there that Ruddy has to decide to attack or to sit back and wait. The whole game could depend on his choice. It is not a position I would enjoy. He adopts a perfect approach for me. Watch the space and prepare to attack.

Who is this John Ruddy? Norwich fans castigated our choice of goal keeper. I still have the emails full of jollity and japes. Castigated is a good word to use. Was he happy there? I don't know. Who am I to investigate the knowledge of the average football fan at one end and the dizzy heights of who you choose to play for your team. I am ignorant. But John Ruddy looked long and limber. His groove was unmistakable and felt like something good to me. Commanding and true. Behind me at Fulham someone had a go at him and I whipped around and held them by the throat for a moment while I looked into their eyes. There was nothing there. No knowledge, no debate, eyes blank, phone in hand, I noticed he was checking his bets through his shouted bile and anger. But there was no real anger, just empty words and that chip shop pallor, that swinging gut of unfitness. I threw him back into his seat. Nobody castigated Ruddy after that.

Who are you John Ruddy? His field of view is narrow and fast changing. Decisions have to be made in a micro second. His capacity for error is much larger than say Coady maybe or Boly simply because that's what goal keeping is. He faces an attacking ball that is sent with and attacked by an opposition that have adrenaline rushing through their bodies at the chance of a goal for their team. Mad ball my friends. Fast as fuck decision making, decisions that may tilt the outcome of the game and thus careers, millions of pounds of investment, league places, trophies. I watched his interview with Mikey Burrows the Wolves media bloke and was struck by how scary and intense Ruddy was. Those eyes for fucks sake. He scared me just watching it. He's controlled and resolute, academic for sure, empirical again…but what happens to him when the magic comes and he finds his soul?

The thing is as well, I don't even think that Nuno has started on Ruddy yet. I don't think that Nunoism has even touched Ruddy in any way. But if Nuno decides to keep Ruddy and should some of that magic rub off and makes him grow, like Coady and Doherty then we have a master goalkeeper. We will see Ruddy in the Premier maybe? There is talk of a very good Goalkeeper on the radar. Probably tempted by the DVD Nuno gave him.

Supporting this team we have in front of us isn't hard, it's easy. But there are indeed times when expectations can outrun ability for sure and all those variables within the team can tangle up and become a knot of sorts. We saw it with Lambert. Cavaleiro and Costa struggling to understand this dour shift mentality. Games running away from us. Burton last season and before that. Trudging out of Molineux thinking what the fuck, shit, bollocks. Now of course this.

Social media was awash with short bitter paragraphs about John Ruddy and they are within their rights of course to discuss errors and flaps. That's the beauty of social media and it's ugliness. Here we are all pundits, all safe in the afterglow, the hours after the game to wax our bars about members of the team or the way we play. Hours, that's the keyword. John Ruddy works on split seconds, keeping track of the ball and three or four players barrelling into his ends. Are we not happy with John Ruddy? I am. I am quite happy with him and I'll stand and say it, the same way I defended Helder and Benik when it seemed like all were about to storm the castle at Compton demanding action, I suspected bedsheets to be ripped off beds and spray painted with with badly spelled propaganda.

John Ruddy has my support, of course he does, he always will while he plays for my team. Every player will have it as long as they trudge out onto the hallowed turf in my teams colours but I offer that support on one condition and that is that you learn to love this team and if not love nod a head to the beauty of what Nuno is doing here. Learn John Ruddy. Not the nuts and bolts of how to keep goal, not the players screaming into your box, not concentrate on the balls that fly across the face of your goal but learn about the spaces in between. This is where the greatest goalkeepers find their fertile ground, and this is where the summit of your ability will be climbed. Coady has done it, Doherty, Morgan Gibbs White is doing it, Benik has cast himself in front of his Master and has said 'teach me'. Thus they have reaped the glory of their own climbs to the summit. Relax John Ruddy and open your mind, look into the spaces.

I awoke and watched Conor Coady with his arms aloft. It is slow motion. Cavaleiro slowly walks across the image and then Coady reappears. He has just slipped a Neves quality ball through to Costa for the first goal. The camera refocuses and Conor is sharp. His shirt is stretched up to his belly button. Slowly gazing at the bench he starts to smile and my tears are fucking flowing. I'm crying again. Now I know we are promoted. Now I'm sure. Help me as I follow my team on that Coach as it winds it's way through Wolvo in May, help me out a bit, I'm going to be a bit unsteady and my eyes will be blurry.

International breaks are weird and strange things aren't they? Like all voids in our Wolves related lives we tend to fill that void with awful shit. I was arguing with somebody about Danny Batth last week. I don't really care about Danny in many respects. I'm not sure about his current skill set but that's it. I just wasn't sure. I didn't have the data or the skillset to comment about the whys and wherefores of Dannys footballing groove. But…international break. The void. Of course I waxed lyrical. Then the doughnut disagreed with me. Then we started arguing.

This was in Poundstretcher too. Nans and fat women getting their multipack groove on. Buying shit lampshades and shittier rugs. Christ almighty. And there was me and Sid Snot going at it like hammer and tongs. International break. We fill the void with shit because we love throwing stuff in holes. Amazing offers on Pringles today, Sour Cream and Chives £1.50 for two. Amazing. Love a handful of Pringles at night. Having a scoff. Danny Batth a distant memory even though Sid is still waxing.

Thing is folks. It's been a bloody long season and to be fair to myself I thought it was too long by October and I'm sure I waxed about it somewhere. It was long because of expectation. It's cool all the Nuno chilled out vibes and the team getting it together. The funky videos we watch on Social media and the chats we have when we have won. It's brilliant. But underneath all that shiny happy people bollocks is a deeper angst.

We are expectant and we are ready. We have been for months. We have been for fucking years. We know that the season is running out and we are getting angsty and a bit crazy. Are we there yet? Kicking the seat in front. Not letting your siblings have an extra 1mm of space on the back seat. Your Dad is on a slow boil watching the thermometer of the engine which is creeping up because of this fucking traffic. The kids are getting angry and nibbly in the back. You've packed half of the house into the boot. The duvet on the parcel shelf doesn't block out the twat that's driving a few feet off your bumper. Wolves. End of season shit this is. Madness. What even is a caravan in Great Yarmouth? This division of course. Next season the wife and kids will fuck off somewhere else and it will all be voluptuous models in San Tropez, red snapper and a divine saffron scented salad with fresh olive oil. You hold your gut in as the beautiful people walk past your table but we deserve to be here too for sure. Even if we are eating our ice cream dessert with the soup spoon.

Who is a bigger Wolves fan is a current favourite purely for the entertainment of course. How do you quantify it? I know an old fella that gets to maybe six or seven games a season when he can afford it and when his health is good. He's 86 years old. I know the pain he has going to the match. I know he hardly has the strength to lift his pint if I see him in the pub. He watched Stan Cullis and Billy Wright years ago. Remembers things, important things. He remembers matches when I cant even remember last weeks. He's a Wolves fan. So is a dude I know who lives in student halls a stones throw from the ground. He will hit two or three games a season because the ticket money is all he allows himself for food. He doesn't flush his toilet for days because he's on a water meter. He dresses like a freak in a video game. He's a fan for sure.

I could go on. Dudes who get to every away game and home. They attend the dinners and the hand shaking ex player stuff. That's cool too. Most of them have their own businesses and can afford it. They can afford to dedicate their existences to Wolves and they become in essence Wolves. The club is everything to them. But the attendance at these games and events doesn't make them a bigger fan than my old fart mate and my student mate. There is more to these two than football. More to them than spending their hard earned money razzing up the motorway to games hundreds of miles away. Sometimes it is more important to watch your daughter careen around at dance class for three hours on a Saturday afternoon. Sometimes you have to watch your lad play some weird under 11s football in a dog shit splattered pitch in the cold rain. Sometimes the hall stairs and landing have to have that fresh covering of autumn gold emulsion from Untouchables while your team are getting beautiful on a pitch somewhere while you try to balance on a milk crate and you notice the dog is speckled in Autumnal hues too.

The angst is amplified by the unknowing void of the weeks when we don't have a game because England and other national teams are playing and to be honest we really don't care about what England are doing. I care even less about Portugal and what part Neves has to play in that squad. I don't even understand the magic Neves ladles out at Molineux yet alone on some pitch I've never heard of. Amplification of Angst is further strengthened by Social Media. Fucking hell what a place that is. This week I have watched meltdown after meltdown as fans have been at each others throats over the wrong word or opinion. Opinions are like assholes, everybody's got one. And boy those little errant letters tapped out by a gnarled thumb on a phone screen don't half get some knickers in a twist.

I've just read another threat of violence in a tweet over some comment lost in the fog of the timelines. On Facebook I know there has been a straightener offered. So two doughnuts will be rolling around on a pub car park somewhere punching the fuck out of each other. Be constructive lads, offer tickets, proceeds to Carls charity. Lets make it constructive at least. Raise some money. Offset the horror of pallid guts spilling out of polo shirts wrangled from the wrestling section of the straightener.

Remember we are on the last lap now. It's nearly done you know. A few games and that promotion is just there at our fingertips. This next few weeks will define what we are to be in the future and we have to hang tough, we have to close together because that's what a Wolf pack does under duress. This is the time when all those away trips to these featureless Lego stadiums in business parks make a little sense. This is where we wave goodbye to Reading, Preston, Barnsley all those shitholes. The Premier league eh? Arsenal, Tottenham, Manchester etc. We are going to have to be at the top of our game at these places for sure. If you think the Talksport propaganda is harsh just wait until the Premier league mouthpieces start spewing the bile. Wait until those creative less donkeys at Match of the Day or SSN start on us. Now we should be consolidating what we are as fans, linking arms and discovering who we all are and again in essence what we are, the link that drives all of us is that we are supporters of Wolverhampton Wanderers and we all share that love regardless of what financial position we are in and how many games we got to. They are going to be coming for us and if we are in a state over some off the cuff tweet or some derogatory post about uber fans then it's all going to go to shit there's no doubt about it. We have to stick together, we have to be strong.

Here we have owners who have firmly nailed their colours to the Wolves mast. We have a Manager/Coach who is part Philosopher and part Footballer. We have assembled a team that stupefy me every time I watch them. They have made me cry during games. I have begun to love certain players and have favourites again. I look upon this team and that includes all of the staff at Molineux as something we haven't had for a long time and I am amazed by it. It's a once in a lifetime experience this is. We will tell tales of it to our Grandchildren hopefully. We will spend idle moments thinking about Neves or Coady or Bennet or Douglas or Jota. We will think about Nuno too and say 'Ah well, when Nuno was Coach…' and people will roll their eyes again, the same as us when an old 'un goes on about Peter Knowles or Mike Baily. These are precious times.

So in conclusion. Just take what you read on social media with a hefty dose of salt. People have had long seasons. Some people have Wolves that firmly entwined in their DNA that any post will provoke a reaction. Don't judge people unless you have walked a few miles in their shoes. Everything will come good I promise. When we get promoted I promise you that you will be hugging strangers next to you with tears in your eyes. You will be running on the pitch next to people you have spent the last few weeks threatening on Twitter or Facebook. It's all cool man. Take some deep breaths and trust each other. It's coming. I can feel it in my bad leg. The bones are knitting together. Things are afoot.

Player of the Season. POTS we abbreviate it to. It's come around fast. I remember voting for Richard Stearman, former defensive Hero...it was meant to be ironic but nobody got the joke.

 It's easy to see the fume and the aggro such an acronym causes. We all have our favourites I suppose. Outside the house sitting on my bench in the odd bits of sun and the dogs are licking each others balls. Last year I sat in the same place and thought about starting a blog where I can talk about Wolves in a way that's never been done. Where I could throw out to the public a few maybe esoteric reasons why Wolverhamptons number 1 team is what it is. Some way to describe the madness that was to come. Now here again. A busted leg encased in dayglow plaster. Shaky Jake asking me if I need any help. For fucks sake the season hasn't even finished yet. Shaky is fresh from a Heroin withdrawal thing and he's giving me help, offering, being a human.

Neves. Our Ruben. He's a thing isn't he? I don't remember another player down here with such silky skills. He's often the reason I go home after a match shaking my head and laughing to myself. In fact I'm that confused about his football I tend to forget him when I'm writing about a match. What actually does he do? He does the Ruben thing of course. Effortless football. Dinking those passes from side to side. Pushing and pulling players out of position. He's a Magician. And we walk away dumbfounded, at least I do. Yet he's always on my mind even if that picture I have of him prowling the midfield is often blanked out by my ignorance of actually what he is and what he does. My puerile footballing knowledge can't even begin to nibble away at what Neves is.

He came here with some fine words attached to him and he unrolled the scrolls of his skills on the pitch too. Some of his goals have been sublime and the finest art. His movement low centred and poignant. Emotional too if only to point at opposition fans and say 'look at this you bastards, this is exactly what we are'. It's not filthy it's beauty and balance all combined to unveil an idea of what football should be and we here are witness to it. Would he get my vote? No. Neves is beyond platitudes and plaudits. Beyond statements like POTS. Give me a poll that says 'Player of the Decade' and maybe I would dink that big X in whatever box you want, with a smile too.

Jota. Little Wolf. His courage has been phenomenal to me. How many times has he been on the floor rolling after Reg Gluehair has run him over. How many fucking times have we took in breath and held it, watched him closely to see if he was going to get back up. When he did get to his feet he would shake himself down and seconds later he would be doing his thing in the box. His delightful turns, the shoulder drop, the forensic perfectly weighted pass to a team mate. This isn't learned stuff. This isn't coached ability. This is pure spirit and innate knowledge of where that ball has to go. Psychological football for sure. Moves he plays are a few seconds ahead of his teammates sometimes but we see them. Up there in the stand we see exactly what he means. Where Neves is so advanced we struggle to understand, Jota we fully know. Would I vote for Jota? No. His skillset is natural and beautiful, brave and resolute, creative dynamic and for fucks sake I run out of things to say about both of them. I could do a painting I think or maybe write some music that might deal with the both of them. But words? Nah. You have to see it for yourself and delve into the madness of it. I spoke to a Leeds fan when we played them at their place a few weeks ago, who asked me about Neves and Jota and I couldn't answer him. Just said 'They are brilliant, I've never seen anything like it'. I'm sorry Leeds bloke, I haven't a clue how to describe how both of them do what they do. I'm an idiot, you should go and talk to somebody else who understands it.

So we have Cavaleiro, Doherty, Bennet, Douglas. I could bung a vote in for Cav for sure. He's been fantastic, my kind of player. Running around like a mad cunt and getting in players faces in a pure footballing sense. Some of his runs are breathtaking. He breaks down attacks too. I watch him do it every week. He's not brilliant at it for sure but he's there every time and he has that link with Costa too. Another player who I could chuck a vote into the hat for. The thing is man, I'm voting for this player, then that one, then somebody changes my mind again and I'm going hell for leather Neves, then Costa, his injury, but Doherty. Then before you know it all these faces are swirling around your mind like a fucking carnival ride or you've just stepped off a neck breaker of a ride at Alton Towers and the five quid burger you just ate is threatening to come back up. For fucks sake…

Coady. Now I'm reticent to wax lyrical about Coady too much. Most people know I love him to bits. But for reasons I can't explain. I've been in his position before. Castigated and sad, not knowing which direction to go into. Thinking maybe I wasn't good enough to do what I was doing. All that self doubt, all those crazy voices going blah blah blah in your mind until you want to sit upstairs in the quiet away from everything. I suspect that's where Coady was at the arse end of Lamberts reign. Jesus Christ he played in some positions didn't he? But he would always do his best there and I loved him for it even if like Neves I didn't quite understand what he was doing but for all different reasons.

I think nobody represents the season I'm watching more than that link that Coady has with Nuno. Mr Santos has taken Coady from the drudgery of Lambertism to new heights and Coady has fully embraced every single idea that Nuno has given him. Coady represents the ideas of Nuno and channels them into solid memes like 'Progression' and 'Improvement' all the buzzwords that Mikey Burrows chokes out of Nuno at every interview. Coady represents the ability of the team to learn new ideas and often complicated ones. Who would have thought that this Scouse nutter would embrace the ideas of Nuno with both hands, utilising them to become one of the great players of this season. Could we say a vote for Coady would be a vote for Nuno too?

I suspect that Jota/Cavaleiro/Neves/Costa always were great players and that is why they were picked to play in this concept Nuno has given us. But the real work has been done between Nuno and Coady and this is where the whole concept has borne fruit for me. God knows what went through Coadys mind when he sat down with Nuno and his staff to discuss the whys and wherefores of Nunoism. This lad from Liverpool who we may hang all the stereotypes we love about Scousers. But here in him we see the architecture of the concept Nuno is building for us. And yes he has improved massively since the Lambert days. He has progressed so much it's hard to see a similarity between him now and the player we brought to be a midfield master. Progression my friends. This is what I see and love. The way he has embraced Nuno and these ideas has staggered me and I feel a little jealous too. I would love some direction, somebody to point me in the right direction as Nuno has with Coady. Yes. I would vote for Connor. Simply because a vote for Coady would also be a vote for Nuno and his idea.

There will be much fume about voting and many will be castigated for voting for whoever. Yes, Carl deserves to be player of the season too but his battle is personal and tougher than a game of football. His gift wont be a trophy but will be fresh air on his face when he walks out of that Hospital cured and free. Trust me when I say that battle is the toughest and a trophy will mean little to him. Now we have to decide who will take that award and I think I am going for Coady. I think he is a lynchpin of the team, I think he represents this season for me at least. I enjoy watching him play. I enjoy watching him lead my team in that special way he does. I think in the years to come he will continue to improve until we can't see another player in that position. I think now is the time to give our appreciation. But Referees eh? This is going to be a rant. Glass of cheap whisky, a roll up. Angst.

I don't even want to write that fucker Atwells name. A Referee? He disgusts me. What an inept show, what a total disregard for the rules and regulations. He looks like he owns one of those off road Landrovers. He fucks off to Wales with his mates to rollock around country tracks scaring the wildlife. She unbuttons her shirt when she goes to the car wash because she loves the Kurdish lads…is that enough? I think so. Fuck you Atwell you bubble. Why do we always get these doughnuts? I mean I love conspiracy theories but fucking hell I wonder sometimes. That tackle on Cavaleiro at the Middlesbrough game was assault. Same old same old. We have to get out of this place. This isn't our home, up there is, the dizzy premiership, that mad as fuck place.

We haven't won at Boro for ten thousand years. The last time we won there we were probably still inventing agriculture. What is a Middlesbrough? Chemical warfare that's what. Pulis with his shitty baseball cap looking like one of those burglars trying to jemmy open your patio doors while you watch him through your night vision CCTV camera. He always has trouble. What are you Pulis? Why did you tell your players to kick the shit out of my team? You must have done that. You knew the Referee was weak and had a penchant for your team. You knew the lack of your idea would be overlooked and ignored. You knew the play could be ugly and Atwell wouldn't care. Your team have no honour. There are a few in it that would be wise to avoid this town in the future. But I think we knew what would happen. Deep down, us who have seen Pulisball and the emptiness of their hearts. What a decrepit system he plays, what sadness, what shamefulness.

We react of course. Have we not suffered enough? How often can you turn the other cheek. I suspect that Nuno in all his Holiness has as well a dark side and a shadow Nuno. Here is untapped potential and gone are the ideas of gallantry and divine philosophies, instead he is redolent and powerful. He instigated this defence and this resoluteness not through respect only but fear. Did you see him at the end of the match? Warrior stock, animalistic, rage, and victory. This came out of him from the touchline and started as Cavaleiro gets hacked in half. It must be a sending off? No? What? But Nuno.

He boiled and plotted, he himself knew that what was to happen. The whole play had been written in those first ten minutes as Wolves player after Wolves player crumpled under the woeful Pulis commanded boot of Boro. But Nuno knew. I guess he would have taken both our goals happily because he knew that now Boros time was short. He had Mr Boly. What a magnificent display from this Prince among men. He bought a matt black Rolls Royce. The car would have gone 'oooh' when he saw Mr Boly. The Great Wall Of Boly'.

I'm sick by now. I'm still trying to work out where Neves is. I can't listen to Don Goodman, he's a lunatic. I've turned the volume down. Costa goes down again. Shit did I actually see him get tripped? Replay. Boro player obviously treads on him. Atwell. I find myself watching him and not the match. I'm being malevolent and giving him bad vibes through the lap top. Wanker. Are we in the second half. I went for a piss which takes ten minutes and Doherty has gone. What's going on. Now I'm confused and I'm looking to see who we've got fucking left. Jesus Christ. I still don't know where Neves has gone. I see our flag and I start laughing but cut to Nuno and he's got his arms crossed and he looks angry as fuck. Malevolence. But now our shape is compact and formidable and nobody is shirking a tackle any more. This is pure English Championship football. The crucible where these Portuguese players can gather their children around them in years to come and explain the horrors of it to them. And those children will look upon Grandpa Cavaleiro/Jota/Costa/Neves with eyes that are full of love for the bravery of their beloved Grandfather.

Jesus Christ we dug in. Costa smashes into this big Boro lunk who's got his head down and just charges with the ball. No pass for him. Things are hard as fuck in there. It's a mosh pit. Boro pressing. Last ten minutes but I remember little of the match at all. It's been that crazy. What the fuck? Shot of Atwell being a prick again. Fuck off.

But something else is at work here too. The Kwan, I talked about it in my first writings when I was planning this book. Kwan is the power at work here. Nine men. Nine fucking men against eleven Boro Heretics and one Referee. But Kwan. It knits and flows through this team. Their playmaker gets sent off. No heads dip but new shapes are formed on the pitch and everybody knew what to do? They knew everything Pulis presented to them. Every shoddy biro and a fag packet tactic Pulis put forward Nuno and his team reciprocated with a better, newer more ductile shape. Attacks were being sniffed out before Boro players had formulated them. There were moments of course. The Coady clearance. The bravery and brilliance of Coady. Smashing into each other. Fuck it was like a Wolves Fancast wrestling podcast not a football match. But the Kwan.

You see the Kwan on Coadys face when we score or when we win, we score, You see it in Wily Boly walking cool as fuck barely displaying emotion but you know he has it coiled within him, but he can't let it out not yet. You see it in little Helders smile, Douglas furrowing his eyebrows, Ruddy concentrating hard, Saiss shuriken sharp. That crazy Kwan took Nuno onto the pitch at the end and show us what he is made from and what he feels. Those ten seconds tell us more than any interview will ever do. Nunos thoughts and hopes as well as his dreams are all there on the pitch and wear the colours of Wolverhampton Wanderers. His past is probably there too, entwined in every pass and movement. Maybe it is like that, beyond words and everything is winning but winning beautifully. Maybe that stoic defending we did looked ugly and crazy at times. But I think this was what was needed. This was a statement match. This is the match that other teams fans would watch and hope that in the face of such ignorance we would crumble. Then Warnock, Holloway and Bruce would sit and watch too and their dried desiccated hearts would shiver as the time ticked on and we stood and faced the barrage of idiocy and stinging attacks.

Statement match this was. Now the rest of the Championship can fuck off. You have thrown everything at us this season. Shitty referees. You let our players get assaulted, you cast lies and accusations, you belittled yourselves in the information wars. Your propaganda has failed. Your soul sucking grounds have failed. Your fat media friends have failed. Man you are going to shit your pants at our successes in the future. You will have to say 'Wolverhampton' a fucking lot. It's going to choke you and every time you say it you will look like you trod in shit and I will laugh loud at your discomfort. Nine fucking men you made us play with. Nine fucking men. Yet they still held the line and stood in front of your attacks. Man what can I say. We've done it haven't we? It's basically happened. I can't see any other outcome. I'm not looking at points and games but I'm looking at the team and the passion of them. This shit you can't buy. If you could then fifty million quid could buy you a lot of passion. But it doesn't. Boro are an expensive crew. They spent.

But within them with their boot on the Wolfs throat they paused for a second. Unsure, wondering. And the Wolf quickly flipped it's head and chewed the fuckers foot off. This doesn't happen to us. There's another reason and the Gods do finally love us and have smiled down on our town. And there's nothing all the fucking Warnocks and Bruces in the world can do about it. You had nothing at all either of you except bile and untruths. You have been found out. The good guys always win in the end lads.

The nutters I watch games with, get drunk with, and people I never met got together after they heard about my injury. They clubbed together and bought a big fuck off Southbank Resistance flag. It's massive. I saw it on the telly today and nearly cried. It was massive. I hope in some way that the love I felt for them at that time was a big thing for me. It took me over a little. I wondered whether any of the players looked over at it and saw the word resistance? Perhaps a couple of them did. Perhaps the word ideas and resistance could have been a subliminal memetic command in some way. Maybe it rolled around their brains as they played. Maybe, who knows? I like to think so. I predicted a 1-2 win for us. They couldn't take our flag to it's first game and we don't win. That's not how it works. Now that cloth has lost it's virginity and has taken on a distinctly holy groove. It's first game was a battle and a victory for good against evil. What emotions soaked into that cloth once lifeless but now holding the emotions of two thousand Wolves fans on the edge of hysteria. Now we can take that flag into Europe and hang it up in some German bar while we wax lyrical about matches like these. Drink that strong beer and get giggly. Try to explain to some German football fan where Middlesbrough is and give them a warning never to visit there. I hope they fluff the play offs.

"This is where the greatest goalkeepers find their fertile ground, and this is where the summit of your ability will be climbed. Coady has done it, Doherty, Morgan Gibbs White is doing it, Benik has cast himself in front of his Master and has said 'teach me'. Thus they have reaped the glory of their own climbs to the summit. Relax John Ruddy and open your mind, look into the spaces."
'Look into the Spaces John Ruddy' – Southbank Resistance March 18th 2018

How? What do I say? I actually held my hands up to the sky and said to God.

'Dude? Forget about the concept of victory and of rewards and look at our faces. Look at our hands and bodies scarred from this season. Look at our hopeful faces. For isn't hope also love?' I hoped he would look at us and think yeah. Fuck it. Let them have some love and some hope and maybe it is more important than football. Maybe it is a victory of good over evil. I suspect God may have thought also that here is a man in Nuno who's thoughts also transcend the concept of football that his mind seeks and discovers new ways of loving the game and that these concepts are like Gods own thoughts and everything is good. Let that ball be saved by John Ruddy. Didn't I love you when they all denigrated you?

Yes John Ruddy have the courage and the intellectual almost telepathic ability to stroke that ball away. Oh my days. Look into the spaces John Ruddy. Feel the path of that ball before it is struck, use the power of the idea to see into the future and sweep your hand across the face of the goal, caress the ball past the post. His face is a picture and Coady is almost crying with relief that he was not to blame for an equaliser. But I would never blame you Conor, never. You stand here with me and I will be proud.

Is this the greatest of games? Can we say that it was a victory more important than sport and the concept of stylised combat? Warnockian bad vibes permeated all of it but more importantly and in my mind what changed the outcome was that Warnocks team had stopped believing in him. You could see it in their faces.. drawn, pale and tired. Bereft of belief. They were cattle driven over the edge of the cliff by the harsh ministrations of their leader. They fought in a fashion, they humped the ball like ping pong. Boingy bollocks.

You could see their lack of passion exhibited in every errant hoof back up the pitch. Neves rarely had a tackle to make. He instead chose to take his second free kick. What was this goal? What was it seriously? I was a glide of passion held aloft in the air inch perfect. As graceful as a Russian ballet dancer. It was in the air for hours I thought. Time did indeed stand still as it floated across that green stage into the top corner. The Cardiff goalie got a fingertip to it and I bet you it burned his fingers. He seemed reticent to touch it, I suspect it was that beautiful a free kick that the Goalie was embarrassed to touch it, to put his unclean hands upon it. Bang, One fucking nil. I see our flag in the corner where the Wolves fans are and I look for my friends but I cant see anything through the tears. Oh Ruben you beauty. How you too have blessed us. I've never seen a player like you at this club. Holy you are and perhaps one day you too will look back and say these days were some of the best you had.

At Hull I watched John Ruddy make a save that was unbelievable and twisty, getting his arm around his back, underneath him to palm away a shot. I was yards away my friends and I had a little moment for sure. Last night John Ruddy gave us something I think. He definitely channelled that feeling that inescapable feeling and groove that perhaps yes, it was a time when the Gods looked down on us and smiled I suppose. But what else could the metaphysical universe do when faced with the charnel house football that Warnock gives us. Hope again I suppose, that yes ideas are the most important thing, and good ideas must trump bad ones, perhaps evil ones too. But the team.

I know Coady was popping a zit on the Cardiff players back when he went over in the penalty area. It was the softest of touches and the colour drained away from Coadys face as the whistle was blown for a penalty. But what say you Coady? Trust. That's what I had. I know you well Conor Coady, at least the player you are. My heart broke at your pain brother but I knew you would pick yourself up and put your shoulder to the wall again. John Ruddy gets to his left and palms away the ball. I stand up forgetting I have one leg again and I fall onto the rug that is full of Bonio crumbs and half chewed pieces of rawhide bone. My face is in that carpet and I'm screaming into it in pain and in absolute fucking joy. It is what must happen.

We can't let these mother fuckers win. This is our time. How dare you Mike Dean you bald headed little freak. The ball is pinging around. It's injury time plus surely and I'm trying to get back up but I cant and I'm stuck. I can feel the Bonio crumbs on my face and my leg is shooting pains right up to my hip. The ball comes in, it's a scramble a fucking mosh pit of bodies. They should score yes? No they can't the ball pings off to the left and one of their players goes down on the edge of the box. I don't see any contact at all in the replay as I brush the crumbs off and try to stop the dogs from licking my eyes as I struggle to regain composure. The laptop is on the floor too. I'm stuck. Dog lick wet face second penalty. I don't know what to think but I know now that this is not Warnocks time. There is only so much fucking rage voodoo you can use to 'inspire' your players Warnock. Only so much rage fuel you can use to instigate your team. But that fucking fuel is running low Warnock. The Cardiff body steps back. Shoots. hits the bar, they missed. I shout again. These words have no meaning except joy and I watch this with belief now. I'm not surprised by any of it. Boro showed me. Bristol away showed me.

I have a brief negative feeling that I'm not there but my battle was at Villa park. My season defined there in pain and rage. This is for my friends who travelled down and this is the very least they deserve. My heart swelled for them, those miles they have travelled up and down the country and for a moment their joy inside that stadium travelled through the ether and affected me as well. I was there, I knew what the feeling was, the joy, the madness and the limbs. I knew what was happening in their hearts and that was communicated to me like a glowing ray of golden light up the motorway off at the junction at Oldbury. Up the Birmingham new road, straight to me. Jesus Christ man. Horace rings me minutes after the game has finished and I can hear the emotion in his voice, he is close to weeping too but I'm being brave, I was insulated by distance but Horace has closed those miles between me and Cardiff and the emotion is raw and 'there' and we talk about the match. I want this for him and for everybody else. I want them to feel the joys and the pleasure of this victory.

Nuno is beating his chest and the badge in front of Wolves fans. Here is our warrior. I've said before you can transpose Nuno into any ancient warrior King and he would not lack anything. Whatever Nuno does in the future he will always remember this season. The letters to the EFL, the assaults on his players, the snide back biting from his supposed equals, the dodgy and bent Referees, the propaganda, the endless fume and castigation of his idea and of his team. He will remember this for sure and this season will give him hope for the future that good can transcend evil. The British coaches do lack many things. Ideas for sure, they mistake bitterness and violence for passion, they profess ideas too that whither away in the cold light of day. They provoke noting but embarrassment at the state of our home grown managerial nous.

At the end of the game Nuno gives an interview that is loaded with an honest humility and the offer of an Olive branch to Pulis and Warnock. I salute this, in fact it makes me want to weep again and I'm sitting down now still rampant and adrenalin fuelled. Humility and beauty, that's what Nuno showed. This man is greater than anything I have ever known. I suspect that maybe Nuno was brought to us as a gift not just an appointment. Now I would build a statue to him and I would put it right in front of the subway at the back of the Southbank. Nuno will be shielding his eyes as he looks towards the West and the setting of the sun. What honours has he brought us? Nothing yet of course in terms of trophies and trinkets, but he has brought us hope and has taught us the meaning of greatness, of ideas that are stronger than the opposition. A legacy too maybe, and a model that will be followed by others that come after him. He gives us hope that dark clouds do have a sun behind them, and that sun will peek out at one point and we can turn our faces to it and feel the warm rays touch us. Hope.

Fucking hell how we have hoped. The ghosts of Molineux don't wail any more for sure. Those ghosts shine for us now and light the paths ahead of us and the trials to come.

It was all emotional and I don't really know what to say. Sometimes words are just senseless things that try to describe concepts that are far greater than could ever be described. This is one of those times I think. I sit here and see Nuno running onto the pitch to celebrate. Fucking hell, the passion of this man. How do you write about that? How do you describe his face? His technical staff glaring at Warnock? How do you describe Doherty grinning at Warnock? How do you describe the limbs in the corner of the ground? How can you describe Warnock telling everybody to fuck off?

We thought Boro would be a defining moment in our season, a game to end all games and yet we are presented with this too? How can we deal with it? I don't know, I haven't got a fucking clue. The way I do it is by knowing we will be playing 'those' big teams next year. There will be more moments of madness and more fume from other Managers. There will be pantomimes like we have never seen but we must also remember that the whole steel of the Wolves teams to come will be forged in games like this, hardened off and made strong in the crucibles of Warnock/Pulis bongoball. God bless Nuno, thank fuck we have him to hold our hands and lead us through this madness.

I wake up this morning and I still have Bonio crumbs in my hair after last nights contact with the living room rug. My leg hurts. But my heart is swollen with love and yes it does take away the pain a little, it does make the day seem brighter.

Football isn't something we invented but it is something we (as a club) now understand. It is a very complex sport and I sometimes struggle to understand it, often needing others to explain integral events and parts of the game I remain ignorant about. I have never played football at a competitive level. But I do suspect that Nuno and the 'kwan' around the club has a more important and meaningful part in our current success that I previously discussed. I think Nuno means more than we can easily understand. Football here at the moment transcends the idea of football as we know it and understand it. Although we may wax lyrical about the 'front end' of the play i.e. the players and tactics. I suspect there is something else at play too. Something different. Can we make statements about a subject so close to our hearts without fear? Perhaps. Nuno has discussed the bond between players and the crowd. It becomes metaphysical then and intimate, all memes which should have no truck with the quantitative point accumulations of the games we have played.

I suspect that there are aspects of this Nunoism that we may forever be lost in the fogs of our ignorance. The facets which he displays in his post match celebrations, the measured tones during interviews, his humility, his unforgiving destruction of the opponents ideas. If Nuno has this relationship with our support then it is transcendent of both football and politics. So it becomes a fourth dimension. 4th Dimensional football in other words. We have been imprisoned by our past and our fears for the future so we inhabited a lone space and were held by it, especially during the Morgan era. Now of course Nuno only waxes a little about previous games, he does not dwell on them, he always looks forward. I would like to call this the 'directions of Nuno' always forward, always looking towards the next match and the next battle. Everything driven on towards the future. But it is not entropy, the movement of an ordered system towards chaos and disorder but actually the reverse. Chaos towards Order. This is a 'meta-statement' where Nuno has not only galvanised the styles of football we play but also affected the way we watch it and interact with it. Often the crowd noise at Molineux this season has been subdued somewhat apart from when we play a rival or a neighbour. It is subdued I suspect because we haven't mentally caught up with what we are watching. Nuno has created a veritable dream world of football. The last minute winner at Bristol City away, Cardiff the other night, the Battle of Boro. All benchmarks of the dream world he has made us and one in which few teams even in the Premiership have experienced. Nuno, his technical staff, FOSUN, Jeff Shi, the staff at Molineux have all come together to give us an experience of being at last totally alive when it comes to watching our team. In essence this direction of Nuno can cut back into the past, the present and the future all ensconced in the endless push forwards into the future. It has confused us within the stadium and it has brought opposition fans to a state of apoplexy and confusion which results in an endless tirade of ill thought abuse from them and from the media a typical ham fisted and insult ridden dogma of self destructive polemic crap.

Even if the football and ethos we have is built from the familiar and traditional aspects of the game every single match is used as a building block for the next part of the story, the next match always. We are in a dream world of Nunos making and it will only be when we are awake and the season is finished we will be able to look back and see that Nuno had indeed hypnotised us with his magical skills. We will see that most of the matches were dreams, mixed in with a few nightmares just to balance it out. The stadium is the stage where this whole drama is played out and we watch it with eyes wide until we shuffle out when promotion is gained, we will rub our eyes and wonder what happened, why we are happy and some have tears in their eyes.

The rhythm? Wolves have been temporal in their football this season. Every pass has a beat to it and its own cadence. We watch and the pass here and to there is ordered and defined, hypnotic. We are being lulled by beautiful football that I suspect if we count the passes and the tackles would exactly match our own heartbeats. Thus we are hypnotised and we are taken into a netherworld of Nunos making. In the Lambert and Saunders/Hoddle years we were ostracised from this experience. We never really felt part of the whole thing. The results of course reflected our own disenchantment with the way the club was being run. But we were louder then. We did feel it. but how much did we actually feel if we were pushed away so much by boardroom bullshit? So now our return to the Premiership is seen less as a return to a place where we deserve to be and is our spiritual home but more of an observation at the time that has passed since we were there. See the famous banner unveiled at Cardiff when we were promoted. 19 years. Time has trapped us, it has moved around us and through us even if we were trapped within the stadium and intent on the dramatics of games and transfers etc.

We will travel to the Premiership on a tide of glorious victories but we will enter that place changed. It will not be as it was before. The Premier will be alien to us and strange because we have suffered for so long being away from it. The cold of Barnsley away and the desolate identikit stadiums around the country will still ache at us and remind us of where we have been but the directions that Nuno has given us 'forward' should annihilate the memories of them in the end for sure. But those memories will be relentless. The 1-5 Albion game, the times when we were destroyed by teams evidently more attuned to the ideas of football than Mick Mcarthy ever was. Those pains of the past we drag with us as we travel towards the new dawn of Nunoism. The speed in which he drives us towards success will pull those memories with us in our slipstream.

But even if we can't escape the memories of the past we can transcend them to some extent and that is what Nuno has given us. We can transcend the memories of the past by making newer more positive ones. Coady slowly raises his arms after his beautiful pass to Helder Costa during the Burton game. Nuno running on the pitch after the Cardiff game, pick any you want. Do you remember turning to your mate on the stands and hugging them tight, shouting in their ear, do you remember singing in the dark streets after a game? The songs we sing?

The footballing moments that left us speechless? Now we have to utilise these positive moments to construct a new idea of what we are and how we play football. These are the constructs of positivity that will propel us through the games we will play in the future. The bad memories too. How often have I read on social media posts about games we lost so badly, days where it seemed there was no release from this existence as a sad Wolves fan. The last minute equalisers, the crumbling of our ideas and the days of decrepit dinosaur players and coaches. They are still important and yes, they are building blocks as well. For we have to experience the blackness to understand the light. We transcend the ideas of football by zipping backwards and forwards through the years and experiencing each moment through a photograph, a piece of film, even the corner shop song. Thus transcending we move ourselves higher and higher. Transcend but do we lose a connection with what's going on at Molineux? Maybe a little.

There is so much negativity in the past sprinkled with positive moments that we are confused about our place within the whole idea. I suspect this is why we have Nuno. With him we may look upon this confusing landscape and see specific parts and occurrences, incidents and events, we can make sense of them because Nuno has become an interface for our experiences in the past with our expectation of the future. Surely as well our memories are only made concrete by the scars we have suffered too? These scars I know only too well and they pull you back time and time again to periods of pain. We have been scarred by Morgan and Moxey and we return to them constantly to make sense of this new beginning and Nuno (although he never mentions them) displays their inadequacy by shining that bright light in the darkest shadows of Molineux.

When Nuno runs onto the pitch at Molineux in delight it is he that shows us the connection between those days and these. It is Nuno when showing passion and humility lays bare the stoic ministration and misery of the Moxey years. It is Nuno that connects us to our past although he himself is abstracted from it. It is our love for Nuno that builds a bridge between the future and the past so that we may make sense of all of those years in the wilderness. In these times now we will discover who we are and what our relationship with this club actually is.

There will be no more ignorance, no more confusion. We now have the ability to assimilate the past with our future and we may be unstoppable due to this metaphysical transformation of our club and team. Our love for our team will tangle with our own lives and we may see at last how important our club and town is to us as we stumble through this strange trip called life. We will come to know that every tear we spilled in the past is just as important as our joys and laughter. This is art in it's greatest form. The ability to transcend a mere sporting event, a football match, a few hours sinking beers with people you love is the greatest of art works on a par with the greatest art works ever presented to the world.

This art should give us courage for the future and Nuno is the artist that drives this passion. It should give us hope for the trials that come because we now know our team and this place called Molineux is our life and does give us meaning as we gather the madness of the past with the hopes for the future. It's an art that is total love and will always transcend ideas. In the future most of these feelings may be lost in our day to day lives, destroyed under the forensic eye of the caustic medias and the sports page, the blog and the tweet. It is our duty to save this love and to keep it safe within our own minds as the world outside seeks to trample them under the foot of banality and clicks.

Nuno will see this next few weeks as a challenge and will not let these strange philosophical thoughts endanger his idea. He is a Warrior and that's what warriors do. But we must hold onto every memory we have of this season to prepare for the next. We do that with trust and love, creativity and dynamism. We must display in the stands around Molineux what Nuno does within it. But Derby next. They are a strange side. The night is weird too. Misty and otherwordly. It's spooky and I feel like something is about to happen.

Douglas puts in a corner, it's the second half. I'm not sure what to expect. Those corners Duggo sticks in slices the air always, Afobe stands ready to flick on for whoever has thrown themselves into the box. The air is misty with pyro madness, smoke and mirrors this side. Who knows what to expect. The ball hangs for sure. Time is just slices and moments of anticipation with this team and we stand and observe. Our hearts are nailed to these moments. Every part of these divine seconds is heavy with anticipation of course. We demand it. We require the magical and the esoteric.

We need these moments to exist and the holy movements are writ again large on the field of play. It is as if these moments, heavy as they are have their own ethereal existence and the quantitative empirical permutations of the act of winning are thrown down at our feet. But Neves is aloft from this, he sees the magical art and the possibility of novelty and creative passion restored to the turf, to the shuffling feet, the expectation is magnificent and holds on to your belly in a tight grip. No way, surely not, not today, this is not us, this is us, this is them, these are our days…surely not.

It was the second time I had jumped out of my wheelchair, stepped into the puddle of water at the bottom of the North bank, smashed my toes against the concrete barrier and the pain arced up my leg right into my hip. The pain actually made me feel sick. I wondered for a second if I was actually going to vomit as I felt the edges of my fractured bones grate against each other. I wanted to shout out to the universe and to the Gods above that this, this was what football was. This my friends was the totality of things, the azimuth of idea, the critical point where football, Wolves football had turned into the religious. Fuck, how I have waxed about poise and beauty, how I have sat here and typed out reams of cack about how fucking great we are and then this.

I know Neves is pointing at his head because that's what he does, and I'm doing it too as the whole of Molineux erupts. The Steward in front of me is looking at the pitch with disbelief. I've got my plaster wet again. I don't care.

Jota had scored and it was beautiful. I sat back down in my wheelchair and idly thought about how I would write about it. It was good. The through ball from Boly was threading a needle type shit. He had resigned the Derby midfield into sightless mannequins. He had made them redundant with that ball to Jota. So Jota did his thing, the jink, the turn and goal. Bang. Straight out of the chair and smash into the concrete. Yes, this was what it was all about. Still we hadn't got out of second gear really and we were ascendant. We were chilling and I couldn't be surprised by anything at all but…

A Derby defender heads away out of the box and everything is still. You see I'm on my feet by now. Bones smash against bone. Fractured legs are nothing compared to this…something. What is about to happen? I'm not sure but I can feel it in the pit of my stomach. Something is going to happen. Intuition or something. Deja Vu? I'm not supposed to stand up but here I am. That pain is nothing. Because Neves. Our Ruben is in space. All the Molineux is a stage right now but the spotlight is on him. There is a strange silence.

I am sure I can hear the flags flapping on top of the Steve Bull stand. The ropes tapping against the flag poles. Is it not said that in battle often there are quiet moments? Precious moments where the world stops for a second? I think God goes to sleep during those divine slumbering seconds, Gods eyes are shut and what dreams that goes through Gods eyes are possibly made real here in this world we inhabit. These dreams that God has are writ on the green grass where the wafts of pyro smoke linger as a mist almost. Subtle but magnificent dreams they are for God at least. But they are made real here tonight.

Ruben Neves. He is in space because that is his place here. Everything is channelled into this moment. The culmination of Nunos Heresies. The epitome of delights. We have suffered have we not? Have we endured the pain of the past for this one moment? The days shuffling out of the Southbank for beauty such as this? The Lamberts, the Saunders, the players who came and refused to believe in anything apart from themselves. The Morgans and the Moxeys, Sir Jack broken by strife his heart still full of love but his mind broken by this insane love of Wolves we have in which he shared totally to the extent he has alienated his own blood?

I suspect as that ball hangs in the air that even the Gods stop their governance of the universe and pause for a second to cast an eye upon him. The ball falls. Every player is motionless as they are about to witness something they will never see again. We stand motionless. Watch the video replay. Watch the crowd. Listen to the audio. There is a hush. There is a moment of intense anticipation and time is flowing on but slower and more refined in some ways. It slows down because for some reason we have already anticipated something divine and magical. Wizardry this is. Not Harry Potter bollocks but something deeper, something more divine.

Something is happening to the universe. Something is different in the wide schemes of surviving and eating, fucking, working, drinking, looking, hearing. Something is going to happen. We knew it and everybody knew it. His first touch is errant. A fumble if you will. It's the dark side of the whole thing but an integral one. I alluded to the shadowy parts of our play. Sometimes you have to see the darkness for what it is to recognise the light. The errant touch that Neves had moved the ball slightly behind him. It was not optimal, it was not perfect but it was right in the wider scheme of things. It was a part of the whole delicious thing, the experience.

He drifts his right foot back pivoting a little. It is the chaos variable, the crack we hardly see in a marble carved by Michelangelo. This tangle is an errant slip of Gods chisel perhaps. But we must have these gentle reminders that even within the most beautiful things there is a thread of angry imperfection in which Mankind struggles. An errant brush stroke hidden in the canvas. But Ruben already knows. He has already seen the final product because he is the artist.

What should he do? Pass? There is a tangle of players in the box. He has to shoot, it is ordained in the wider topics of this season that he shoots or has a pop. He has to adjust his weight, it is too far forward now so his weight is balanced by swinging his right foot back further than it should comfortably be so his left leg and foot is now off the floor to give him the freedom to move that foot back to connect. He swings his foot in a beautiful arc.

This arc has it's own mathematics and I am reminded of the 'Golden Mean' the beauty of nature and of the natural world. It swings easily. It connects. These seconds are hours to me and I can watch every delicious movement, every sinew and muscle stretch like a ballet dancer. Balance and poise but more importantly belief and effort. He sees it. He knows it. It's there Ruben in every gasp of the crowd and the urge for you to unleash that belief at last. To make history and to stamp your existence deep into the Molineux turf.

The thing is my friends we knew straight away that it was a goal before he had even connected. Why? Because it was such a beautiful goal carrying such pathos and gravitas that time flowed forwards to a split second after the ball had hit the back of the net and recoiled back through time to the moment he hit it with his foot. My arms were aloft. Ruben isn't even looking at the goal. There is nothing except him and the ball. He could be in the middle of a deserted landscape. The smoke dissipates a little and he is shining gold and black. There is only him in focus on the pitch, only Ruben exists. Only the ball too. I see the ball, his foot, his whole existence personified by this moment. The blood roars through my ears as I haven't taken a breath for a few seconds. My hand is halfway to my face to push my glasses further up my nose. It will never get there of course. I am too slow, too material. This is a Holy communion between

Ruben and the dreams of God and I am not invited yet. The arc of his movement has begun and it's not a prelude, not a beginning yet but as his foot and leg begins that beautiful arc it's like an orchestra slowly building to a crescendo of sorts when the conductor holds his baton still and then slowly it rises as he controls and defines the explosion of sound.

The bones creaked, here was the moment of course. He hits and the ball flies in slow motion. There isn't much spin on the ball but it revolves slowly. Time is relative now and flexible. It seemed like twenty seconds to me as I wasn't allowing myself a breath but I was filling my lungs ready. Intake the air, the sour smell of the pyro, the stink of somebody vaping nearby, the stink of the brackish water that collects at the bottom of the North bank concourse. This air filled me. The ball arced and fell as all bodies must do under the dominion of gravity but only enough, only the amount it needed to creep under the crossbar and beyond the outstretched fingers of the Derby goalie.

My arms rose too, did everybody else's? I'm not sure, my eyes are on the ball. Faced with such magnificent beauty for a second I didn't believe it. I didn't recognise it at all and there was a second where all the negative energy rolled around my soul. Of course no, not here, this is Wolves mate. You might have seen some good football this season but are you taking the piss? This isn't for you imbeciles. Goals like this are what you watch on telly where beautiful players score, where beautiful stadiums erupt. Where other people reach those ecstatic heights. This isn't for you mate, this isn't yours and never will be.

A frozen tableau. Players static and unconnected with this event. We were too and then an eruption, a moment when all those dark days of the past were obliterated by such an intense burst of light that it seemed like the demons were blasted out of every dark corner of Molineux in that moment leaving the ghosts and us, the team and Nuno. This was the act of baptism, a cleansing of the soul, total immersion in the waters of football so gracious and holy that no evil could withstand it. It was our moment, we could also take part in the communion between Ruben and the nap of God, the dreams, the sense of belonging to both and they too belonging to us. Ruben beckoned to us to join in with the joy of it.

Neves wheels away pointing to his head. He does that because he knows that beauty lies in creative though, in the dynamic and the novel. Three pounds of meat. That is what the brain is. It nestles inside bone and defines our lives with moments such as this. What is promotion? What is going up as Champions? What concepts could be greater than this goal? I turn to Horace and just say 'Fucking hell' because that is all in my infinite ignorance I could say. The stadium erupts, the flags wave..We've got Neves…Ruben Neves, I just don't think you understand….

Who can understand this? Who can make any sense out of it? I can't. I've never seen a goal like it. I've never been dumbstruck by anything, I've always had an opinion or some fucking senseless waffle to give out to anybody that would listen. But this I can't. It has happened a lot this season. You know the stories, you can read them here. But this? No fucking way. Every moment in the future when I am watching football I will think of this madness. This interplay between Ruben and the ball. Every movement is scored into my brain and I think everybody's. The benchmark of a beautiful goal of course. We will wax lyrical in the years to come to younger people and we will be old and slightly insane with life. They will have the blood and the fire in their veins as they watch a goal scored in the future and they will grab onto us and say have you ever seen anything like it?

We of course will just smile as our knees threaten to buckle and that pain in the hip cracks through us as lightning. We will smile and nod but I think we will keep the memory of that goal to ourselves and our minds will replay these moments as precious memories, glorious times in our past. Because the young will never understand what it looked like even if they watch it replayed on TVs and phones. They will never understand because the goal was an epiphany of enlightenment that only us that have suffered will understand. But we will look in those times for people that were there and they will be old like us and we will perhaps find some fellowship and share maybe a knowing wink at each other and say 'good goal, but not a patch on Rubens against Derby'.

I couldn't even watch the Fulham Brentford game. I don't even comprehend the importance of it now thinking about it. It rolls within the other meaningless games I've watched when other teams are fighting for themselves. I have a lack of empathy for both teams. I struggle to puke up some element of caring. Then I remember. Promotion day. This result will send us up. But I know we are anyway. This is just an idle full stop on the whole mad crazy train. Somebody please pull the fucking emergency cord.

I sat in the garden and was in a state of suspended animation it felt like. The fucking sun had come out. I had forgotten what it looked like. The dogs were licking each others balls on the grass. My plaster cast leg glowed. How many weeks has it been since the cold street outside that cursed Villa ground? The grass was sweet for sure. A bumblebee. I had asked my daughter to tell me the score when I went in and sat quiet. I couldn't concentrate on anything other than just sitting and waiting. I knew it was going to come…it would arrive. She came in 20 minutes ago and told me and I wept. For me? For Wolves? I don't know. But emotional doesn't give any service to the feeling I had right there in the pit of my stomach…it's a soul thing ay it. Snot and tears, years and fucking years. Glen fucking Hoddle. Dean fucking Saunders. How we have suffered. How we welcomed the Chinese men in Hugo Boss suits and the Italian shoes when years ago we would have turned our faces away. How they have transformed us with their ideas.

Little old Wolverhampton eh? The way people take the piss out of our accents, the way people come from villages on our outskirts instead of saying 'Yeah I come from Wolverhampton'. Us, once the powerhouse of world industry, we made such beautiful things. Motorcycles, cars, the best tools in the world. We slaved in those dark places now ground down and lost. I suppose we lost something too. The decline of our town mirrored in the decline of our team. No more. This is important now and I feel different to previous promotion days. This is a lot fucking different. People around the world will soon know our name and what we stand for. This isn't the place where we should bow our heads and be mindful of our place in the world. We are about to be a powerhouse beyond even my fevered imagination. My fucking town will overcome the castigations we have suffered for years. My Wulfrunian pride will not buckle under such scrutiny when it comes because I will point to my team and say 'Look at them, how proud and fine they are, how brave and how magnificent. I will also point to the skyline of my city and say 'This is where I live and I have always been proud despite the mockery and the laughter. This is Wolverhampton, and I have never know a place so entwined with it's team. I heard a woman on the phone once. 'Yes I come from a Village near Stafford called Bushbury'.

Before, after other promotions we would sidle up to the table where the rich men sit and beg for a point here, or a win there. They would throw down a few scraps for us and we would be content for a week or two before our slide down the Premier League leached the life from us. We were further and further away from the table at times. Mocked, vilified and insulted. But this? This my friends is different. I feel something different. I feel that instead of pulling our forelocks at the tables of the great and good we have cast a chair out and sat heavily within it. I look around that table and I look at the faces of the great and good of this league and I hold the gaze of every one of those mother fucking big teams and say this 'We are not afraid any more'. Thus we can kick up our legs and put our dirty war boots on their clean tablecloth and light that cigar. Because shit is going to change. It will change because we have a philosophy now. We have an understanding that things are different in the world, much different. This isn't Mick buying a few crocked semi famous faces to grind our way through the season to come. This is us with a new idea and a new way. We look beyond this table of the English Premier League as a stepping stone to greater more lofty paths.

We are scarred for sure. Warnock, Holloway, Bruce. Jota rolling on the floor, Coady being sent off, Neves leaving the field of play after a ridiculous red card. The Referees we have endured, the ire of clubs PR machines planting stories in the press. The Leeds chairman vilifying us, sending letters to the EFL. Bruce,

Dr fucking Xi or whatever his face is. Bristol away, Bennett. Cardiff, when they tried to crush us under the last minute penalties, the 40 yard throws, the evil ministrations of Colin Wanker. There have been times when the team were still learning and a defeat here and there lead to nervous breakdowns among a few. But I never stopped believing. You have to be honest and true to attain victory and we have done that even if they will accuse in the future. Nuno has done this. Humility in the face of crushing blackness, honesty in the face of lies, innocence under the judgement of liars and thieves. I am proud to have you representing our town. Nuno you are a treasure in the heart of our City.

We have come together as a fan base, we have believed too and we have fought as well as the team. Those journeys up and down motorways, trying to find a pub, strange roads and traffic systems, the cold always the fucking cold. But together we have fought other battles. Rumours on social media, the accusations shot down from the ether with facts and research, well defined answers and come backs, humour, art, and often brilliant new ways of restating our position in the world. It is no longer an abyss we step at the edge of. That experience is now Steve Bruces. He will look upon the bottomless pit and fucking forsake his very existence and that of his club. We will be at the foot of a great mountain and we will be fresh, ready to climb, and we are laughing. Top ten next season? Who would get ahead of themselves and think such a thing? Me I suppose. I see us as being unstoppable now. Fosun, Nuno, all the warrior like ideas now unleashed will be a hard storm to survive for many teams next year. May I think like this? Well I did at the beginning of this season. Something in the whole soul vibe of this club speaks to me. Tells me to fucking hang on because it's going to be crazier than ever.

What do we do now? We plan. This is one great battle in a greater war. This is the way we and Nuno do things. Promotion is done and tonight I have some Jamaican Rum I want to get acquainted with while I plot. Because there will be battles to come. Nuno will know this. Hasn't he said that he only thinks of the next match, the next battle? I will allow myself one drunken night tonight. Tomorrow another stepping stone, another thankless Championship team. Another idealess footballing side as opponents. By God we have some soul in this team don't we? Who would have expected the magic of Neves/Jota/Cavaleiro/Costa/Saiss or N'Diaye/Doherty/Douglas/Bennett/Ruddy or that we would have a Captain like Connor Coady. I'm speechless. The art of Wolves, of Nuno writ large upon the desolate football grounds we have gone to. The shit beers, the awful facilities and now we have gone through the fires and come out forged much harder and tougher I'm sure. I know one man will. You Carl Ikeme, what say you? I want you here now with us and perhaps that chemo burn and fatigue will stop you but when we are Champions in my mind at least you will be there in the hearts of everyone who rejoices and I pray to God that the love we feel for you will give you strength and power.

But tonight this is for my team and my wafflings will not do justice to the beautiful edifice Nuno and the Wolves staff has built. Tonight I will raise my glass to them in thanks. This is for Shaky Jake who kicked his smack habit this season. This is for Gaz Mastic who struggles to pay for his season ticket but still manages every year. This is for Horace and everybody who has helped me through this intense season and you know who you are. Stepping stones brothers and sisters.

Throughout this book I've talked about an energy that seemed apparent around Molineux and that the energy seemed like it was causing some kind of sea change in the zeitgeist of the place. Promotion. It happened in some shit hole London ground hundreds of miles away from us. It happened on the Internet for me, you see I was checking scores and throwing HobNobs down my neck as fast as I could. It's the way I roll man. Then, a last minute header and it was done and dusted. I would love to say I jumped up and face planted the rug again, but I didn't. I sat there and nodded slowly to myself that it was done. It was Karma for sure. Karma for the shit we have had to deal with this season in terms of referees and clod hopping world war one football espoused by the likes of all the usual suspects. We know who they are. I don't want to talk about them any more. I would like to cleanse my mind of their football if I can. Kind of gather a new blank slate kind of mindset for the season to come.

Birmingham City was a reminder of the season. It was like a highlights reel of what has gone on for months. You can see why we had to get out of here, why we had to move ourselves along. I'll be honest with you, I don't think I could have hacked another season of watching teams like City, Cardiff, QPR et al. My mind was nearly broken by it. Jota rolling around after getting his ankle nearly snapped again did it for me. I was up out of the wheelchair waxing insults from the bottom of the Northbank again.

They sang though, these North bankers. They had a right shout at times, but it's always too late of course. Now you sing. Blah. I want to get back in the Southbank thanks. Among my people. But it was a great place to watch Matt Doherty racing down the touchline. He is very physical this lad. I was close you see. Close enough for Dohertys sweat to sparkle as it flew through the air and he out muscled some Brummie doughnut to get a foot on the ball and a beautiful cross. Did Saiss bunk him the ball? I'm not sure but it was forensic for sure. Bonk, right on him. Jota points to the sky. I wave at him like a dickhead. Laughing.

Close up as I was, you get to see the subtle and the sublime movements of a player. He was five yards away maybe? He had that stare going on and he only looked up for the merest second before sliding that ball over to Jota. Of course Jota didn't fuck about with it. Straight in thanks. Jota didn't even look hassled by the effort. It's second nature to him now. These movements are refined and magnificent. His movement is classical, like a ballet dancer. His shots like a bear hug off a brickie. One nil and the script is there for everybody to see. Elbows fly in from Birmingham city players. The beards and the shit trims eh? Only the strip changes, never the lack of idea. They are fighting for their lives. I've seen tougher battles getting your hand stuck in a Pringles tube. Jesus Christ. Why did they bother? Who pissed on their parsnips? I don't care it's funny.

Twenty minutes in and Digga Davis former Wolves man and now arch villain of the Southbank is huffing and puffing. Looking like you just found him in your shed carrying your hover mower in one hand and your strimmer in the other. You can have the strimmer Dave, it's shit. They always are, just like you really. Your footballing ability is the same as the strimmer string. Liable to snap and get tangled every few seconds. Oh Digga you poor sod. Of course the 'dingleboys' insult was going to come and bite you on the arse. It had to. Your shit tattoos. Your wide eyed realisation that this whole footballing carousel you have been looning around on for the past few years is about to stop. It was slowing down during this match. Soon he will be climbing down from those gay painted steps, the horses wide eyed and mouths open, the cacophony of the jingly music. He will step into the faceless crowd and be gone. Just another doughnut. He will attend a few supporter get togethers with the rest of the Lulus at some shit social club in Northfield. Good bye Digga. Watch what yam doin'.

The City fans were only a few yards from me. Ordinarily I would have been throwing some shapes at them. Having a few insulting waxes thrown back. All these Brummies looked the same. Bowl haircuts, black puffa jackets, tight black jeans, Nikes. Madness. Like angry clones. One of them made a cut throat gesture at me and I laughed. It would have been funny outside, me being chased in my wheelchair by Brummie bowlheads. It would have made a funny headline.

Aside from this Costa was making me laugh too. Man that dude jinks and turns lovely. He was knotting the Bluenoses up for fun. They didn't have a clue did they? The ambience was good and wholesome for him. He was revelling in it. I think our Helda could play through the Summer and not get pissed off. It was lovely to see. Especially after his trials and tribulation coming back from injury when everybody slagged him off. He turns again and a Bluenose tumbles to the ground twisted up. He puts his head on the grass and just crouches there for a few seconds. You've been fucking Helder'ed mate. There isn't any cure for it. To nobble him like you want to you have to catch him. And we call him little Helder…pffft. Massive player.

Big Alf who came on for Jota. Yes, I love big Alf. He's a treasure. So physical yet so refined. He dinks a ball through to Benik in the second half and my black Prince chips the goalie and it's all done and dusted really. Will we keep Benik? I hope so. He's learning strange Nuno things, wizardry I suspect. Benik is praying at the feet of Nunoism but it's early of course. What else will he learn over the summer? What freedom will he find in the Premiership? Much I think. Buy him yes. I would.

I think City didn't even know what was happening to them. The match took on the aspects of an exhibition match. A display of total football. I don't think we broke shape once. Nuno kept everything on the down low. No madness, just pure unadulterated love ball. Sliding balls through their midfield with aplomb. Even the Blue Jota looked impressed, though he must have wondered what the fuck he was doing in this side. But how much did their Jota cost? Millions I bet. Poor sod. Sitting in his hotel room, the beaches and beauty of his ends reflected back at him as he looks through the window at the dystopia of Birmingham below him. He flicks on the TV. It is a sad existence. You could tell in his face, he looked resigned. He will be phoning his agent after this game. Talking tactics and escape plans. I wonder if he's building a glider on the roof like Colditz. Plotting airborne escape. There is no escape from Luluism young man. Ya fucked. Look at Digga, look into his eyes. Deep. You're fucked son.

At the final whistle there was cacophony, there was madness. Three dudes got on the pitch and we had a bit of kiss chase with the stewards. Fair play to them I suppose. The madness of youth. They probably wont be watching Wolves for a few years and those few seconds on flicking the V's at the miserable Lulus will seem a long forgotten memory I suppose. I cheered. Clapped a lot. The delight of getting promotion would have been nice with a win right there in the ground. You can't have your cake and eat it I suppose. I knew we were going to be promoted all season, I'm not joking. You can read the past posts on here to see it between the lines. I celebrated when the team were playing in Austria, watching it on the web stream. Watching these young men go through their paces. I was happy to sit back in my wheelchair and just groove to other people enjoying themselves. Especially the kids. Now they can wear their Wolves shirts proudly and people will know what team they support. People will now know us.

Me? Well I've been here before. The joy is tempered by experience of course. I've already seen the likes of Manchester United and Liverpool getting dicked at Molineux. Tottenham, Everton, all of them. My emotions have run riot all season. Tears have been shed, pain has been felt. I've met beautiful people. forged friendships that will last forever. Talked about the football, loved the football. Taken away memories of goals that will stay in my mind forever. Bennet, Bristol City. This is what I will celebrate, this is what I will remember.

Seeing our South Bank Resistance flag on the stand I love made me weep. There can be nothing bigger than this for me....apart from that Neves screamer, you know the one....maybe watching Benik score.

You see, the club will progress and will grow. The times we have had this season will be the most important of things and I sat there, in the chair with a few sad thoughts really. The whole zeitgeist will change now. The whole club will be changing and creating new paradigms for us to try and get our heads around. Premiership football for Gods sake. I can't quite get my head around it of course, can't quite understand it. I know the season tickets wills rise in price. How will we deal with that? Fuck knows. But we always do. Maybe it will be by pre drinking maybe, have one beer in the pub. Maybe get rid of Sky Sports, keep the car for another year, do some overtime, be a bit scruffier this year, tell the kids that Weston-Super-Mare is a great place to go on holiday as you clip out and save the Sun holiday vouchers...fuck knows. We will be there of course in August. Still singing and shouting, watching all the new sexy players Nuno will bring in. Keeping the belief strong and the passion flowing. Because at the end of the day it's only money, worthless by itself. You could start a shit brief fire with nearly 500 squid. Go on holiday to Spain or somewhere. Cook your head in the Mediterranean sun as you chug cold weird lager out of the bottle. But for fucks sake, the feelings this club give us, the love, the hate, the holding your head in your hands, grabbing strangers and kissing them. That's what it's all about. Fuck the ticket rise. You can have my money. Take it. Give me love and pride back and we will call it quits. I watch the Lulus stream out of the ground. Sad bitter little faces. But they are envious too. Most people will be envious next season too. I want to watch it, want to breathe it all in again. I want Nuno to take me to heights of joy I have rarely felt in this past decade.

Bolton next. McGinlay. We have never forgotten. This is what we live for. The journey has only just begun. Soon we will be back on Nunos Crazy Train.

Did we need a leader like him? Of course we did. Watch him stalk the touchline. Animated at times and at others he stands with his arms crossed like Napoleon watching his troops fight the battles he himself has dictated for them. Behind them his coaching staff cajole, inspire and whisper in his ear about events that are judged in seconds and minutes, a reply given, the twist of a tactic and the tweak of a position. Fulham have fallen under the strength of 'idea' and of 'love'. And does not love conquer all?

The Heresy of Nunoism: Southbank Resistance November 4th 2017

It was darkness wasn't it? 1995 and McGinlay. All week I've been thinking about that fat bastard and now this. Revenge? Yes, I think it is, I think they have had such a fucking thumping today that ghost of 1995 has been well and truly banished. The only bad thing is that I would have loved nothing more than to have been in the press box where I would have slapped his fucking head back right into the desk in front of him. Jesus Christ. Bully with his head down. Knackered. Desolate. Out of the play offs and Steve Bulls last chance to play Premiership football.

Enough of that shit. We have done it haven't we? At last. It's been a right journey and a tough one. How they denigrated us at the start of the season eh? How they mocked us and cast their slurs at us. Nuno 'untried' or 'one of those European fly by night Coaches'. Man every time you clicked on an article it was full of shit. We don't wonder why Nuno sits behind the desk at these press conferences and looks at these doughnuts with disdain like he's just stepped into a hot dog turd in bare feet. He knows them well. He's read the crap and the lies all season. He's tired you can tell. Keeping the hyenas away from his Wolves. I say 'His Wolves' because they are his. How he has transformed a crazy bunch of second stringers and league one players into this team before us is nothing less than majestic. I am speechless.

I knew something was up. I knew that we had something golden and real in front of us. The games we have seen, the play, the goals all penultimate, all magical, all fantfuckingtastic. There is a time I suppose when I will sit down and write about it and try and make sense of it. The book I've been threatening maybe. But this moment, this absolute demolishing of accepted norms by this team is a thing I will remember for the rest of my life.

Of course I had to have a trip up to the top of the garden. It's where I go to weep. I've done it a lot this season. There's a compost heap up there with a spot that's moulded to the shape of my arse. It's where I go to reflect. It's under an apple tree. It's peaceful. At full time I went up there and sat down, covered my face with my hands and sobbed. Happy. Yes, I was happy but also sad. Emotional but stoic inside at the same time. Triumphant emotional moments like this always get me right in the heart. Because this is bigger than the team. It's a whole experience for me and one in which the town too gets enveloped in the glow of this success. But it's more important than just winning or just being Champions. It's a victory for all of us that really is a triumph of Good over Evil. It's that time again when there does seem something right in the universe that confuses us and in the end crushe us. Good does fucking prevail and the Gods have given us this moment and at Notlob too, where we stand and raise our hands and everything is good, in fact it's brilliant.

The fact that Coady smashed in number four made me shout so much the neighbours over the road stopped jet washing their drives and cutting their lawns. I didn't care. What do they know? What do they know about the freezing cold away games we have attended? What do they know about Fulham and the desolate capital? What do they know about those years behind us when we stood in the Southbank and urged our players on under the tutelage of buffoons and idiots. It's an outpouring of emotion now of course. The time when we stand proud at the top of the table and look down at the Villa and laugh loud. Yes, I laugh very loud at them. How dare they question our hearts and our minds, our plans and our tactical supremacy. How dare they cast their lack of idea and bitterness on our club. I laugh loudly at them because they are doomed. This is a present to myself. I know I shouldn't mock the afflicted but I am.

How many teams below should I mock? All of them. We are sitting on a golden mountain at the feet of a great Master. This Nuno…

I suspect that there are aspects of this Nunoism that we may forever be lost in the fogs of our ignorance. The facets which he displays in his post match celebrations, the measured tones during interviews, his humility, his unforgiving destruction of the opponents ideas. If Nuno has this relationship with our support then it is transcendent of both football and politics. So it becomes a fourth dimension. 4th Dimensional football in other words.

I wrote much in praise of this Nuno and I never regretted any of it. Even if the spark wouldn't have struck and we would have struggled this season I would have sat at his feet and listened. Simply because his idea is new and dynamic, it is different and it is new. He blasts the cobwebs of this footballing nation away with aplomb, humility and with intent so strong and forceful that the Warnocks and the Holloways found ways to galvanise their teams against him initially anyway. This was the last gasp saloon for this grotball. Now the ideas of Nuno will spread around this league system like wildfire. It's an overlap or a bleed through of Nunoism. Now he has set the template for how to run a football team, how to galvanise and how to inspire. We knew he would do this. There was something different about him, something strange and attractive. Something that made us love him as soon as he spoke. We saw in him a method and a litany of beauty that we could relate to. He has done us proud and I sing for him and I am inspired myself to create similar art and songs.

Even if the football and ethos we have is built from the familiar and traditional aspects of the game every single match is used as a building block for the next part of the story, the next match always. We are in a dream world of Nunos making and it will only be when we are awake and the season is finished we will be able to look back and see that Nuno had indeed hypnotised us with his magical skills. We will see that most of the matches were dreams, mixed in with a few nightmares just to balance it out. The stadium is the stage where this whole drama is played out and we watch it with eyes wide until we shuffle out when promotion is gained, we will rub our eyes and wonder what happened, why we are happy and some have tears in their eyes.

He looks ahead to the next match and I also look ahead too. Champions we are. But this has gone now for me. I let my joy out in the garden sitting among the dog eggs and the hot compost. Now is the next stage. Domination of the Premier league. The Mastering of those teams we see adorning the back pages of our newspapers or the glossy magazines. The funky web pages and the adverts on TV. Who there will have ideas bigger than our Nuno? Who will step up to debate the art of football with him? Who will stand in front of our players with more belief than them. I don't see anybody. All I see are mercenaries who lack these ideas, who lack Kwan.

We will travel to the Premiership on a tide of glorious victories but we will enter that place changed. It will not be as it was before. The Premiership will be alien to us and strange because we have suffered for so long being away from it. The cold of Barnsley away and the desolate identikit stadiums around the country will still ache at us and remind us of where we have been but the directions that Nuno has given us 'forward' should annihilate the memories of them in the end for sure. But those memories will be relentless. The 1-5 Albion game, the times when we were destroyed by teams evidently more attuned to the ideas of football than Mick Mcarthy ever was. Those pains of the past we drag with us as we travel towards the new dawn of Nunoism. The speed in which he drives us towards success will pull those memories with us in our slipstream.

We will go to these palaces of football next year a lot better armed than we were in previous years. We have owners with an incisive learning mind. They absorb knowledge like a sponge. They learn and they act fast. Just like the team and just like Nuno. They learn and they act and they destroy the vapid ghost like ideas of others. They will be unstoppable and we will be unstoppable too. These heights will be lofty and tall, sometimes we will find ourselves trying to find meaning in it all and we will stand firm with the idea that everything is learning, everything is training. What doesn't kill us will make us stronger. But while we are there at the top of the mountain we must never forget what went on before. Fingles at the forefront of a mass of gold and black that never ran. The bloke who cut a Wolves head into his lawn in Low Hill. Everybody getting the Bully cut. The four thousand of us that never stopped supporting our club when the wind ripped around that half empty Southbank. The way we always said we were proud to wear our shirt on holiday. They mocked us then, but now? The ghosts are triumphant and I know that they watch us and love every minute of what is happening. I know it man. This is for them not me. This is for those we have lost on these mad travels.

Gaz Mastic was at the bottom of my path today after the match and I went out slowly on my crutches to see him. He was beside himself and Gaz isn't a bloke who's emotions run free.

'Wim Champions Mikey' he said, and I swear his lip quivered a little bit and I dropped my crutches and gave him a big love over the gate. I crushed him a bit I was so happy. He was smiling and showing me the gaps in his teeth. This is why I'm happy. I'm happy for him and for us. This is the time we grab each other and love each other because that is the only way we will navigate the madness of next season. And it's ok to cry a little bit through the laughter too. Thank you Wolves. Thank you Nuno. Thank you Jeff. Thank you Laurie. Thank you Horace for protecting me in more ways than one. Thank you Greeny and Bigmon. Thank you Rikky and Sophie, Andy Powell, Kate and Neil. Thank you to Southy and Ian Powell who gave me the courage to write about this season and teaching me about how football really works. You have all given me my heart back.

Wreathed in Black and Gold smoke

I felt the heat of the pre game pyro technics on my face. I was gibbering a little. Bottom lip quivering. For fucks sake. It's only football. 22 blokes booting a bag of wind around a rectangular bit of green with thirty thousand half pissed ecstatic doughnuts cheering on every pass and move. But it's not really like that is it? It's more important, far more important. That is until it's not. Being pushed down Molineux alley in my wheelchair I was talking about the whole thing being in flux. What do I mean by that? Things have been changing fast at our club, for the better yes. Changing fast, can we keep up with it without losing our heads? I've already lost mine a few times already over these past few months.

I loved the smoke bombs. I love the chaos. I love to see the little kids on Dads shoulders being hoisted above the swirling madness. Their little hands trying to wave the smoke away to see Neves or Jota or Nuno, these dudes who's names have been repeated to them by their parents for months. I loved seeing the people I love in the middle of all the videos posted up on social media. I loved everything yesterday. Fucking loved up mate. But I've got one eye on those Premier league bastards don't worry. I'm watching them with one eye while the other one has tears streaming down it.

The smoke catches you in the throat. The team Coach is appearing and everything is flux emotionally. The players get off one by one with faces like they are in shock. The match itself had the same groove. It's been a long fucking season hasn't it? I'm not going to go through the whole litany of what went on. You can catch the podcasts where I talk to people I love about that. But man, what a long strange trip it's been. But Nuno is smiling and I've never felt warmer and more secure with him in charge. God bless you Nuno our Sanctus Espiritus. Not our 'special one' but our Holy one. We prayed for you and you came although at first we did not realise who you were.

In the Concourse at Bristol City I was soaked in beer dancing around like an idiot. Bennett scores. Last minute stuff. I'm crazy and try to run on the pitch but the boingy stuff they stretch across the empty seats in front of us is like one of those dreams where you are chasing something or being chased and your legs don't move. I yell and scream and am lost in that metaphysical golden smoke bomb love but it's all in my head at that time. You see after that match at Bristol I relaxed. I knew we had done it. There is a tenacity in this team. A yearning for greatness. There IS a philosophy. How we lacked that with Mick and Magoo. Now there is something else. As I walked out of Ashton Gate I knew we had done it. I knew it had come, this time it's for real and it's all about the now.

The front of the Northbank is a strange place. Especially with the wheelchair dudes and women. I'm afraid some Southbank madness has been transplanted straight into an ocean of calm. I mean the Northbank is quiet at the best of times but down there at the front it's very laid back. Apart from when I'm in it. Here I can denigrate and insult 'them' the opposition. Foresteiro-ee-eye whatever his face his. The little cheating git. He's right in front of me the little shithead. Doherty runs to the byline and he's so close I can practically touch him. Golden Gods become real there. So I can plant a few insults in their players heads. 'What a shit fucking haircut' or 'My Moms got more muscle in her withered leg' maybe 'Oi Shitbeard' possibly 'you little cheating bastard fuck you'. Something like that. Just something to taken a few inches of pace, maybe make them check their hair or beard in the mirror at halftime. A bit sad.

I have never forgotten the Sako thing. I haven't forgotten when your team nearly cut Conor Ronan in half last season either. My cast bangs against the concrete wall and I don't care. If I had a good leg….OK I'm not talking about it. This match is when she's still gobbling away after you've bust your nut and it feels weird, you want it to stop. We've had our fun, we have had our laughs and tears and now we just want to bask in the glow like a Walrus, fat and happy on a fucking rock being baked by the sun and cooled in the sea spray.

Forestry or whoever he is dinks and turns. I watched him do it for a few years now. Two years ago I though fucking hell we need something like him. He seemed luxurious and real, a player, twisting and turning. He pissed me off. He had some of that flair stuff I liked. He's a good looking sod too.But yesterday I wasn't as insulting. I actually felt sorry for him to be honest, because he looked bloody average compared to what delights we plonked on the green rectangle. In fact he looked a bit crap. They had a neck of a player on too, that Serbian. Jesus Christ mate, what's the weather like up there ahk? When he ran I kept giggling because he was using his head as some weighty momentum device…but there's the keyword for today. Momentum.

Through the smoke and the flares. The spangly arch of victory, the TV cameras. Kids on the pitch, the pyro ribbons which nearly tripped Coady up a few times, families. Nuno going crazy. Everybody on the pitch going up to the Southbank….oh. I laughed. So we weren't going to get any Cup waving love from the lads. I perched myself on the wall and chatted to Horace for an hour while we waited. But I didn't care much. You see the Southbank is the heart of Molineux. This is where all the passion comes from. This is the most important place in Molineux because the Southbank although it's in Molineux has a deeper meaning in our hearts and obviously those of Nuno and Company.

While the coach wound it's way up Waterloo road I was reminded perhaps of it's namesake battle. The smoke and the passion, the emotion, the madness. Fucking hell I love smoke bombs. This is where we really staked our claim to the premiership, as fans any way. This is what we will be like when Real Madrid come here when he play them in the Champions league. We will instigate chaos like it's never been seen before. Not the choreographed dancing of Dortmund et al, but the insanity of Wulfrunia, the outpouring of passion that we hold tight in our hearts in times of lean. Was I there? Nah. I was in the bar around the corner talking about when the Southbank didn't have a wall in the concourse separating fans, about how the bar sold glass bottles of Bass for 23p a bottle. How those bottles became projectiles and weapons. How everything became violent and real in that darkness underneath there lit but a few shitty bulbs and wire mesh windows dotted here and there to illuminate the insanity. I was with two very precious men from those days and you know who you are, you nutters, a bit quieter now, but you still had that gleam in your eyes.

Momentum. My brain was clicking through the permutations of the months to come. Who will strengthen the squad. Who will leave. What will be our ideas next season. We've had it fucking slick this season apart from the grotball and the shit refereeing. We've had it bloody easy. So among the madness of our victorious campaign this year I'm still underneath the Southbank, in the half light, thinking tactically. Next season will be tough. We will be playing some of the best teams in the country. We will have to think on our feet and instigate our ideas, as lofty as they have been this year, against other ideas that have an abyss between themselves and the teams we have played this season. These ideas will be as strong as ours and will be as dynamic. We will be standing among equals now.

The Manchester's and the Liverpool's, Tottenham's and Arsenals. How strong are their ideas? Bloody strong mate. How dynamic? Crazy fucking dynamic. But still…what will Nuno bring to this table of greats. He's a Maverick for sure. Implementing a team cohesion that will make those greater teams shiver. The Premiership lot are a lack lustre bunch. The demonic lure of cash and TV rights, the merchandising etc has turned their ideas into a many headed beast which they struggle to control. A loss here and there can turn their fanbase into slathering entities of grief. They are vocal in their castigations. That's good for us. We have momentum and we have a stand at Molineux which is a throwback to when every club had a stand where the nutters stood. The songs got sung and the volume of our love would give strength to the team. We have Momentum in that a bond has been struck between the owners and us. We have to carry it on. We will get battered at times next season no doubt. Times when the opposition click into some perfect flowing loveliness. You've seen them do it on Sky. These teams can dismantle others at will...sometimes. These victories for them will be against us when maybe we are a bit lacklustre. We can't be brilliant all the time ya know. There will be times when everything goes to shit. But there will be times when we click too and we will walk out of Molineux heads held high and lofty.

Now it's all about next season for me. Has been since Bristol. Billy Wrights statue gets wreathed in smoke. It's orange smoke but it's really gold, in our minds anyway. There is black smoke too. The detritus of spent rage and of blackness in our hearts. The golden feeling that we have stood our ground and have seen the light. The two sides of the Wolves story. Next season we take this theology of Nuno. This togetherness and we must make it stronger, we must also take our part in the whole unfolding of these new chapters. We must play our part. Support the team next season. Through the black and the gold. Trust the people you stand with in that ground. Trust the players and the staff. Trust in Nuno and Fosun. Be strong and link arms against the new threats that will face us. Use the momentum of this season to propel us into the stratosphere of new challenges. This is what was on my mind yesterday. Plans and tactics for the season to come. We must make every visit to an away ground an event where we 'own' that places they put us to watch the team. Support 100%. Sing until you cant sing anymore. Clap until your hands fall off. Denigrate the opposition. Remind them how shit their towns and cities are. Let them know our ideas. Let them know who Nuno is.

The End

Thank You

When you attend a football match or follow a team inevitably you gather a group of trusted friends along the way. People you share a love with, and those people become very precious. This book would not have happened without these people. In fact I probably wouldn't be alive without a few of these people too. So strap in while I wax friendship love.

My friend Horace. He argued for me from day one. Whether it was in a cold Birmingham street as I lay motionless at his feet or in the Hospital where the Surgeons were debating cutting off my leg. Horace you are a treasure and a brother. I owe you so much.

Ian Powell and Pat Russell. These are my Podcast co hosts and every time I sit down with them I learn more about the art of football. From day one they have placated my fears as I tried to write about this madness called Wolverhampton Wanderers. I owe them a debt that can never be repaid.

Mark Green and Carl Evason. The dynamic duo. There generosity and love kept me going a few times...well a lot of the time. They fed me and they kept me half pissed. Mark made stickers and flags total madness. But more importantly they both showed me how they love their club. Bless your hearts.

Neil and Kate Wright. Neil you have supported this mad project and others through your graphical skills and your chilled outlook. Many times you have made me laugh when all I wanted to do was cry. Kate, you too are a little Wolf, defending our club on Social Media has made me proud to know you.

Others have entered my life too and made some large and some small impacts on my life and they are all important. I would like to bow down to Andy 'Knocker' Powell, Charlie Hickman, Rich Lamine, Ian Mundy, Roy Poole, Sophie, Simon Rickard, Steve Plant, Pottsy, Russ Cockburn, Simon Sinclair, Neil Goff, Julie Harrison, Perth Dave, Darcy and Liv Harrison, Dis Harrison (for cheering me up in Hospital), Harrison Coady, Ryan Leister, Downer, all the Staff at Sandwell Hospital and finally the Southbank Molineux. Never have I felt more at home than when we are playing at home and I am right in the middle of all the madness.